HUSBANDRY TO HOUSEWIFERY

HUSBANDRY TO HOUSEWIFERY

Women, Economic Change, and
Housework in Ireland,
1890–1914

JOANNA BOURKE

CLARENDON PRESS · OXFORD

1993

Oxford University Press, Walton Street, Oxford OX2 6DP

Oxford New York Toronto
Delhi Bombay Calcutta Madras Karachi
Kuala Lumpur Singapore Hong Kong Tokyo
Nairobi Dar es Salaam Cape Town
Melbourne Auckland Madrid
and associated companies in
Berlin Ibadan

Oxford is a trade mark of Oxford University Press

Published in the United States
by Oxford University Press Inc., New York

British Library Cataloguing in Publication Data
Data available

Library of Congress Cataloging-in-Publication Data
Bourke, Joanna.
Husbandry to housewifery : women, economic change, and housework
in Ireland, 1890–1914 / Joanna Bourke.
p. cm.
Includes bibliographical references and index.
1. Women—Ireland—History 2. Housewives—Ireland—History.
3. Women—Employment—Ireland—History. 4. Ireland—Social
conditions—History. I. Title.
HQ1600.3.B68 1993 305.4'09415—dc20 93–7539
ISBN 0–19–820385–3

1 3 5 7 9 10 8 6 4 2

Typeset by Graphicraft Typesetters Ltd., Hong Kong
Printed in Great Britain
on acid-free paper by
Biddles Ltd., Guildford and King's Lynn

Preface

I AM very grateful to many friends and colleagues for reading portions of my work or arguing with me at conferences and seminars. In particular, I am indebted to Nicholas Brown, Danny Church, Manning Clark, Louis Cullen, David Dickson, Marianne Elliott, Richard Evans, Iain McCalman, Avner Offer, Anna Pierre, Dorothy Porter, Eric Richards, Edward Sands, Hilary Sapire, F. B. Smith, Kosmas Tsokhas, and Bill Vaughan. At Oxford University Press my editor, Tony Morris, was splendid. There are a few to whom I reserve special thanks: Oliver MacDonagh of the Australian National University, David Fitzpatrick of Trinity College, Dublin, and Jay Winter of Pembroke College, Cambridge. At crucial times during the writing of this book I have received help from colleagues, staff and committees at the Australian National University, Emmanuel College, Cambridge, Flinders University, Queen's College, Belfast, and Trinity College, Dublin. The guidance of staff working in libraries and archives in Australia, England, and Ireland was also invaluable. I am especially grateful to staff at the Australian National Library, British Library, Cork Archives, Irish Folklore Commission Archives (University College, Dublin), National Archives of Ireland, National Library of Ireland, Public Record Office of Great Britain, Public Record Office of Northern Ireland, Registry of Friendly Societies, Trinity College Library (Dublin), and the Ulster Folk and Transport Museum Archives. Permission to use material from previously published work has been given by the editors of *Irish Historical Studies*, *Eire-Ireland*, *Agricultural History Review*, and the *Journal of Interdisciplinary History*. Finally, I wish to dedicate this book to my family: Stafford, Ella, Paul, Sharline, Mark, Lisa, David, and all my nieces and nephews.

J.B.

London
September 1992

Contents

List of Tables

Abbreviations

AER	*American Economic Review*
CDB	Congested Districts Board
DATI	Department of Agriculture and Technical Instruction
DED	District Electoral Division
EHR	*Economic History Review*
HC	House of Commons
IAOS	Irish Agricultural Organization Society
IH	*Irish Homestead*
IIDA	Irish Industries Development Association
JEH	*Journal of Economic History*
JEI	*Journal of Economic Issues*
JEL	*Journal of Economic Literature*
JPE	*Journal of Political Economics*
JSSISI	*Journal of the Statistical and Social Inquiry Society of Ireland*
NAI	National Archives of Ireland (formerly PRO, Dublin)
n.p.	no pagination
PRO Kew	Public Record Office, London
PRONI	Public Record Office of Northern Ireland, Belfast
RCCI	Royal Commission on Congestion in Ireland
RCL	Royal Commission on Labour
UFTM	Ulster Folk and Transport Museum
UI	United Irishwomen
WNHA	Women's National Health Association

Introduction: Women, Economic Change, and Housework in Ireland, 1890–1914

I N the generation prior to 1914 Irish women transformed their position within society: bidding farewell to labour in the fields and in other men's homes, they enlisted for full-time work in the unpaid domestic sphere. A haughty young boy welcomed them in their new role: 'Girls, generally speaking, are very useful for indoor or household work, a great deal more than boys. This, of course, is not an exaggeration, for boys are so careless about household business while the girls are otherwise.'[1] Rather than asking their daughters, fathers hired male labourers to help them bring in the harvest. Scorning paid domestic service, young women thronged to classes in rural housewifery. In 1901 only 430,000 women in Ireland were employed, compared with 641,000 twenty years earlier. Single women performed housework, free of charge, for fathers, brothers, and uncles. Or they emigrated. Married women nursed their children and strove to improve the standard of services that they provided to their family, while widowed women competed with their children's spouses in the production of domestic goods. Female labour came to be dominated by housework.

At the same time, the rural Irish economy was booming, and living standards were improving. According to economists, economic growth entails improved well-being. Economic growth increases happiness either by satisfying wants or by widening the range of choice.[2] Although a distinction is made between economic welfare and total well-being, economists generally agree

---

[1] Letter addressed to 'My Dear Aunt Polly' of the 'Children's Cosy Corner', from D. J. Buckley, *Irish Weekly Independent*, 30 Apr. 1910: 7.
[2] *The Collected Writings of John Maynard Keynes,* ix. *Essays in Persuasion* (1972), 326, and W. Arthur Lewis, *The Theory of Economic Growth* (1955), 420.

that economic welfare is 'an approximate index of total welfare'.[3] Such a position can be maintained only by taking the market-place and 'economic man' as sufficient metaphors for human experience. The market is a model of human relations. The price of commodities is an indicator of their relative worth. The 'factors of production', including human labour, receive their economic value in the process of exchange.[4] People choose on the basis of 'rational' analysis of economic conditions and prospects. In a growing economy, 'rational' behaviour is followed by increased well-being.

The economic approach poses problems for the historian trying to understand the decisions that Irish women made in the period prior to World War I. Are housewives 'economic men'? Does economic rationality have any meaning for women who choose to move outside paid market relationships? Clearly, people make decisions based on notions of what they perceive to be 'best' for them. How can we understand the decision of many Irish women to become full-time, unwaged houseworkers? This book investigates the interaction of female well-being, agricultural production, and labour.

WELL-BEING: SOME THEORETICAL ISSUES

A model of well-being needs to consider three aspects: material production and private consumption, non-economic factors, and distributional factors.

Production and Consumption

Historical analysis of production and consumption in Ireland is under way, but it remains concerned with those urban areas central to the dominant political and nationalist debates. The most prominent exceptions are works that frame their questions

---

[3] E. M. Ojala, *Agriculture and Economic Progress* (1952), 7. See also A. C. Pigou, *The Economics of Welfare* (1920), 11.

[4] Douglass C. North, *The Economic Growth of the United States, 1790–1860* (Englewood Cliffs, NJ, 1966), and North's article with Robert Paul Thomas, 'An Economic Theory of the Growth of the Western World', *EHR*, 2nd ser. 23/1 (1970), 1–17.

in terms of political movements.[5] Only Louis Cullen's explora-
tion of rural life over four or five centuries shows economic and
social trends without political signposts.[6] The books by Raymond
Crotty and Cormac Ó Gráda on Irish agriculture surpass anything
previously written, but neither deals directly with labour, and,
although Ó Gráda graces the jacket of his book with a depiction
of female potato-diggers, the experience of women workers is
ignored.[7] The neglect of female labour in economic analyses is
a serious lapse, especially if we are concerned with private or
material consumption. Housework is crucial for economic development.[8] Improvements in housing, diet, and the consumption
of household goods are crucial determinants of welfare.

Economic variables tell us a great deal about well-being, but
they do not tell us enough. Increased production and consumption
do not always improve individual well-being. Rising incomes
may be bought at a high cost. In Ireland, the development of
home industries increased the flow of income into the household, but at the cost of long hours of monotonous labour. Rising
productivity led to unemployment. Once the basic human needs
for food, shelter, and clothing have been fulfilled, wants change
in line with a shifting of expectations.[9] Richard A. Easterlin argues
that this constant shifting of expectations negates any positive
impact that economic growth may have on well-being.[10] The
production and consumption of more goods do not necessarily

---

[5] David Fitzpatrick, *Politics and Irish Life, 1913–21* (Dublin, 1977), and Samuel
Clark, *Social Origins of the Irish Land War* (Princeton, NJ, 1979).

[6] See the following books by Louis M. Cullen: *An Economic History of Ireland
since 1660* (1972); *The Emergence of Modern Ireland, 1600–1900* (1981); and *Life in
Ireland* (1968).

[7] Raymond D. Crotty, *Irish Agricultural Production: Its Volume and Structure*
(Cork, 1966), and Cormac Ó Gráda, *Ireland before and after the Famine* (Manchester,
1988).

[8] The terms 'growth' and 'development' are not identical. In this book, 'growth'
refers to changes in the income level of rural households. 'Development' is used
much more broadly to refer to a series of changes that might result from increased income. I reject both liberal and Marxist development models with their
notion of 'stages'. I see no reason to assume that changes resulting from rising
incomes need to follow any pattern across time or between cultures.

[9] Adam Smith, *An Inquiry into the Nature and Causes of the Wealth of Nations*
(New York, 1937), bk. 1, Ch. 11: 164.

[10] Richard A. Easterlin, 'Does Economic Growth Improve the Human Lot?
Some Empirical Evidence', in Paul A. David and Melvin W. Reder (eds.), *Nations
and Households in Economic Growth* (New York, 1974), 89–125.

lead to a better life. Alexander Irvine recounts Sir Walter Scott's story of a caliph who attempts to find happiness by wearing the shirt of a happy man. After travelling the world, he finally found a happy man—in Ireland, shirtless.[11]

Furthermore, the conventional methods of determining 'value' prove to be an inaccurate guide to the particular uses that people make of time. American research concerning the 'comparative worth' of male and female employment reveals the extent to which wages do not reflect an objective 'market value'. 'Value' seems to be related to the socially defined status of the person performing the work rather than to the economic worth of the output. Although these American debates tend to be restricted to the paid labour market, placing excessive weight on descriptive models of socialization, they have implications for any study seeking to move beyond the conventional accounting of paid markets.[12]

Sectors of the economy that do not conform to these conventional ways of modelling economic behaviour are often ignored by economic historians, who choose narrow definitions of 'economic variables'. Until recently, these narrow definitions have led to the neglect of unwaged forms of work. Histories of women frequently deny the importance of domestic labour: wives and mothers are said to be non-participants in 'social production',[13] and their daughters 'largely redundant'.[14] The economists' view

[11] Alexander Irvine, *The Souls of Poor Folk* (1921), 10–11.

[12] Paula England and Bahar Norris, 'Comparable Worth: A New Doctrine of Sex Discrimination', *Social Science Quarterly*, 66/3 (Sept. 1985), 629–43; Daphne Greenwood, 'The Institutional Inadequacy of the Market in Determining Comparable Worth: Implications for Value Theory', *JEI* 18 (June 1984), 457–64; Danielle P. Jaussaud, 'Can Job Evaluation Systems Help Determine the Comparable Worth of Male and Female Occupations', *JEI* 18 (June 1984), 473–82; Robert Livernosh (ed.), *Comparable Worth: Issues and Alternatives* (Washington, DC, 1980); Elaine Sorensen, 'Equal Pay for Comparable Worth: A Policy for Eliminating the Undervaluation of 'Women's Work', *JEI* 18 (June 1984), 465–72; and Donald R. Williams and Charles H. Register, 'Regional Variations in Earnings and the Gender Composition of Employment: Is "Women's Work" Undervalued?', *JEI* 20 (Dec. 1986), 1121–34.

[13] Margaret Ward, 'Marginality and Militancy: Cumann na mBan, 1914–1936', in Austen Morgan and Bob Purdie (eds.), *Ireland: Divided Nation, Divided Class* (1980), 96.

[14] David Fitzpatrick, 'The Modernisation of the Irish Female', in Patrick O'Flanagan, Paul Ferguson, and Kevin Whelan (eds.), *Rural Ireland, 1600–1900: Modernisation and Change* (Cork, 1987), 164.

that housework is not 'work' can be blamed on the pervasive influence of Thorstein Veblen.[15] Veblen argued that as income increases, so does the consumption of leisure, allowing families to enhance their social status by keeping 'redundant' wives at home. Thus, the social and economic position of women is basic to the nature of the economic system not because they 'work', but because they consume. This type of analysis is rapidly changing in response to debates in economic theory.

Economists have sporadically considered housework. Many of these earlier economists recognized the importance of domestic labour to the economy. In his classic *Principles of Economics* Alfred Marshall argued that housework was so crucial to the economy that women must be retained in the domestic sector. Marshall was prepared to integrate traits such as 'feminine selflessness' into his analysis of economic production.[16] In 1930 Lionel Robbins heralded the modern theory of labour supply with the notion that labour decisions were made as a result of individuals rationally allocating their time between market work and leisure.[17] Jacob Mincer extended the approach to female decision-making. For women, the choice was not simply between work and leisure, but between work in the home, work in the market, and leisure.[18] Family income determined the total number of hours worked, but the individual's relative productivity in the home and in the market determined the location of their work.[19] Gary S. Becker integrated housework into neoclassical economics, and, by applying concepts such as comparative advantage, maximizing behaviour, and equilibrium markets to the family, he attempted to answer the question: why do married women concentrate their labour in the unwaged markets, while married men concentrate theirs in the paid markets? According to him,

[15] Thorstein Veblen, *The Theory of the Leisure Class: An Economic Study of Institutions*, first published in 1899 (New York, 1934), and his essays 'The Beginnings of Ownership', 'The Barbarian Status of Women', and 'The Economic Theory of Women's Dress', in Leon Ardzroone (ed.), *Essays in our Changing Order* (New York, 1964).

[16] A. Marshall, *Principles of Economics*, 8th edn. (1930).

[17] Lionel Robbins, 'On the Elasticity of Demand for Income in Terms of Effort', *Economica*, 10 (1930), 123–9.

[18] Jacob Mincer, 'Labour Force Participation of Married Women: A Study in Labour Supply', *Aspects of Labour Economics* (1962), 63–105.

[19] Arleen Leibowitz, 'Education and Home Production', *AER* 64/2 (May 1974), 243–50.

the decisive factor is the relative efficiency of each sex in its sphere of labour.[20] Thus, unmarried women might 'rationally' allocate more time to housework than unmarried men. The central problem with his work concerns causality: the sexual division of labour as described by Becker can equally be explained as a *response* to customs or institutions that offer lower pay and provide fewer choices for women in the employment market. Irrespective of the weaknesses of these approaches, the new economics of the family has done us a favour by incorporating housework as an essential element in the analysis of labour. These economic studies suggest that greater emphasis should be placed on the household as a unit of production (rather than of consumption).[21] This view is not new,[22] but it has radical implications for the historical study of labour that have not yet been examined.

Economic approaches to the family are not restricted to neoclassical expressions. The approach called 'transaction costs' complements 'new household' neoclassicism. Transaction economists pronounce the internal structure of the organization to be decisive. Hierarchical structures within the family are emphasized. Individuals are not caricatured as being anonymous agents: rather, they recognize other economic agents, and are recognized in turn.[23] In contrast to Becker, this institutional approach addresses the problem of social status. For instance, John Kenneth

[20] Gary S. Becker, 'A Theory of Marriage: Part I', *JPE* 81/4 (July 1973), 813–46, 'A Theory of Marriage: Part II', *JPE* 82/2, ii (Mar.–Apr. 1974), 11–26, and *A Treatise on the Family* (Cambridge, Mass., 1981). For critiques, see William J. Goode, 'Comment: The Economics of Non-Monetary Variables', *JPE* 82/2, ii (Mar.–Apr. 1974), 27–33, and Michael T. Hannan, 'Families, Markets, and Social Structures: An Essay on Becker's *A Treatise on the Family*', *JEL* 20 (Mar. 1982), 65.

[21] Economic analyses that confirm that households do not 'only' consume include Gary S. Becker, 'A Theory of the Allocation of Time', in Gary S. Becker (ed.), *The Economic Approach to Human Behaviour* (Chicago, 1976), 89–114; Daphne Greenwood, 'The Economic Significance of "Women's Place" in Society: A New-Institutionalist View', *JEI* 18 (Sept. 1984), 663–80; K. J. Lancaster, 'A New Approach to Consumer Theory', *JPE* 74 (1966), 132–57; and R. T. Michael and Gary S. Becker, 'On the New Theory of Consumer Behaviour', in Becker (ed.), *The Economic Approach to Human Behaviour*.

[22] Margaret Reid, *Economics of Household Production* (New York, 1934).

[23] Yoram Ben-Porath, 'The F-Connection: Families, Friends, and Firms and the Organization of Exchange', *Population and Development Review*, 6 (Mar. 1980), 1–30, and Robert A. Pollack, 'A Transaction Cost Approach to Families and Households', *JEL* 23 (June 1985), 581–608.

Galbraith's *Economics and the Public Purpose* linked the role of the wife as the manager of consumption to that of a crypto-servant. Galbraith made the simple discovery that increased consumption requires greater inputs of time. At this point, however, he swerved away from an economic approach, and described the force that drives women to perform housework as social virtue rather than economic reward.[24]

A different question is tackled by Marxist feminists. Starting with the assumption that houseworkers provide the necessary labour for the reproduction of labour (on both a daily and a generational basis), they attempt to demonstrate the contribution of housework to capitalist accumulation.[25] More than other economists, they are concerned with the role of domestic labour in the external economy rather than for the individual woman or the individual household.[26] Their analysis has become increasingly abstract and semantic: those who argue that housework produces 'use values' are challenged by those who argue that housework either contributes to, or directly produces, surplus value.[27] Empirical verification is lacking even in clearly empirical issues such as their assertion that the 'manufacture of housework' came about by the transfer of production *from* the home and *to* the factories.[28] As we shall see, this doctrine is based on a particularly flexible notion of 'housework' and of how women

[24] John Kenneth Galbraith, *Economics and the Public Purpose* (Boston, 1973).

[25] Mariarosa Dalla Costa and Selma James, *The Power of Women and the Subversion of the Community* (Bristol, 1973), and Wally Seccombe, 'The Housewife and her Labour under Capitalism', *NLR* 83 (Jan.–Feb. 1974), 4.

[26] The best review of this literature has been written by Nona Glazier-Malbin, 'Housework', *Signs*, 1 (1976), 905–22.

[27] Margaret Coulson, Branka Magas, and Hilary Wainwright, 'The Housewife and her Labour under Capitalism: A Critique', *NLR* 89 (1975), 59–71, discuss use values. The following writers argue that housework contributes to surplus value: Veronika Bennholdt-Thomsen, 'Subsistence Production and Extended Reproduction', in Kate Young, Carol Walkowitz, and Roslyn McCullagh (eds.), *Of Marriage and the Market* (1984), 41–54; Jean Gardiner, 'Women's Domestic Labour', *NLR* 89 (1975), 47–58; John Harrison, 'The Political Economy of Housework', *Conference of Socialist Economists*, bull. 1 (1974), 35–52; and Seccombe, 'The Housewife under Capitalism', 3–24. In contrast, Costa and James, *Women and the Subversion of the Community*, argue that housework directly produces surplus value.

[28] Barbara Ehrenreich and Deirdre English, 'The Manufacture of Housework', *Socialist Revolution*, 5 (Oct.–Dec. 1975), 5–40; M. Kay Martin and Barbara Voorhies, *Female of the Species* (New York, 1975); and Ann Oakley, *Woman's Work: A History of the Housewife* (New York, 1974).

came to be underemployed in the home.[29] Another version links
housework to the threat that early industrialization posed to the
reproduction of labour. When conditions in industrial cities deteriorated to such an extent that the working class was unable to
reproduce itself adequately, men of all classes had an interest
in encouraging women to 'return' to the home.[30] Explanations
for such extraordinary cross-class male unity are varied: housework is said to increase the male worker's efficiency in the
workforce, to provide an outlet for the release of tensions inherent
in capitalist life, and to ensure the reproduction and production
of labour. The other side to this argument belongs to the doctrine
called the 'reserve army of labour'. While the class–gender argument says that capitalism needs domestic labour, this doctrine
states that secular shifts in the participation of women in the
labour force reflect changes in the need of capitalism for wage
labour. Thus, married women become a latent 'reserve army'.[31]
What the Marxist feminist debates never explain in economic
terms is why *women* perform housework: in the final analysis,
the selection of houseworkers is explained by ideological rather
than economic factors.

Very few economic analyses of female labour in and outside
the household are constructed solely from the standpoint of
economic production and material consumption. Non-economic
factors constantly intrude.

Non-Economic Factors

Non-economic factors such as status, approbation, work satisfaction, religion, health, leisure activities, domestic harmony,
sexuality, and education dominate the experience of well-being.

[29] An example of this approach is Margaret Benson, 'The Political Economy of
Women's Liberation', *Monthly Review*, 21 (Sept. 1969), 13–27.

[30] Ellen Malos (ed.), *The Politics of Housework* (1980), introd. 17. See also Patricia
Connelly, *Last Hired, First Fired* (Toronto, 1978), 37–41; Costa and James, *Women
and the Subversion of the Community*; and Heidi Irmgard Hartmann, *Capitalism and
Women's Work in the Home, 1900–1930* (Ann Arbor, Mich., 1975).

[31] This argument was developed initially by Harry Braverman, *Labour and
Monopoly Capital* (New York, 1974). It has been extended by Connelly, *Last Hired,
First Fired*, and Marilyn Power, 'From Home Production to Wage Labour: Women
as a Reserve Army of Labour', *Review of Radical Political Economics*, 15 (Spring 1983).

As we have already seen, attempts to provide strictly 'economic' analyses slide (often subtly) into non-economic explanations. Thus, 'human capital' economists implicitly argue that women enjoy housework (especially child-rearing) and choose 'easy', less demanding, flexible—and, therefore, low paid—employment so that they can continue as houseworkers.[32] At the other extreme, many theorists let notions about 'patriarchy' either within the family or in the wider community explain female work.[33] Arguments that imply that women make the best of bad options require at the very least that economic forces should be modified by 'tastes', which reduce the effectiveness of the market in providing optimum levels of employment. W. Elliot Brownlee, for instance, maintains that the discrimination faced by women in the paid labour market increases the attractiveness of domestic work.[34] The argument that narrowing the gap between women's wages and men's wages reduces the demand for female labour requires an explanation of why it is that female workers are not remunerated in the same way as male workers. The elasticity of substitution is not simply an economic variable; it has political and social determinants.

These other determinants cannot be ignored. What is the role of payment in labour? Housework is not valued in the same way as familial farm labour or paid employment.[35] Were women 'better off' working full-time as unwaged houseworkers? Did education for the home increase the work satisfaction of housewives? While economists shy away from these value judgements, partly because many of these variables cannot be quantified, historians have more licence to explore beyond the boundaries of quantification.

[32] Gary S. Becker, *The Economics of Discrimination* (Chicago, 1957), and Jacob Mincer and Solomon Polachek, 'Family Investments in Human Capital', *JPE* 82/2 (Mar.–Apr. 1974), 76–108.

[33] Julia A. Heath and David H. Ciscel, 'Patriarchy, Family Structure and the Exploitation of Women's Labour', *JEI* 22 (Sept. 1988), 781–94.

[34] W. Elliot Brownlee, 'Household Values, Women's Work and Economic Growth, 1800–1930', *JEH* 39 (Mar. 1979), 204.

[35] Thus, the comment by Fitzpatrick that the increased importance of the dowry in post-famine Ireland was a reflection of the 'diminished economic importance of women' is legitimate only if 'economic' labour refers to a very limited range of activities: Fitzpatrick, 'The Modernisation of the Irish Female', 169.

Distributional Factors

We need to know how the satisfaction of needs is distributed over the population. A change that improves the well-being of one group may have the opposite effect on another group. Development or growth is not neuter. A few people argue that women may benefit *more* from economic 'development' than men.[36] Most question whether 'development' is good for women.[37] Certain types of development *increase* inequality between men and women; as economists like Ester Boserup have documented, women's power in many Third World countries was eroded by European developers who planned their programmes with culturally specific beliefs of 'women's place'.[38] Although most of these studies pinpoint industrialization as the crucial variable, my work looks at what can happen in a rural context. Gender must be examined separately, especially since female poverty is often unlike male poverty. As we shall be examining in this book, changes in the Irish dairy industry may have led to improved well-being in terms of increased income or standards of living for the household as a unit; but within the household these changes might have led to a decline in female status. Similarly, although the value of poultry-rearing in Ireland increased, female status in the poultry industry declined as managerial control came to be vested in men.

Any distributional analysis of the impact of 'development' on women must concentrate on the impact that it had on housework. Specialized studies of housework tend to equate 'development' in the home with the technological impact of industrialization in this sphere, thus giving precedence to appliances and mass production.[39] There is a stress on the reduction in the amount of

[36] Jane S. Jaquette, 'Women and Modernization Theory: A Decade of Feminist Criticism', *World Politics*, 34/2 (Jan. 1982), 267–84, and Lewis, *The Theory of Economic Growth*, 422.

[37] Lisa Leghorn and Katherine Parker, *Women's Worth: Sexual Economics and the World of Women* (1981), 33–59.

[38] Ester Boserup, *Women's Role in Economic Development* (1970).

[39] Jenni Calder, *The Victorian Home* (1977); Ruth Schwartz Cowan, *More Work for Mother* (New York, 1983); Caroline Davidson, *A Woman's Work is Never Done* (1982); Susan Strasser, 'An Enlarged Existence? Technology and Household Work in Nineteenth Century America', in Sarah F. Berk (ed.), *Women and Household Labour* (Beverly Hills, Calif., 1980), 29–52; and Susan Strasser, *Never Done: A History of American Housework* (New York, 1982).

time spent cleaning, cooking, and washing, and an increase in the amount of time spent in the 'labour of love', such as child care, talking to one's spouse, and making love.[40] Marxists argue that industrialization of the household had a profound effect on female labour.[41] However, these writers have only vague notions about the relationship between technology and the *work* of housework, and about how the 'gains' of domestic industrialization are shared between the members of the household.

The three aspects of well-being—material production and private consumption, non-economic factors, and distributional factors—need to be considered simultaneously for practical as well as for theoretical reasons. If we had to deal solely with quantifiable inputs, a great deal would be lost.[42] The three aspects interact with each other. For instance, non-economic well-being is liable to be modified by the manner in which income is earned and spent.[43] Similarly, non-economic variables exert a great influence on economic well-being. People do not live in isolation: the well-being of one individual may directly affect that of another. Overall well-being depends not only on economic growth, but also on non-economic factors and, most importantly, on how the benefits are distributed.

[40] Brownlee, 'Household Values and Economic Growth', 199–209; Peter Lindert, *Fertility and Scarcity in America* (Princeton, NJ, 1978); Theresa McBride, 'The Long Road Home: Women's Work and Industrialisation', in Renate Bridenthal and Claudia Koonz (eds.), *Becoming Visible* (Boston, 1977), 286, and Mary Lynn McDougall, 'Working-Class Women during the Industrial Revolution, 1780–1914', in Bridenthal and Koonz (eds.), *Becoming Visible*, 275; and Wally Seccombe, 'Domestic Labour and the Working Class Household', in Bonnie Fox (ed.), *Hidden in the Household: Women's Domestic Labour under Capitalism* (Toronto, 1980), 25–99.

[41] This need not be a dramatic revolution; it could be a gradual process, as is argued by Seccombe, 'Domestic Labour and the Working Class Household', 25–99. In contrast, some Marxists argue that industrialization had little impact on women's lives in the home: see McBride, 'The Long Road Home', 286, and McDougall, 'Working-Class Women during the Industrial Revolution', 275.

[42] Historians seldom have detailed knowledge of labour demands on family farms (see Chs. 5 and 6). Much of the guesswork about this has to be taken from evidence regarding paid employment. For instance, the evidence about the decline of female labour as dairymaids on other people's farms (Ch. 3) also applies to women's involvement in dairying on their families' farms. Thus, the division of the book into three 'parts' (Paid Workers, Subsistence Entrepreneurs, and Houseworkers) is not rigid. A similar problem is experienced in the more speculative section estimating the number of houseworkers (Ch. 7).

[43] Pigou, *Economics of Welfare*, 14–17, and F. Thomas Juster and Frank P. Stafford (eds.), *Time, Goods and Well-Being* (Ann Arbor, Mich., 1985).

WOMEN AND AGRICULTURAL PRODUCTION IN IRELAND

> 'But you know, pa,' said the farmer's daughter, when he
> spoke to her about the addresses of his neighbour's son,
> 'you know, pa, ma wants me to marry a man of culture.'
> 'So do I my dear, so do I; and there is no better culture in
> the country than agriculture.'[44]

With the theoretical issues discussed in the previous sections in
mind, we can consider some of the fundamental features of Irish
agricultural history in the generation prior to World War I. Although the conclusions are applicable to the urban sector, the
emphasis in this book is on the Irish rural sector. Over half of the
Irish population were directly engaged in agriculture. In 1911
less than one-third of the population lived in towns, compared
with four-fifths of the population in England and Wales. This
said, it will become clear in the course of this book that the
particular experience of the inhabitants of the Irish countryside
was similar to the experience of men and women in Irish towns
as well as in other countries.

Demography

Any analysis of well-being requires careful examination of the
peculiarities of a country's demographic history. This is particularly true in the case of Ireland, whose demographic patterns are
regarded as perverse. The two unusual features of Irish household strategies are the importance of celibacy and the level of
migration. Irish population growth was not controlled by postponing marriage or by using contraceptives. Irish men and women
married later than their contemporaries in England, but at very
similar ages to men and women in Germany, Belgium, and
Norway. On average, at the turn of the century, Irish men married
when they were 30 years of age, and women married when they
were 26 years. Once married, Irish mothers reproduced at almost
as fast a rate as the Hutterites of Northern America. In Ireland,
by the time a mother reached the age of 45, she would have
given birth to five or six children. Instead of limiting their fertility once married, a large proportion of Irish men and women
simply did not marry. In 1911, 27 per cent of men aged between

---

[44] 'Items of Interest', *IH*, 14 Dec. 1895: 666.

45 and 54 years and 25 per cent of women in this age-group had never married. Unmarried rates in England and Wales in 1911 were significantly lower, at 12 per cent for men and 16 per cent for women. Furthermore, the proportion of single men and women had increased during the nineteenth century. In 1851, 12 per cent of women aged between 45 and 54 years had never married; in 1871, 16 per cent; in 1891, 17 per cent; jumping to 22 per cent in 1901 and 25 per cent in 1911. This increase in spinsterhood was accompanied by very little change in the age at which those who married did so. Women from the generation born between 1821 and 1831 married only one year earlier than those who were born between 1861 and 1871.[45]

The high rate of non-marriage in Ireland was largely a product of the relationship between the marriage market and the economic constraints imposed by impartable inheritance patterns. In general, the ability of a man to marry was dependent on inheriting land, while the ability of a woman to marry was dependent on possessing a dowry. In Ireland the dowry moved along generations rather than flowing between generations. The father of the bride gave the dowry to the father of the groom, who generally used it to facilitate the emigration of other offspring or to dower a daughter. In a typical household of six children, two daughters would be unable to marry.

Single siblings could either remain in Ireland or they could emigrate. The propensity of Irish men and women to emigrate was as remarkable as their propensity to remain unmarried. Whereas surplus siblings in many other European countries could be dispersed to urban centres, in Ireland they emigrated to America, Canada, England, or Australia. In the period we are discussing, over 20,000 Irishmen and over 20,000 Irishwomen emigrated every twelve months. In 1891 there were 2,386,000 women in Ireland; twenty years later, there were 2,198,000. Most of the female emigrants left the country on their own, most were between the ages of 18 and 26, and most were unmarried.[46]

---

[45] David Fitzpatrick, 'Marriage in Post-Famine Ireland', in Art Cosgrove (ed.), *Marriage in Ireland* (Dublin, 1985), 129–30.

[46] This book is concerned with women who remained in Ireland. For superb studies of Irish emigration, see David Fitzpatrick, *Irish Emigration, 1801–1921* (Economic and Social History Society of Ireland, 1984); id., 'Irish Emigration in the Later Nineteenth Century', *Irish Historical Studies*, 22/86 (1980), 126–43; and Kerby A. Miller, *Emigrants and Exiles: Ireland and the Irish Exodus to North America* (Oxford, 1985).

The unusual aspects of Ireland's demography are important in understanding the context of the changes examined in this book. However, they cannot explain the changes. To do this, we need to turn elsewhere. What this sketch of Irish demographic patterns does illustrate, however, is that we must be careful not to generalize from Ireland to other countries.

The Irish Rural Labour Market

The three sectors of the labour market in Ireland are paid workers, subsistence entrepreneurs, and houseworkers. If women are left out, the difficulties of writing Irish economic history are the same as they are for other histories. This discussion about Ireland has a bearing on the contemporary history of other countries. The paid worker is the category of worker usually encountered in labour histories. It includes all those who are paid predominantly in money (although payment may be partly in goods). When writing about 'employed' and 'unemployed' people, I am referring to this group. The term 'subsistence entrepreneur' is used to designate small-scale agricultural production by a worker who aims at maximizing returns not only for a local, national, or international market, but also for his or her own consumption and pleasure. In other words, the subsistence entrepreneur is a consumer as well as a producer. In the Irish case, the term 'subsistence' is used to indicate the scale of operations and the informal (although not absent) market relations. It chiefly refers to work performed by members of the household on the family farm.

The term 'houseworker' is the most difficult to define. What is 'housework'? 'Housework' suggests work inside the 'house', although not necessarily one's own house, but what are the boundaries of the 'house'? Child care takes place in meadows as well as inside houses. If a mother enjoys taking her child for a walk, should her activity be called housework or leisure? In rural households, what is farm work and what is housework? Housework is not clearly different from other economic tasks carried out by rural women. Is an Irish woman who feeds chickens from her front door performing housework if the eggs are to be consumed by the household rather than sold? Much 'farm work' is performed inside the house. Marxists frequently define housework as 'use value' production, that is, production for the household rather than production for the market ('exchange value'),[47] but this terminology is inappropriate to a small farming economy where much of what is produced 'in the fields' is consumed by the household. Use of these terms results in the rather empty conclusion that, in rural communities, housework is 'use value' production that can be carried out just as well in non-agricultural households as agricultural households.[48]

Casual alternation between the terms 'housework' and 'housewife' confuses the issue of unwaged domestic labour. Much housework is performed by single women (such as daughters and nieces) or by women not married to the 'male head of the family' (such as mothers, sisters, and female in-laws). Furthermore, men also perform housework. The term 'housekeeper' has certain ideological overtones drawn from a later period; and 'domestic workers' are liable to be confused with 'domestic servants'. It is more appropriate to call people who perform housework 'houseworkers', irrespective of marital or familial status. However, to work in a house is not enough. Paid domestic servants and piece-workers need to be excluded. For the purposes of this study, housework is defined as those uses of household time, outside the arrangements of paid markets, which are aimed at the production of goods and services that might be replaced by market goods and services. Crucially, housework can be performed by a paid servant without any reduction in its utility (unlike leisure activities).

Definitional problems hide a basic consensus about what houseworkers actually do. They work for 'the family'. They prepare food, organize consumption, and ensure some degree of post-consumption cleaning. The home and the ground immediately around the home are their responsibility. In the words of Rosie Hickey, a schoolgirl from Kilgarvan High School (county Kerry), in 1910, housework involved living up to the old rule: 'A place for everything and everything in its proper place.'[49] Clothing and furnishings are often produced by houseworkers and are

---

[47] See e.g. Benson, 'The Political Economy of Women's Liberation', 13–27.

[48] This is the definition of housework used by Christine Delphy, *Close to Home: A Materialist Analysis of Women's Oppression* (1984), 85–7.

[49] Letter from Rosie Hickey of the Kilgarvan High School in county Kerry, in *Irish Weekly Independent*, 6 Aug. 1910: 9.

generally serviced by them. Houseworkers take care of the family, manage the household, and attempt to ensure that the relationship between 'the market' and 'the household' remains amicable. They are managers of capital and human resources. Their role as mediators between the patriarchal 'head' and the 'children' cannot be ignored. Housework is the reproduction of labour power; that is, it reproduces the capacity for work on a daily and generational basis. Labour power is used up daily: the value created by housework re-creates labour power. Its use value is transferred into exchange value whenever labour is sold.[50] If housework were seriously regarded as 'work', it would be the largest sector of the labour market. The value created by housework is often estimated as exceeding half of the conventional valuations of national income.[51] The cost of maintenance and reproduction is much smaller when it is performed by a houseworker than it would be if these goods and services had to be bought on the market.[52] Consumption cannot occur without housework: it transforms income into consumable goods. Housework is production.

WELL-BEING IN THE IRISH COUNTRYSIDE

Agricultural Production

Between 1890 and 1914 the Irish rural sector experienced rapid economic growth, as measured by the value added of agricultural products and by levels of investment in the rural economy.[53]

[50] Bennholdt-Thomsen, 'Subsistence Production and Extended Reproduction', 41–54.

[51] For one of the earliest economic works to impute values for housework, see Colin Clark, 'The Economics of House-Work', *Bulletin of the Oxford University Institute of Statistics*, 20 (1958), 205–11.

[52] For a discussion of the relationship between housework and the accumulation of capital, see Coulson, Magas, and Wainwright, 'A Critique', 59–71; Terry Fee, 'Domestic Labour: An Analysis of Housework and its Relation to the Production Process', *Review of Radical Political Economics*, 8/1 (Spring 1976), 1–8; Gardiner, 'Women's Domestic Labour', 47–58; Ira Gerstein, 'Domestic Work and Capitalism', *Radical America*, 7/4 (July–Oct. 1973), 101–28; Harrison, 'The Political Economy of Housework', 35–52; and Seccombe, 'The Housewife under Capitalism', 3–24.

[53] The rural sector is defined narrowly as including the farming sector and excluding forestry and fishery.

In the two decades before 1890, large-scale foreign competition was influencing the British market. New techniques in marketing had revitalized Continental agricultural production. The depression in agriculture lasted from the 1870s until the middle of the 1890s, after which farm prices began rising.[54] Agriculture in Ireland underwent rapid change in the two decades before World War I. Erratic but vital growth had occurred throughout the century, but the cumulative impact of these changes hit Ireland at the end of the nineteenth century. Rapidly improving standards of living across a wide spectrum of classes in the countryside were expressions of this growth.

Gross national product (GNP per head) is the most common measure of economic growth. As the sum of final products, GNP represents the flow of traded resources and their potential to satisfy human needs. No GNP series exists for Ireland before World War I. Since this book is concerned with the rural community, agricultural output is taken as a proxy for rural GNP. The value of Irish agricultural output grew rapidly between 1860 and 1870, before commencing a decline that was not halted until the 1890s. Overall agricultural production increased by 20 per cent in the two decades between 1890 and 1910.[55] Total annual output for each agricultural worker increased from £50 in 1880 and 1890 to over £71 by 1910.[56] Output increases were not achieved by an expansion in labour or land inputs. The number of people 'engaged in agriculture' declined from 936,000 to 780,000 in the same twenty years. The amount of land in tillage between 1890 and 1910 decreased by 0.4 million statute acres, and the acreage in pasture decreased by 0.5 million. Between 1890 and 1910 agricultural output of crops increased by 24 per cent, while the percentage of the total area used for crops decreased by 6 per cent. In 1890 every acre of land under crops and hay produced yields to the value of £2 (on average). By 1910, the value of the output of each acre had increased by almost one-third. In terms

---

[54] For a discussion of the long-term trends, see Liam Kennedy, 'The Rural Economy, 1820–1914', in Liam Kennedy and Philip Ollerenshaw (eds.), *An Economic History of Ulster, 1820–1940* (Manchester, 1985), 1–61.

[55] For an in-depth analysis, see my 'Husbandry to Housewifery: Rural Women and Development in Ireland, 1890–1914', Ph.D. thesis (Canberra, 1989).

[56] This was calculated by dividing output per acre by the number of workers per acre.

of gross production, every acre of land under crops and hay produced 15 hundredweight of crops in 1890 and 18 hundred-weight of crops in 1910. Gross statistics on export trade in agricultural products reflect these changes. The total valuation of exports of butter, beef, pork, bacon, hams, poultry, and eggs increased from £5,472,000 to £12,258,000 (or by 63 per cent) in nine years.[57] There are many reasons for this growth in the agricultural sector; but the massive capital investment channelled through state and private institutions such as the Congested Districts Board (CDB), the Irish Agricultural Organization Society (IAOS), and the Department of Agriculture and Technical Instruction for Ireland (DATI) cannot be ignored. Their extensive intervention in the rural economy included schemes designed to raise the fertility of the land, improve livestock breeds, and promote the sale of high-quality seeds.[58]

Human Capital

Investment in people was the most important non-economic factor affecting agricultural productivity. Although human capital outlays are not always motivated by the desire to increase income (people sometimes educate themselves for pleasure), investment in human understanding and health often has pecuniary effects. While the volume of labour input in Irish agriculture declined, the *quality* of labour inputs improved. Irish workers were healthier, stronger, better fed, and more educated.[59] Farmers and farm labourers shared in the overall improvement in basic literacy.[60]

Much of the investment in human capital was motivated by ideas that remain influential today about the urgency of developing human resources as an integral part of general developmental

[57] Across all products, the value of exports increased by 22% between 1904 and 1913.

[58] See my 'Husbandry to Housewifery' for a history of the CDB, the DATI, and the IAOS, and for a detailed description of the intervention.

[59] Cullen, *The Emergence of Modern Ireland*.

[60] Data taken from the census tables of 1891 and 1911, as published in the British parliamentary papers. For example, in 1891, 44% of boys aged 12 and 47% of girls aged 12 attended school. Twenty years later, the figures were 70% and 73% respectively. The *Census of Ireland, 1911: General Report* (Cd. 6663), HC 1912–13, cxviii. 286, notes that the % of boys attending school for more than 100 days a year increased from 40% in 1871 to 56% in 1891 and 64% in 1911. The corresponding figures for girls were 41%, 58%, and 65% respectively.

planning.[61] All reforming institutions in Ireland invested in agricultural education. By the 1890s, agricultural instruction was compulsory for boys in all rural national schools.[62] Irish farmers gained access to information about improved farming techniques through the services of itinerant instructors, model farms, and agricultural schools. The DATI and the CDB distributed pamphlets widely. The effect of these educational improvements is impossible to measure.

Distributional Factors: Land and Tenure

In agriculture, the distribution of these economic and non-economic benefits broadened, particularly through widening access to credit facilities and through government intervention in land allocation. There is some hint of the distributional changes in the fact that, while Irish bank deposits in the entire country increased more than fourfold between the 1880s and the 1910s, post office deposits in the poorer, 'congested' districts increased ninefold.[63] An important aspect in capital formation was the improvement in credit facilities.[64] One example is the co-operative credit societies, which began with a total membership of 71 in 1895, but had grown to nearly 20,000 within sixteen years. In 1911 they granted loans for agricultural development to the value of over £56,000.[65]

The distribution of land was more important than that of credit.

[61] For a summary of the literature, see Theodore W. Schultz, *Investing in People: The Economics of Population Quality* (Berkeley, Calif., 1981), and Darim Albassam, *Investment in Human Capital and its Contribution to Economic Growth and Income Distribution in Developing Countries* (East Lansing, Mich., 1973).

[62] *Programmes of Instruction in Agriculture in National Schools* (Dublin, 1896), and *Report of the Recess Committee on the Establishment of a Department of Agriculture and Industries for Ireland* (Dublin, 1896), 89.

[63] DATI, *Report of the Departmental Committee on Agricultural Credit in Ireland* (Cd. 7375), HC 1914, xiii. 39, and W. L. Micks, *An Account of the Constitution, Administration, and Dissolution of the CDB, from 1891 to 1923* (Dublin, 1925), 221–2. In *Irish Agricultural Production* Crotty argues that this capital was not reinvested in the farm. However, if, as Crotty suggests, the increased savings were used as dowry payments, then the investments probably did increase productivity by spreading payments across the rural population.

[64] Liam Kennedy provides an excellent summary of credit facilities in the 1890s: 'Retail Markets in Rural Ireland at the End of the Nineteenth Century', *Irish Economic and Social History*, 5 (1978), 46–63.

[65] DATI, *Report of the Committee on Agricultural Credit*, xiii. 128.

Other historians have dealt at length with the effects of the land acts in Ireland.[66] The most influential statutes date from the 1880s. By the Land Act of 1881, the Purchase of Land (Ireland) Acts of 1885–8 and 1891–6, and the Wyndham Land Act of 1903, rents were dramatically reduced.[67] The Wyndham Land Act of 1903 (extended in 1909) enabled tenants to buy their land through annual repayments, and landlords were compensated in a lump sum by the state. By 1905, virtually all the land except leasehold was either subject to judicial rents or vested in the occupiers. These changes ensured farmers both security of tenure and compensation for improvements. It increased their incomes to the extent that judicial rents or the Land Commission's annuities were lower than competitive rents. While the number of holdings remained stable, the proportion of owner-occupiers amongst farmers increased from around 3 per cent in the third quarter of the nineteenth century to 66 per cent by 1912. Most of those who remained as tenants were in possession of secure leaseholds.[68] The land reform measures reduced the cost of the fixed land input in agricultural production by as much as 20 per cent between the third quarter of the nineteenth century and 1914. Land ownership also affected the willingness of farmers to invest in the land.[69] In tillage districts, the effects were seen in early ploughing, cleaning of ditches and fields, trimming fences, re-making farm roads, and reclaiming land.[70]

The social effect of these reforms in land tenure is equally important. In the words of one of the commissioners examining the effects of the land reforms: 'The first and in many respects the most important outcome of purchase is the feeling of contentment

[66] See e.g. B. Solow, *The Land Question and the Irish Economy, 1870–1903* (Cambridge, Mass., 1971), and W. E. Vaughan, *Landlords and Tenants in Ireland, 1848–1904* (Dundalk, 1984).

[67] *Return Showing, by Counties, the Average Number of Years' Purchase under the Different Land Purchase Acts, 1885 to 1903* (357.), HC 1908, xc. 1–5.

[68] J. Huttman, 'The Impact of Land Reform on Agricultural Production in Ireland', *Agricultural History*, 46 (1972), 355, and DATI, *Agricultural Statistics, Ireland, 1912* (Cd. 6987), HC 1913, lxxvi.

[69] *Report of Mr William F. Bailey, Legal Assistant Commissioner of an Inquiry into the Present Condition of Tenant Purchasers* (92.), HC 1903, lvii. 5–6. See also DATI, *Report of the Committee, on Agricultural Credit*, xiii. 320.

[70] *Report of Mr William F. Bailey*, 6. See also *First Report from the Select Committee of the House of Lords on Land Law (Ireland)* (.249), HC 1882, xi. 63, evidence by Denis Godley, secretary to the Land Commission.

which it has given the people. Their minds are at ease. The anxiety as to the future which formerly oppressed them has disappeared.'[71] The commissioner went on to say that low repayments and the 'greater self-respect that has followed proprietorship' meant that tenant purchasers had a higher standard of living than their rent-paying neighbours.[72] In Leinster and Munster the extra income was diverted into improving the productivity of the land rather than increasing consumption. In the poorer western areas, surpluses were absorbed into the household: increased consumption was a prerequisite for increased productivity.[73]

The 20 per cent rise in the value of agricultural production between 1890 and 1910 reflected improvements in the productivity of land and labour. Capital investment was a significant factor in the growth of the rural economy. The general increases in living standards that resulted from the increased production were not necessarily immediately reinvested in agriculture. In poorer areas particularly, capital surpluses and land reforms influenced the rural economy indirectly by being absorbed into the household.

While this book is primarily an attempt to explain changes in female labour experience in Ireland from the last decade of the nineteenth century, the increased concentration of female labour in housewifery in Britain and Europe in this period is clearly relevant. This analysis of Irish trends is a step towards a broader understanding of the separation of men and women in the paid and unpaid labour markets. Although Ireland was primarily a rural society in the late nineteenth century, the relationship between housewifery and rising living standards in Ireland is consistent with trends in women's work in urban Britain.[74] The greater diversity of wealth in Britain makes the shift of female labour to full-time housewifery seem slower there. However,

[71] *Report of Mr William F. Bailey*, 12–13.
[72] Ibid. 14. See also DATI, *Report of the Committee, on Agricultural Credit*, xiii. 323.
[73] *Report of Mr William F. Bailey*, 15.
[74] Joanna Bourke, 'How to Be Happy Though Married: Housewifery in Working-Class Britain, 1860–1914', *Past and Present*, forthcoming; Jane Lewis, *Women in England, 1870–1950* (Brighton, 1984); Angela V. John (ed.), *Unequal Opportunities: Women's Employment in England, 1800–1918* (Oxford, 1986); Louise A. Tilly and Joan W. Scott, *Women, Work and Family* (1975); and Jane Lewis (ed.), *Labour and Love: Women's Experience of Home and Family, 1850–1940* (Oxford, 1986).

working-class women in Britain also began to invest progressively more of their time in housework from the 1890s. This shift occurred earlier among middle-class women.

For both Ireland and Britain, the primacy of economic motivations rather than some vague notion of 'patriarchy' or 'respectability' is stressed. The crucial element is *time*. Women's time spent in housework competes with alternative uses of time. Changes in domestic production and productivity increased the time required to perform housework. The issue of choice, though not irrelevant to the discussion, is set aside, since, by the last decades of the nineteenth century, housework was already seen as the *primary* responsibility of women. With the increasing amount of time required to fulfil this primary function, women moved into full-time work in the unwaged household sector.

The structure of this book follows the argument advanced in this introduction. First, the world of paid work in extra-domestic and domestic sectors is examined. Part Two discusses women and farming practices, with special reference to household agriculture and poultry-rearing. Part Three is concerned with the history of housework. To conclude, we return to the theoretical issues and the implications of this study for economic development, the history of women, and Irish history in general.

PART ONE:

PAID WORKERS

1

Paid Employment

Because men have become so effeminate that they wish to
do women's work, it is no reason why women should en-
deavour to become so masculine as to invade the sphere of
man.[1]

HISTORIANS and economists still prefer to define 'labour' narrowly as paid employment. From whatever standpoint, analysis
of well-being within market-orientated societies gives a peculiar
dominance to market labour. Increasingly, scholars have been
entering the treacherous arena of sex, labelled 'spheres' of labour,
and have increased our understanding of the work process for
women as well as for men. Nearly all men and most women
spend part of their life engaged in production for the market.
The well-being of both sexes is heavily dependent on the
availability of employment, the type of employment, the conditions of employment, and the appropriate remuneration for
employment. Life choices (and chances) are influenced by per-
ceptions of employment. Money is needed to buy many of the
basic human needs. Unemployment can mean dependency or
poverty.

Rapid swings in employment participation, choices, and status
for any large group are obviously important. For Irish women,
the crucial period was the two decades after 1890, when there
was a shift of their labour out of paid employment markets
and into the unpaid sphere. This chapter traces one side of this
shift; that is, their movement out of paid employment. There was
no *one* explanation for the changes traced in this chapter, and
detailed analysis of the relative weights that we should give to
possible explanations is left to other chapters. At this stage, it is
necessary to document shifts in female labour within the major
sectors of the employment market, to introduce complexities
relating to life cycle and regionalism, and to evaluate some of the

[1] 'A Ratepayer', 'Women's Suffrage', *IH*, 6 Apr. 1912: 277.

broader explanations for women's increased exclusion from paid employment.[2]

The fundamental change can be summarized in one sentence: between 1891 and 1911 the figure entered in the Irish census for the percentage of all men with designated occupations remained steady at 64 per cent, which contrasts with a rapid decline from 27 to 19 per cent in the numbers of women with designated occupations.[3] Documenting this unusually rapid decline of female employment in Ireland is hampered by incomplete and inaccurate data. Published census data are discouraging. The exclusion of 'farmers' wives and daughters' from the census statistics, and the ambiguity of categories such as 'agricultural labourer', 'indoor farm servant', and 'domestic servant', have encouraged historians to examine only urban trends, despite the predominantly rural nature of Irish society in this period.[4] The available data simply ignore certain types of labour. Neither the censuses nor the agricultural statistics can be relied upon for estimates of labour on family farms. Part-time workers may or may not be included. People are rarely credited with more than one occupation. Establishing the number of females causes particular problems. Until 1926, Irish censuses say nothing about houseworkers. Census forms were usually filled in by men, either in their capacity of 'heads of families' or as census enumerators. Can they be trusted? For instance, Bridget Heslin lived in the Keeldra district (county Leitrim). In the 1901 census her stepfather said that she was a farmer's daughter. Ten years later, he repudiated this familial link with her (although he was still married to her mother), and claimed that their relationship was that of master

[2] For a much more detailed statistical analysis, see my 'Husbandry to Housewifery: Rural Women and Development in Ireland, 1890–1914', Ph.D. thesis (Canberra, 1989).

[3] An estimate has been made for the number of women in professional occupations in 1891 to make it comparable with the 1911 figure, which excludes students.

[4] For a summary of some of the problems faced by historians of rural employment, see David Fitzpatrick, 'The Disappearance of the Irish Agricultural Labourer, 1841–1912', *Irish Economic and Social History*, 7 (1980), 66–92. Mary E. Daly, 'Women in the Irish Workforce from Pre-Industrial to Modern Times', *Saothar* 7 (1981), 74–82, provides a superb analysis of urban trends.

Table 1.1. Number of men and women with designated occupations, 1841–1911 (000s)

Year	Women	Men	Total
1841	1,169.6	2,342.2	3,511.8
1851	938.2	1,903.4	2,841.6
1861	845.7	1,827.4	2,673.1
1871	817.3	1,665.4	2,482.7
1881	814.6	1,571.9	2,386.5
1891	641.4	1,504.3	2,145.7
1901	549.9	1,413.9	1,963.8
1911	430.1	1,387.2	1,817.3

Source: Censuses of Ireland, 1841–1911.

to servant. Kate Carr also lived in Keeldra. In 1901 Kate and her husband were both called farmers. In 1911 her husband again wrote that she was a 'farmer', but this was crossed out, presumably by the census enumerator, and Kate was placed in the 'unoccupied' category of the census.[5] One of the advantages of using manuscript household data is that we can identify different 'hands' at work, adding to, or deleting from, the forms. The researcher has to be cautious, however, seeking confirmation outside the statistical tables.

The limitations of the census do not make its analysis unprofitable. What does the census tell us about employment? While it severely underestimates the number of people engaged in subsistence production, and ignores unwaged domestic occupations, it does provide a broad indication of the numbers of those claiming to be engaged in 'gainful employment'. Table 1.1 sets out the figures for the number of men and women entered as having designated occupations in the census between 1841 and 1911.[6]

[5] Manuscript census returns for Keeldra DED, NAI, 1901 and 1911, nos. 20 and 147.

[6] A few adjustments have been made in the census statistics to make them more comparable. Because of the radical changes in the way in which occupations were recorded in the 1871 census, I have subtracted the 'wives' category from the total number of women entered as having designated occupations in 1871. Those 15–19-year-olds who were classified as 'literary and scientific' persons in 1881 and 1901 were placed in the 'unoccupied' category to make the statistics comparable with the 1901 and 1911 censuses.

Employment statistics vary significantly between rural and urban areas, with rural women less liable to claim employment. The mean percentage of women employed between 1881 and 1911 ranged between 17 and 30 per cent in all areas, but only between 15 and 23 per cent in rural areas.[7] Outside the cities, female employment was highest on labour-intensive small farms in crop-producing districts. The southern central counties of Tipperary, Kilkenny, Carlow, Kings', and Queens' retained higher levels of employment. Very low female participation in the workforce characterized the western counties, especially Mayo. By 1911, only the northern counties, the Dublin hinterlands, and the counties of Limerick, Waterford, and Kilkenny employed even one-sixth of their rural female population. In no county did more than one-quarter of rural women claim an occupation.

Female employment is strongly related to the cycle of youth, marriage, child-rearing, maturity, and old age. These life-cycle aspects can be examined by analysing the age structure of the employed cohorts.[8] The percentage of women with a designated occupation in the 1891 census peaked at the 15–19 age-group and then dropped rapidly, levelling off or increasing slightly after age 44. By 1911, proportionately more women aged between 20 and 24 were employed than between 15 and 19, and female participation was lowest in the middle years between marriage and maturity (that is, between the ages of 20 and 44). Once again, there was a levelling-off or increase in the proportion of women aged over 25 in the occupational statistics. The poorest province, Connaught, was remarkable for the increase in the proportion of women aged over 44 who were entered as having designated occupations. Among men, the pattern is very different. Participation levels stabilized after the ages of 19 (1891) and 24 (1911). Male participation rates declined only for the elderly.

Provincial patterns in the age structure of the employed female population are striking. Within each age category, the lower rate of participation in Connaught differentiates this province from the other three. This disparity only disappears for the elderly.

---

[7] 'Rural' areas exclude all urban county districts and towns with over 1,500 inhabitants.

[8] Strictly speaking, age-specific data reflect changes over time as well as life-cycle effects. We are comparing different cohorts, not the same cohort at different ages.

Furthermore, in the decades 1891–1901 and 1901–1911, the percentage of women of each age category in employment declined more rapidly in Connaught than in any of the other provinces.

The occupational participation levels of men and women under the age of 20 show greater homogeneity. Not only did fewer members of both groups claim occupational affiliation, but the total percentage of employed men and women in this age-group was closer (the male percentage ranged from 16 to 28 per cent, and the female from 13 to 22 per cent). The highest percentage of employment for all women under the age of 20 was found in Ulster, followed by Leinster, Munster, then Connaught. Taking into account changes in the total population of young people, the employment participation rate of men under the age of 20 decreased by between 24 and 28 per cent in every province. The corresponding change for young women was between 32 and 48 per cent. The largest changes in participation occurred in Connaught and Munster.

The marital status of these workers is more difficult to ascertain. Between 1881 and 1911 the published census data do not break down employment by marital status; nor do they tell us anything about the relationship between family structure and employment. In 1871, however, tables were provided showing the employment of married women and tabulating the number of female 'farmer's relatives'. In the whole population, between 9 per cent (Leinster) and 17 per cent (Connaught) of women in the occupational tables were married. The large numbers of married women within each age-group who were entered as having an occupation are surprising. One-third of wives between the ages of 15 and 19 appeared in the occupational tables, and this proportion increased at each age category, exceeding half in Connaught in the 25–34 age-group and in Ulster in the 35–44 age-group. The employment of married women was lower in Munster and Leinster. The high proportion of married women in the paid labour force in Ulster can be explained by the high concentrations of married women in the linen and textile industries. However, Connaught had little employment in these industries; 83 per cent of the wives in Connaught were listed as being engaged in agricultural pursuits, most of them as the wives of farmers and graziers.

Data dealing with a later period can be extracted from the

manuscript census returns for households for 1901 and 1911. Eight district electoral divisions (DEDs) in the counties of Waterford, Limerick, Galway, Leitrim, Donegal, Monaghan, Fermanagh, and Kings' have been examined.[9] As shown in Table 1.2, the most rapid decline in female employment occurred in the north-western community of Ards. The smallest declines occurred in the eastern districts. In 1901 unmarried women were generally categorized as farmers' relatives; married women were usually given no occupation; and widows were classed as farmers. By 1911, women were largely placed in the unknown or 'no occupation' category, regardless of marital status. However, almost half of all widows were still likely to be farmers, and nearly one-fifth of single women were domestic servants. The number of married women in Woodstown and Rathmore who had designated occupations *increased* between 1901 and 1911, despite the overall decrease in the aggregated figures for married women in the eight communities. The increase in these two eastern communities was caused by the number of married women who entered into domestic or farm service. If we accept the definition of the census commissioners of 'occupied' as excluding women in the unknown category and those enumerated in the census as relatives of farmers, scholars, or in unwaged domestic occupations, the proportion of 'occupied' women declined within each marital category. In the ten years between 1901 and 1911 the number of 'occupied' single women

[9] The manuscript census returns for 8 DEDs were examined in 1901 and 1911. Seven districts were chosen at random, with limitations: the districts had to be rural and in different counties. The district of Belleek was deliberately chosen to facilitate my study of home industries. The census data for the districts were matched with the house and land valuation records held at the Valuation Office in Dublin.

District	County	Number of individuals		Number of households	
		1901	1911	1901	1911
Rathmore	Limerick	280	279	52	52
Tullamore	Kings'	446	514	104	113
Kilconickny	Galway	446	428	90	88
Ballatrain	Monaghan	516	530	128	126
Woodstown	Waterford	546	560	120	117
Ards	Donegal	672	659	211	126
Belleek	Fermanagh	797	686	194	171
Keeldra	Leitrim	833	559	170	131
TOTAL		4536	4215	1069	924

Table 1.2. Marital status of adult women with designated occupations, 1901 and 1911 (%)

	Unmarried	Married	Widowed
1901[a]			
Ards	40.4	3.4	53.3
Woodstown	52.5	4.4	52.4
Tullamore	30.0	8.1	71.4
Keeldra	13.0	7.3	78.6
Kilconickny	14.3	4.8	58.3
Bellatrain	40.2	13.0	70.7
Belleek	49.3	10.9	46.7
Rathmore	47.5	3.3	75.0
1911[b]			
Ards	24.5	1.0	29.6
Woodstown	45.7	13.6	41.4
Tullamore	27.9	2.9	45.5
Keeldra	9.4	2.4	40.6
Kilconickny	7.2	1.6	53.8
Bellatrain	33.8	7.8	60.5
Belleek	36.7	7.7	25.6
Rathmore	37.3	12.1	45.5

[a] n (no. in sample) = 743, 612, and 250 for the unmarried, married, and widowed categories respectively.

[b] n = 688, 581, and 211 for these categories.

Source: Manuscript census returns, NAI, 1901 and 1911.

declined by 9 per cent, that of married women by 2 per cent, and that of widowed women by 20 per cent.[10] The small decline in the proportion of married women with designated occupations was due to the low initial level of that category. As will be shown later in this chapter, married women with designated occupations had particular characteristics that set them apart.

SECTORAL ANALYSIS OF EMPLOYMENT

Different rates of change occurred between occupational categories. There was a declining proportion of women in domestic,

[10] This analysis only includes women over 15.

Table 1.3. The representation of women within occupational 'classes', 1881–1911 (%)

'Class'	1881	1891	1901	1911
Professional	31.3	35.1	24.9	26.6
Domestic	92.0	86.5	88.1	84.9
Commercial	2.1	2.6	5.1	8.8
Agricultural	9.6	9.7	9.8	7.6
Industrial	38.0	38.4	36.5	29.1
Indefinite or non-productive	65.5	68.2	68.5	68.7

Source: Censuses of Ireland, 1881–1911.

agricultural, and industrial fields, while their representation in the commercial and professional category increased (see Table 1.3).

The 'commercial class' was the only sector where female participation increased significantly. It was a small category. In 1891, only 2,161 women were involved in commercial occupations, and although this number increased to 9,747 over the next twenty years, they still constituted less than 9 per cent of all people in commercial occupations. The number of commercial men increased from 81,012 to 101,396. 'A. G. C.', writing to the *Irish Homestead*, expressed the typically ambivalent attitude towards women in commercial occupations:

No sensible person wishes women to do men's work, but the progress of machinery has and is changing our ideas as to what should belong to each. The typewriter, for instance, has displaced many men clerks. This may not be undesirable, but it is no more unjust than the usurpation of women's home work by men working in factories.[11]

'A. G. C.' was correct: changes in the number of commercial women could be traced to an influx of female clerks. Thus, in 1891, 42 per cent of the women in commerce were clerks. By 1911, over 80 per cent were clerks. It was both a small occupational category and, for the purposes of this book, marginal in another way: it was an urban occupation, and rising female representation did not benefit women residing in rural areas.

[11] 'A. G. C.', 'Women's Suffrage', *IH*, 30 Mar. 1912: 256–7.

The only other occupational category to experience an increase in the proportion of women was the professional category. These statistics need careful examination, however, since the criteria for admission into this class changed between the censuses of 1891 and 1901. In 1901 the enumerators transferred 'scholars' aged over 15 from the 'literary and scientific' category of the professional class to the 'persons of no specified occupation' class.[12] Adjusting the 1891 figure, we can conclude that female representation in the professions increased slightly. In 1891 they constituted 22 per cent of all professionals, compared with 25 per cent in 1911.

This change was caused by the movement of women into the teaching profession. In 1841 women constituted 32 per cent of all teachers, but this had increased to 63 per cent by 1911. Despite discriminatory wages policies and a glutted market, school teaching was widely billed as 'the most important profession open to women'.[13] Promotion was easier for women than for men. Women constituted over half of all school principals in the counties of Meath, Waterford, Dublin, Westmeath, Kings', Kildare, Wexford, Kilkenny, and Carlow, primarily due to the large number of small, single-sex schools in the south and east.[14] Promotion was less open in the northern counties.[15] An analysis of age statistics shows that, although female teachers were marginally more likely to die early, their promotional chances in certain grades were improving. Between 1880 and 1900 female teachers were slightly older than their male counterparts when receiving promotion. But in 1901 women tended to be four years younger when they were promoted to Class 1(1), and almost a year younger when they were promoted to Class 1(2). Men and women were almost the same ages when they were promoted to Classes 2 and 3. In 1901 female teachers were older than male teachers. They had been almost a

[12] *Census of Ireland, 1901*, ii (Cd. 1190), HC 1902, cxxix. 22.

[13] Joseph P. O'Kane, *Leader*, 4 June 1910: 368, and Miss Cummins (winner of the Gold Medal from the Cork University Philosophical Society), *Irish Citizen*, 18 July 1914: 66.

[14] *Education (Ireland): Report of Mr F. H. Dale on Primary Education* (Cd. 1981), HC 1904, xx. 36.

[15] NLI, 'Minutes of the Proceedings of the Commissioners of National Education at their Meeting on Tuesday, 3 March 1914', 61; statistics taken from a list of the numbers of principals, assistant teachers, and junior assistant mistresses in 1912.

year older than men when they resigned or were dismissed, but
in 1901 they were almost a year younger. However, women were
reappointed to their jobs at a younger age. The age of retirement
increased for female teachers. Between 1880 and 1900 women
tended to retire six and a half years earlier than men. This differential declined to under four years by the turn of the century.[16]
For rural educated women with some familial or local support,
teaching was one of the few expanding possibilities. The expansion, however, was slow, and it was a fortunate woman who
found a good job.

All other occupational categories were experiencing a decline
in the proportion of women. The most significant decline in female
employment occurred in industry. Although the wages of Irish
women in industry in the 1860s were often less than one-third of
their British counterparts, industry was much more 'feminized'
in Ireland.[17] In 1861, over half of all Irish people with designated
industrial occupations were female. However, from the end of
the nineteenth century men began to predominate. By 1891, the
percentage of women in Irish industries had decreased to 38, and
then it dropped further to 29 per cent by 1911. The decline in the
proportion of women engaged in industry was less steep for
those under the age of 20, where the proportion of women fell
from 48 per cent in 1891 to 44 per cent by 1911. Industry as a
whole was depressed, affecting even male workers. In no county
did the number of men in industrial occupations fall by more
than 16 per cent, and in the south their numbers rose by up to
thirty per cent. The number of female industrial workers declined
in all counties, falling by over 60 per cent in Leitrim, Roscommon,
and Cavan. Women were less affected in county Dublin (excluding
the city) and Louth. This geographical pattern is largely explained
by the collapse of the linen market, affecting both factory workers
in the north-east, Waterford, and Kildare, and cottage workers in
Roscommon, Leitrim, Cavan, and Fermanagh.

It is simplistic to talk about 'industrial occupations' as a whole.
Within this category, the pattern is not uniform. For women
working in the industrial sector, the most important occupations

[16] *Appendix to the 68th Report of the Commissioners of National Education, 1901*, ii
(Cd. 1444), HC 1903, xxi. 91.
[17] RCL, *Fifth and Final Report* (C. 7421-i), HC 1894, xxxv. 476, app. 3, Mean
wages of women in factories and workshops, 1891–1892, by district.

were milliners, stay-makers, dressmakers, shirt-makers, and seamstresses. The number of milliners, stay-makers, and dressmakers
increased between 1891 and 1901, before declining in the following
decade. Between 1901 and 1911 the number of women in the
millinery, stay-making, and dressmaking trades declined by 35
per cent, and the number of female shirt-makers and seamstresses
(a profession already experiencing difficulties by 1881) declined
by 52 per cent.

Although the industrial sector saw the fastest declines in female
representation, the trends in domestic service were more significant. Domestic service—employing the largest proportion of all
occupied women—slumped both numerically and proportionately. In 1891, 220,100 women were engaged in domestic occupations, dropping to 193,300 by 1901, then to 144,900 by 1911. As
a proportion, female domestic servants declined by 33 per cent,
compared with a decline of 8 per cent amongst male domestic
servants. Women in Connaught were hit hardest. As regards the
number of women in employment, however, the female percentage scarcely changed. In 1891 and in 1911, approximately one-
third of all employed women were domestic servants. In terms
of actual numbers, male indoor domestic servants declined more
rapidly than female servants in the last decade of the nineteenth
century, then increased between 1901 and 1911, when the decline
in the number of female indoor domestic servants was especially
rapid. These changes are crucial to understanding the position of
Irish women in employment, and they are examined in greater
detail in Chapter 2.

Agriculture, including farmers, agricultural labourers, and farm
servants, was the largest occupational sector. Overall changes in
the number of men and women employed in this sector are shown
in Table 1.4. Again, the decline in the number of men in agriculture was minor compared with the decline experienced by
women. The fastest falls occurred in Cork and Waterford, where
the number of male agricultural labourers declined by about 13
per cent in both counties, compared with female declines of 16
per cent in Cork and 29 per cent in Waterford. Within the female
agricultural population, the fastest declines occurred in Waterford,
Meath, and Dublin, and the slowest declines in Donegal and
Westmeath.

The significance of these changes is hard to judge: women

Table 1.4. Male and female employment in the agricultural sector, 1861–1911 (000s)

Year	Women	Men	Total
1861	84.1	904.7	988.8
1871	93.6	891.9	985.5
1881	95.9	902.0	997.9
1891	91.1	845.7	936.8
1901	85.6	790.5	876.1
1911	59.2	721.7	780.9

Source: Censuses of Ireland, 1861–1911.

made up a very small proportion of the total numbers designated as being engaged in agricultural pursuits. Their high representation in Cork and Tyrone was unusual. More commonly, women constituted between 2 and 5 per cent of all those said to be engaged in agricultural occupations. In part, the seeming insignificance of this category was caused by the fact that female farmers' relatives were eliminated from the census tables, but male farmers' relatives were included. Due to this definitional sleight of hand, over half of all occupied men were categorized as being employed in agriculture, compared with less than one-sixth of all occupied women. The percentage of all women engaged in agriculture declined from 4 per cent to 3 per cent between 1881 and 1911, compared with a decline of 35 to 33 per cent in the proportion of all men in agricultural occupations.

Clearly, different ways of portraying changes in the presence of women in agriculture need to be found. We can find evidence for a reduction in the number of women in the fields by looking at the age structure of the female agricultural labour force. In 1881, 16 per cent of the male agricultural population were aged under 20, compared with 11 per cent in 1911. Among the female agricultural population, 15 per cent were in the younger age-group in 1881, compared with only 2 per cent by 1911. No other occupational category experienced such a radical ageing. Young women just entering the occupational labour force were choosing not to perform agricultural labour.

Within the category 'engaged in agriculture', it is helpful to

Table 1.5. Number of male and female agricultural and general labourers, 1871–1911 (000s)

Year	Agricultural labourers		General labourers[a]		Total	
	Men	Women	Men	Women	Men	Women
1871	446.7	62.7	194.8	19.8	641.5	82.5
1881	300.1	36.0	104.6	9.4	404.7	45.4
1891	258.0	22.0	82.8	4.6	340.8	26.6
1901	217.7	14.2	76.9	2.2	294.6	16.4
1911	195.9	4.0	101.0	1.1	296.9	5.1

[a] In the case of general labourers, labourers listed in the 6 county boroughs have been excluded.

Source: DATI, *Agricultural Statistics, Ireland, 1909–1910* (Cd. 5033), HC 1910, cviii. 7.

distinguish between farmers and labourers.[18] The number of female farmers and graziers increased in the decade 1891–1901, a time when the number of male farmers and graziers declined. In the decade 1901–1911, though, the number of female farmers and graziers declined by 23 per cent. The number of male farmers and graziers remained stable.

An even more dramatic change in the agricultural sector occurred amongst labourers (see Table 1.5). In the decades 1891–1901 and 1901–1911, the number of women who gave their occupation as agricultural labourers declined by 35 and 72 per cent respectively, compared with declines of 16 and 10 per cent among male agricultural labourers. Similarly, the number of female farm servants (indoor) declined in these decades by 28 and 75 per cent, while male numbers declined by 26 and 19 per cent.

These changes were not lost on contemporary observers. Women were accused of 'looking down' on agricultural employment. Female members of the small-farmer class had begun to regard certain types of agricultural work as inappropriate forms of female labour. Employers complained that women, who had been the 'sheet anchor of the farmer in harvest', now preferred

[18] For the problems associated with this procedure, see Fitzpatrick, 'The Disappearance of the Irish Labourer', 66–92.

emigration to agricultural labour.[19] This theme dominates reports on agricultural labour. For example, the steward to Lord John Browne, William Davidson of Westport, complained that: 'You cannot now get a woman to work at any price. They all go to the American mills . . . Boys have taken the place of women in weeding and cutting thistles.'[20] Commentators agreed that women would not work as wage labourers except during peak seasons, and some alleged that this shortage of female labour was the cause of the decline in tillage.[21] Not everyone thought that the trend was bad. Many reformers promoted the exclusion of women from rural labouring occupations. Men such as George Russell (the assistant secretary of the IAOS) praised the co-operative women's guilds for attempting 'to make women in rural Ireland less like men, less agricultural labourers and more a social force'.[22] In the view of some people, it was 'a cruel thing to see women in the fields digging potatoes and putting them into big hampers which they have to put on their backs . . . some of these sacks are over two cwt.'[23] Explanations for the declining numbers of women in agricultural occupations are examined in Chapters 3–6.

This summary of changes in the occupational strength of women as noted in the censuses and by contemporary observers neglects many kinds of paid work. Occupations severely underestimated in the census—indeed, generally ignored—include prostitution and begging. The census only counts prostitutes and brothel-keepers in custody. It is easier to establish the nature of

---

[19] RCL, *The Agricultural Labourer*, iv. *Ireland*, IV. *Reports by Mr Arthur Wilson Fox* (C. 6894–xxi), HC 1893–4, xxxvii/1: 125–6, report on the Poor Law Union of Delvin (Westmeath), comment by Mr Ramage of Craddenstown.

[20] Ibid. 81 (421), report on the Poor Law Union of Westport (county Mayo).

[21] Ibid. 109 (449), report on the Poor Law Union of Skibbereen (county Cork); *Earnings of Agricultural Labourers: Second Report by Mr Wilson Fox* (Cd. 2376), HC 1905, xcvii. 118; and RCL, *The Agricultural Labourer*, iv. *Ireland*, II, *Reports by Mr W. P. O'Brien* (C. 6894-xix), HC 1893–4, xxxvii/1: 113, report on the Poor Law Union of Mountmelick (Queens' and Kings' County).

[22] Henry Summerfield (ed.), *Selections from the Contributions to the 'Irish Homestead' by G. W. Russell—A. E.*, i (Gerrards Cross, 1978), 238, quoting from *IH*, 30 Apr. 1910. See also George W. Russell's comments in *Co-operation and Nationality: A Guide for Rural Reformers from This to the Next Generation* (Dublin, 1912), 63–9.

[23] RCCI, *Appendix to the 9th Report* (Cd. 3845), HC 1908, xli. 80–1, evidence by Patrick Sweeney, a general merchant living at Achill Sound.

prostitution in cities than in the countryside; however, we are told how 'living sins' plagued rural Poor Law authorities, and we hear stories of local rural harassment of prostitutes.[24] Problems of measurement, however, cannot be overcome, so we are left with the rather unsatisfactory statement that, although working outside conventional economic and social structures, prostitution continued to be an option for women living in country towns. The short supply of prostitutes in small communities probably had more to do with fears of community retribution and limitations of scale than lack of demand.[25]

Other unenumerated occupations included begging, peddling, and the gathering of saleable goods on the sea-shore or on the bogs. Pedlars would sell anything from whelks, to eels, to turf.[26] Begging was an occupation for women and children during slack seasons and during times of agricultural distress.[27] It could be

[24] See the paper given by Dr Denham Osbourne at the conference on Women's Work on 10 Dec. 1913, reported in *Irish Citizen*, 20 Dec. 1913: 253. See also Cyril Pearl, *Dublin in Bloomtime* (1969), 10; *Census of Ireland, 1861*, iv (.3204-iii), HC 1863, lx. 685–714; Revd Thomas N. Burke, *Lectures on Faith and Fatherland* (Glasgow, 1874), 71; Local Government Board for Ireland, *Copies of a Report from the Local Government Board, 1883, with Regard to Distress in Ireland* (.92), HC 1883, lix. 3, report from Dr Stewart Woodhouse, Local Government Board Inspector, referring to the parish of Glencolumbkille (county Donegal); *Third Report of Her Majesty's Commissioners for Inquiring into the Housing of the Working Classes* (C. 4547-i), HC 1884–5, xxxi. 28 and 55, evidence by the Revd J. Daniels and the Revd Robert Conlan of Dublin; W. A. Greer, '18 Years, 1896–1914', unpublished autobiography of life in East Belfast and Crossgar, county Down, 1896–1914 (1967), PRONI T3249/1: 60; and a story recounted by John Kenny of Carrowmurragh (parish Kiltoon, Barony Athlone, county Roscommon), aged 76, in Irish Folklore Commission (hereafter IFC) MS 1836: 158–9.

[25] A very full report on the 'Conference of Public Morals' and prostitution in Ireland is to be found in *Irish Citizen*, 5 Oct. 1912: 158, 1 Mar. 1913: 1 and 322, 31 Mar. 1913: 10, 12 July 1913: 60, and 5 Dec. 1914: 1. See also Agnes Halpin Downing, 'Women's Part', *Harp*, Dec. 1908: 4; *Irish Worker*, 9 Mar. 1912: 2; and *Report from the Select Committee on the Law Relating to the Protection of Young Girls* (.448) HC 1881, ix. 154.

[26] W. H. Paterson, *Irish Tenants at Home: Tenant Farmers and their Poverty. What we Saw in the West of Ireland* (1881), 9; Meggy-the-eels of Bruff (county Limerick) in Mary Carbery, *The Farm by Lough Gur: The Story of Mary Fogarty (Sissy O'Brien)* (1937), 20; W. R. Le Fanu, *Seventy Years of Irish Life, Being Anecdotes and Reminiscences* (1893), 52; and Samuel Laing, *A Visit to Bodyke, or, The Real Meaning of Irish Evictions* (1887), 11–13.

[27] RCL, *The Agricultural Labourer*, iv/II, *Reports by Mr W. P. O'Brien* xxxvii/1: 20, 63, and 113, report on the Poor Law Unions of Mountmelick (Queens' and Kings' County) and Cashel (county Tipperary).

remunerative.[28] Although some of these people may have been classified as 'rag-gatherers', most census enumerators described them as 'unoccupied'.

Faced with erratic and incomplete data, we are still able to conclude that women of all ages, at every period of their lives, and throughout the country were either moving out of employment or were being affected by the movement of other women out of employment. Women who remained in rural areas were unable to take advantage of expansions in commercial occupations. Teaching remained an option for a small proportion. However, more women expected to find work in domestic service, industry, or agriculture, and the representation of women in these sectors was declining.

STRUCTURES AND PREFERENCES

The two dominant explanations given by historians for changes in female participation in market employment are inadequate. One group glosses over reductions in female employment by saying that they were 'not surprising' given the structural vulnerability of the female sector of the market. This vulnerability was most clearly expressed in the concentration of female workers in a narrow (and narrowing) band of occupations. For instance, in Ireland, 80 per cent of female workers were to be found in ten occupations.[29] Between 1881 and 1911, 2–6 per cent of employed persons worked in occupations whose workforces consisted solely of women. The number of occupations composed solely of men was not minor. In 1891, 460,000 men—or 22 per cent of the total number of all workers—worked in all-male occupations. By 1911, this had increased to nearly 600,000 men, or 34 per cent of the total working population. In a country with a slight excess of

[28] RCL, *The Agricultural Labourer*, iv. *Ireland*, III, *Reports by Mr Roger C. Richards* (C. 6894-xx), HC 1893–4, xxxvii/1: 69, reports on the Poor Law Union of Bailieborough (county Cavan). See also S. Elliott Napier, *Walks Abroad: Being the Record of the Experiences of Two Australians in the Wilds of the United Kingdom* (Sydney, 1929), 263–4; James H. Tuke, *A Visit to Donegal and Connemara in the Spring of 1880: Irish Distress and its Remedies. The Land Question* (1880), 58–9; and Thomas H. Mason, *The Islands of Ireland*, (1936), 88.

[29] Farmers, agricultural labourers, indoor farm servants, domestic servants, flax and linen manufacturers, milliners and dressmakers, seamstresses, washing and bathing attendants, schoolmistresses, and general shopkeepers or dealers.

women, less than 5 per cent of working women were involved in occupations with a fairly equal distribution between men and women.[30]

Confirmation of the employment vulnerability of women could be found by noting the lack of formal employment networks for women. Associations to protect the interests of women workers were based in cities such as Dublin (such as the Governesses' Association) or Belfast (such as the Linen Workers' Trade Union). With the exception of organizations promoting cottage industries (which are dealt with in Chapter 4), the Irish Central Bureau for the Employment of Women was the chief association aimed at improving the employment prospects of rural women. This association was founded in 1903 by Lady Dudley to bring prospective employers and women seeking employment into communication. However, it had closed within three years, after finding places for only 9 per cent of women applying for work.[31] Arguments based on the 'vulnerability' of female workers cannot tell us *why* women were unable to develop employment networks to serve their interests. The circular reasoning at the heart of this type of argument is unhelpful.

The other type of argument dominating discussions of female labour-force participation refer to 'tastes'. This type of argument tackles questions of women's work in a more satisfactory manner, despite relying heavily on ideological explanations. In fact, the 'tastes' school can be conveniently divided into three strands, based on similar premises but differing in emphasis. Two of the strands refer to changing tastes of female workers (a supply-based model). The other strand refers to the tastes of employers (a demand-based model).

The supply-centred arguments assert that, at a particular point in time, women decided that they no longer wanted to work for money — that such activity was outside their desirable 'sphere', that it was not appropriate behaviour for them. While economists tend to use 'tastes' as a catch-all word to account for unmeasurable variables, feminist and Marxist historians are most inclined to view 'taste' as a product of socialization. This argument is compatible with the claim by the Irish Central Bureau for the Employment

---

[30] 'Fairly equal' is defined as between 45 and 55%.
[31] Myrrha Bradshaw (ed.), *Open Doors for Irishwomen* (Dublin, 1907), 3.

of Women in 1906 that their failure to find jobs for more than 9 per cent of applicants was due to the fact that women no longer wished to be gardeners: they preferred working as domestic economy instructresses.[32] Of course, 'tastes' do not only apply to potential or actual female workers; *male* decision-makers may have a function. Contemporaries sometimes referred to the status bestowed on 'fathers' with 'redundant' adult daughters. Female leisure was a status symbol for the father: 'public opinion forces him to maintain her at home'.[33]

In the Irish context, the 'tastes' of the clergy may be seen as an important variable. For instance, much of the debate by teachers against the rule severely restricting the employment of pregnant women originated among teachers in the north of Ireland, who resented what they saw as 'interference from the Catholic south'.[34] Were the 'tastes' of the Catholic clergy responsible for the low proportion of married women in the workplace? Clearly, the clergy included many men who opposed the employment of women. Bishop O'Dwyer's 1912 Lenten pastoral condemned the employment of women except in the case of extreme hardship, and then only that of unmarried or childless women.[35] The Revd L. McKenna was the most vehement protagonist of employed women.

It is clear that the law of work, though it binds all human beings, has a different application to men and to women. Hence, any application of that law of work which would be incompatible with women's nature—for example, the imposing on women of work which by its character or by its severity would endanger women's social function—would be contrary to God's ordinance and would be essentially wrong . . . To the man he assigns external work, the production of wealth; to the woman, motherhood and its consequences, home work and the training of her children.[36]

But religious influences were minor. Nearly all married women in the eight DEDs were Roman Catholic. In all provinces except Connaught, Roman Catholic women were more likely to be employed

---

[32] *The Times*, 12 Feb. 1906: 14.
[33] 'H. B.', *Letters from Ireland* (Dublin, 1902), 128–9.
[34] Irish Protestant Teachers' Union, Minute-Book, 19 Feb. 1913, PRONI D517.
[35] 'Working Women's Column', *Irish Worker*, 9 Mar. 1912: 2.
[36] Revd L. McKenna, *No. 3: The Church and Working Women* (Dublin, 1913–14), 43–4.

than adherents of other religious groups. In Connaught, women classified as holding 'other' religious beliefs and as Presbyterians were more likely to have a designated occupation. It was Methodist (not Roman Catholic) women in Leinster who moved most rapidly out of employment between 1891 and 1911. Perhaps more pertinent in the analysis of change over time, there is no evidence to suggest that the clergy became more vocally opposed to female employment between 1891 and 1911, or that the laity became more inclined to obey.

Furthermore, explanations dependent on 'tastes' are unconvincing in Ireland, where the rapid decline in female employment precludes any argument based on radical swings in consciousness. There is no clear way to understand the process through which this particular 'ideology' was transmitted. In addition, 'tastes' were not consistent. While some contemporaries portrayed the employment of married women as evil, their views were not shared by everyone. Women might be expected to be more sympathetic to the plight of other women attempting to make a living for themselves and their children, with or without husbands present in the household. A series of letters in the *Irish Weekly Independent* in 1911 suggested that women were *more* likely to hire an older woman with young children as a charwoman (*even if* she were a poor worker), than a young, strong unmarried woman.[37]

Another version of the supply-centred 'taste' argument, and one that is more plausible, introduces the notion of income effect. Here, the assertion is that 'tastes' were always opposed to female employment and that, when average household income reached a certain level, this 'taste' was able to be acted upon; or, that there was a threshold effect whereby those who reached a certain income level always disliked female employment and, as more households reached this level, more women withdrew from paid labour. In the Irish context, this explanation is not totally persuasive. There does seem to be a broad relationship between wealth and female propensity to find paid employment. Taking the total valuation of land, houses, and outhouses in six DEDs as

[37] *Irish Weekly Independent*, 8 Sept. 1911: 9, letters by M. Grene, 'Lily', M. E. Reily, 'A Sister', and Miss Bridget M'Inerney. See also RCL, *The Employment of Women* (C. 6894-xxiii), HC 1893–4, xxxvii/1: 329, and *Third Report on the Housing of the Working Classes*, 55, question to Revd Robert Conlan of Dublin.

Table 1.6. Female employment and property valuation, 1901 and 1911

Valuation of property (£)	'Occupied' women (%)	
	1901[a]	1911[b]
0–1	20.0	33.3
1–4	31.8	11.9
5–9	22.4	18.5
10–14	26.4	13.7
15–19	26.9	22.4
20–4	14.8	12.9
25–9	11.5	8.9
30–4	22.2	9.1
35–9	0.0	12.5
40–4	36.4	7.7
45–9	14.3	10.0
50 +	18.7	8.7

Note: These figures only cover adult women living in their own household.

[a] n (no. in sample) = 1,028.
[b] n = 1,009.

Source: Manuscript census returns for 6 DEDs, NAI, 1901 and 1911; Valuation Books at the Valuation Office, Dublin (nearest year to 1911).

a proxy for wealth, there is a negative relationship between this valuation and the propensity of adult female members of the conjugal household to be described as holding a designated occupation in the census.[38] In 1901, 26 per cent of women resident in households with a valuation of less than £24 were described thus. This contrasts with just over 18 per cent of women resident in households with a valuation of over £24. In 1911 the respective percentages were 16 and 9. Table 1.6 shows, however, that the disparity between households of low and high valuation was not constant. The broad correlation between wealth and employment may just as reasonably be ascribed to other factors, such as

---

[38] The analysis excludes all non-relatives such as domestic servants, farm labourers, visitors, and boarders as well as ignoring households for which no valuation could be found.

increased timidity about declaring an occupation in wealthier households, or the likelihood that larger and wealthier farms were pastoral farms with low labour requirements.

Discrimination arguments are concerned with 'tastes' as experienced by the employers rather than by the employees. This demand-based explanation for changes in female employment has been influenced by Gary Becker's discussion of the 'taste' for racial discrimination.[39] It typically focuses on only one side of the equation, ignoring the possible preference of women for employment in all-female occupations. This neglect results from conceptual problems: the admission that labour decisions may be affected by self-discrimination leaves no way to discriminate between such decisions based on the free choice of the employee and those based on the imposition of 'discrimatory taste' by the employer.[40] The explanation is flawed in the same way as the other 'tastes' debates. What determines 'tastes', and how quickly can the 'tastes' of employers change? In the Irish context, discrimination is a powerful argument when examined in the context of *new* forms of labour from which women might be excluded. Chapters 3 and 6 provide examples of attempts by reforming organizations to move men into new positions opening up in the dairy and poultry industries. However, as the reorganization in poultry-farming illustrates, the gender preferences of employers or reformers were not automatically translated into reality. Another example of discrimination could be taken from commercial occupations. The 'feminization' of this sector has been noted, but the movement of women into clerical positions did not proceed smoothly. In 1910 the Metropolitan Water Board, for instance, decided not to employ any more female typists, 'because they become hysterical in times of rush and are nervous wrecks before they are two years in the firm'.[41]

Discrimination could also work in favour of women, as in primary teaching, where women benefited from the notion that men were unfit to teach children under 7 years of age.[42] Even in secondary schools, female teachers had an advantage. Katherine

[39] Gary S. Becker, *The Economics of Discrimination* (Chicago, 1957).
[40] For a more detailed analysis of this contradiction, see Francesca Bettio, *The Sexual Division of Labour* (Oxford, 1988), 4.
[41] 'Anti-Sweater', 'Working Women's Column', *Irish Worker*, 7 Oct. 1911: 2.
[42] *Education (Ireland): Report of Mr F. H. Dale*, xx. 36.

Roche, a secondary school teacher and organizer, concluded a speech with the provocative statement: 'I consider teaching essentially a woman's work, and one in which few men will be able to compete with her. I am not advocating the suppression of the male teacher, as I have no wish to oppress men. Besides, I am a believer in the doctrine of the survival of the fittest.'[43] Despite this, the place of women in the teaching profession was contradictory. The idea that women made 'better' teachers because of an 'innate' relationship between women and child-rearing was not seen to conflict with the view that *mothers* should not be teachers. On 4 April 1911 the Commissioners of National Education decided that, from 30 June that year, female teachers were to be forced to stop teaching three months before childbirth. Furthermore, pregnant teachers were responsible for providing a qualified substitute if their absence coincided with the teaching term. Female teachers protested angrily. They argued that three months was a ridiculously long period of time, given that one month's leave of absence without stoppage of salary had been sufficient in the past.[44] Others were furious with the commissioners' insistence that the women themselves find substitutes.[45]

The debate widened to include a long-standing resentment against some managers who forced their teachers to resign upon marriage or pregnancy.[46] Female teachers were anxious about the promotional implications of the new move by the commissioners. In a speech to the 1912 Teachers' Congress in Cork, Mrs O'Shea noted that a teacher was unlikely to win the final merit mark from the inspector (enabling promotion) if she were forced to hand over her teaching to a substitute for three months. She was also concerned with the eugenic implications of the rule,

[43] Katherine Roche, 'Another Aspect of Training', *Irish Educational Review*, 11/5 (Feb. 1909), 289.

[44] 'Minutes of the Proceedings of the Commissioners of National Education' 123. For a small sample of the uproar, see the protests by teachers in Baltinglass, Tralee, Galway, Kanturk, and Donegal in the minutes for 27 June and 31 Oct. 1911: 216 and 372. In 1893 medical officers who recommended three months' compulsory suspension for pregnant linen workers also noted that such a policy would be fought vigorously by the workers: see RCL, *The Employment of Women*, xxxvii/1: 329.

[45] 'Women Teachers and Substitutes', *Irish School Weekly*, 29 Apr. 1911: 86.

[46] 'Educational News of the Week', ibid. 23 Sept. 1911: 704.

arguing that the mental and physical distress caused to the mother would affect the child. Punishment of the mother seemed to be the order of the day. In her words:

Then begins a series of fines. The teacher is fined in the salary she pays her substitute. The required merit mark is not obtained. She is fined in her reputation as an efficient teacher, not through her own inefficiency, but thoroughly through that of her substitute, who is probably a perfect stranger to her. She is fined in not securing an increase of salary. In fact, her punishment extends through the whole term of her natural life, as the loss of promotion will reduce the amount of her pension—should she live long enough to claim it.

Female teachers wondered how attaining 'the right to the highest and holiest name in our language . . . that of a virtuous and honourable mother', merited such punishment.[47] Faced with the fury of female teachers, coupled with demands for equity, the commissioners opted to let the rule slip. Discretion was given to the local manager. Some salary 'fines' that had already been paid were refunded.[48] In spite of the confusion, female representation in schools increased during this period. Many female teachers in single-sex and convent schools remained unthreatened. More employed women were unmarried. However, the response of female teachers to the threat does provide an illustration of resistance to the attempts of employers to discriminate against them.

Structural vulnerability and the preferences of potential and actual workers and employers are important in understanding employment, but, as explanations for changes in women's employment, they have only a limited usefulness. As in the case of teachers, workers may resist the 'preferences' of employers. 'Tastes' are not automatically translated into the workplace. In some sectors women faced discriminatory employers; in other sectors there was a high demand for their labour, but potential women workers refused to be mobilized. The catch-all word 'tastes' cannot grasp the subtleties of their decision-making.

[47] Speech by Mrs O'Shea reported in 'The Maternity Question', ibid. 26 Apr. 1913: 185–6.
[48] Catherine C. Mahon, 'Inquiry and Other Matters from the President', ibid. 7 June 1913: 377; Catherine C. Mahon, 'The Maternity Rule', ibid. 21 June 1913: 440; and T. J. O'Connell, 'Married Women Teachers', ibid. 19 Apr. 1913: 154.

HOUSEHOLD DECISION-MAKING AND
FEMALE EMPLOYMENT

Nearly all researchers agree that the clue to understanding changes in female employment lies in the family. The work of economists such as Gary S. Becker in modelling the relationship between the domestic household economy and the market economy has been crucial. An important function of the familial unit involves the care of the house and the people within it. Customarily, this function has fallen to women and is thought to reduce female opportunities for employment in other occupations. Children require labour, and some people believed that a woman (preferably the mother) gave this attention best.[49] Unsurprisingly, therefore, where alternatives to child care by female family members were restricted, women living in households with young children were less likely to be entered on the census as having an occupation than women living in households with no or few young children (see Table 1.7).[50]

The importance of the family life cycle in regulating female employment can be seen by looking at households in the eight DEDs in 1901 and 1911. Just over 700 households were matched in this way, that is, nearly 80 per cent of the households in 1911 were matched with households in 1901. Of all the women in 'matched' households, 13.9 per cent had the same occupation in 1901 and 1911, 1.1 per cent changed from one occupation to another, 25.3 per cent did not have an occupation in 1901 but did

---

[49] RCL, *The Employment of Women*, xxxvii/1: 329, and *Report from the Select Committee on Distress from Want of Employment* (.321), HC 1896, ix. 84, evidence by Anthony J. Staunton (general merchant, farmer, Poor Law Guardian and chairman of the Swinford Union, county Mayo).

[50] An adult woman was defined as any woman over the age of 15. Women designated as 'scholars' were omitted from the analysis. Strictly, the years 1901 and 1911 should not be compared, since a significant proportion of women with designated occupations in 1901 were 'farmer's relatives', an option not open to women in 1911. Women were categorized as having 'no occupation' if the space for occupation was left blank or if one of the following designations was given: 'housewife', 'domestic duties', 'helping about the house', or 'domestic work at home'. For a discussion on alternatives to familial child care in rural areas, see 'Irish Mothers and their Critics', *IH*, 22 Feb. 1913: 150, and Revd Denis Kelly (Bishop of Ross), *Women's Share in the Industrial Revival of Ireland* (Dublin, 1905), 19.

Table 1.7. 'Occupied' women within households with (and without) children, 1901 and 1911 (%)

	1901		1911	
	'Occupied'	Not 'occupied'	'Occupied'	Not 'occupied'
No. of children under 5				
0	82.9	68.0	79.4	69.1
1	7.6	14.1	6.0	12.4
2	7.0	10.1	8.9	10.8
3 +	2.5	7.8	5.7	7.7
No. of children under 15				
0	56.2	45.4	64.9	47.4
1	16.2	17.6	11.5	16.8
2	10.0	10.2	6.3	10.1
3	5.5	9.6	7.8	9.3
4	4.9	5.0	3.4	6.5
5 +	7.2	12.2	6.1	9.9

Source: Manuscript census returns for 8 DEDs, NAI, 1901 and 1911.

in 1911, and 59.7 per cent had an occupation in 1901 but did not by 1911.[51] Each of these categories will be examined in turn.

Nearly 14 per cent of women were doing the same job in 1901 as in 1911 (see Table 1.8). Most were widowed or unmarried. Half of those who kept their occupational status were either the only employed person in the household or they resided in all-female households. Overall, 111 women 'gained' an occupation in 1911 which they did not have in 1901. Of these women, one-quarter were too young to have found employment in 1901. In one-third of the households, the 'head' had died between 1901 and 1911, presumably increasing the need for an extra wage-earner. Entry into the labour force generally occurred along two lines. First, approximately one-quarter entered employment in 1911 as female 'farmers'. Their entry was stimulated by the death

[51] Women without an occupation in either year were excluded. The number of women gaining employment, losing employment, and remaining in employment between 1901 and 1911 were 72, 155, and 48 respectively.

Table 1.8. Consistency of employment and marital status, 1901 and 1911

Marital status	%[a]
Unmarried, 1901 and 1911	37.7
Married, 1901 and 1911	4.9
Married, 1901; widowed, 1911	6.6
Married but husband absent, 1901 and 1911	6.6
Widowed, 1901 and 1911	44.2

[a] no. in sample = 61.

Source: Manuscript census returns for 8 DEDs, NAI, 1901 and 1911.

of the head of the household, usually their husband. In many cases it is clear that the change in occupational title from 'none' to 'farmer' entailed little real change in function.[52] Second, 36 per cent of the women entering the workforce became domestic servants; and 40 per cent of the domestic servants finding employment in 1911 entered households with either a large number of elderly people (and no compensating younger person) or a large number of very young children who had not been there in 1901.

Almost 60 per cent of the women in these districts had an occupation in 1901 but not in 1911. One-fifth of those losing their occupations presumably retired, as the farm and the title of 'farmer' were taken over by the son. In 16 per cent of the cases it can be presumed that an elderly woman's 'disappearance' from the 1911 household was due to her death, especially since a relative (usually the son) had generally taken the title of 'head'. This is even clearer in the subset of women categorized as 'farmers': 90 per cent of the women who *became* farmers in 1911 after having no occupation in 1901 did so after the death of the male 'head' (generally the husband), while another 90 per cent of those who *relinquished* the title of 'farmer' had either retired in favour of a male relative or had died.

---

[52] In 1926, 77% of female farmers in the Republic of Ireland were widowed, compared with 10% of male farmers (of *all* women over the age of 12, 12% were widowed, compared with 5% of all men).

Table 1.9. Loss of employment among domestic servants between 1901 and 1911

Presumed cause for loss of employment	%[a]
No explanation: a young, unmarried member of family	20.5
Replaced by another female domestic servant	30.4
Replaced by a male domestic servant	6.5
Children in household grown up	16.3
Servant married by 1911	1.1
Servant has children by 1911	2.2
Death of head of household	3.3
Elderly servant in 1901, presumed retired	9.8
Elderly servant in 1901, presumed dead	3.3
New female relative doing domestic work in 1911	2.2
Household no longer employing domestic servant	2.2
Multi-servant household in 1901, 1 servant cut	2.2

Note: Where there was more than one possible reason for the servant's 'disappearance', an assumption has been made about the probable importance of the explanations. For instance, it was common to find households with elderly servants (presumed to have retired) as well as grown-up children by 1911. In this case the former explanation was assumed to be dominant. Similarly, the category 'household no longer employing any female servants' could have been used to explain a number of the changes, but it was only used where no other 'explanation' fitted.

[a] no. in sample = 62.

Source: Manuscript census returns for 8 DEDs, NAI, 1901 and 1911.

Looking at the other large occupational category that women had entered in 1901 and had left by 1911—domestic service—the striking factor here is not retirement or death (although this may have affected 13 per cent of the sample), but rapid turnover (see Table 1.9). Two-thirds of the domestic servants in the sample lost their job between 1901 and 1911. Only one-third were replaced with another female servant. More surprising was the substitution of a male domestic servant for a female servant in over 6 per cent of the cases. The 'no explanation' category generally comprised young, unmarried daughters who had simply 'disappeared' from the household by 1911, perhaps by finding a live-in

Table 1.10. Household size and changes in female employment, 1901–1911 (%)

No. in household (excluding servants)	Occupational changes		
	Gained[a]	Lost[b]	Remained[c]
1	6.1	6.1	8.8
2	8.1	12.7	19.3
3–4	34.4	35.9	31.6
5–6	26.2	22.2	21.0
7 +	25.2	23.1	19.3

[a] n (no. in sample) = 99.
[b] n = 212.
[c] n = 57.

Source: Manuscript census returns for 8 DEDs, NAI, 1901 and 1911.

position in another household, or by getting married and commencing work in their own household, or by emigrating. This group is examined in detail in Chapter 2.

An analysis of the family structure of households where women moved either in or out of the workforce or remained in the same occupation reveals interesting patterns. Over 80 per cent of the households where the woman remained in the same occupation between 1901 and 1911 were headed by a woman, compared with half of all those households where women 'gained' employment between 1901 and 1911, and one-quarter of households where women left employment. Although part of the differential relates to the fact that women in female-headed households would be more likely to *claim* an occupation (their labour was more acceptable), the large differential also implies that women in female-headed households were more likely to have to find paid employment in order to maintain living standards.

Households where women entered the labour market were larger than those where women left the market or remained in the same occupation (see Table 1.10). As expected, households with small children were more likely to demand the attentions of a woman with no other employment. Thus, women who remained in the same occupation between 1901 and 1911 were most likely to be residing in households with fewer children.

Less than one-fifth of households where the woman remained employed or found a job between 1901 and 1911 contained children under the age of 5, compared with one-quarter of households where a woman left her job between 1901 and 1911.

Examining changes in female occupational status in individual households within a ten-year period illustrates numerous potential motives for changes in female employment. Household structure is most important in explaining why women moved in and out of the paid labour force. As will be argued later, shifts in paid employment cannot be separated from shifts in unwaged forms of labour. Thus, women entering the paid workforce between 1901 and 1911 were more likely to come from houses that required less work; that is, small, 'third-class' houses. Less than 1 per cent of women entering the workforce were from large, 'first-class' houses, compared with over 4 per cent of women who left the occupational workforce or who remained in the same employment between 1901 and 1911. Women leaving employment were most likely to come from larger houses.[53] Chapter 7 argues that it was not wealth (or rising living standards) *per se* which caused women to withdraw from the market. It is plausible, however, that increased living standards, as represented by larger and 'better' houses, stimulated the workloads in the unwaged domestic sphere. The relative importance of factors introduced in this chapter, such as sectoral shifts, discrimination, and household labour, are examined in the rest of the book.

[53] For each decade between 1841 and 1911 census enumerators collected data on the 'class' of inhabited housing in rural and urban areas. Houses were divided into four categories according to the number of rooms, the number of windows, and the materials from which the house was built: fourth-class houses were small mud huts; third-class houses had windows and 1–4 rooms, and they were also made of sturdier materials; second-class houses were often good farm houses, with windows and 5–9 rooms; first-class houses were the most superior houses.

2

Rural Service

> Jane McArthur was in my service for upward of four years
> as House and Parlour Maid. I found her a faithful servant
> in every respect, capable of doing her work, willing and
> obeying. She left me more than two years ago to get married
> to my coachman, latterly she had charge of my laundry and
> in that situation gave me every satisfaction.[1]

JANE MCARTHUR represents an élite of servants: she was no
general slavey. Typical of women in her occupation, she was
a local girl who had filled the years between adolescence and
marriage by working as a domestic servant. After marriage, she
had exchanged full-time service in the home of her employer for
full-time service within her own home, supplemented by doing
laundry for her former employer. Henry Meteor accredited her
with the three traits desired in a servant: she was capable,
malleable, and obedient. Within two decades of the composition
of his letter, domestic service was declining. Although the term
'domestic servant problem' came into vogue in the 1890s, the
decline of service scarcely merited comment from most former
employers and employees. The 'servant question' was answered
by the substitution of unwaged labour for the cash nexus.

Although domestic service has attracted many British and
American scholars, explorations of service in these countries
contribute little to an understanding of this kind of employment
in rural Ireland. Most historians of domestic service concentrate
either on explaining urban patterns or on examining the habits
of wealthy employers. Even when considered carefully within
the context of wealthy households, many explanations are unconvincing; when used to explain the decline of service in Ireland, they are inadmissible. J. A. Banks, for instance, attributes
the collapse of service to an attempt by employers during the

[1] PRONI D2957/7, letter of recommendation for laundry work from Henry
Meteor, 13 Aug. 1877, Fort Williamspark.

depression to maintain the 'paraphernalia of gentility' by reducing expenditure on servants. Not only does this demand-based
argument conflict with evidence that could be drawn from British
wage data, it also fails to account for the timing of the decline,
and places excessive stress on the motivations of wealthy employers. Pamela Horn, M. Ebery, B. Preston, and Theresa M.
McBride emphasize supply factors. From the last three decades
of the nineteenth century, they argue, the availability of new
forms of employment drew women out of domestic service. In
addition to problems in making this argument fit the timing of
the expansion of employment opportunities in England, it is
obviously inapplicable for Irish females, who faced declining
alternative opportunities for employment.[2] Heidi Hartmann argues that the decline in domestic service was due to expanded
capitalist production, which saw goods and services previously
produced in the home transferred to the market-place. She also
argues that a 'taste' for expensive commodities (such as cars)
competed with domestic service for scarce income.[3] Again, her
timing is wrong. Domestic service was unimportant by the time
that mass private transport took off. Furthermore, she ignores
expanding production in the home, and seems to consider 'shopping' as a form of leisure rather than labour. Similarly, Edward
Higgs's argument that the labour of the servant moved out of the
home and into the factory, while the houseworker began to buy
products rather than hiring a domestic servant to produce the
product, did not apply to Ireland.[4] There was little substitution

[2] J. A. Banks, *Prosperity and Parenthood: A Study of Family Planning among the
Victorian Middle Classes* (1954); C. Davidson, *A Woman's Work is Never Done* (1982),
164–82; Faye E. Dudden, *Serving Women: Household Service in Nineteenth-Century
America* (Middletown, Conn., 1983); M. Ebery and B. Preston, *Domestic Service in
Late Victorian and Edwardian England, 1871–1914* (Reading, 1976); Pamela Horn,
The Rise and Fall of the Victorian Servant (Dublin, 1975); David M. Katzmar, *Seven
Days a Week: Women and Domestic Service in Industrializing America* (New York,
1978); Theresa M. McBride, *The Domestic Revolution: The Modernisation of House-
hold Service in England and France, 1820–1920* (1976); Daniel E. Sutherland,
Americans and their Servants: Domestic Service in the United States from 1800 to 1920
(Baton Rouge, La., 1981); and Donna L. Van Raaphorst, *Union Maids Not Wanted:
Organizing Domestic Workers, 1870–1940* (New York, 1988).
[3] H. I. Hartmann, *Capitalism and Women's Work in the Home, 1900–1930* (Ann
Arbor, Mich., 1975), 180–1.
[4] Edward Higgs, 'Domestic Servants and Households in Victorian England',
Social History, 8/2 (May 1983), 201–10. He also suggests that the decline in servants
was simply a replacement of the term 'domestic servant' for 'shop assistant' in
retailing households. This did not occur in the 1901 and 1911 census sample.

of processed foods for domestic servants in Ireland.[5] In fact, Chapter 7 argues both that the labour involved in domestic food production *increased* as the number of domestic servants decreased and that the time costs of shopping (for instance) were as high as the time costs of primary production. A popular explanation for the decline of service in Ireland is the failure of Irish cities to grow significantly. Since, however, most Irish servants were employed in rural areas, this argument is unconvincing. Clearly, new explanations must be called upon if we are to understand the role of servants in rural Ireland.

NATURE OF SERVICE

A key to understanding rural domestic service is that the work was not necessarily 'domestic'. Rural domestic servants were expected to do a wide range of activities, both indoor and outdoor:

The kitchen maid can work or play
At certain times when not engaged
Some times she puts the hens to lay
And more times rock the cradle
Some times she puts the gees to hatch,
And other times she is cleaving fleas
She'l dress the beds both soft and flat
And sleep til day is breaking.[6]

For the sum of 25s. a month, with the right to eat in the kitchen but not to board with the family, Miss Harker of Kings' county was expected to teach three children, mind two infants, cook the dinner, wash the dishes, and clean the knives. She was eventually forced to leave because of a row which developed after the family refused to allow her any holidays.[7] Like Jane McArthur at the beginning of this chapter, Miss Harker was part of an élite of servants: she did not have to work outdoors, and the cleaning and laundry were done by another servant. The 'all-purpose' servant girl had a different life:

---

[5] Harvey A. Levenstein, *Revolution at the Table: The Transformation of the American Diet* (Oxford, 1988), ties in the decline of servants with dietary changes.

[6] Spelling as in original: 'A New Song on the Hiring Fairs of Ulster' (n.d.), Australian National Library, q.320.945 I68, Box 46/844c. For accounts, see Molly Byrne, 'The Life of a Servant Girl', *Grand Old Limerick Journal* (Spring 1983), 29–30, and 'L. de K. K.', 'On Furnishing Bedrooms', *IH*, 1 Nov. 1905: 833.

[7] 'The Governess', *Kings' County Chronicle*, 10 July 1890: 3.

I must have been about ten years old, and in those days there was no school act and you could come and go as you pleased. A neighbour's wife took me in, and I helped her with the little jobs around: calves and pigs, bringing in the cows and housework of every sort. I tell you it would be ten o'clock before your eyes were closed and you had your clothes off. You'd be that worn out. But you'd never complain, because there were lots of young people watching out for the first little job that was coming. I was not unhappy, they were nice and good people. I got ten shillings a month and stayed ten years. They had old style ways then, and I was young and didn't take any notice. It was all washing a' scrubbing down the floors, plucking fowl and any other little thing . . . I can't remember growing up . . . [sic] you were young, and then suddenly you were old and there was little or nothing in between. 'Come here, Annie. Go there, Annie.' The only free moment in any day was Sunday when I was let off for two hours. 'Be back around six,' the Mistress would tell me, 'because of dairying the cows'.[8]

No clear distinction can be made between women called 'domestic servants' and women called 'farm servants'. Analysis of the type of work that servants performed illustrates the overlap between farm and domestic service. For example, 'Murphy of Ballygarret' (county Kerry) hired a woman called Mary Sullivan to be a servant:

It was the harvest time and they were cutting the oats and he was out in the cornfield one day and his father was inside and this girl walked in the door to him. He welcomed her and he asked her what was her business.

'I'm looking for work,' says she.

'Well,' says he, 'can you milk cows?'

'I can,' says she.

'Can you bake and keep house?' says he.

'I can,' says she.

'Well,' says he, 'as you can do all those things you say I'll keep you for three months.'

And out in the evening she was snapping the oats from the scythe. She was a great servant—able to do everything around the house.[9]

Nearly 90 per cent of the respondents to the Ulster Folk and Transport Museum's questionnaire on hiring-fairs included indoor

[8] Peter Somerville-Large, *Cappaghglass* (1985), 24–5, interview with Annie Sullivan, ex-maid, aged 82.

[9] Interview with 'Jack Dick', aged about 75, a farmer from Lixnax Parish in Clanmaurice (county Clare), May 1950, talking about Mary Sullivan (county Kerry), IFC MS 1177: 2–3.

tasks in their list of the activities of female farm servants. Female farm servants cooked, cleaned, washed carpets and blankets, made jams, knitted, baked bread, spun, took care of children, and carried tea to labourers in the fields. Indoor tasks overwhelmed the time schedules of women hired in autumn to a greater extent than of those hired in spring. While male farm servants rarely did housework, female farm servants performed agricultural work in addition to housework. Respondents noted that female farm servants dropped, gathered, and washed potatoes. They cut and stacked turf, threshed, cleaned cattle-houses, harvested corn, pulled flax, made hay, fed animals, milked and churned, thinned turnips, tied corn, boiled potatoes for the pigs, took care of the poultry, and 'some of the sturdier types would even mow with a scythe'. As a woman from Gilford said: 'No job too hard. No job too dirty. No consideration for women.'[10]

However, if domestic and farm service are interconnected, what about that category of workers called 'agricultural labourers'?[11] Indoor female farm servants were much more likely to perform household work than women called 'agricultural labourers'. Agricultural labourers were more important as short-term harvest workers. In the eight DEDs that we have studied, less than half a dozen women called themselves agricultural labourers: all were elderly, landless women, dependent on hiring themselves out for casual labouring work. This chapter concentrates on domestic servants and female indoor farm servants.[12]

Our problems do not end with definitions. As we have noted before, the use of census data limits our analysis. How would a

[10] Ulster Folk and Transport Museum, Questionnaire on Hiring-Fairs, No. 2 (1977). The two quotations come from respondents in Kilrea (county Londonderry) and Gilford (county Down). Richard Breen, 'Farm Servanthood in Ireland, 1900–1940', *EHR*, 2nd ser. 36 (1983), 87–102, also notes the high proportion of domestic duties involved in the work of female farm servants.

[11] The total number of agricultural labourers is made up of those called 'agricultural labourers' in the census, plus those living in rural areas who were simply called 'labourers' in the 'indefinite' section of the census tables.

[12] Only female indoor farm servants were examined, since the argument about household work does not apply to male indoor farm servants, who only performed farm work. However, it must be noted that young boys hired as farm servants often worked for the mistress, performing such tasks as collecting firing, running messages, picking up the groceries, milking cows, and preparing pigfood: see the reminiscences of Michael MacGowan, *The Hard Road to Klondike*, trans. Valentin Iremonger (1962), 29–30. The agricultural explanations given in this chapter could, of course, be applied to female agricultural labourers.

Table 2.1. Number of female indoor farm servants, by province, 1861–1911 (000s)

Year	Leinster	Munster	Ulster	Connaught	Total
1861	12.7	18.9	7.3	12.8	51.7
1871	8.4	14.4	11.9	10.6	45.3
1881	3.9	6.3	5.9	3.5	19.6
1891	1.9	4.7	3.6	2.5	12.7
1901	2.0	3.4	2.4	1.3	9.1
1911	0.3	1.2	0.7	0.1	2.3

Note: The 1861 statistic is not strictly comparable with later statistics. The 1861 figure used here is the number of female 'farm labourers and servants'.

Source: Censuses of Ireland, 1881–1911.

woman who migrated seasonally to Scotland as a labourer classify herself? A dairywoman could be called a domestic servant, an indoor farm servant, or an agricultural labourer. She might be given no occupation. Some employers hired male agricultural labourers on the condition that a female member of the family milked the cows, or fed the poultry, or helped during harvest. These women would probably be listed as 'unoccupied'. We can only assume that women working full-time for a wage as a domestic servant were liable to have been given that occupation in the census.

The first part of this chapter examines general trends in domestic service and indoor farm service in order to establish the extent of national demand for servants. The main source for this section is published and unpublished census data. Then, wage data, household statistics from the eight DEDs, and other contemporary sources are used to examine explanations for the decline of rural service.

THE DECLINE OF SERVICE

Indoor farm service employed a small number of women (see Table 2.1). Between 1891 and 1911 the number of women so

Table 2.2. Male and female employment in the 'domestic class', 1861–1911 (000s)

Year	Women	Men	Total
1861	309.0	47.4	356.4
1871	343.1	34.5	377.6
1881	392.1	34.1	426.2
1891	220.7	34.5	255.2
1901	193.3	26.1	219.4
1911	144.9	25.8	170.7

Source: Censuses of Ireland, 1861–1911.

engaged declined by 82 per cent. In 1911 farm service employed just over 2,000 women. The number in Munster declined less rapidly because the demand for dairymaids remained relatively buoyant.

By contrast, domestic service was the single most important occupation for women (see Table 2.2), employing 11 per cent of all women. It was a female occupation. The percentage of all employed men who were domestic servants dropped from 2.1 per cent in 1891 to 1.7 per cent in 1911, that is, from 31,950 to 23,077. The 'domestic class' in the census included domestic gardeners, private lodge- and gatekeepers, private park-keepers, inn and hotel servants, servants in colleges and clubs, non-governmental office-keepers, non-domestic cooks, charwomen, washing and bathing attendants, hospital and institution servants, as well as general 'indoor domestic servants'. Between 86 and 90 per cent of all women in the 'domestic classs' were general indoor domestic servants. This chapter limits itself to these workers.

Employment in this sector underwent a crisis between 1891 and 1911. In 1911, 72,000 fewer women worked as indoor domestic servants than in 1891. Domestic service was the only occupation in the census sample in which women regularly claimed to be 'unemployed'. For instance, Bridget Leahy was an 'unemployed cook' in 1901. By 1911 she had descended to being a 'cocklepicker'.[13]

[13] Bridget Leahy lived in the Woodstown DED (county Waterford): manuscript census returns, NAI, 1901 and 1911.

Women in every province left domestic service. In Connaught and Ulster the proportion of female domestic servants almost halved, and in Munster and Leinster their numbers fell by 70 and 42 per cent respectively between 1891 and 1911. Since employment also contracted in all other occupations, however, domestic service increased slightly as a proportion of women *in employment* in Leinster and Munster, and declined slightly in Connaught and Ulster. The decline of domestic service is most apparent in recruitment. Progressively fewer young women aged between 20 and 24 entered domestic service. In Roscommon, Sligo, and Longford the number of female domestic servants in this age-group halved at least between 1891 and 1911. Only in the areas around Belfast and Dublin were young women recruited at at anything like their former levels, and, even there, young domestic servants decreased in number by 14 and 20 per cent respectively. Declining proportions of domestic servants in younger age-groups coincided with an increase in the age categories 25–44 and over 65. Still, domestic servants were young by comparison with other employed women. Over half of domestic servants were aged between 15 and 24, while 38 per cent of all employed women belonged to this age-group.

Domestic servants tended to be single. In 1871 less than 4 per cent of the domestic servants in the entire country were married. Approximately 7 per cent of domestic servants in the eight DEDs sampled were married, while over 82 per cent were unmarried. The decline in the domestic servant population between 1901 and 1911 did not significantly affect the proportion of married servants, but it did affect the number of widows in service. In 1901, nearly 11 per cent of the female domestic servants in the eight areas were widowed, compared with 4 per cent ten years later. Both demand and supply factors may explain this change. Most widowed domestic servants would have entered service before marriage, left when they married, and then resumed service after their husband's death. The increasing difficulties associated with returning to service after marriage suggest a declining demand for servants. Old-age pensions made it less necessary for elderly widows to find employment, and provided younger relatives with an incentive to welcome such women into their homes to perform household chores and to look after children without payment.

EMPLOYERS

Who employed servants, and what do the changes in the characteristics of employers tell us about the changing nature of
service? Between 44 and 50 per cent of households with indoor
servants on the day of the census were 'headed' by farmers.
Local clergymen, barristers, JPs, magistrates, and land-agents each
employed their share of domestic servants. Women who gave
their occupation as 'ladies' hired up to 10 per cent of indoor
domestic servants. However, the employment of a servant in the
household was not a prerogative of the wealthy. An elderly,
unmarried agricultural labourer in Ards in 1911 had a resident
servant to do his chores. As the valuation of his land was only
£1, 40-year-old Hannah O'Donnell probably had to be content
with little more than her keep. Although around 60 per cent of
all indoor servants in the DEDs worked in households with a
total valuation of over £30, one-quarter resided in households
with a land valuation of between £1 and £9. Indoor domestic
servants were over-represented in households with a valuation
of more than £30. The proportion of households with resident
domestic servants increased for larger farms between 1901 and
1911. The decline in domestic servants hit households on holdings
of between five and thirty acres. In 1901, 12 per cent of households on such holdings employed resident domestic servants,
compared with 9 per cent in 1911.

A different pattern emerges for *farm* servants. The number of
households with at least one indoor male or female farm servant
remained stable at 8–9 per cent in the DEDs between 1901 and
1911. This statistic masks the rapid decline in the number of
female farm servants. Because female farm servants were rarely
employed, and, when required, resided on large farms, it was
holdings of more than one hundred acres that were most affected by the decline in female farm service. At the same time,
farms over five acres in size hired *more* male farm servants (see
Table 2.3).

One of the most significant features about the change in domestic service is that employers were increasingly wealthy. In
1911, 8.4 per cent of all households in these eight districts hired
three or more domestic servants, compared with half that number
in 1901. Domestic servants were also increasingly likely to reside

Table 2.3. Farm service and farm acreage, 1901 and 1911 (%)

Farm acreage	Households with female servants[a]		Households with male servants[b]	
	1901	1911	1901	1911
1–5 acres	0.0	0.0	2.4	2.0
5–15 acres	1.0	0.9	3.0	6.2
15–30 acres	4.3	1.9	9.5	11.4
30–50 acres	1.3	0.0	16.0	17.5
50–100 acres	9.1	1.8	29.1	33.9
100 + acres	18.5	4.2	40.7	54.2

[a] n (no. in sample) = 415 and 437 for 1901 and 1991 respectively.
[b] n = 415 and 437 for 1901 and 1911 respectively.

Source: Manuscript census returns for 6 DEDs, NAI, 1901 and 1911; Valuation Books at the Valuation Office, Dublin (nearest year to 1911).

with their employers rather than with relatives: another indication, perhaps, of the growing wealth of employers. In 1901, only half of domestic servants lived with their employer, compared with 80 per cent ten years later. Further support for the contention that wealthier households were employing more servants can be found by studying the birthplace of servants. The eight DEDs show an increase from 12 to 16 per cent in the proportion of domestic servants who were employed in counties outside the one in which they were born. There was also a rapid increase in the proportion of servants who came from outside Ireland. By 1911, 35 per cent of all servants in these districts were born outside Ireland, compared with 14 per cent in 1901. Of those servants born in Ireland, just over one-third were born in neighbouring counties.

Using English data, Edward Higgs suggested that many of the servants residing with relatives were actually working (without wages) for those relatives.[14] By excluding those women who

[14] Edward Higgs, 'Domestic Service and Household Production', in Angela V. John (ed.), *Unequal Opportunities: Women's Employment in England, 1800–1918* (Oxford, 1986), 131.

described themselves simply as 'housekeeper' from my statistics on domestic servants, the likelihood of this confusion is reduced. Higgs was using census enumerator forms rather than the original entries by heads of households. If his hypothesis was valid for Ireland, the declining proportion of domestic servants residing with relatives would suggest a reduction in the 'employment' status of unwaged housework. The increase in the number of dependent females within households between 1901 and 1911 could have been a result of the transfer of relatives from the 'domestic servant' category to the 'unoccupied' category. This reclassification occurred in only one household in my sample of matched households in the eight DEDs, so it cannot account for the widespread shift of servants into their employers' house-holds. This movement may have resulted in employers having greater control over their servants, with a corresponding aliena-tion of the servant from her own class and familial ties.

We are now in a position to examine the reasons for the de-cline in rural domestic service. As we saw in Chapter 1, changes in the sex ratio and in total employment would lead us to expect a small decline in the number of women in domestic service (less than 11,000 between 1891 and 1911), whereas changes in distri-bution would lead us to expect a large fall in the number of women in domestic occupations (between 21,000 and 33,000). Why did this change in distribution occur?

SUPPLY OF SERVANTS

Preferences of Employers

By the turn of the century, middle-class Irish women had iden-tified a 'domestic servant problem'. For them, the problem was straightforward: good servants were unobtainable. The employ-ment columns of the newspapers are full of requests for servants and of women seeking employment. Although I have used these advertisements for information about wage rates, their validity with regard to questions of supply and demand is doubtful. Only the occasional employable domestic servant and prospective mistress would resort to newspaper advertisements. Further, we do not know to what extent Irish mistresses and servants were addicted to 'playing at general post'—that is, perpetually giving or receiving notices.[15] My sample of advertisements in the *Irish Times* indicates that, up until the turn of the century, the number of women advertising for employment generally equalled the number of prospective employers looking for servants. After 1901, there were about 1.3 positions for every servant asking for work.[16] Newspaper testimonies stress the shortage of servants. The employment and retention of servants were a major concern for the wealthier women in the community. They complained that servants packed their bags without warning to take up employment with the highest bidder.[17] The servants, confident of their status as scarce workers, made their mistresses groan under their independence.[18] Naïve people muttered that the solution was the substitution of gas fires for coal fires.[19] Others decided that education was the solution. So long as housework was regarded as a menial occupation, mistresses would be denied satisfactory domestic servants.[20] A few disagreed, maintaining that servants were 'too damn educated' now, and that the illiterate, malleable 'girl' of the past was to be preferred.[21] These people were a minority, however, and recognized themselves that it was impossible to re-create their vision of an idyllic past.

In opposition to this view, other commentators argued that

[15] Board of Trade, *Report by Miss Collett on the Money Wages of Indoor Domestic Servants* (C. 9346), HC 1899, xcii. 15.

[16] My sample of advertisements (from the *Irish Times*) for domestic servants, taken every 3 years between 1883 and 1913 on 3 and 10 or 11 Apr., included an analysis of 1,379 women asking for employment and 1,506 employers requesting servants. This sample includes all women enumerated on these days. As not all advertisements contained wage rates, the sample used later in this chapter is smaller.

[17] 'A Baffled Employer', 'Masters and Servant', *IH*, 26 May 1900: 330.

[18] 'The Domestic Service Grievance', *Kings' County Chronicle*, 4 Nov. 1886: 4. For other comments about the shortage of domestic servants, see Katherine Roche, 'The Lady Teachers' Own Page', *Irish School Weekly*, 17 May 1913: 270; Margaret T. Downes, 'The Munster Technical Dairy School', *Irish Textile Journal*, 15 Aug. 1893: 91–2; 'N. J. D.', 'The Woman Emigrant', *United Irishman*, 9 Aug. 1903: 5; and RCL, *The Agricultural Labourer*, iv. *Ireland, IV, Reports by Mr Arthur Wilson Fox* (C. 6894-xxi), HC 1893, xxxvii. 19, 57, 91, 109, and 125–6.

[19] 'Moira', 'Household Hints', *IH*, 28 July 1906: 619.

[20] 'Kelm', 'Order and Method in the Household', ibid. 24 Nov. 1900: 770.

[21] RCCI, *Appendix to the 8th Report* (Cd. 3839), HC 1908, xli. 84, comment by Maurice Fitzgerald, smallholder in Dromod and Prior Parish (county Kerry); 'Geraldine', 'The Irishwoman's Attitudes', *Irishman*, 15 Jan. 1916: 4; and 'A Kerry Woman' (of Killarney), 'The Irishwoman's Attitudes', *Irishman*, 1 Mar. 1916.

there was an ample supply of servants who could not find jobs. In response to criticism of female emigration, Helen Hawthorn (women's columnist for *Ireland's Own*) retorted that girls were forced to do so because they could not find employment as servants, and that there were too few alternative options.[22] In the early 1880s, Vere Foster used the low demand for servants as a rationale for his Female Emigration Fund.[23] The wife of the unpopular land-agent S. M. Hussey never had difficulties hiring servants, at the turn of the century, even during a boycott.[24] Enthusiastic throngs of unemployed women and girls applied for a place at the training-schools for domestic servants which were opening by the 1890s.[25]

We can attempt to assess the patterns of employers' demands by concentrating on regional and class differences. Wealthier urban women found the supply of servants insufficient. Their problem was exacerbated by unreliable links of communication with potential servants. Urban employers advertised in newspapers. Rural girls were more likely to hear of employment opportunities through the 'American letter' than through the Dublin press. Unlike their English counterparts, urban employers in Ireland were not anxious to attract rural girls into service. The work involved in training a rural girl to be an urban servant was too great. Even in the countryside, servant girls were thought to be incompetent.[26] A 78-year-old farming woman, Eileen O'Shea, summed up this attitude: 'Sometimes I had a girl to help me, but God knows, more often than not they were poor slatternly creatures, and it was more hard work looking after them than any little service they did. Some of the things they did, or rather, didn't do would keep me talking for weeks.'[27] Rural employers wanted 'superworkers'. For a subsistence wage, they expected

---

[22] Helen Hawthorn, 'Dress, Gossip, Cookery and Household', *Ireland's Own*, 9 Mar. 1904: 12.
[23] *Mr Vere Foster's Irish Female Emigration Fund, under the Auspices of All the Clergy of All Denominations in the West of Ireland* (Aug. 1883), PRONI D3618/D/10/12.
[24] S. M. Hussey, *The Reminiscences of an Irish Land Agent*, compiled by Home Gordon (1904), 224 and 237.
[25] Patrick Dougherty, 'Carrigart Housekeeping School', *IH*, 24 Mar. 1900: 185.
[26] Board of Trade, *Report by Miss Collett*, xcii. 9.
[27] Interview with Eileen O'Shea, a farmer's wife, aged 78, in Somerville-Large, *Cappaghglass*, 21.

women willing to invest as much of their labour in the farm as
themselves. If they advertised for cooks, they demanded that she
would feed the pigs, milk the cows, and take care of the children.
They wanted their parlourmaids to be tall and sophisticated, as
well as strong laundresses. Nurses were to have impeccable
accents as well as being experienced seamstresses, making all the
children's clothing and doing all the family's laundry.[28]

Good servants were 'rarer than white blackbirds': 'Perhaps the
upbringing in the cottage home may not have been of a kind to
foster habits of industry.'[29] In the middle of an article promoting
domestic service as a profession, Kathleen Ferguson suddenly
launched into a tirade against the typical domestic servant, revealing that she feared not a shortage of servants, but a shortage
of 'respectable' women willing to accept employment in this low-
paid, menial occupation:

Of course the dirty, ill-kept slattern servant, with shaggy locks, shoes
down at the heels, dirty apron, dirty face and hands, is a creature to be
looked down on. But why does such a being exist? It is because the
respectable girls won't go into service, therefore many servants come
from the very poorest classes, and they continue in their servant life the
life they were brought up to in the back slums by ignorant, idle parents,
given very often to drunkenness.[30]

Typical of her class, Frances Moffett swore that servants were
frequently pregnant spinsters, commonly alcoholics, guaranteed
to disturb the household with 'superstitious' fears, and, without
exception, incompetent.[31] Such attitudes led to proposals that girls
should be imported from the 'North of Ireland, Scotland, or
foreign parts' to work as domestic servants, with a view to
marrying them to local Irish farmers. As one writer reasoned,
such a policy would benefit the entire community: the imported
servants would improve the standard of domestic service by
setting a good example within vulgar society and by rearing a
superior stock of future servants.[32]

---

[28] Every column included such stipulations.
[29] 'Fireside Cat', 'The Home-Keeper', *IH*, 3 Sept. 1904: 739.
[30] Kathleen Ferguson, 'The Nobility of Domestic Work', ibid. 19 Dec. 1903:
1039.   [31] Frances Moffett, *I Also Am of Ireland* (1985), 98–101.
[32] 'A Well-Wisher of Ireland', 'Home Life in Ireland: Some Suggestions for its
Improvement', *IH*, 20 May 1899: 353.

Who was responsible for the disappearance of the 'good' servant? Employers blamed the decline in quality on the disintegration of the patronage system in the countryside. This, in turn,
was the fault of nationalists. In the indistinct but relatively recent
past, according to these accounts, a woman of 'a superior culture'
and 'a little goodwill' might allow peasant girls to visit her home,
where they would be taught 'that civilization demands that this
thing and that thing in the daily contact of life must be done
in a particular way, but also the reason why civilization so demands it'.[33] These were the days when 'Little Biddy' would cry
out to local 'Grand Lady': 'Open your door to me, give me a
chance!', and the grand woman, hearing the cry, would pity the
child, draw her into her home, and begin teaching and punish-
ing her until she ripened into the ideal domestic servant.[34] Clearly,
local 'ladies' needed to renew their commitment to the 'Biddies'
of their community. Practically, potential women of the 'grand'
class were assured that local girls would be satisfied with only
a few pounds a year (or no wages at all) for the honour of instruction in servanthood; and the mistresses must stifle their sense
of generosity and pay not one penny more than this minimum
stipend.[35] In some cases, the employer might profit on the deal.
Ladies like 'Mrs A.'—who 'lives in a good sized house in the
country; her means are small, she has to keep up a certain style
of living, and finds it difficult to pay the numbers of servants
which are necessary for her work and for her happiness'—should
send their name to a bureau, saying that they would allow two
country girls inside their house to work, without wages and,
until they had amassed experience training a number of girls,
without charge. As the anonymous writer blandly commented:
'the advantage to the employer would naturally be that they
would get such domestic service for nothing in return for the
training given.'[36]

These schemes, exploitative and fantastic, provide some in-
sight into the nature of the 'domestic servant problem'. Large

[33] 'L. de K. K.', 'The Homestead and its In-Dwellers,' ibid. 14 Jan. 1905: 33.
[34] 'Fireside Cat', 'The Home-Keeper', ibid. 3 Sept. 1904: 739–40.
[35] 'A Woman Worker', 'Notes of the Week', ibid. 28 May 1898: 455.
[36] 'Training for Domestic Work: Some Suggestions', ibid. 2 July 1904: 556–7. See
also 'An Irish Lady', 'Suggestions for the Technical Education of Young Irishwomen', ibid. 26 Dec. 1896: 715.

landholders had been moving out of the countryside and into the cities of Ireland, Great Britain, and the Continent for decades. However, the departure of rich landholders only accounts for part of the change, since the employment of domestic servants was decreasing faster in less wealthy households than in wealthy households.

Preferences of Employees

Girls and women who, in previous decades, might have gone into service increasingly regarded it as an inferior type of employment: 'Many an intelligent farmer's daughter considers it a great comedown in the world, a disgrace even, to become a domestic servant. A sense of slavery and servitude seems to have attached itself to the idea of domestic service.'[37] Servants recognized their subservience. Tenant farmers objected to marrying former domestic servants.[38]

There is a great reluctance on the part not only of daughters of small farmers, but also the daughters of labourers to go out to service. This springs partially from pride such as deters farmers' sons from service, and partially from its becoming an obstacle to marriage. In service they become accustomed to a style of dress and a manner of living such as small farmers and labourers cannot or will not afford; hence, if a girl looks forward to marriage she will eschew service.[39]

Reminiscing about her childhood as a servant, Molly Byrne recalled how the clothes of the servants could not be dried next to the clothes of the farmer's household.[40] Mrs Mary McConnell of Enniscorthy bitterly commented:

This is a matter about which I feel very deeply—nothing gives me more pleasure than to see grass growing on the hearth stones of a farmer's

---

[37] Charlotte Dease, 'Domestic Service as a Profession', *New Ireland Review*, June 1903: 219. See also the speech by George Fletcher at the opening of the school for domestic servants, in 'Northlands School of Housewifery, Londonderry (in Connection with Victoria High School)', *DATI Journal*, 4/4 (July 1909), 713, and Katherine Roche, 'The Lady Teachers' Own Page', *Irish School Weekly*, 25 Jan. 1913: 880.   [38] 'M. L. T.', 'Homelife in Ireland', *IH*, 27 May 1899: 376.

[39] RCL, *The Agricultural Labourer*, iv. *Ireland*, III, *Reports by Mr Roger C. Richards* (C. 6894-xx), HC 1893–4, xxxvii/1: 40, report on the Poor Law Union of Roscrea (county Tipperary).   [40] Byrne, 'The Life of a Servant Girl', 30.

house where servant boys and girls were badly treated—Even yet in our country farmer's sons and daughters would not dance with a boy or girl whose parents or grandparents had been hired hands, and this in 1978![41]

Unsurprisingly, girls preferred 'business', that is, employment which placed them securely and respectably behind a counter, or sitting at a desk playing 'that entertaining musical instrument', the typewriter.[42]

Maurice Fitzgerald's evidence to the Royal Commission on Congestion hints at the reasons for women's attraction towards other occupations. Despite offering an annual salary of £12, he had to search three parishes before finding a willing servant. His difficulties stemmed from women's refusal to perform one of the most important tasks of a domestic servant—milking cows: 'It is not easy to get a girl to do rough work now, and they would prefer to be at a place where there were no cows kept, for more money. We farmers blame Waterville [county Kerry] a good deal for that, because they say that they have the easier life in Waterville than they have with the farmers.'[43] Employers of domestic servants imposed too many rules: servants resented having to fight for one night off a week.[44] Employers responded by blaming 'misplaced pride and also ignorance' for the attitude of the complaining servants.[45] There could be no easy solution. Servants attempted to restrict their duties. Some would 'take no washing'; others would work 'only in a small family'. More impertinent servants demanded a minimum wage.[46] The average wage requested by prospective employees in the *Irish Times* was 18 per cent higher than that offered by employers. There were calls to mistresses to treat their domestic servants with more respect—only by doing this, could they plug the flow of servants.[47]

[41] This note was written by Mrs Mary McConnell, and has been added to the box containing the Ulster Folk and Transport Museum, Questionnaire on Hiring-Fairs, No. 2 (1977).

[42] 'Brigid', 'Domestic Service as a Profession for Women', *IH*, 8 Feb. 1902: 113.

[43] *Nationist*, 22 Feb. 1906: 329.

[44] 'D. L.', 'Working Women's Column', *Irish Worker*, 11 Nov. 1911: 2.

[45] Ferguson, 'The Nobility of Domestic Work', 1039. See also the defensive comments of members of the Governesses' Association of Ireland, all of whom were employers of domestic servants, *Warder and Dublin Weekly Mail*, 7 May 1881.

[46] Every column includes such stipulations: see *Daily Express*, 24 Feb. 1885: 8, and 3 Mar. 1885: 8.

[47] 'L. de K. K.', 'On Furnishing Bedrooms', *IH*, 1 Nov. 1905: 833.

DEMAND FOR SERVANTS

The Household and Relative Costs

Some contemporaries argued that the decline in the number of domestic servants was due to retrenchment in household expenses. The emigration of potential employees to America, attracted by higher wages and better conditions, left the Irish rate of pay for servants high, and the standard of service low. 'As a consequence of the higher cost of domestic help, without any corresponding increase of efficiency in service, many Irish housewives have in recent years discarded hired help and do their own work—a desirable social revolution, provided the housewives are physically equal to the task undertaken.'[48]

Economists view wages as signals about the allocation of scarce resources.[49] What can wage trends tell us about the changing numbers of domestic servants? There are only two sources of wage data for servants in Ireland: newspaper advertisements and wage-books. Each has its own advantages. Wage-books provide profiles of servants, allowing us to look at individual households over time and at wage differentials on the farm. We shall examine these first. Newspaper advertisements provide a longer 'run' over time and allow us to differentiate between types of servants.

William Boyd of the Blackstaff Flax Spinning and Weaving Company paid his cook and his maid £18 a year. His groom received £30. Wages for the cook and the maid were the equivalent of one-quarter of the monthly amount spent on 'hunting trains' (during the season), and one-eleventh of the sum given to himself for his personal expenses.[50] Mrs Annet was hired for 4s. a week, and her employer informed her that this sum included

free lodging and fire during the time you are with me but if you do not suit the position you will have to leave at a fortnight's notice. Your duties will be: First to keep the house clean and tidy outside and inside

---

[48] 'The Man of Figures', 'Domestic Servants', *Ireland's Own*, 7 Jan. 1903: 7.

[49] For a discussion of the role that cultural beliefs and practices play in wage determination, see D. J. Treiman and Heidi I. Hartmann (eds.), *Women, Work and Wages: Equal Pay for Jobs of Equal Value* (Washington, DC, 1981). Adam Smith also dealt with the way in which non-money characteristics of jobs affect wages: *Wealth of Nations* (New York, 1937), 99–100.

[50] PRONI D1534/5 and 6, Household account-books (1901–11) of William Boyd of the Blackstaff Flax Spinning and Weaving Company.

and have such things as windows clean and nice. Second, when people go down [to their country house] you must be kind and good natured with them even if they are disagreeable sometimes. You will have to wash their sheets and bed things but you need not cook for them unless they specially arrange with you first and pay you a little.[51]

Despite the low proportion of personal expenditure devoted to female servants, these wages were higher than those paid by most rural employers. John Keane, a farmer in Baltacken (county Westmeath), hired a *male* yard servant on 30 October 1912 for an annual wage of £14. A month later, Bridget Poker commenced work as a general servant under Mrs Keane for £8 a year.[52] Mary Boyce worked as a parlour-maid for T. M. Green in the Ballymoney Rural District in 1892 for £13 per annum. This sum was not fixed at the beginning. For her first month of service, Mary Boyce was paid less than 7s. This was raised to £1 a month in August, then to £13 a year in October.[53]

New servants were expected to work for very little, to appreciate the 'training' that they were receiving in the hands of their mistress.[54] In 1899 servants under 18 years of age were generally paid half as much as servants over 30.[55] The higher average wages of the older servants may not be a result of benefits incurred by increased efficiency. A more satisfactory explanation focuses on the higher proportion of young servants in poorer, single-servant households. Older servants were generally found in households with a larger number of servants and in more specialized service categories, and for this reason they commanded a higher average wage. In 1899 a cook in her twenties could claim a wage of £17 a year, while her kitchen-maid, the same age, was paid £11. A general servant received a pound less. At the other extreme, a 'lady's maid' could receive £24 a year.[56] Younger servants also worked in larger households. Thus, in 1901 and 1911 the average size of households with servants under the age of 20 was seven persons, while households employing servants over 40 generally

[51] PRONI D2956/1, copy of letter-book (out) of J. N. Richardson, Mount Caulfield, Bessbrook, letter dated 9 Mar. 1876: 177.

[52] Cork Archives Institute U251, John Keane, Baltacken, Myvore, Mullingar (county Westmeath).

[53] PRONI D1835/4/101–11, T. M. Green, solicitor, Ballymoney Rural District.

[54] 'A Woman Worker', 'Notes of the Week', *IH*, 28 May 1898: 455.

[55] Board of Trade, *Report by Miss Collett*, xcii. 11.   [56] Ibid. 13 (13).

Table 2.4. Average wages and number of domestic servants, 1899

No. of servants in household	Average wages (£)			
	Dublin	Belfast	Cork and Limerick	Ireland
1	10.8	12.6	9.5	11.3
2	13.5	13.9	11.1	13.3
3	15.3	16.7	13.9	15.5
4	16.6	17.1	14.7	15.9
4 +	19.8	19.7	17.4	18.7

Source: Board of Trade, *Report by Miss Collett on the Money Wages of Indoor Domestic Servants* (C. 9346), HC 1899, xcii. 10.

contained four persons. Household size increased only in homes employing elderly domestic servants.[57] Poorer households could only afford to hire young girls.[58]

Clearly, wage differentials varied with the income of the employing family and with the type of duties expected from the servant. Thus, households that could afford a few domestic servants paid higher wages (see Table 2.4). Such households would employ women for specialist duties such as those of parlour-maid, cook, governess, and children's nurse. The 'display' function of servants in these households would also prompt higher wages, so the servants could afford the 'paraphernalia of gentility'. General domestics in one-servant households performed functions similar to those of labourers, and were paid accordingly.

Table 2.5 gives the average wage offered in advertisements for general domestic servants and 'specialist servants'. The latter category is divided into Class 1 (cooks, lady's maids, nurses, dairymaids, and sewing maids) and Class 2 (kitchen-maids,

[57] Note that household size here includes relatives, visitors, and boarders, but does not include those whose relationship to the 'head of the household' was that of servant.
[58] I have excluded households for which I could find no valuation. Where there was more than 1 servant within the same age-group in the household, I included only 1 servant in my calculations. These procedures have not changed the relationship between the age-groups in any significant way.

Table 2.5. Annual wages and 'class' of domestic servants, 1880–1913 (£)

Year	General servants[a]	Specialist servants[b]	
		Class 1	Class 2
1883	9.7	20.5	12.0
1886	—	22.8	16.0
1889	7.3	15.5	9.8
1892	8.9	14.9	14.2
1895	8.6	11.7	14.7
1898	9.7	17.6	14.3
1901	12.4	16.4	14.9
1904	11.6	21.2	14.0
1907	11.1	20.1	13.7
1910	12.4	19.1	16.2
1913	13.1	23.8	18.1

Note: The wages for 'specialist servants, Class 1' were dominated by the wages of cooks.

[a] n (no. in sample) = 155.
[b] n = 126 for Class 1, and 155 for Class 2.

Source: *Irish Times*, 3 and 10 or 11 Apr. 1880–1913.

parlour-maids, housemaids, laundresses, child-minders, and scullery-maids), as advertised every three years in the *Irish Times* on 3 and 10 or 11 April. These wage data suggest a declining demand for female domestic servants, as their wages rose less than the average for all workers, despite a fall in the number of servants per family. The higher relative price of personal services could be expected to decrease demand for domestic servants. The fact that it cost more to keep servants than it did to maintain full-time unwaged 'houseworkers' tipped the balance in favour of houseworkers.

Agriculture and Service

The demand for servants must be examined in two distinct spheres: the agricultural and the domestic environment. The coincidence of change in these areas radically reduced demand for female servants. The agricultural factors will be discussed in

Chapter 5. The remainder of this chapter examines influential household factors.

The Household and Service

Changes in household structure may have reduced demand for paid labour in the household. As we have already seen, the number of domestic servants in the eight DEDs declined by 12 per cent. However, these changes mask marked differences between districts. In Tullamore, Woodstown, and Rathmore, for example, the number of domestic servants increased slightly. This contrasts with Keeldra, Ards, and Bellatrain, where servants declined by over 60 per cent. Domestic servants in Kilconickny declined by one-third, and the number of Belleek servants declined by 17 per cent. The following few pages will deal with changes in familial structure in the eight DEDs which may help to explain the decline of service in some of these areas.

Domestic servants were over-represented in households with a low proportion of women. For instance, in 1901, 15 per cent of all households had a male to female ratio of less than one to three, whereas 29 per cent of all households with resident domestic servants had a male to female ratio of more than one to three.[59] The corresponding figures for 1911 were 18 per cent of all households and 21 per cent of households with resident domestic servants. If the proportion of households with a sex ratio biased towards men decreased, so would the need for domestic servants. This does not fit the sample districts. While the number of domestic servants was decreasing, there was an increase in the proportion of households containing a low ratio of women. Although the percentage of all-male households rose from 6 to 8 per cent, someone other than a domestic servant was beginning to do the housework.

Domestic servants were more likely to be found in larger households. While one-fifth of all households had seven or more members in 1901, over one-third of households with domestic servants had seven or more members.[60] Similarly, 7 per cent of all households in 1901 and 1911 had over nine members,

[59] The ratio excludes female domestic servants.
[60] The corresponding figures for 1911 were 22% of all households and 39% of households with domestic servants.

compared with almost one-fifth of all households with resident domestic servants. As the proportion of large households declined between 1901 and 1911, we would expect the proportion of resident domestic servants to have declined as well. As households became smaller, the 'head female' (generally the wife, but frequently a mother or sister) could manage the housework without hiring a servant. Looking at the DEDs individually, this occurred in six of the eight districts. The district experiencing the most rapid decline in domestic servants (Keeldra) was the district experiencing the fastest decline in household size. The three districts that did not experience a fall in the number of domestic servants were the three districts that saw small increases in the proportion of households with seven members or more. The two exceptions were the northern communities of Bellatrain and Ards, which saw small increases in the size of households, yet also saw a decline in service.

We may hypothesize that servants were needed in households with a large number of children. Resident servants were over-represented in households with children. For instance, in 1901 households with three or more children under the age of 5 were twice as likely to have at least one resident domestic servant as households with fewer than three children under the age of 5.[61] At first sight, this hypothesis does not seem to hold for the eight districts, since, given the *increase* in the percentage of all households with three or more children, we would expect an increase in domestic servants. However, once we have broken the statistics down into their districts, this becomes less of a problem. Areas experiencing a rapid decline in the number of households with at least three children under the age of 5 also experienced a decline in domestic servants. The exceptions were Ards and Bellatrain. In Bellatrain there was a 38 per cent increase in the number of households with at least three children under the age of 5, but an exceptionally rapid decline in the number of domestic servants. In part, this resulted from the choice of criteria. The number of households with *any* children under the age of 5 declined between 1901 and 1911. Ards is the anomaly. In Ards there were fewer young children in the household, yet domestic service still declined. Although the fall in the number of young

---

[61] The corresponding figures for 1911 were 7% of all households and 11% of households with resident domestic servants.

Table 2.6. Employment for 'head females', 1901 and 1911 (%)

District	'Occupied' head females	
	1901[a]	1911[b]
Woodstown	24.1	21.9
Ards	26.8	11.6
Tullamore	39.8	18.1
Kilconickny	61.2	14.8
Rathmore	29.2	21.6
Bellatrain	36.8	25.9
Belleek	32.4	26.8
Keeldra	36.8	16.3
All districts	35.2	19.5

[a] n (no. in sample) = 920.
[b] n = 800.
Source: Manuscript census returns for 8 DEDs, NAI, 1901 and 1911.

children in the household—either through a spacing of children, a reduction in family size, or a tendency for married siblings to move away from the parental household with the birth of a child —can explain some of the declining demand for servants, it is insufficient by itself.

The most important explanation for the decline of domestic service lies in increased labour by unwaged family members in the household. The growing numbers of adult females without an occupation ('houseworkers') reduced the demand for paid domestic servants. The increase in houseworkers can be calculated in two ways. First, we can look at the number of households where the 'head female' was not entered as having an occupation. Table 2.6 provides a percentage figure for 'head females' with designated occupations.[62] Between 1901 and 1911 this figure dropped by 50 per cent.

---

[62] If the head of the household was female, she was designated as the 'head female'. If the head of the household was male, the 'head female' was defined as his wife if he was married, or as the oldest adult female (generally his mother or sister) if he was unmarried. Non-relatives, such as servants or visitors, were excluded. Some households had no 'head female' and were excluded from the analysis. A 'head female' was deemed to have no occupation if she was entered as 'unoccupied' or as 'housewife', 'engaged in home duties', or 'farmer's relative'.

Table 2.7. Households with 'unoccupied' adult females, 1901 and 1911 (%)

District	1901[a]	1911[b]
Woodstown	72.5	72.6
Ards	72.7	88.1
Tullamore	53.8	78.8
Kilconickny	38.9	87.5
Rathmore	65.4	82.7
Bellatrain	60.1	69.8
Belleek	64.4	79.5
Keeldra	64.7	80.1
All districts	62.6	79.4

[a] n (no. in sample) = 987.
[b] n = 924.

Source: Manuscript census returns for 8 DEDs, NAI, 1901 and 1911.

Table 2.8. Households and houseworkers, 1901 and 1911

No. of houseworkers	Households with 'unoccupied' women (%)	
	1901	1911
0	37.4	20.6
1	51.1	52.2
2	9.6	21.0
3 +	1.9	6.2

Source: Manuscript census returns for 8 DEDs, NAI, 1901 and 1911.

Second, the number of houseworkers can be calculated by looking at the number of adult women (over fifteen years) within each household who were not employed (see Table 2.7). From this, we can see that 17 per cent more households had at least one houseworker in 1911 than in 1901. The percentage of all households with no 'unoccupied' women decreased between 1901 and 1911, while the proportion with more than one dependent female increased (see Table 2.8).

The emphasis has been twofold. On the one hand, demand for female domestic servants was reduced. Agricultural reasons for the decline in demand are examined in Chapter 5. On the domestic side, the lower demand for servants was a function of the rising price of domestic service which resulted in a transfer of that labour to unwaged family members. Women increasingly performed domestic labour within their own households rather than for another family. On the other hand, the supply of domestic servants dropped as women who might have gone into paid service remained in their own homes to produce those goods and services increasingly necessary to the efficient functioning of households (this aspect is examined in Chapter 7). Taking up David Fitzpatrick's comment that labourers became less and less distinguishable as a class from farmers as they progressively consisted of smallholders and their sons, it can be maintained that a similar movement occurred for women, except that they moved from waged domestic and farm labour to unwaged domestic and farm labour as the wives, sisters, and aunts of male farmers.[63] The significance of the decline in domestic service is that housework was increasingly being done by members of the family. The extra burden of housework did not fall evenly on all members of the household, and so-called 'labour-saving devices' did not come to the rescue.

[63] David Fitzpatrick, 'The Disappearance of the Irish Agricultural Labourer, 1841–1912', *Irish Economic and Social History*, 7 (1980), 82.

3

Dairymaids

ON 16 October 1892 Denis Hurley wrote from Carson City to his sister in Cork about their brother:

I believe Tim is foolish to be postponing his marriage so long under the circumstances. As dairy farming is the most profitable, he should get a good looking and affectionate wife that would make first class butter. If you cannot help him to get one in Cork, why I will give him a letter of recommendation to go wife seeking down to Connaught.[1]

Denis had emigrated to America twenty-two years earlier: his advice was becoming dated. Butter prices had been declining since Hurley left Ireland in the 1870s. They rose briefly in 1891 and 1892, before falling again. Prices did not pick up until the turn of the century, and then they remained relatively stagnant for another decade. However, the industry was vital to the Irish economy. In 1912 the production of butter and milk made up 2 per cent of the total agricultural income of Ireland.[2] Astute publicists could see that, with regard to female participation in dairying, the industry was changing. By the beginning of the twentieth century, the practice of farm women milking cows, making butter for family consumption, selling the surplus in markets and shops, and using the money to pay off shop debts was no longer the dominant pattern.[3] A technological and managerial revolution in the dairy industry was affecting female farm labour in large parts of the country. This chapter examines these changes. The first section discusses the declining participation of women

---

[1] Cork Archives Institute U170, Hurley emigrant letters, letter from Denis Hurley to his sister Kate, dated 16 Oct. 1892. His family was from Clonakilty (county Cork). Denis emigrated in 1870.

[2] DATI, 'Council of Agriculture, 27th Meeting, Tuesday, 4 May 1915, Report of Proceedings', 6.

[3] *Committee on Butter Regulations* (Cd. 1039), HC 1902, xx. 175–8, 154–6, and 181, evidence by (respectively) the Department's instructresses Miss E. Dundon of county Limerick, Miss K. A. Brown of county Donegal, and Miss Ethel Sarsfield of county Cork.

in milking and butter-making. What caused women to move out of these sectors? Historians of the dairy industry stress its rapid growth in this period.[4] The cost of these changes was high. Women were driven out of the industry. Contemporaries responded to increasing unemployment among women in two ways. Rural reformers attempted to educate women in improved forms of butter-making. These schemes failed. More realistically, they attempted to divert 'redundant' labour into three areas: home industries, poultry-rearing, and housework. The economic and social situation meant that the promotion of housework was the dominant (and successful) response.

As we noted in the last chapter, job definitions were flexible. Dairymaids could find themselves working for part of every day or year in the kitchen or in the fields. For example, Mary Sheehan worked on the Mount Trenchard estate. According to their wage-books, which cover the years 1882 to 1887, between thirteen and twenty people were employed on the estate each week. All employees were men, until Mary Sheehan appeared on 6 January 1883 as a milker. While the men worked for six days, she worked for seven days, for a weekly wage of 1s. 6d. The men were paid between 4s. and 11s. a week. Her husband spread manure, cut bog, and gardened. By 1884, Mary Sheehan's weekly wage was raised to 2s. She was employed irregularly during the year, depending on whether or not the cow was dry. In March of every year she spent a few weeks cutting and then dropping seed in the fields. During these weeks her wage was 6s. a week.[5]

WOMEN AND MEN

Census statistics provide information on the sexual division of labour within the dairy industry. People involved in milking and butter-making might be categorized under a number of

[4] Raymond D. Crotty, *Irish Agricultural Production* (Cork, 1966); Liam Kennedy, 'Aspects of the Spread of the Creamery System in Ireland' in Carla Keating (ed.), *Plunkett and Co-operatives: Past, Present and Future* (Cork, 1983), 92–110; Cormac Ó Gráda, 'The Beginnings of the Irish Creamery System, 1880–1914', *EHR*, 2nd ser. 30/2 (May 1977), 284–305; and Trevor West, *Horace Plunkett: Co-operation and Politics: An Irish Biography* (Gerrards Cross, 1986).

[5] NLI MS 580, Wage-Books of the Mount Trenchard Estate, Lord Monteagle Papers, 1882–6.

occupations. The decline of female domestic and agricultural servants has been examined in Chapter 2. Women explicitly given dairying occupations were placed in different categories in 1881–91, 1901–11, and 1926. In 1881 and 1891 they could be called milk-sellers and dairywomen, or cheesemongers and butter-women. In 1881 women made up 43 per cent of all persons within these categories. Ten years later, this had declined to 31 per cent. If we then turn to the heading 'milkseller, dairywoman' in the 1901 and 1911 census, the percentage of women declined from 26 per cent in 1901 to 16 per cent by 1911. The 1901 and 1911 census included a separate category for creamery workers. Women con-stituted almost 30 per cent of this category in 1901, and only 12 per cent by 1911. Only 1 per cent of the employers and managers of creameries in Ireland were women in 1926. By 1936, this had decreased even further to 0.5 per cent. There were no forwomen or female overlookers in creameries. Women were concentrated in the general category of 'creamery workers' (where they made up 34 per cent of those enumerated) and in the category for skilled makers of food in creameries (60 per cent of all skilled creamery-makers). If we take all those occupations explicitly labelled as employment in creameries or as concerned with milk and dairy products, over 40 per cent of this workforce in 1881 was female, compared with less than one-sixth by the end of the period.

MILKING

Men began to take a larger role in dairying. Wealthier house-holds altered their practices first. Women in these families began delegating dairying tasks to hired male labourers.[6] The first widespread change occurred in milking practice, as this was an outdoor job and one that was more easily redefined as men's work. The 1848, 1853, and 1860 editions of the *Agricultural Class Book* encouraged young boys to read the chapter entitled 'The Cow—The Dairy—Milk—Butter—Cheese—Pigs', with the words: 'possibly some *boys*, on reading the heading of this lesson, may be so foolish to think it is a fit study for *girls* only.' It went on to

[6] J. P. Sheldon, *Dairy Farming: Being the Theory, Practice and Methods of Dairying*, 1st edn. 1879 (1888), 360.

say that, although girls milk, make butter, and scour milk vessels, the boys should still read the chapter so that they could perform their role of feeding and attending to the cow, helping with particularly heavy churning, and supervising the women if necessary.[7] Although women regarded the dairy as their 'traditional' province, and although folklore conferred 'natural', superior milking skills on women,[8] commentators agreed that, increasingly, men were doing the milking.

Long ago it was the women milked the cows, but in later years it was done in a lot of cases by the men.[9]

In days gone by cows were all milked by women. There was no such thing as a man milking a cow. Men would not consider it their work to milk a cow. Whatever be the cause, women have gone out of the business, and in a great number of cases, therefore, cows have got to be milked by men and boys.[10]

Although it is easy to perceive the general movement of men into milking activities, precise identification of the timing and locational aspects are more elusive. The evidence is impressionistic and often contradictory. For example, in 1911 a dairy farmer in Bangor stated that male milkers had completely replaced females; but he later added that the wives of milkers assisted their husbands in large dairies.[11] Similarly, in 1911 the vice-chairman of the North Down Agricultural Society said that young boys grew up learning to milk, and were engaged in that occupation as

[7] Commissioners of National Education in Ireland, *Agricultural Class Book* (Dublin, 1848), 240–1, (1853 and 1860 edns., 288–9).

[8] See the story told by Mickey Crowley of Carrigroe (county Cork), aged 95 years, recorded between Aug. and Oct. 1942, IFC MS 843: 88. See also evidence by R. A. Anderson and Henry S. Guinness of Stillorgan (county Dublin), in Department of Industry and Commerce, Saorstát Éireann (hereafter DIC), *Commission of Inquiry into the Resources and Industries of Ireland* (Dublin, 1919), 25 and 50–3, and Helen Blackburn (ed.), *A Handy Book of Reference for Irishwomen* (1888), 84–5.

[9] IFC MS 1024, discussion by John Cullen, aged 71, labourer of Bailieborough (county Cavan), collected by P. J. Gaynor of Bailieborough in Jan. 1948. See also the comments by Mrs Anne Prunty, aged 82, housewife of Dromond Parish (county Longford), collected by J. G. Delaney, ibid. 357–8.

[10] DIC, *Commission of Inquiry into the Resources of Ireland*, 9, evidence by R. A. Anderson, secretary of the IAOS.

[11] Vice-Regal Commission on Irish Milk Supplies, *Appendix to the 1st Report* (Cd. 6684), HC 1913, xxix. 268, evidence by M. Shiels of Bangor. It was very common for a male labourer to be hired on condition that his wife would milk the cows, see *Cork Constitution*, 19 Jan. 1886: 4, and Mary Carbery, *Farm by Lough Gur* (1937), 9.

adults. This assertion was followed by the comment that the wives of labourers frequently supplemented the family income by milking.[12]

Two questionnaires provide some indication of the changes. In 1958 the Irish Folklore Commission issued a questionnaire on the social aspects of work. Question 5 asked whether milking was considered 'beneath the dignity' of the 'average farmer' in their district; 87 respondents replied by specifying whether men or women milked. The questionnaire on hiring-fairs that was sent out by researchers at the Ulster Folk and Transport Museum asked for lists of work performed by male and female agricultural labourers; 82 replies stipulated whether men or women milked. Examination of the questionnaires reveals a mixed pattern. Men rarely replaced women entirely in the business of milking. Poorer classes of women were more likely to be engaged in milking. Women did not milk in those places where male wages were high. If the milk was used merely for household consumption, women were more likely to milk as part of the housework. With the advent of creameries, which regularized production and marketing, men were increasingly likely to take over the milking. Furthermore, with higher wages for male labourers, and the rapid substitution of casual labourers for indoor servants, farmers were more likely to hire men who could be employed at other agricultural work during slack milking months. Thus, we see an increase of *male* farm servants in households with dairies. In the eight DEDs that have formed our sample, 10 per cent of all households in both 1901 and 1911 had dairy sheds. In 1901, while only 8 or 9 per cent of *all* households in the areas had either a domestic servant or a farm servant, 35 per cent of households with dairies had servants. By 1911, 40 per cent of households with dairies had servants. The number of domestic servants and farm servants in these households remained stable; what changed was the sex composition of farm servants. In 1901, 27 per cent of farm servants on holdings with dairies were female. Within ten years, only 11 per cent were female.

---

[12] Vice-Regal Commission on Irish Milk Supplies, *Appendix to the 1st Report*, xxix. 173, evidence by Revd W. Wright, Presbyterian clergyman at Newtownards and vice-chairman of the North Down Agricultural Society.

CREAMERIES AND FEMALE EMPLOYMENT

Milking was only the first of many jobs in which a predominantly female workforce was replaced by men. The traditional way of making butter, with women churning the milk or cream, was gradually replaced (in all areas except the east) by large-scale creameries—co-operatively or privately run.[13] The move to creameries was particularly strong in Limerick, Tipperary, Kilkenny, Sligo, Cavan, Monaghan, Cork, Leitrim, Kerry, and Waterford.[14] Creameries were initially established in Limerick. Canon Baggot started the first Irish creamery in 1884. In 1889 two partners erected a creamery at Limerick Junction. Farmers in northern Cork and county Limerick opened joint-stock creameries. The English Co-operative Union also set up creameries in Ireland under the Industrial and Provident Societies' Act. The sudden upswing in large-scale butter production came with the growth of the co-operative movement under the managerial guidance of the IAOS. The creameries were managed by a committee elected by the shareholders. Farmers took shares in the co-operatives, and profits were shared. People supplying milk were paid the highest market price consistent with creamery survival. In most co-operative creameries, the farmer was paid in proportion to the amount of butterfat in the milk. The milk was separated, by centrifugal separators, and the skim milk was given back to the supplier. By 1908, nearly all societies were adopting a 'binding rule' whereby the supplier had to sell all this milk to the society in which she or he held shares. There was also the tendency to restrict the acceptance of milk from non-shareholders.

By 1915, the dairy societies of the IAOS had a membership of over 45,000 with a turnover of £3 million.[15] Proponents of the creameries argued that they were the only salvation for a dairy industry depressed through generations of poverty and land

---

[13] Co-operative creameries accounted for, at most, half of the total butter production: Cyril Ehrlich, 'Sir Horace Plunkett and Agricultural Reform', in J. M. Goldstrom and L. A. Clarkson (eds.), *Irish Population, Economy and Society* (Oxford, 1981), 281.

[14] DIC, *Agricultural Statistics, 1847–1926: Report and Tables* (Dublin, 1928), pp. xx–xxi.

[15] Ministry for Reconstruction, *Summaries of Evidence Taken before the Agricultural Policy Sub-Committee* (Cd. 9080), HC 1918, v. 93, evidence by R. A. Anderson, secretary of the IAOS.

insecurity, and facing strong international competition.[16] In addition, Irish dairying required creameries, because Irish women could not make uniformly high-quality butter. Without creameries, the best butter was exported and sold at the same price as the 'rancid productions evolving from a smoky cabin, where one churning lay gathering for weeks'.[17] The industry could not survive if it continued to produce butter that tasted of peat.[18] What was the good of dairy farmers in Limerick or Cork having 'grass so rich you could grease your boots on it', if no market would accept their butter?[19] Even if women had the training and facilities for making high-quality butter, the lack of uniformity in farmhouse butter meant that it would not secure the highest price. Creameries increased the profits of dairy farmers. It was claimed that they raised the average price of the farmers' butter by about 4*d.* per pound, and increased output by as much as 10 per cent.[20] Creameries were said to be superior to the factory (or blending) system, because 'responsible' butter producers received the milk straight from the cow's teat, so to speak, with no intermediate peasant woman to dirty the milk through her methods of setting, preparing, and churning.[21]

You would have to reform the conditions of Irish dairy farming altogether if you wanted to adopt the factory [that is, blending] system, and you would have to teach every woman who makes a pound of butter

[16] *Report from the Select Committee on Industries (Ireland)* (.288), HC 1884–5, ix. 211, evidence by William John Lane, Cork butter merchant. See also the letter from Mrs Ernest Hart republished from *Daily Graphic* in *Irish Farming World*, 4 Dec. 1891: 788. Kennedy, 'Aspects of the Creamery System', 92–110, provides a convincing analysis of these processes.

[17] Sarsfield Kerrigan, *Leader*, 7 Mar. 1908: 39. See also Trinity College, Dublin, MS Library, 'Confidential Report [Baseline Reports], CDB, County of Donegal—Union of Inishowen, Report of Major Gaskell, Inspector, District of North Inishowen', 3, and RCCI, *Appendix to the 8th Report* (Cd. 3839), HC 1908, xli. 72, evidence by the Very Revd Canon Humphrey O'Riordan, representing the bishops, the Cahirciveen Rural District, and the fish-curers.

[18] *Committee on Butter Regulations*, xx. 154, evidence by Miss K. A. Brown, dairy instructress for the DATI in Donegal.

[19] Augusta Gregory, 'Ireland, Real or Imaginary', *Nineteenth Century* (Nov. 1898), 771.

[20] Creameries extracted 10% more butter out of the same amount of milk used in home churning: *Leader*, 21 Mar. 1908: 73–4.

[21] The factory or blending system meant that farm women churned the milk in their home, then brought the butter to the factory, where it was mixed with butter made by other women in the district, and then marketed. Creameries separated the milk and churned the butter.

in Ireland how to make it properly, you would have to build new dairies on special and proper principles, and you would have to have a system of inspection which would insure the dairies being properly clean. You must recollect that the bulk of butter which comes from Ireland is manufactured in districts where the people are untidy. I have known cases where some of the butter made in County Kerry was stored in a room where there was a patient suffering from typhus fever.[22]

Historians have generally accepted this view of creameries, portraying them as economically desirable (because they are 'efficient') in areas with a sufficiently large milk supply.[23] However, creameries drastically reduced the income potential of many women and girls. Creameries lowered female employment.[24]

The inevitable effect of the general adoption of such institutions [creameries] in this country must be, I apprehend, to remove from the wives and daughters of the farmers a healthy, and at the same time, most valuable source of industrial occupation and training; in every way peculiarly adapted to their condition and habit of life for which it will not be easy to discover in any other direction, an equally suitable or sufficient substitute, and the want of which now, on the part of these by no means insignificant classes of the working population, may—it is quite conceivable—in the many possible contingencies of the future, be found to ultimately result in serious loss to the farmers themselves.[25]

Local controversies developed as to the relative advantages and disadvantages of replacing home-made butter production by creameries.[26] This aspect was summarized in the *Irish Nation*.

The co-operative creameries . . . have and are taking away what was the main occupation and the mainstay of many of the women in this country. Without in any way entering into the comparative merits of home butter-making and calf-rearing, and the co-operative system, it will easily be seen that no farmer's daughter will find working under factory conditions a welcome change from being, as she was after all, mistress of her time, her capital and her labour.[27]

[22] Royal Commission on Agriculture, *Minutes of Evidence*, iii (C. 7400-iii), HC 1894, xvi/3: 393, evidence by R. A. Anderson.
[23] Ó Gráda, 'The Beginnings of the Creamery System', 284–305.
[24] *Irish Peasant*, 28 Apr. 1906: 6, and 'M. G.', 'Economic Thoughts for Irishwomen', *Irish Nation*, 13 Feb. 1909.
[25] RCL, *The Agricultural Labourer*, iv. *Ireland*, II, *Reports by Mr W. P. O'Brien* (C. 6894-xix), HC 1893–4, xxxvii/1: 37, report on Kanturk (county Cork).
[26] Ibid. 66 (198), report by W. P. O'Brien on Cashel; 'Killeagh', *IH*, 15 June 1901: 407; and throughout the reports on co-operative meetings in *IH*.
[27] 'M. G.', 'Economic Thoughts for Irishwomen'.

This argument is deceptive, however, because few farmers' daughters were given employment in creameries. The IAOS defended the increase in female unemployment by advising farmers to calculate the economic value of the time of their daughters. When a farmer learned about the value of time,

then he will be able to judge more truly what the creamery system means; where the cream from a 1,000 farms is churned in two churns instead of 1,000, and where two or three girls do the work of many hundreds, and the selling of tons of butter is done at less cost of time and money than the selling of pounds by individuals, and more important, perhaps, still, where you have only one good quality instead of 1,000 of all sorts.[28]

In a labour-surplus economy, such reasoning was unhelpful.

Women were also absent within the creamery labour structure. None of the twenty-seven creameries and dairy societies examined in the Registry of Friendly Societies had a woman on a managing committee.[29] Female shareholders were also rare. They were usually women who had taken over shares after the death of their husband. Single women frequently transferred their shares to their husband after marriage.[30] Only 6–9 per cent of the shareholders in the Ballyrashane Co-operative Agricultural Dairy Society (county Londonderry) between 1908 and 1924 were women.[31] Table 3.1 has been constituted from lists of members found within the Registry papers in Dublin. With the exception of the last three societies listed in the table, these statistics show

---

[28] Arthur S. Lough, 'The Creamery Movement in Ireland', *Irish Technical Journal*, 1/10 (Dec. 1903), 142.

[29] The following creameries and dairy societies were examined at the Registry of Friendly Societies: Dublin, Pettigo, Killowen, Centenary, Poles, Mayo Abbey, St Johns's, Drumholme, Moycartkey, Ardrahan, Ballyhadereen, Kill, Kilnaleck, Kiltoghert, Lower Ormond, Toher, Kildimo, Thurles, Ballinfull, Ballinode, Busna, Inver, Bruree, Corcaghan, Newtownards, Ballinaglera, and Bennettsbridge. I have detailed accounts for all these societies. They were chosen because they were the only societies for which such information existed; thus, they represent 'successful' societies.

[30] See e.g. the letters of Eliza Robinson and Ellen Convoy in PRONI D3076/ BA/1, papers of the Deerpark Co-operative Agricultural and Dairy Society Ltd., Glenarm, county Antrim.

[31] PRONI T3132/BA/1 and 2, Minute-Book of the Ballyrashane Co-operative Agricultural and Dairy Society, Ltd., Coleraine (county Londonderry), 28 Feb. 1908–17 Apr. 1924. Note the scarcity of female shareholders in the list in PRONI D3076/BA/1, Deerpark Co-operative and Dairy Society Ltd.

Table 3.1. Female shareholders in creamery or dairy societies, 1914–1919

File no.	County	Year	Female shareholders (%)
153	Tipperary	1916	3
371	Roscommon	1919	4
924	Donegal	1914	5
1172	Limerick	1919	5
1172	Limerick	1916	6
972	Kilkenny	1919	6
152	Tipperary	1916	6
638	Monaghan	1916	8
638	Monaghan	1919	8
280	Mayo	1914	8
109	Kerry	1916	9
774	Cavan	1916	10
1097	Limerick	1919	15
230	Tipperary	1919	16
693	Cork	1915	27

Note: I have only included those lists which consistently give both forename and surname.

Source: Registry of Friendly Societies, Dublin.

the low representation of women in dairy societies. The last three, however, in Limerick, Tipperary, and Cork, seem to have a large proportion of female shareholders. These societies were the only ones that set out to encourage membership by dealing in eggs and poultry as well as in milk and butter. The larger proportion of female shareholders in these societies reflected their role as collectors and sellers of eggs.[32]

Few women were employed in creameries. A photograph in the Public Record Office of Northern Ireland shows a dairyman and an all-male staff. Men sit and stand around carts stacked with cans delivering milk. The only females in the photograph are two small girls with pails, obviously waiting to buy skim milk for the family.[33] In the twenty-seven creameries examined

[32] This is discussed in Ch. 6.
[33] PRONI D3057/ib/2, photograph of creamery.

in detail, eleven hired no women, and the remainder employed only one or two. The societies hiring no women were scattered throughout the sample, as likely to be found in Tipperary and Cork as in Leitrim and Roscommon. Most creameries hired more than two men. Creameries had to be significantly larger to warrant the employment of another dairymaid, while new male workers might be required after only a slight increase in production. Furthermore, the larger a creamery, the more likely it was to prefer men to perform the functions previously designated to women. Technology has been blamed for this. The heavier machinery necessary in a very large creamery required 'masculine' strength:

I do not think that in a large creamery a woman could do the work as effectively as a man. Two women might. I think this is the reason there has been a tendency on the part of creameries that have a large output, to replace women by men. The management would naturally say that it would be better to pay a man once and a half the salary of a woman, than to pay two women their salaries for the work that only one woman previously did. That, and the fact that the work is heavy, that the physical labour is heavy, accounts for it [the decline of female employment in creameries].[34]

Technological arguments have their weaknesses. Even where physical strength was no prerequisite—such as in managerial posts—women were marginalized. Photographs show groups of 'Creamery Managers in Training', all male.[35] Of course, these patterns should not be exaggerated. Regional variations in practices were important. A distinction must also be drawn between creameries and blending societies. Miss Eustace was manageress of the Drumlease Co-operative *Blending* Society.[36] Conventional creameries (as opposed to blending co-operatives) were reluctant to employ female manageresses. In 1899 the Erne Co-operative Dairy Society was the first full-scale creamery to accept a woman on its committee.[37] In reply to a question from a female reader as to whether women were eligible to become creamery managers,

[34] Evidence by Mr O'Connell, 'Commission on Technical Education, Typescripts of Evidence, 1927', 5th instalment, no pagination, but 3–4 pages into the evidence given by Mr J. Mahony, agricultural instructor in county Clare and chairman of the Irish Agricultural and Technical Instruction Officers' Organizations, NLI MS 48–9.   [35] *IH*, 17 Mar. 1906: 203.

[36] 'Creamery Notes', ibid. 1 Jan. 1898: 890.

[37] Emily Atthill, 'Notes of the Week', ibid. 12 Mar. 1899: 228.

the editor of the co-operative newspaper *Irish Homestead* replied affirmatively, but warned that the work was 'exceedingly laborious' and hardly suited to anyone not willing to 'rough it with a vengeance'.[38] The editor commented that, although women were dairy instructresses, 'we have not heard so far that any of them were daring enough to visit creameries and see that the managers kept them in proper order.' Similarly, they had not heard of women being employed by creameries to travel and solicit orders for butter.[39]

The registers of cow-keepers, dairymen, and purveyors of milk provide another way of measuring the extent of female participation in dairying. Although some local districts anticipated the nationwide legislation by as much as eight years,[40] in 1907 the Local Government Board for Ireland issued regulations imposing compulsory registration of all dairies, cowsheds, and milk shops in an attempt to stamp out disease and to raise standards of cattle, milk, and butter.[41] The 'vexations' connected with registration caused many farmers to give up selling milk, while others simply ignored the legislation and hoped for a benevolent inspector.[42] Despite these biases, the registers give us some indication of the proportion of female owners of dairy cows and sellers of dairy products, at least in the north of Ireland. I have examined four complete registers: Enniskillen Rural District (county Fermanagh), Newcastle Urban County District (county Down), Strabane Rural District 1 (county Tyrone), and Lisburn Rural District (county Antrim). As shown in Table 3.2, women made up a small proportion of registered dairy owners in all districts except in the urban district of Newcastle, where women would own a couple of cows in order to sell the milk in the city. Women owned fewer cows than men, and the average size of their herds increased more slowly than those of their male counterparts.

[38] 'Creamery Notes', ibid. 4 June 1898: 482.

[39] 'Traveller', 'Query and Reply', ibid. 6 Jan. 1905: 13.

[40] e.g. Larne Rural District, *Regulations Made by the Larne Rural District Council with Respect to Dairies, Cow Sheds, and Milk Shops, in the Rural District of Larne* (Carrickfergus, 1900), PRONI LA 44/1E/1.

[41] Particularly tuberculosis—their legislation was tied to the Tuberculosis Prevention (Ireland) Act, 1908.

[42] 'The First Human Duty', *IH*, 20 Apr. 1912: 309, and the reports of the committees of the Newtownards Rural District Council, 22 Oct., 1, 17, 18, and 27 Dec. 1909, in PRONI LA 61/3c/1.

Table 3.2. Women in the dairy industry, 1908–1933

District and date	Total no. of registered female owners	%	Average no. of cows owned	
			Women	Men
Enniskillen				
1912–13	136	13.2	4.9	5.2
1930	178	13.4	5.7	6.0
Newcastle				
1908–12	43	27.9	1.8	3.1
1921–3	28	21.4	2.2	4.7
Strabane				
1910	208	9.6	5.2	8.5
1933	125	7.2	5.8	7.6
Lisburn				
1908–12	131	19.8	6.6	18.8

Source: Registers held in PRONI, Belfast.

FACTORY ACTS

Public debate about the hours and conditions of work of women in creameries further weakened the position of the few women in this industry. The factory acts that restricted the employment of women came at the same time as accusations of sweated female labour in creameries and dairies. A writer for the *Irish Homestead* responded to criticisms of this kind with regard to co-operative creameries:

The only fact which might have given the slightest colour to the accusations is that although the hours during which a dairymaid is at work are by no means unduly long, they have sometimes been spread over a longer period of the day than is permitted by the Factory Acts, and that dairymaids are obliged to work on Sundays. There is, owing to the very nature of the work, a long interval in the middle of the day during which there is nothing to be done, and cows in Ireland have a habit of giving milk on Sundays as well as week-days, but even where the letter of the law has been broken, the Inspectors have freely admitted that there was no violation in spirit. The case was simply one which the Acts did not contemplate, and efforts are being made to procure a slight amendment of the law so as to make it consistent with the necessities of the manufacturer.[43]

Speaking at the third annual general conference of delegates from co-operative dairy and agricultural societies, R. A. Anderson confirmed the need to lobby the Home Secretary to exempt creameries from the general rules regarding female labour.[44] For the first time, the IAOS was able to turn criticism levelled at creameries on its head: far from the IAOS having reduced female employment through establishing creameries, government legislation, so it claimed, had blocked its attempts to employ women in the creameries:

If the Factory Acts were strictly enforced, it would be impossible to employ women at all in creameries.[45]

Factory and workshop legislation bore so heavily on creamery work as virtually to penalise the employment of young girls under the only conditions on which it was, in most cases, practicable to provide them with occupation in creameries.[46]

The IAOS received considerable sympathy for its arguments. Even *The Times* referred to Irish dairymaids. On 2 July 1901 Lady Frances Balfour wrote a letter to *The Times* on behalf of the Freedom of Labour Defence League and opposing the Lord's Day Observance Committee:

To the Lord's Day Observance Committee it may seem immoral to do any work on Sunday, or it may only be immoral in their eyes to work for hire on that day; but how have they solved the problem of paid domestic service in which the duty of preparing and preserving food is as important on Sundays as on week-days? Is there not a tendency in specialising of this kind, to overlook the true balance of things—to put all weight of immorality on the side of a supposed breach of Sunday observance by Irish Dairymaids, and nothing at all on the domestic service side of Sabbath-breaking for wages in their own homes?[47]

A committee appointed by the Irish creamery proprietors was successful in amending the legislation to allow women and young

---

[43] 'Notes of the Week', *IH*, 17 Sept. 1898: 7780.
[44] IAOS, *Annual General Report, 1898* (Dublin, 1899), 53.   [45] Ibid.
[46] 'The Factory Act and the Creameries', *IH*, 18 Oct. 1902: 813.
[47] Her letter was reproduced in 'Irish Dairymaids and Sunday Work', ibid. 13 July 1901: 463–4.

persons to be employed between 6 a.m. and 9 a.m.[48] Creamery managers and co-operative officials argued, however, that this new order of 2 June gave 'a quite insufficient time for the performance of absolutely necessary work in connection with the business of a dairymaid in a creamery'.[49] A further amendment allowed women to be employed for three consecutive hours on Sundays; the managers could choose any time between 6 a.m. and 7 p.m.[50] Even so, prosecutions continued, as creamery managers employed dairymaids outside of the three hours they had fixed.[51] These infringements were treated lightly by the magistrates: often the managers simply received a caution. Opposed to any form of restrictive legislation, creamery managers continued to complain:

The special exemption allowed under Section 42 of this Act [Factory and Workshops Act] is availed of by a good many creameries, including ourselves, and as we found it impossible to do the necessary work during the three hours on Sunday, we arranged to have one of our dairymaids work from 7 a.m. to 10 a.m. and the other from 9 a.m. to 12 noon, thereby giving ourselves two hours longer for working, and giving one of our dairymaids a decent opportunity of attending early prayers and the other late. The Factory Inspector will not allow this, maintaining that only one period of employment can be worked by all the women, and all at the same time, nor will the Government allow different meal hours for women and young persons. We have been summoned for this Sunday working, and convicted.[52]

The losers in this legislation and the debate surrounding it were the dairymaids. The DATI listed eighteen creameries which claimed that they could not reduce their requirements for a dairymaid to only three hours on Sundays. To maintain their levels of production, they were going to replace their dairymaids with men. It also listed another fifteen creameries which had

[48] Statutory Rules and Orders, 1902: 465, 2 June 1902.

[49] 'The Factory Act and the Creameries', 813, and 'Manager', 'Sunday Work in Creameries', *IH*, 29 Aug. 1903: 715.

[50] Order of the Secretary of State, 23 Oct. 1903,' Granting Special Exemptions: Creameries'.

[51] 'Creameries and the Factory Act', *IH*, 27 Aug. 1904: 703, concerning the Effin Co-operative Dairy Society; 'The Factory Act and the Creameries', 813; 'Manager', 'Sunday Work in Creameries', 715; and D. Meehan (manager of Pilltown Co-operative Dairy), 'Factory and Workshops Act', *IH*, 1 Oct. 1910: 816–17.

[52] Meehan, 'Factory and Workshops Act', 816–17.

'recently' replaced female dairymaids with male operators.[53] There is no reason to think that these lists represent the full extent of the substitution. Larger dairies were more likely to be affected than smaller ones, and creameries were likely to be more affected in summer than winter. Extracts from the creamery instructor's notes tell the same story:

Most of the creameries have solved this by employing males. Three hours are not long enough on Sundays in summer.

In the North West district women are not employed at work on creameries. In the South West I consider that five hours are required to carry out the work during the summer months.

It would be impossible for female buttermakers in large creameries to get through the work in three hours on Sundays.[54]

The agitation came to little. During the war, the legislation was allowed to lapse.

EDUCATIONAL DISCRIMINATION

Given the importance of the dairy industry and the large number of reforming institutions dedicated to agriculture, it is not surprising that the dissemination of knowledge concerning 'scientific dairying' was an official policy. The revival in the dairy industry was actively promoted by state organizations. The DATI encouraged the scientific breeding of dairy cattle, instigated schemes to improve tillage and the production of dry feeding stuffs, supplied farmers with the latest information on farm improvements, inspected dairies, and provided credit for the purchase of equipment and for construction work. Each year the Council of Agriculture spent over £3,000 on butter-improvement schemes.

[53] From the papers of the DATI in NAI MS A13881/16 and A20703/19.
[54] DATI Papers in NAI MS AG1 A20703/19. All these reports were confidential reports from instructors of dairying. The name of the instructor has frequently been omitted, but the second quotation has been taken from a letter from Thomas Scott (dairy instructor in Liverfovill), and the final quotation came from a report by A. Alcorn (dairy instructor in Ballymullen, Tralee). See also the letters between the secretary of the Department and Eliot F. May (Inspector of Factories), in NAI.

The classes in practical dairying were the most significant of its reforms.[55] The introduction of butter-making classes was a response to popular fears that standards of housekeeping would drop as women ceased making butter.[56] The educational schemes were paid for by the Department and run by county committees, which appointed itinerant instructresses and supplied them with equipment. Between 1901 and 1912 the number of instructresses increased from one to thirty-three.[57]

It is difficult to assess the effect of these classes. In November 1904 the dairy instructress in Dromore (county Longford) had fewer than ten pupils.[58] The classes were accused of attracting only the better dairy workers. There was a fundamental contradiction in these educational schemes: why, if 'home dairying is a thing of the past', was all this money being spent on itinerant instructresses?[59]

In addition to itinerant instruction, colleges providing training in farm work were established. At first, it seemed as though the colleges would promote men at the expense of women in its training schemes. The Albert Agricultural College had provided a special dairying course for women in 1883. By 1895 a course for creamery managers was started—largely attended by men. Finally, in 1899, it was decided to discontinue all courses for women. It was claimed that running a course in dairying for women and a course in agriculture for men in separate halves of the year was expensive, duplicated staff, and led to inadequate

[55] The Department was not the first organization to institute dairying courses for the 'ordinary farm woman'. On a much smaller scale, individuals and philanthropic organizations had been providing local courses. For instance, clergy in several areas taught their female parishioners new dairying techniques: see DATI, *Departmental Committee on the Irish Butter Industry* (Cd. 5093), HC 1910, viii. 464.

[56] The 'discipline' of butter-making stems from the need to keep the place where the milk is stored and churned exceptionally clean. Reformers feared that, without this economic incentive, farm women would become careless about household cleanliness: RCCI, *Appendix to the 9th Report* (Cd. 3845), HC 1908, xli. 163–4, evidence by Revd John McDonnell, representing the National Directory of the United Irish League.

[57] DATI, *5th Annual General Report, 1904–1905* (Cd. 2929), HC 1906, xxiii. 25, and DATI, *12th Annual General Report, 1911–1912* (Cd. 6647), HC 1912–13, xii. 50.

[58] 'Spectator', 'Things in General', *IH*, 12 Nov. 1904: 95–6, on Dromore (county Longford).

[59] 'Dairymaid', 'Home Dairying v Creamery Co-operation', ibid. 7 Oct. 1905: 743.

training of the men.[60] However, female students were not left un-catered for. Classes for women continued at the Munster Institute:

The Munster Institute fulfils for female students the same function as that discharged by the Royal College of Science and Albert Agricultural College in respect to male students. The course of instruction embraces the subjects in which a girl of the farming class needs to be proficient, either for the performance of the work of her own home or for the discharge of the duties which may be allotted to her if she obtains employment in a dairy or a creamery.[61]

Applications for admission increased each year. A period of over a year elapsed between application and acceptance.[62] Students came from all over the country. For example, in 1902, al-though 37 per cent of all students came from Cork, 9 per cent came from both Cavan and Limerick, 5 per cent from Kerry, 4 per cent from Clare, and 3 per cent from each of the counties of Kilkenny, Galway, Sligo, Londonderry, and Kildare.[63] In 1908 the Ulster Dairy School at Loughrey (county Tyrone) accepted its first pupils. This was similar to the Munster Institute, teaching dairying, poultry-keeping, cooking, laundry work, sewing, and cottage gardening. However, between 1905 and 1913, the Mun-ster Institute was the only training-centre in Ireland for instruc-tresses in dairying.[64]

Other schools were established for farm women. With financial help from the DATI, communities of nuns set up small schools training women in dairying, poultry-keeping, and domestic work. The Department helped to establish the schools, paid the teachers' salaries, and contributed towards the cost of pupils. The most successful of these were the residential schools at Portumna (county Galway), Westport (county Mayo), Ramsgrange (county Wexford), Claremorris (county Mayo), Swinford (county Mayo), and Clifden (county Galway), rather than the non-residential

---

[60] DATI, *Report of the Departmental Committee of Inquiry into the Provisions of the Agricultural and Technical Instruction (Ireland) Act, 1899* (Cd. 3572), HC 1907, xvii. 22.

[61] DATI, *6th Annual General Report, 1905–1906* (Cd. 3543), HC 1907, xvii. 21.

[62] DATI, *7th Annual General Report, 1906–1907* (Cd. 4148), HC 1908, xiv. 21–2.

[63] Munster Dairy School and Agricultural Institute, Cork, *Report of the Gover-nors and Statement of Accounts for 1902* (Cork, 1903), 10.

[64] After 1913 the Ulster Dairy School began to provide similar training for women.

schools at Loughglinn (county Roscommon) and Beneden (county Clare). The Department also helped private individuals to set up schools to train women in farm work (such as the school at Killashandra, county Cavan). However, the success of these schools depended more on their role in teaching domestic arts than on the dissemination of new dairying skills.[65]

The ambivalence of the reformers with regard to training women in dairying was revealed most strongly in the debates about the link between emigration and creameries. By reducing female employment, creameries were accused of increasing female emigration. Furthermore, since women did not have to prove that they were going on to farms, unlike the men attending the Albert Agricultural College ('because a girl cannot very well guarantee to get a husband who is a farmer'), some of the female students were said to be using the school as a stepping-stone to emigration. Given that it was unrealistic for graduates of the school to expect remunerative employment in Ireland, that demand for their services was not increasing, and that the days of roving instructresses were nearing their end, agricultural reformers perceived that there was only one solution: women were to be trained as skilled rural *wives*. This aim was most explicitly carried out in the itinerant dairying classes and in the schools of rural domestic economy, but even the Munster Institute determined that its students should not become preoccupied with waged labour. Its aim was not so much to train dairy servants as to train women to share the labour of their household's farm in a more efficient manner; in particular, these women required instruction in such domestic arts as cookery, laundry, and needlework. Between 1880 and 1901 the committee responsible for domestic training spent almost one-fifth as much money on the promotion of housework as the governors spent on experiments on water in butter, organizing butter shows throughout the country, bestowing prizes on pupils, paying salaries to lecturers, and so on.[66]

---

[65] Munster Institute, *Report and Accounts for 1902*, 9. This aspect is examined in greater detail in Ch. 8.

[66] RCCI, *Appendix 4th Report* (Cd. 3509), HC 1907, xxxvi. 53, evidence by Professor J. R. Campbell. The more popular argument was that creameries encouraged emigration by inflating the number of unemployed females of emigrating age: see 'The Problem of our Future', *IH*, 25 May 1901: 336–7.

WORK FOR WOMEN OR MEN?

In the early years, the reforming organizations complained about men's lack of interest in dairying. It was 'women's work'. Professor Carroll commented that 'one of the principal difficulties that had to be overcome in the establishing of dairy instruction in the country is the small amount of interest taken in the subject by the male population; indeed . . . a man who knew anything about practical dairy work was looked upon almost with contempt.'[67] For this reason, women were trained as instructresses, even though men were moved into all prestigious positions and managerial posts. Even the Commissioners of National Education, who were responsible for the Munster Dairy School before it was taken over by the Department, had been concerned with getting *men* managerial posts in dairying. The 1885 report of the Commissioners of National Education argued that:

As a rule, in this country, this important industry [dairying] is carried on by the female portion of the farmer's family, the men knowing very little of the subject. The women, confined to the narrow circle of the home, without time for reading or opportunity of seeing improved methods, and frequently having no knowledge of the various qualities of butter required for the market, could scarcely be expected to contribute much towards improvement in buttermaking. It should not be considered that it is desirable that women should be superseded by men in the work of the dairy. The largest portion of dairy work is eminently suited to women, but, taking into account the vast importance of the industry, and that intelligent direction in the dairy would be useful, the question as to how far the training of men in dairy management is advisable is deserving of serious consideration.[68]

That 'question' had been decided by the following year. The commissioners introduced the first course in dairy management for men at the Albert Institute. Its policy of pushing men into managerial positions was continued by the Department, which went a step further in promoting men at *every* level of dairy work.

This policy created strained relations in the 'real world' of creamery management, where managers and dairymaids were frequently antagonistic towards one another. Women 'considered

[67] Professor Carroll, 'A Brief Account of the Progress of Dairy Instruction in Ireland', app. 4; DATI, *Departmental Committee on the Irish Butter Industry*, viii. 464.
[68] Quoted in ibid. 464 (476).

that they "knew all about it", and so despised any attempts at teaching by men'.[69] The most detailed exposition of the conflict is found in a letter by 'Majerist':

It is unfortunate that in a good many of our creameries, young intelligent men are installed as managers, who, through lack of sufficient training and experience under expert tuition, are subject to the anomaly of being subordinated to the dairymaid in the primary department of his work, and under his supervision, and consequently his full responsibility for the full control and management of the creamery in such cases is only nominal. With a dairymaid whose qualifications are inferior, under such conditions the management of the creamery can be better imagined than described. It therefore behoves us to make all our young, intelligent creamery candidates pay, first and foremost, attention to the dairymaid's duties, particularly the handling of the cream, so that he may be in a position to assume full responsibility for the proper and efficient carrying out of her work, as well as that of the rest, and that he may be able to dictate instead of being dictated to, and also if necessary that he himself may be capable of performing the work without having to receive instructions first from the dairymaid. Our average dairymaid's understanding of the use of starters and their preparation is very limited, and as in not a few cases her training dates rather far back, since a considerable number of them retain their office not so much by virtue of their qualifications as by ties of kinship, it cannot be presumed that the average dairymaid is qualified to impart instructions to the manager on the scientific principles of up-to-date methods in the treatment and preparation of cream and cream-starters.[70]

In the following issue of the *Irish Homestead*, an angry 'Munster Manager' replied to this criticism of dairymaids in creameries, arguing that dairymaids were more skilled than managers. It was the creamery managers who were employed for familial or political reasons: 'This is what has spoiled the reputation of our Irish butter — an auxiliary manager taken into central creameries without knowing how to wash his face. This is how the annoyances arise in creameries. He comes in and dictates to the dairymaid how to make butter, who has never made a bit in his life.'[71]

[69] Ibid.
[70] 'Majerist', 'The Handling of Cream before Churning, VIII', *IH*, 20 Jan. 1905: 52.
[71] 'Munster Manager', 'Dairymaids', ibid. 27 Jan. 1906: 75–6. See also NAI, ICOS file 1088/5/4, report on the Achonry Creamery by R. S. Tarrant, dated 10 Nov. 1902.

Other changes were driving women out of dairying. In Wicklow, Carlow, Kildare, and Longford (as well as in most eastern counties) the number of milch cows in each county declined by as much as one-quarter between 1891 and 1911. The practice of employing the wives and daughters of male farm workers as milkers during the summer season remained undisturbed in many areas, but increasingly this work was being performed on large farms with a number of labourers, rather than on farms with a small family herd.

TECHNOLOGY

Crucial to all the reforms were technological advances. The invention, in 1878, of a centrifuge 'separator', capable of efficiently separating cream from milk, provided the chief way of improving farmhouse and factory butter-making. Here, as well as in the educational schemes, the Department attempted to resolve the contradiction between home and factory dairying. It promoted equipment at every level of dairy organization. Beginning in Cork in 1902, small farmers could purchase hand-separators with the help of loans from the committees.[72] Instructresses sold equipment—especially thermometers—for butter-making at reduced cost to women in their classes.[73] Dairy societies and creameries also benefited from departmental loans amounting to almost £5,000 for the purpose of erecting pasteurizing plants. Twenty-six loans were sanctioned, with low interest rates and repayment schemes spread over five years.[74] The Department also encouraged creameries with schemes whereby instructors visited installations, policed their registration, provided courses of instruction for creamery managers, awarded certificates to the managers held 'Surprise Butter Competitions', and conducted experiments.[75]

---

[72] John Donovan, *Economic History of Livestock in Ireland* (Cork, 1940), 327. The 1902 loans were limited to Cork farmers. Even after this date, most of the loans were accepted by farmers in Cork.

[73] DATI, *3rd Annual General Report, 1902–1903* (Cd. 1919), HC 1904, xvi. 23–4.

[74] DATI, *Report of the Departmental Committee on Agricultural Credit* (Cd. 7375), HC 1914, xiii. 316.

[75] DATI, *7th Annual General Report*, xiv. 57–8.

NEW WORK FOR WOMEN

Those in favour of creameries had to face the problem of unemployed wives, sisters, and daughters. Initially, the plan was that
women made redundant because of creameries would be given
alternative employment. However, policies designed to develop
alternative industries either failed or, in many areas, were never
started. The Reverend Terence C. Connolly of Manorhamilton
(county Leitrim) confessed that:

I was one of the men who committed what some call the sin of doing
what I could to start the co-operative creameries. I spent a good many
hard days at it. The idea was where a girl was deprived of the industry
of churning she would be turned over at once to a cottage industry like
lacemaking or sprigging or something of that kind. I think that matter
has not been sufficiently followed up, simply because after the Department of Agriculture was started, those who had asserted it before
said, 'There is enough money now; we will do nothing.'[76]

Reformers, creamery managers, and larger dairy farmers hastened
to reassure critics, asserting that, although creameries denied farm
women an important area of productive employment, 'the farmer's wife has enough employment to keep her out of mischief
without making butter.'[77] George F. Trench reasoned:

Another objection to creameries is that women of the farms have less to
do. This is the ordinary complaint that follows the introduction of any
kind of machinery in field or factory; but the wants of men are so many
that the female part of the farm family have abundance of occupations
with rearing the children, milking, feeding calves, pigs and fowl, keeping
everything clean and tidy, needlework, etc.[78]

In particular, poultry-rearing and increased domestic work were
advocated as the main ways in which women could occupy their
time. A biting defence of poultry-rearing as an alternative to
dairying was published in the *Irish Homestead* on 29 September

[76] RCCI, *Appendix to the 6th Report* (Cd. 3748), HC 1908, xxxix. 148, evidence by
Revd Terence C. Connolly, representing Manorhamilton Rural District Council
and the fishermen of the Leitrim coast. The failure of lacemaking and sprigging
classes is discussed in Ch. 4.

[77] 'Homely Wrinkles', *Ark*, 6/53, Feb. 1914: 7.

[78] RCCI, *Appendix to the 8th Report*, xli. 55, evidence by George F. Trench. See
also 'Home Industries in Relation to Agriculture', *IH*, 7 Feb. 1903: 102.

1906. After noting the chief charge brought against creameries, the writer commented:

Many good people have shaken solemn heads over this decay of industry in the home. They have had visions of women yawning about the house, and ready to fall easy prey to that power which finds some mischief still for idle hands to do. Better bad prices, hard work, and muscles aching from the churn, than ease and affluence. The dear old geese who talk like this are quite sincere as they cackle about the good old days when the domestic industries were in full swing. One would suppose that there was nothing to replace the churn, that emigration was inevitable, and that women were a useless adjunct to the farmer's family. These dear old geese have forgotten the poultry yard, where, indeed, many of them should have been born and where they could have cackled to their hearts' content without doing any harm.[79]

The muscular arms of the butter-churning maid will give way to 'a slim young miss looking after poultry':

' We declare . . . that churning as it used to be done was a most inhuman labour to put women to, especially in the winter and when the whole milk was churned. Anyone who has seen these women, often those about to become mothers, labouring for a couple of hours, and almost fainting over their work, would agree with us that all this talk about home employment of the sort is the worst kind of nonsense [*sic*]. Our anti-co-operators would have it that if a woman wasn't sweated over a churn she has nothing to do which is a fit and womanly employment for her. We say that the more she has to do with the churn the worst for Ireland, and the more she has to say to the poultry yard the better for Ireland. These silly journalists seem to think that labour-saving machinery is bad for a country and bad for the farmer. We, on the contrary, assert that any device which will enable four hands at a creamery to do work which 100 women were engaged in is good for the country, because those 100 wives do not emigrate . . . but they now make the farm more profitable by devoting their spare time to poultry-keeping, by which Ireland gains quite as much as it does by its butter production. We like to hear of an industrious household, but Heaven save us from cant about it all; from the silly, sanctimonious tongue that wags because people have more leisure in their lives and do not sweat and faint from

[79] 'A Great National Industry: Home Employment in Plenty', ibid. 29 Sept. 1906: 790. See also 'Among the Societies', ibid. 9 Mar. 1895: 6, for an address by R. A. Anderson to a meeting of tenant farmers and others about setting up a co-operative dairy in Tralee, and IAOS, *Annual General Report, 1897* (Dublin, 1898), 58.

their labour; which calls farmers lazy because they adopt labour-saving machinery, and wives idle because they are less beasts of burden and can go to bed at night without every joint aching, and can live so that they still preserve some appearance of gracious womanhood at forty, and are not already wrinkled and gnarled and bent like old trees on a seashore.[80]

Although the extension of poultry-rearing was frequently thrown up as an alternative occupation for redundant butter-makers, another argument was more prevalent. The removal of butter-making from female work schedules left women more time to devote to their 'proper' duties—housework. At a large meeting of the Dromore Co-operative Home Industries Society in July 1904, the political economist and ardent supporter of co-operation Father T. A. Finlay asserted that the diversion of female labour into housework was ample justification for the existence of creameries.[81] Lady Londonderry, speaking at the annual meeting of the Ulster branch of the IAOS, praised the introduction of creameries for leaving women more time for recreation and their 'proper domestic duties'.[82] A 'County Cork Woman' argued that freeing women from butter-making was the only way to improve the 'semi-barbarous condition' of rural homesteads. She suggested that home butter-making had led to the 'deterioration of the breed of women and children': the transfer of this 'drudgery' to creameries 'saved a needless sacrifice of life, and has protected both mother and child from ill-health'.[83] Critics of the creamery movement included urban journalists: rural households were less likely to disparage the transfer of the energies of women to housework.[84] The success of the farm depended on the housekeeping skills of farm women:

They [critics] should know that there was a difference between nominal wages and real wages, one man might be receiving only half the nominal wages of another man, but yet may be receiving equal or more of real wages, for wages for labour depended on the amount of conveniences

[80] 'Mass Movement against Co-operation', *IH*, 27 Mar. 1909: 242. The poultry industry is examined in Ch. 6.

[81] 'Co-operation and the Home', *IH*, 30 July 1904: 622–31.

[82] 'Ulster Branch of the IAOS', ibid. 23 Apr. 1910: 345.

[83] 'Creamery and Female Labour', ibid. 11 May 1901: 303.

[84] 'The Education of Munster Farmers', ibid. 18 May 1901: 317–18.

and the requirements of life which the man enjoyed. Take the man with an income of £50 a year and an unskilled wife: all he was getting out of that income would not represent, perhaps, as much of the real advantages of living, of the conveniences and necessaries of life, as his neighbour with a skilled wife was getting from £25 a year. For that reason, it was an advantage to the farmers that the women were set free from the rather strenuous task of churning to devote themselves to the study of their proper business in the home.[85]

Related to this stress on housework was the response of the co-operative societies to criticisms that creameries were responsible for the shortage of milk, particularly for young children.[86] The creamery was satirized as 'a horrible ghoulish monster' snatching milk out of the lips of starving children and frantic parents.[87] This argument, although repeated constantly by the anti-creamery faction, was treated with contempt in IAOS publications. The Vice-Regal Commission on Irish Milk Supplies showed that, rather than creameries being responsible for the milk shortage, the Dairy and Cowsheds Order was to blame, since registration and inspections reduced the number of farmers willing to sell milk.[88] Despite the lack of substance behind the accusation that creameries denied children milk, the argument recurred periodically because of its critique of female competence in the home: if Irish women were better housekeepers, they would welcome the opportunity to devote more time to such activities as child care, and they would wrest milk for their dependants out of the grasp of creameries.

[85] 'Cavan District Conference', ibid. 22 June 1912: 510, speech by Father T. A. Finlay. See also 'Homely Wrinkles', 7.
[86] RCCI, *Appendix to the 7th Report* (Cd. 3785), HC 1908, xl. 148–9, evidence by P. E. Mallon of Doobally, county Down, representing the Enniskillen Rural District Council 2 and the Doobally branch of the United Irish League; 'M. O'B', *Leader*, 14 Mar. 1908: 58; and 'Inquirer', ibid. 21 Mar. 1908: 73.
[87] 'The Creamery Vampire', *IH*, 4 May 1907: 347. See also 'Milk for Labourers' Children', ibid. 2 May 1908: 349; 'Should we Blame Separators or Souls?', ibid. 16 May 1908: 388; Sarsfield Kerrigan, *Leader*, 7 Mar. 1908: 39, and ibid. 28 Mar. 1908: 91; a report on a speech by John Clancy, in 'The Bishop of Elphin and the Co-operative Creameries', *IH*, 13 June 1908: 470–3, where he links shortages of milk to the creameries, and says that this is why people drink too much tea and porter in the fields; 'Wexford Women in Council', ibid. 17 Jan. 1914: 45–6; and Harold Barbour, *The Work of the IAOS* (pamphlet printed from *IH*, Dublin, 1916), 6.
[88] Vice-Regal Commission on the Irish Milk Supplies, *Appendix to the Final Report* (Cd. 7134), HC 1914, xxxvi. 1 ff.

Of course, many women continued to make butter. Not all areas were provided with creameries.[89] Many women churned for family consumption, using the weekend milk supplies.[90] During World War I Irish women took up butter-churning again on a large scale, resulting in a massive decline in the amount of milk taken to creameries.[91] The dairy industry, however, had changed. Farming households were more likely to buy butter than to make it.[92] Some indication of this change can be seen in the increasing amount of butter being bought from the creamery by their own suppliers, suggesting that they were no longer retaining some of the milk to churn at home for household consumption.[93] Women were liable to find that their training in the dairy schools increased their wages to such an extent that demand for their labour declined; farmers realized that seasonal labour requirements favoured the employment of men, who could be given other occupations when milk production was low (that is, during winter). If women made butter, they were more likely to be found as the solitary female in large dairies or creameries, overseen by male managers, than in their own homes. The home churn became a less prominent feature of the farm household. Women lost a dominant forum for discussing matters of community interest.[94] Less obviously, a tradition of folklore and folk-charms fell into disuse. The 'good people' were not invoked in creameries.

[89] RCCI, *Appendix to the 9th Report* (Cd. 3845), HC 1908, xli. 72, evidence by the Very Revd Canon Humphrey O'Riordan and Mrs Maxwell (of Dungloe United Irishwomen, county Donegal); 'Opening of the Dungloe Co-operative Hall', *IH*, 26 Nov. 1910: 976–7.

[90] *Leader*, 28 Mar. 1908: 91, article by Sarsfield Kerrigan. For other examples of women churning for household consumption, see the evidence given by the manager of the Ballyhaise Creamery, Mr C. F. Costello, in DIC *Commission of Inquiry into the Resources of Ireland* (Dublin, 1919), 121, and Martin Murtagh, *Proud Heritage: The Story of Imokilly Co-op* (Dublin, 1986), 11, referring to the 1920s.

[91] DATI, *Report of the Departmental Commission on the Decline of Dairying* (Cmd. 808), HC 1920, ix. 7.

[92] Vice-Regal Commission on Irish Milk Supplies, *Appendix to the Final Report*, xxxvi. 80, evidence by James Stewart of Strabane.

[93] Taken from an analysis of the dairy accounts in the Registry of Friendly Societies, Dublin.

[94] For examples of the role played by groups of women who met to churn or mix butter ('choring'), see the interview of Mrs Dore (of county Limerick), aged 60, carried out by P. Ward in Jan. 1939, IFC MS 591: 484–6, and 'Athea, 24 March General Meeting', *IH*, 30 Mar. 1895: 53.

May-morning charms, prayers, and spells lost their efficacy: 'The advent of the separator has, I fear, destroyed nearly all the poetry of these times, and with it the power of the butter witch.'[95] Butter-making had become 'as scientific a business as brewing', and women were moved out.[96]

Both absolutely and relatively, female workloads in dairying were reduced, along with access to control over cash income. Organizations set up to strengthen the rural economy lamented the declining work opportunities for women, but they decided that the Irish farm woman had enough work to do in looking after her family. In most cases, the reforms instigated by these organizations benefited the communities as a whole. The Irish dairy industry was strengthened by the rationalizations insti-gated by the DATI and the IAOS. But the adverse affects of the reforms fell disproportionately on the female members of the rural communities. No one said it as well as 'Peper' in the *Ark*:

Where is the maiden all forlorn
That milked the cow with crumpled horn?
She has gone to the town
Where she's now holding down
A job as a skilful typewriter.[97]

As we have seen in Chapter 1, the skills of the milk maid were less likely to be appreciated in the shops and offices of the towns and cities of Ireland, England, or America, but they were more valued when channelled into the home. Although Humphrey James's story *Paddy's Woman* was written at about the same time as Denis Hurley's letter at the beginning of this chapter, James showed more foresight by identifying the element that was to become dominant by the first decades of the twentieth century. Paddy and Barney discuss the marriage prospects of Titia, a skilful dairywoman:

[95] R. A. Anderson, 'The Influence of Co-operation on Dairying', *IH*, 4 June 1904: 469. For lengthy descriptions of the folklore and folk-charms associated with dairying, see IFC MS 80, collected by Padraig Mac Greiue of Ballinalee, Edgeworthstown (county Longford), Nov. 1929, 45–50, and MS 1340, collected by James G. Delaney from James Dermody, aged 54, of Columcillen Parish (county Longford), in the 1950s, 41–2.

[96] 'Gilt-Edged Butter', *IH*, 22 June 1912: 497.

[97] 'Peper', *Ark*, 3/5, Dec. 1913: 1.

'And she's as good as she's nice and clean.'

'Them that'll get her, will have a bargain, for if she's so nice and clean, and can sing so well, she can hardly be expected to milk the cows and make the butter,' said Paddy, laughing.

'I'm thinking you and me'd be rich, Paddy,' said Barney, 'if we had half the cows she could milk or make butter from—according to what Mickey Coulter, her mother's servant boy, tells me. Besides, any steel of a girl can feed the pigs and wash the veshels [sic].'

'Ay, but not everyone of them can make it a pleasure for a neighbour to come into your house, and kaly at your fire,' said Pat.[98]

[98] Humphrey James, *Paddy's Woman and Other Stories* (1896), 107–8.

4

Home Industries

They were pretty, good, and cheerful, and supported themselves and an aged mother by working embroidery or
'sprigging' for Mrs Finlay of Churchill, who was an agent
for an English firm. On certain days fixed by that lady for
receiving and paying for the finished work, and giving out
fresh material, one of the sisters always attended, bringing
with her the beautifully-flowered pieces into which the deft
hands of her sisters and herself had converted the flimsy
pieces of drapery supplied by Mrs Finlay; and returning
with the scanty price of their ill-paid industry.[1]

THE central elements of this chapter are contained in P. T.
McGinley's fairy tale, 'The Three Sisters'. The story began with
Donegal women earning a living through skilled embroidery.
One day, a fairy took pity on their plight and assumed control
of their work. His intentions were noble, but ultimately unproductive. In late nineteenth-century Ireland the rural reformers
played the part of the kindly fairy. Home industries were promoted on an unprecedented scale. This chapter examines the
impetus to develop female industries. Various promotional
schemes were started, but they failed to secure a market for the
products. What caused the collapse of home industries? Equally
pertinent, why did many women continue working at home
industries? Female home industries were inseparable from housework. In the minds of the promoters, the schemes achieved their
major aim: to serve as an intermediate form of work between
agricultural labour and housework.[2]

---

[1] P. T. McGinley, 'The Three Sisters', in *Donegal Christmas Annual, 1883, Containing Stories by Donegal Writers* (Londonderry, 1883), 42. Churchill is in Kilmacrenan
Barony (county Donegal).
[2] The theoretical debates surrounding 'proto-industrialization' have not proved
useful for understanding Irish home industries. Shortage of space for the discussion
of what will be a negative conclusion prevents an independent analysis of the
theory. For an explanation of the theory and a critique, see D. C. Coleman, 'Proto-
Industrialisation: A Concept Too Many', *EHR*, 2nd ser. 36 (1983), 435–48; Rab

PROMOTING HOME INDUSTRIES

Home industries were not new in rural Ireland, although most can be traced to philanthropic efforts rather than to commercial trade.[3] The industries examined in this chapter—lacemaking, crochet, embroidery, sprigging (white embroidery), and knitting—existed precariously in Ireland at the beginning of the nineteenth century. They were revived during and slightly after the famine years, then collapsed in the 1860s and 1870s. The exception was the sprigging industry in Ulster, which was introduced in the 1830s and only declined substantially from the 1890s. Beginning with small-scale projects, then expanding with the CDB and other state and private organizations, home industries were artificially stimulated again from the 1880s. This chapter examines the failure of these schemes.

Numerically, it is difficult to estimate the extent of these projects. Most homeworkers were not given an occupation in the census. Of the fifty-one women active in the Belleek embroidery and lace class (county Fermanagh) during January 1911, 56 per cent were given no occupation in the 1911 census manuscripts, and 4 per cent were given occupations other than industrial workers (one domestic servant and one 'farmer's sister').[4] Statistics like this illustrate the caution with which we must view any attempts to generalize about female employment from the census. Keeping these limitations in mind, what does the census tell us about home industries? Home industries were classed under 'dress and textiles'. In 1871, over 276,000 women were employed in this *broad* category. This number had more than halved by 1911. An unknown proportion of these women worked at home. Some homeworkers can be found within separate categories in

Houston and K. D. M. Snell, 'Historiographical Review: Proto-Industrialization? Cottage Industry, Social Change, and Industrial Revolution', *Historical Journal*, 27/2 (1984), 473–92; and Lennart Jorberg, 'Proto-Industrialization: An Economic History Figment', *Scandinavian Economic History Review*, 30 (1982), 1–2.

[3] Ben Lindsay, *Irish Lace: Its Origin and History* (Dublin, 1886), 6, and Elizabeth Boyle, *The Irish Flowerers* (Belfast, 1971). This chapter ignores the work organized by Poor Law Guardians in workhouses, where home industries were used as a way of separating the 'deserving' and 'undeserving' poor: *Second Special Report from the Select Committee on the Cottage Homes Bill* (.271), HC 1899, ix. 13 ff.

[4] The Belleek Needlework Industry (also called the Belleek lace class or lace and crochet class) in county Fermanagh was chosen for this study because of the mass of data on the class in PRONI MS D2149. The process of matching this data with the census manuscript data is discussed later in the chapter.

the census. There were 557 lacemakers in 1891, and the numbers increased by 500 each decade until 1911. Those employed in embroidery decreased between 1891 and 1901, and then increased between 1901 and 1911 to a level only slightly higher than the 1891 figure; 4,500 women were employed in embroidery in 1911. Less than 450 women were described as hosiery manufacturers in the censuses of 1891, 1901, and 1911. Home industries were concentrated in Donegal, Londonderry, Down, Monaghan, Cork, Limerick, and Wexford. In the three southern counties, the employment gains apparent between 1891 and 1911 had vanished by the next census. According to the 1926 census for Saorstát Éireann, there were fewer women employed in these three industries than there had been in 1891.[5] The official statistics suggest that there was a temporary but minor increase in some home industries. The census records only small numbers of women employed thus. The statistics ignore the thousands of women provided with a subsistence income, or an auxiliary income in the home industries established by the reforming organizations. From small beginnings in the 1880s, reformers rapidly moved to large-scale projects.

Initially, attempts to promote home industries were the work of individual philanthropists, small groups of wealthy women, and school authorities. Early promotions were directed at 'ladies'. These included the Royal Irish School of Art Needlework, established in the 1880s by the Countess Cowper, the Home Arts and Industries Association, formed in 1883, and the Irish Distressed Ladies' Fund, established in 1886 to help ladies suffering from the non-payment of rent by tenants and from the agricultural depression.[6] Private philanthropists like Mrs Alice M. Hart, who provided employment for Donegal women in producing knitted gloves and Kells art embroidery, were influential in the late 1880s.[7] Mrs Hart was followed by more professional industrial promoters

[5] We cannot estimate the numbers for Northern Ireland. In 1926 embroidery was combined with hemming. The lacemaking and hosiery trades in the north increased between 1891 and 1911, rising from 177 to 703 women.
[6] Helen Blackburn (ed.), *A Handy Book of Reference for Irishwomen* (1888), 52–3 and 82, provides a summary of these organizations.
[7] Mrs Alice Hart was married to Dr Ernest Hart, editor of the *British Medical Journal*. For further information about her work, see *Londonderry Sentinel*, 10 Sept. 1887: 3; *Union*, 13 Aug. 1887: 3, 3 Sept. 1887: 1, 10 Sept. 1887: 1, 24 Sept. 1887: 3, and 15 Oct. 1887: 3; Mrs E. Hart, *The Cottage Industries of Ireland* (1887); and the papers of Bishop Michael Logue, which include letters to Hart, in NLI MS 13827.

such as Mrs Robert Vere O'Brien of Limerick, Alan Cole of the Science and Art Department at South Kensington, and James Brennan of the Crawford Municipal School of Art in Cork and of the Metropolitan School of Art in Dublin. Irish design in a few communities improved with their efforts.

The Irish Industries Development Association (IIDA), established in 1887, set out to organize home industries, improve communication between local communities, circulate information about competitors and new markets, and provide skilled manual instruction and designs.[8] Its first year was spent collecting information about home industries in Ireland. In 1888, under the management of the Countess of Aberdeen, it succeeded in buying Ben Lindsay's depot for the sale of home products.[9] Its significance thereafter rested in international exhibitions and the co-ordination of sales for other organizations.

Education in industrial arts such as needlework, crochet, lace-making, and knitting was a part of the school curriculum before the 1880s. Convent schools in particular were well known for such classes—the most prominent example being St Joseph's Convent in Kinsale, which introduced lace and muslin embroidery as early as 1847.[10] Serious attempts to promote education in home industries began in 1888, when the Commissioners of National Education appointed the first directress of needlework. The following year they ordered that girls in the higher classes of schools with a female teacher or worker must be taught needlework for at least one hour a day.[11] By the 1890s, over 160,000 schoolgirls were being trained in needlework each year. From September 1900 it was compulsory to teach needlework to female pupils of all ages. By 1911, over 320,000 girls were being instructed annually.[12]

In addition to classroom instruction, national schools set up 'industrial departments' to train girls and women who had left school. Most of these departments attempted to sell the final

---

[8] IIA, *Irish Home Industries Association* (Dublin, 1887), iii, in the Royal Irish Academy.   [9] Blackburn (ed.), *A Handy Book for Irishwomen*, 53–4.

[10] Kinsale Convent of Mercy, extracts from annals of St Joseph's, Kinsale, Sept. 1847, Cork Archives Institute U64.

[11] Office of National Education, *Industrial Instruction: Memorandum*, signed by the secretaries of the ONE, John E. Sheridan and J. C. Taylor, 31 July 1889: 1.

[12] This information was extracted from the annual reports of the Commissioners of National Education in the British parliamentary papers.

products. In 1895, thirty-seven national schools (nearly all of them convents) had industrial departments, of which 64 per cent had been established in the previous six years.[13] Ironically, educational authorities in England had been disparaging lacemaking classes and schools for two decades by this time.[14]

In 1892, the CDB began promoting home industries in conjunction with the IIDA. The IIDA managed the industries, while the CDB provided the capital and instruction. Initially, the Board was only interested in the tweed industry that already existed in Donegal at this time. It modernized the industry by replacing its antiquated looms. The new machines could weave almost three times as many yards a day. The CDB gave loans with easy terms of repayment for the purchase of machinery and tools, and attempted to improve quality by inspecting webs at the monthly fairs of Ardara and Carrick, giving prizes, and holding classes in dyeing and weaving.

Almost immediately, however, it moved into the lace, crochet, and knitting industries. The CDB held classes in Mayo, Donegal, Cork, Leitrim, Sligo, Galway, and Kerry (in descending order of expenditure). By providing the initial investment and working capital, the CDB was able to let the workers keep the full sum paid for their work. Lacemaking classes made up 95 per cent of the classes helped by the CDB;[15] only two were for embroidery. The old hand-knitting industry of Donegal, which had almost disappeared because of mechanized competition from Leicester, was stimulated by the CDB's provision of knitting-machines at cost price and on easy terms. After repayment, workers were free to seek work from the Donegal hosiery merchants.

The lacemaking classes were each attended by around thirty women. Girls would attend classes three or four days a week for about eighteen months. Once trained, they attended the classes once or twice a week for payment. Nearly all of the work was

[13] *Appendix to the 62nd Report of the Commissioners of National Education in Ireland, 1895* (C. 8185), HC 1896, xxviii. 271–82.
[14] Anne Buck, 'The Teaching of Lacemaking in the East Midlands', *Folklife*, 4 (1966), 39–50.
[15] *Report from the Select Committee on Home Work* (1908), 34, evidence by W. J. D. Walker. We have no way of knowing how many of these 'lace schools' switched to knitting during depressions: see William L. Micks, *An Account of the Constitution, Administration and Dissolution of the CDB for Ireland, from 1891 to 1923* (Dublin, 1925), 69.

done in their own homes.[16] The work was sold at the IIDA depot. The system of instruction and marketing that the CDB established for the home industries remained unchanged until the 1930s, when Gaeltarra Éireann was established in Dublin. In 1902 the Board spent over £3,000 on grants for home industries. This sum does not include the substantial portion of the £12,000 for technical instruction that involved home industries. By 1905, earnings exceeded £20,000.

The IAOS also became involved with home industries through the IIDA. Instruction and marketing were to be the main role of the IIDA, while the IAOS dealt with organization.[17] By taking one 5s. share, a woman was admitted to a co-operative society. In 1901, 2,500 women were members of co-operative home industry societies. Societies were managed by committees, in which women predominated.[18] However, home industries were comparatively neglected by the IAOS, which was much more concerned with agricultural co-operatives.[19]

In 1902, the DATI had assisted or established twenty-one home industry societies, employing over 1,000 women annually in eleven counties.[20] Their activities were generally concentrated in Leinster and Ulster. Annual expenditure usually ranged between £2,000 and £3,000. The Department stimulated the establishment of local classes by paying county councils £3 a head for the first ten workers and £2 a head thereafter, and by sponsoring the employment of nearly a hundred industrial instructresses.[21] In

[16] *Report from the Select Committee on Home Work*, 43, evidence by W. J. D. Walker.
[17] IAOS, *Annual General Report, 1898* (Dublin, 1898), 22.
[18] I have examined the accounts, membership lists, and committee memoranda in the Registry of Friendly Societies for the following home industries: Foxford Co-operative Industrial and Agricultural Society (1459 R Mayo), Glencolumcille Knitting Co-operative Society (2980 R Donegal), Ballyakerry Co-operative Home Industry Society (442 R Mayo), Dun Emer Guild Society (767 R Dublin), Moneyguyneen Co-operative Home Industries Society (706 R Kings'), Meath Home Industries Society (615 R Meath), Youghal Co-operative Lace Society (216 R Cork), Dorard Co-operative Home Industries Society (1148 R Limerick), North Donegal Hand-Spinners and Hand-Weavers Society (1190 R Donegal) and New Ross Co-operative Home Industries Society (666 R Wexford). They were chosen arbitrarily.
[19] 'The Organisation of Home Industries', *IH*, 18 July 1914: 578.
[20] William P. Coyne (ed.), *Ireland: Industrial and Agricultural* (Dublin, 1902), 173.
[21] George Fletcher, 'The Functions of the Department in Relation to Rural Industries', *DATI Journal*, 7/4 (July 1907), 666; NLI, 'DATI Council of Agriculture, 11th Meeting, Report of Proceedings, Friday, 17 May 1907', 72; and R. A. Anderson, 'Notes on the Irish Lace and Crochet Industry', *DATI Journal*, 14/1 (Oct. 1913), 54.

1903, the Department set up summer courses to teach the technique of lacemaking. Later, bookkeeping and business methods were also taught, and a more regular school was opened in Enniskillen. It conducted enquiries on the Continent on home industries, and set up exhibitions on Irish products; the policing of trade infringements was also important.[22]

REASONS FOR PROMOTING HOME INDUSTRIES

What explains the promotion of home industries in Ireland from the end of the nineteenth century, peaking between 1900 and 1908 with the policies of the CDB, the co-operative societies, and the DATI? Home industries were adopted because they conformed to the reformers' idealized image of the Irish rural community. In the attempts to improve the life of Irish women and men, personal contentment was linked with economic stability. Female unemployment and emigration were ever-present evils. Home industries were to provide salvation and, just as important, to promote *domestic* contentment. The 'immense advantage' of home industrial development as opposed to factory development was that it protected home life, health, and happiness.[23] Finally, the reformers were working within a limited framework. Choice was limited by their theories about development in general and about Irish social history in particular.

Rising female unemployment provided the main economic motive for the establishment of home industries. Unemployment increased poverty. The reforming organizations recognized that they were partially responsible for unemployment amongst rural women, since 'modern methods in agriculture involved finding work for the female members of the farmer's family', and creameries reduced female employment.[24] In the words of one commentator: 'The whole economic control of life tends more and more to become concentrated in the man of the family and women

[22] Its work in this area can be traced through the *DATI Journal*, which published annual reports on trade infringements and the action taken by the Department against these infringements.

[23] J. M. Harty, 'The Living Wage: Its Ethical Conditions', *Irish Theological Quarterly*, 2/8 (Oct. 1907), 429, and 'Rural Industries Ahead', *IH*, 25 Jan. 1908: 61.

[24] 'Home Industries', *IH*, 17 June 1905: 470.

must be diverted into home industries.'[25] Economic stability demanded that Ireland become 'one of the most eminently female
industrial countries of Europe'.[26] The special difficulties attendant on women finding employment made bureaucratic intervention necessary.[27] Widening employment opportunities for Irish
women was the goal of the Meath Home Industries Committee,
which aimed to enable women 'who would otherwise be obliged
to become a charge on their relatives' to earn a living for themselves.[28] Work was stimulating: women would be saved from
idleness; they would remove the 'brunt of the battle of life' from
the shoulders of male breadwinners.[29]

These economic analyses all identified the chief symptom of
dissatisfaction as emigration. An economic solution was proposed;
Irish women could be persuaded to remain in Ireland if they
were provided with employment in the form of home industries.[30] Home comfort would increase. In the minds of reformers,
the words 'home comfort' embraced both economic prosperity
and interpersonal harmony.

The aim was not to employ women indiscriminately. Rural
industries were particularly suitable because they were home-
based. As a form of employment for women, home industries

[25] Lionel Smith-Gordon and Laurence C. Staples, *Rural Reconstruction in Ireland: A Record of Co-operative Organisation* (1917), 194. Other references include
Hart, *Cottage Industries*, 9–10; DATI, *4th Annual General Report, 1903–1904* (Cd.
2509), HC 1905, xxi. 6; 'Some Unresolved Problems', *IH*, 4 June 1904: 461–2; 'Home
Industries', 470; RCCI, *Appendix to the 7th Report* (Cd. 3785), HC 1908, xl. 16 and
19, evidence by the Very Revd Canon Quinn, member of Armagh County Council, and secretary both of the Newry Agricultural Society and of the Newry Rural
District Council 1 and 2; and Mary E. Connolly, 'Industries: The Gort Industries,
Ltd.', *IH*, 22 Dec. 1900: 715.
[26] Preface by Mary Power Lalor, in Blackburn (ed.), *A Handy Book for Irishwomen*, p. iv.
[27] 'Technical Education for Women', *Hibernia* (Dec. 1882), 177.
[28] 'Meath Home Industries Exhibition', *Warder*, 21 May 1898: 7.
[29] Harty, 'The Living Wage', 429. See also 'A Well-Wisher of Ireland', 'Home
Life in Ireland: Some Suggestions for its Improvement', *IH*, 20 May 1899: 353.
[30] 'Finola', in an untitled article in *United Irishman*, 22 Aug. 1903: 6; 'Mire',
'Industrial Possibilities: Hosiery', ibid. 24 May 1902; 'A Westerner', 'Home Industries and the General Conference', *IH*, 13 Nov. 1897: 765–6; Katherine Tynan, 'The
Cottage Industries of Donegal', in the Countess of Aberdeen (comp.), *Guide to the
Industrial Village and Blarney Castle: The Exhibit of the Irish Industries Association at
the World's Columbian Exposition, Chicago* (Irish Village Book Store, 1893), 56;
'Keilam', 'The Power of the Purse', *IH*, 19 Jan. 1901: 44; 'Clogher Head', ibid. 28
Sept. 1901: 655; and R. A. M'Owenn Bell (of Toomebridge, county Antrim), 'An
Appeal for Handloom Weavers', *Belfast News-Letter*, 13 May 1902.

appealed to rural reformers because they did not contradict the concept that women's economic role in the rebuilding of Ireland was located within the household. After praising female home industries, Helen Blackburn exclaimed: 'Long may Irish [female] workers aim at thus keeping their hold of home, and yet winning self-respect which comes of the power of earning.'[31] Home industries and housework were complementary activities.[32] Many claimed that the introduction of home industries *improved* domestic skills.[33] High-quality lace or crochet could only be made in a clean environment. Neatness was essential. Since much of the white work would be ruined if it had to be washed, housing had to be improved in areas adopting home industries. Roofs were sealed to keep out the rain. Chimneys were introduced 'so that the fair linen might remain innocent of stain from the turf reek'.[34] The small increase in income would allow the houseworker to spend money on domestic fineries, giving her a sense of pride in her home. Rural women would be inspired to achieve feats of model housework by creating fine lace or even sturdy woollen gloves. In 1907 Revd P. J. Dowling asserted that 'every true patriot knows' that economic well-being was only one effect of home industries: there was an equally important moral and social effect:

In the first place, you cannot have such industries without order and regularity in the home. The hand and the eye get a training that shows itself in the dress and surroundings of the worker. In particular, such trades as lacemaking, embroidery, and shirtmaking force order and cleanliness on the house where they are carried on. Then, a great sense

[31] Blackburn (ed.), *A Handy Book for Irishwomen*, 6–7.

[32] 'Women's Work in Irish Homes', *IH*, 24 Aug. 1895: 405; Sylvia Everard (president and hon. secretary of the Meath Home Industries Association in Randlestown, county Cavan), 'Industries: The Meath Home Industries Association', ibid. 4 Mar. 1899: 174; 'Finola', 6; and RCCI, *Appendix to the 10th Report* (Cd. 4007), HC 1908, xlii. 8, evidence by Peter J. O'Malley of Connemara.

[33] IAOS, *Annual General Report, 1899* (Dublin, 1900), 101–2, comment by Lt.-Col. Everard at the fourth annual general conference for co-operative societies; M. J. Hickey of Enniscorthy, 'The Homes of the People', *IH*, 3 Feb. 1901: 73; NLI, 'DATI Council of Agriculture, 1st Meeting, 29 May 1900, Report of Proceedings', address by Horace Plunkett; 'The Value of Cottage Industries', *IH*, 16 May 1903: 398; 'Home Industries', 470; *Report from the Select Committee on Home Work*, 188, evidence by Guy P. Morrish, a Londonderry shirt manufacturer; and CDB, *20th Report, 1911–1912* (Cd. 6553), HC 1912–13, xvii. 28–9.

[34] *Report of the Chief Inspector of Factories and Workshops, 1888* (C. 5697), HC 1889, xviii. 146–7.

of self-respect and self-reliance comes to the man or woman who feels that the bread that is eaten is not idle bread. The idler in the home, who is a kind of parasite on the worker, must have a very low standard of self-appraisement, and must feel very sharply the contrast between himself and the worker. Frugality, too, is begotten in such a home. The material must be husbanded, the profits are small, every suspicion of waste must be checked, and this makes the mind of a frugal bent.[35]

Given the desirability of industrialization, the CDB had no choice but to adopt home industries in districts which lacked transit facilities and local capital. The raw materials and the final product were light enough to be sent by parcel post. Capital outlay was low.[36] However, state legislation restrained the distribution of capital. The CDB could not own or manage any industrial enterprise.[37] Under the act of 1899, the DATI could assist small home industries, but not larger enterprises such as woollen mills.[38] It was allowed to provide technical instruction, but not to offer apprenticeships.

Sentimental attachment to home industries also narrowed choices. This attachment was based on a version of Irish history which focused on a vision of the self-sufficient and innately artistic farming household.[39]

It is only now that we begin to realise what a cruel deprivation the killing of the cottage industries meant. The peasant women took a keen delight in the hand-spinning and weaving. The work refined them, bringing out all the dormant artistic qualities in their nature. These cottage workers never regarded their work as the hard task-master that the mill-hand considers his toil. These hand spinners were like Whitman's 'loving labourer' whose work 'holds him near to God'. They learned to

---

[35] Revd P. J. Dowling, 'Home Industries in Other Countries and their Importance', in *Irish Rural Life and Industry, with Suggestions for the Future* (Dublin, 1907), 64–5; and *Ireland of To-Day, Reprinted, with Some Additions, from 'The Times'* (1913), 332.

[36] RCCI, *Final Report* (Cd. 4097), HC 1908, xlii. 29–32, and Alfred Harris, *The Revival of Industries in Ireland: Notes Made during a Tour in October, 1887* (Dublin, 1888), 33.

[37] CDB, *1st Annual Report* (C. 6908), HC 1893–4, lxxi. 20.

[38] DATI, *Report of the Departmental Committee on Agricultural Credit* (Cd. 7375), HC 1914, xiii. 330.

[39] 'Old Irish Farmers: A Long Way in Advance of the Men To-Day', *Irish Peasant*, 23 Dec. 1905; 'Slaney', 'Work for United Irishwomen', *IH*, 4 Nov. 1911: 871–2; *Ireland of To-Day*, 305; and 'Mire', 'Industrial Possibilities: County Waterford', *United Irishman*, 4 Oct. 1902: 5.

love their work and to put their loves and hearts into it. What painting was to the painter and the sculptor, home weaving and spinning was to the cottage workers of a bye-gone time. And in addition to this gain, there was the material advantage, the money it brought.[40]

The fact that home industries *used* to flourish in Ireland would increase the chances of success—after all, Irish peasants had an 'almost inherited skill in knitting'.[41] Rural reformers had a responsibility to restore home industries to women and to the farming household.[42]

Finally, notions of rural development led reformers to adopt home industries. Ultimately (they acknowledged), economic recovery required large-scale industrialization. Home industries were seen as a precursor to the creation of an industrial Ireland on the Scottish and English model.[43] According to W. J. D. Walker of the CDB, attempting to regulate home industries by imposing legislation aimed at improving working conditions and at controlling wages would

abolish all possibility of later on having larger industrial developments founded on the hereditary skill and application of the trained worker accustomed to a Wages Scale. If you take Hawick and Galashiels, and even Lancashire, the entire industry there is based on the previously existing home industry developed by steam and power into the modern factory, and whenever you find an industry such as in Darvel, or any of those towns in Scotland, you will find that the industry there has grown up from the previously industrially-trained population at hand-work.[44]

Industrial growth depended upon the development of an industrial character. Unlike the Irish, English children grew up in an industrial environment, inheriting a 'natural aptitude' for industrial life.[45] In Ireland the first task was to develop home industries.

[40] 'Slaney', 'Work for United Irishwomen', 871–2.
[41] Hart, *Cottage Industries*, 4.
[42] George Fletcher, 'Rural Industry and Training for Home Life', in *Irish Rural Life and Industry*, 47.
[43] This argument is promulgated by development economists and theorists of proto-industrialization today.
[44] *Report from the Select Committee on Home Work*, 43, evidence by W. J. D. Walker; and *Report from the Select Committee on Industries (Ireland)* (.288), HC 1884–5, ix. 5, evidence by William Kirby Sullivan, president of the Queens' Colleges at Cork and member of the Senate of the Royal University of Ireland.
[45] 'Technical Education', *IH*, 27 Jan. 1905: 64.

THE FAILURE OF HOME INDUSTRIES

The range and financial resources of these organizations did not
guarantee success. Classes and societies were established, thrived
for short periods, then died. After 1906, a society was fortunate to
experience even a short period of affluence. Private charities were
the most unstable. Even the well-managed enterprise of Alice
Hart had disappeared by the early 1890s. The IIDA survived, but
it did not thrive. The generous financial resources of the large
organizations encouraged private groups to withdraw. Eventually,
however, even the large organizational efforts crumbled. Receipts
from the CDB's home industries increased more slowly than
expenditure. In 1904, and drastically in 1906, it was forced to cut
expenditure on home industries.[46] Its work continued, but it never
achieved self-sufficiency.

The number of co-operative home industries in Ireland grew
most rapidly between 1900 and 1902, peaked in 1903 with twenty-
eight societies, but was falling again by 1904. In 1909, sales were
lower than they had been in 1899.[47] Those societies which survived were unstable. Few managed to balance their accounts for
more than a couple of years. For instance, in 1912 sixty members
of the Ballykeery Co-operative Home Industry Society in Mayo
purchased £385 worth of materials, but they could only sell £344
worth of goods. The following year, purchases amounted to £373,
and sales to £371. The Moneyguyneen Co-operative Home Industries Society in Kings' County balanced its books, but with
declining profit margins until 1916. The Meath Home Industries
Society sold lace work and knitted products to the value of £486
in 1912. By 1914, sales had declined to £256, with expenses total-
ling £339. When it closed in 1916 'for the duration of the war' (it
never reopened), it was selling only £42 worth of goods, although
expenses were £68. Sales of the co-operative home industry societies increased from 1900 to 1903, declined suddenly in 1904,
then slowly increased again until 1906. There was no recovery
after 1906.[48]

---

[46] Annual reports of the CDB, as published in the British parliamentary
papers.
[47] Board of Trade, *Report on Industrial and Agricultural Co-operative Societies* (Cd.
6045), HC 1912–13, lxxv. 24.
[48] Registry of Friendly Societies, Dublin, 442 R Mayo, 706 R Kings, and 615 R
Meath.

The home industry classes of the DATI suffered a similar fate. Expenditure peaked in 1902, declined between 1903 and 1910, then temporarily increased until 1913. In spite of the increase in expenditure in the two years after 1910, sales never recovered after the collapse of the crochet industry in 1906.[49] As one worker said: 'The failure of the crochet was as bad as the cattle disease itself.'[50] In 1912 the instructress of home industries for the Department, Miss Anderson, noted that instruction in home industries had almost disappeared from the Leinster schemes and was declining rapidly in the Connaught schemes. In the west, only county Mayo still held classes in home industries. The extension experienced in Ulster was minor.[51]

World War I affected all the home industries. The shirt-making and knitted-wool industries boomed as demand from private commercial firms and the military grew. By shutting off Austrian competition, the war helped sales of coloured embroidery.[52] However, the industries boosted by the war collapsed quickly. Overall, the war sped up the process of decline. Demand for crochet, lace, and sewed muslin waned. Women withdrew from home industries because of increased demand for agricultural labour. The fixed rates of pay instituted by the Board of Trade led experienced workers to leave, while medium-skilled workers found that their goods were being sent to cheaper sewers abroad.[53]

The wages that women received for their work contributed to the failure of home industries. Not only were wages low, they also declined in absolute and real terms. Unfortunately, it is difficult to find wage series for home industries. Work was paid by piece. For the most part (but not entirely), we have to deal with fragmentary evidence. Most important, we usually do not know how many hours women worked for their wages. The examples given here refer only to women working 'full-time' at home industries, although we are still unable to state categorically how

---

[49] From the annual reports of the DATI, published in the British parliamentary papers.

[50] DATI, *13th Annual General Report, 1912–1913* (Cd. 7298), HC 1914, xii. 138.

[51] DATI, *12th Annual General Report, 1911–1912* (Cd. 6647), HC 1912–13, xii. 134, report by Miss Anderson, instructress of home industries.

[52] DATI, *15th Annual General Report, 1914–1915* (Cd. 8299), HC 1916, iv. 84.

[53] DATI, *18th Annual General Report, 1917–1918* (Cmd. 106), HC 1919, ix. 97, *DATI 19th Annual General Report, 1918–1919* (Cmd. 929), HC 1920, ix. 98; and the Belleek Needlework (Lace) Industry, letters between M. A. Dolan and the Office of the Trade Board, PRONI D2149/8/1.

many hours this actually constituted. Further, we have no way of measuring differences in skill. Elizabeth Boyle, the historian of Irish 'flowerers', asserted that 'individual earnings seem respectable'. She claimed that wages in this period ranged between 10s. and £1 per week.[54] My examination of the records shows much lower wages. The women involved in S. E. Donaldson's guipure and appliqué lace industry were earning 10s. a week in 1877 and 1878, but these were peak years, and wages declined thereafter.[55] In 1894 thirty-one elderly and highly skilled lacemakers who worked for Mrs Robert Vere O'Brien of Ennis, county Clare, earned 7s. a week.[56] During the same period, knitters could earn only 3s. a week.[57] Some women in Donegal worked for 18d. a week.[58] In 1899 the minimum wage for an outside hemstitcher working in Banbridge (county Down) was 2s. 5d. A year later, the minimum wage had dropped to 1s. 7d. Folders in the same place earned between 3s. 7d. and 8s. in 1899, and between 4s. 1d. and 7s. 6d. in 1900. Other female workers were paid an average of 3s. a week. No male employee was paid less than 9s.[59] Sewers in Tullamore could earn a maximum of 4s. a week in 1905.[60] Spriggers in Donegal used to earn 8s. a week early in the century, but this had fallen to 3s. or 4s. by 1906. Women were paid 3s. for sprigging a dozen shirts: in 1906 the return was 18d. a dozen.[61] In Rathmullen spriggers were earning between 8s. and 10s. a week in 1906.[62] The Fermanagh sprigging industry brought workers 6s. to 9s. a week.[63] After three months' training, crochet workers in Mayo earned an average of 5s. to 7s. a week in 1907.[64]

---

[54] Boyle, *Irish Flowerers*, 127–8.

[55] S. E. Donaldson (of Crossmaglen, county Armagh), 'Irish Lace', *Irish Textile Journal*, 15 Aug. 1891: 96.

[56] 'Trade in the South of Ireland', ibid. 15 Feb. 1894: 18.

[57] 'Notes of the Week', *IH*, 18 Mar. 1895: 206, and 'Cottage Industries', ibid. 6 Apr. 1895: 75.   [58] Micks, *An Account of the CDB*, 210.

[59] John Johnson's hemstitching factory in Banbridge (county Down), statistics from wage-books of 23 June 1899 and 22 June 1900, PRONI D1042.

[60] *Irish Peasant*, 16 Dec. 1905, speech by William Kennedy at the meeting of the Tullamore Industrial Association.

[61] RCCI, *Appendix to the 2nd Report* (Cd. 3319), HC 1907, xxxv. 38, evidence by Revd James Maguire of Inishowen and Fannet in the parish of Clonmany.

[62] Ibid. 21 (37), evidence by Revd James Gallagher of Rathmullan.

[63] RCCI, *Appendix to the 7th Report*, xl. 145, evidence by Revd J. R. Maguire, representing Garrison in county Fermanagh and the United Irish League.

[64] RCCI, *Appendix to the 9th Report* (Cd. 3845), HC 1908, xli. 83, evidence by Patrick O'Donnell of Newport, member of Mayo County Council.

In 1908 the average crochet worker in Cavan earned only 2s. a week. The maximum wage was 6s.[65] Handkerchief-clipping was one of the most skilled jobs in the sprigging industry. In 1908 a clipper could 'lift' 11s. to 12s. a week. By 1910, no woman could earn as much as half this sum. The wage had been reduced to between 2s. 9d. and 6s. 3d. A clipper commented: 'they just keep reducing and reducing, and when they don't reduce the price they increase the work.'[66] Generally, average wages between 1908 and 1910 ranged between 4s. and 7s. in home industries as diverse as Donegal embroidery,[67] lace making in congested districts,[68] and Limerick lace.[69] As such, these figures fail to indicate extremes. Although the average lacemaker in Kenmare earned between 4s. and 12s., the best worker earned £1, beginners earned less than 4s.[70] Similarly, the range of wages earned in 1908 in the Londonderry shirt industry was between 4s. and 15s. a week.[71] In the same years, rural women lettering handkerchiefs were earning 2s. to 4s. a week.[72]

Let us examine wages for lacemakers and spriggers in Belleek and Cashelnadrea (county Fermanagh) between 1903 and 1917.[73] The first thing to notice is the low average wage. Converting the daily wages of the eighteen women in the Cashelnadrea lace class into weekly rates for the years 1905 and 1906, the most

[65] RCCI, *Appendix to the 7th Report*, xl. 141–2, evidence by Patrick Clark, a farmer and shopkeeper of Swanlinbar (county Cavan).
[66] 'Report of Inspectors re. Sweating in Making-Up and Embroidery Trades', c.1910, probably county Tyrone, Woman no. 36, PRONI D3480/41.
[67] *Report from the Select Committee on Home Work*, 37, evidence by W. J. D. Walker; and Edna L. Walter, *The Fascination of Ireland* (1913), 52–3.
[68] *Report from the Select Committee on Home Work*, 43, evidence by W. J. D. Walker.
[69] L. Reynolds, 'Irish and French Lace Workers', *IH*, 20 Nov. 1909: 943.
[70] RCCI, *Appendix to the 8th Report* (Cd. 3839), HC 1908, xli. 121, evidence by the Ven. Archdeacon David O'Leary.
[71] *Report from the Select Committee on Home Work*, 186–7, evidence by Guy P. Morrish of the Londonderry firm of Welch, Margetson and Co., vice-president of the London Chamber of Commerce, and conveyor of the Manufacturers' Committee of Londonderry merchants.
[72] RCCI, *Appendix to the 7th Report*, xl. 24, evidence by Revd R. J. Murphy; and 'Report of Inspectors re. Sweating in Making-Up and Embroidery Trades'.
[73] The Belleek and Cashelnadrea lace and sprigging classes, set up under the county Fermanagh schemes of technical instruction, have left a daunting array of wage- and account-books in PRONI. Daily wage rates have been converted into yearly, monthly, and weekly totals. Whenever possible, weekly payments are quoted, since this enables comparisons to be made with the wages of agricultural servants.

highly paid worker earned 6s. a week. The average worker earned 3s. The highest wages were paid during the harvest period—presumably to ensure the continued labour of women in the industry during these months.[74] During the months of highest demand for casual agricultural labour, payments to workers exceeded sales.[75] The individual long-term trend of wages is exemplified by Winny Carmy. Carmy joined the Belleek sprigging class in 1903. In her first year she earned 3s. a week. By 1904 this had increased to 5s., then to 7s. in 1907. After this date, her earnings declined. By 1908 she could earn only 1s. a week.[76] Since the number of workers in the Belleek and Cashelnadrea classes remained relatively stable until 1916, the aggregate sums paid to workers provide a useful indicator of wage trends. Wages paid to women increased between 1909 and 1911, then declined rapidly. Thus, in 1912 wages were lower than they had been in 1909. The difference between minimum and maximum wages had also widened. Highly skilled workers were able to maintain their rate of payment, while the average sprigger was paid less and less.[77] Wages increased again at the end of 1913, but this lasted only until July 1914. Detailed figures for seventy-one women confirm that, except for the period October 1913–July 1914, the average wage was less than 2s. a week.[78] The daily payments to twenty-three piece-workers in the Belleek class between August 1903 and January 1915 have also been analysed. They had different levels of skill. They stopped work occasionally, then resumed at later dates. In an attempt to look at general trends, these payments were averaged by month. Trade increased steadily until the middle of 1905, dropped suddenly between 1906 and 1909, rose until 1911 (with a small decline in mid-1910), and then fluctuated at levels much lower than 1904–5. At their peak, women were earning an average of 8s. a week. By the pre-war period, they were lucky to earn half this sum.[79]

Low wages were a source of embarrassment to the promoters of home industries. The CDB was able to justify the wages by reminding critics that the cost of living in congested areas was much lower than in the rest of Ireland. To make the point, they

[74] Belleek Needlework Industry, Wage-Books, PRONI D2149/3/10.
[75] Ibid. D2149/3/3.   [76] Winny Carmey of Foxtown, PRONI D3239/4/1.
[77] Belleek Needlework Industry, Wage-Books, PRONI D2149/3/4.
[78] Ibid. D2149/6/2.   [79] Ibid.

exaggerated the differential, arguing that rent was low, that the acquisition of fuel demanded expenditure of labour and time rather than of capital, that the land provided households with their food, that dress was simple and amusements spontaneous.[80] The co-operative societies, based in wealthier areas such as Leighlin (county Carlow), Youghal (county Tipperary), Carrick-macross (county Monaghan), and Crossmaglen (county Armagh), were more prepared to confess that they never intended to provide a 'living wage', but only to supplement earnings while providing women with 'pleasant and comfortable employment in their own homes'.[81] Home industries were not full-time occupations; women embroidered or knitted before and after housework.[82] Wages were paid accordingly.

The main justification that the institutions establishing home industries put forward for the low wages was that the women were learning skills which were at least as important as the monetary return on their labour. Female labour should not be judged in the same way as male labour. All types of employment for women had to be weighed against their chief form of labour, housework. By knitting or embroidering, women were learning domestic skills; 'small earnings and habits of tidiness and economy are better than no earnings and habits of untidiness and wastefulness.'[83] The relationship between housework and home industries was increasingly emphasized, at the expense of those employed in home industries.

THE PERSISTENCE OF HOMEWORKERS

Why did women continue to embroider or to make lace when their labour was so poorly paid? In depressed areas they had little choice: there was simply no other form of income-earning employment. In the 1887 IIDA pamphlet on home industries, Revd John MacKerna of Pettigo (county Donegal) pleaded for

---

[80] Micks, *An Account of the CDB*, 210–11.

[81] IAOS, *Annual General Report, 1898*, 15, and 'Dromore Industries', *IH*, 9 May 1903: 387, an address by R. A. Anderson to the St Macartan's Home Industries Society in Dromore.

[82] 'Dunleer and Clogher Head', *IH*, 30 Nov. 1901: 798.

[83] Alan S. Cole, *Two Lectures in the Art of Lace Making* (Dublin, 1884), 4.

the establishment of home industries for the unemployed women in his district, 'who have not a day's work to do and who would work for anything sooner than be idle'.[84] Women took up home industries as a 'temporary occupation until some more profitable employment offers'.[85]

We can speculate on the economic motivations of workers in home industries by looking once again at the Belleek sprigging class. I have matched the women employed in the class during January 1911 with the census manuscripts for 1911.[86] In 1911 the Belleek DED contained 171 households, or over 500 adults. All the workers in the sprigging class came from this DED; three-quarters of them came from the townlands of Derrynon Glebe, Belleek town itself, and the Commons. Almost one-third of all households in the Belleek DED had at least one homeworker. The chief factor distinguishing these women from all other women (aged over 15 years) in the DED was that they came from house-holds that might be expected to be poorer than average (see Tables 4.1 and 4.2). Households with industrial workers were larger, had more dependent kin, and fewer males than house-holds without home industries. Child care requirements in households with home industries were lower than in all house-holds. While almost one-quarter of all households had depend-ent children, only 13–16 per cent of households with industrial workers had dependent children. This suggests that home indus-tries were not adopted by women 'trapped' at home because of child care requirements: the shortage of alternative employment opportunities was crucial. The workers' relationship to the 'head of the household' was also skewed. First, homeworkers were much more likely to be the 'head'. Second, fewer were wives and none was a non-relative (whereas 7 per cent of all women over 15 in Belleek DED were servants, boarders, or visitors). Third, a higher proportion of industrial workers were 'relatives' but not members of the conjugal family unit: they were sisters, nieces, mothers living with married sons or daughters, and aunts. More

[84] IIA, *Irish Home Industries Association*, 20.

[85] DATI, *11th Annual General Report, 1910–1911* (Cd. 6107), HC 1912–13, xii. 139, report of Miss L. Anderson.

[86] A matching has only been made where both names agree and where there are no other likely candidates. Duplication of names has meant that I have matched only 72% of the sample.

Table 4.1. Households and home industries in Belleek DED, 1911 (%)

Characteristics of household	Household without home industry	Household with home industry
5 + members	45.1	33.6
Dependent kin	33.4	21.6
Less than 40% men	49.0	32.0
More than 2 children over 15	15.7	24.0
At least 1 child under 5	13.0	24.8
Unoccupied 'head'	26.1	12.0

Note: Since households may contain more than one of the characteristics, the columns do not add up to 100%.

Source: Manuscript census returns for Belleek DED, NAI, 1901 and 1911.

Table 4.2. Women and home industries in Belleek DED, 1911 (%)

Characteristics of adult woman	Employed in home industries	Not employed in home industries
Married	17.6	37.0
Widowed	25.5	11.4
Unmarried	56.9	51.6
'Head' of household	29.4	15.6
Not a member of a conjugal family unit	23.5	15.6
Wife of 'head' of household	15.7	32.8

Note: Since households may contain more than one of the characteristics, the columns do not add up to 100%.

Source: Manuscript census returns for Belleek DED, NAI, 1901 and 1911.

homeworkers were unmarried. The economic vulnerability of homeworkers in Belleek is clear when we note that, while 11 per cent of all adult women not involved in home industries were widows, over one-quarter of industrial workers had lost their husbands. Households containing home industries were more likely to include a larger number of 'unoccupied' adult females, and their heads tended to be older: 26 per cent of households with industrial workers had a head without an occupation, compared with only 12 per cent of households without home industries.

Given the economic vulnerability of households with home industries, even the low wages paid to women could be indispensable to the household economy, particularly if more than one woman in the family were employed in the industry. In the matched group of Belleek workers, one-fifth of all workers in home industries lived in households with more than one industrial worker. The small wages of one or two female members of the household could mean the difference between poverty and the balancing of accounts.[87]

An additional explanation for the persistence of homeworkers lies in the nature of trade fluctuations. Until 1906, depressions in the industries had been followed by periods of stability and even prosperity. Competition required constant application of the manual skills involved in lacemaking and crochet. During the periodic depressions, women had two options: they could learn new skills and spend a few more years on apprentice wages, with a slight hope of 'coming out' during a boom; or they could retain and improve the skills that they possessed, and wait for a resurgence of trade. After 1906, however, trade depressions were protracted, and some industries never revived. In the words of one sprigger: 'We're lost we women that work at home.'[88]

---

[87] CDB, *19th Report, 1909–1911* (Cd. 5712), HC 1911, xiii. 34; 'Home Industries in Relation to Agriculture', *IH*, 7 Feb. 1903: 102; IAOS, *Annual General Report, 1897* (Dublin, 1898), app. F, 'The Second Annual Conference of Delegates from Co-operative Dairy and Agricultural Societies', 38, comment by Mr Flynn of the Ballinagleragh Industries Society; 'Report of Inspectors re. Sweating in Making-Up and Embroidery Trades'; R. M. Martin, 'The Manufacture of Lace and Crochet', in *Irish Rural Life and Industry*, 129–30; 'The Bye-Products of a Home Industry Society', *IH*, 8 Feb. 1908: 106; and NLI, 'DATI Council of Agriculture, 4th Meeting, Thursday, 5 Mar. 1903, Report of Proceedings', 26, comment by R. A. Anderson.

[88] 'Report of Inspectors re. Sweating in Making-Up and Embroidery Trades', Woman no. 50.

Economic reasoning is not the basis for all human action. In trying to explain why women continued to work at home industries despite low wages, creativity cannot be ignored. For some, lacemaking or knitting provided their chief form of self-expression. It was legitimate leisure. They enjoyed the touch of fine threads and linens. Knitting brought a sense of accomplishment. Linen crafts were an imitation of the higher classes of women as portrayed in penny readers and the Bible, and helped to while away the evenings:

These earnings may seem small, but they have brought the margin of comfort to many poor hearths in the past seven years, and that out of time redeemed from mere idling. Nor is the money the sole return. This knitting brings the girls some of the pleasure of skilled, intelligent work. To make a good jersey or a well-proportioned pair of gloves, and to adapt the article to the various requirements of the various customers requires some 'faculty', and gives the work sufficient individuality to save it from the machine-like repetition which is so foreign to the versatile Celt.[89]

The symbolic value of industrial work was also important. In an economy that offered women few opportunities to contribute monetarily to the household, home industries allowed them to snatch some (albeit little) independence. As Miss L. Reynolds (co-operative organizer of home industries) argued in Ballyshannon, women had to establish a lace industry if they were to 'earn money and independence'. Eighty women agreed, and established the industry.[90] The word 'independence' had more than rhetorical value. Home industries were a way of combining the new virtues of housework and domesticity with attempts to earn a living.

WHY HOME INDUSTRIES FAILED

Given the willingness of well-endowed organizations to invest capital and other resources in home industries, and given the docile (even desperate) labour force, why did the schemes to

[89] Ellen Blackburn (of Valencia Island), 'Thoughts on Home Industries', *Union*, 17 Dec. 1887: 5, and 'Slaney', 'Work for United Irishwomen', 871–2.
[90] 'Ballyshannon', *IH*, 22 Dec. 1901: 716, and 'Keilam', 'The Power of the Purse', 44.

promote home industries in Ireland fail? An examination of three relationships provides the answer. The relationship between the bureaucracy and the rural community was fraught with tension. Administrative inefficiency and ignorance contributed to the failure of local industries. This explanation says very little about the intrinsic problems of establishing home industries. The relationship between the rural community and the market was never satisfactory. Homeworkers were inefficient. Their industries were severely damaged by the competition of large-scale factories and home-producers in other countries. Fundamental marketing deficiencies were never remedied. Finally, conflicts within the communities thwarted development.

Local leaders were frequently justified in placing the blame for the failure of home industries on the bureaucracy. Competition between organizations promoting home industries frequently destroyed classes, as in the impassioned conflict between the DATI and the IAOS over the Lissan Co-operative Home Industry.[91] The 'starchy paste-board little men from the Department' often destroyed local plans for extending home industries by enforcing rules rigidly.[92] For example, in 1909 technical school rolls plummeted when the DATI decreed that students of lace and crochet had to attend design classes one evening a week in addition to practical classes. While some were annoyed that their household commitments would not allow them the necessary extra time, others resented being treated as schoolchildren sitting at desks with pen and pad.[93]

Unofficial benefactors also played a role in ruining the industries that they established. Many of the cottage industries were really charities. Their failure was caused by the disorganized dispensation of charitable capital by people unacquainted with business methods, the market, and even with the objects of their benevolence. The instability of such enterprises was frequently exposed during the first crisis: the first attempt to sell the products,

[91] DATI, *Minutes of Evidence Taken Before the Departmental Committee of Inquiry* (Cd. 3574), HC 1907, xviii. 460, evidence by Mr L. Bradley, secretary of the Tyrone Committee of Technical Instruction.

[92] RCCI, *Appendix to the 8th Report*, xli. 71–2, evidence by Canon Humphrey O'Riordan, representing the bishops, the Cahirciveen Rural District, and the fish-curers.

[93] 'A Mere Woman', 'Women's Work in the Technical Schools', *Leader*, 25 June 1910: 401.

a depression in the industry, or the absence of the leading bene-
factor caused panic. The tendency of these fairy godmothers (and
occasionally godfathers) to promote the most ornate, decorative
work also encouraged their economic ruin. Co-operators legiti-
mately accused them of treating home industries as a form of
'personal benefactory', and of leaving 'the sense of personal responsibility unawakened' amongst the workers.[94] Workers no
longer accepted such charity gratefully. Dignity demanded that
a woman earn her own living rather than depend on patronage.[95]

The lack of skilled teachers denied home industries a solid
technical base. Competent technical leadership was lacking. The
ineptitude of amateur organizers of home industries frustrated
potential buyers. For instance, the Belleek home industry depended on large orders from Ireland Brothers and Warings of
London, yet the incompetence of the organizer, Miss M. A. Dolan,
led to annual confrontations which threatened to destroy relations.[96] Co-operative societies relied on the leadership of local
committees; for home industries in particular, an independent,
business-minded committee was essential to direct the workers.
However, a high proportion of employees were on the committee.
Taking co-operative enterprises in Ireland as a whole, less than
1 per cent of the members of committees were also workers.
However, in the Irish lace and embroidery co-operatives, 44 per
cent of all committee members were employees.[97] Given the
economic and social status of workers in home industries, their
near-dominance in the managerial committees was not conducive
to business expansion.

Finally, reforming organizations, although striving to make
the classes self-sufficient, discovered that the cost of establishing
them frequently exceeded the income generated by the industries. Societies were small; management wasteful. The maintenance of the industries entailed a large expenditure of public
money, out of proportion to the earnings. While such expenditure was expected to decrease after two or three years, the com-
bination of trade fluctuations and high emigration rates among

---

[94] 'Home Industries', 470.   [95] 'Rural Industries Ahead', 61.
[96] Belleek Needlework Industry, letters between Miss M. A. Dolan and Ireland
Brothers and Warings of London, PRONI D2149/8/1.
[97] Board of Trade, *Report on Workmen's Co-operative Societies in the United Kingdom, with Statistical Tables* (Cd. 698), HC 1901, lxxiv. 55.

the most skilled workers meant that return on expenditure remained low.[98]

Irish home industries competed unsuccessfully with producers
in other countries. Industry in England, France, Switzerland, Italy,
Lebanon, Syria, China, Japan, the Philippine Islands, Germany,
and parts of the United States was more efficient than that of
the Irish lacemakers.[99] For example, the Austrian government
established profitable home industries amongst its poorer inhabitants, primarily by developing more effective marketing methods.
In particular, the Irish market for raised crochet was affected by
imports of creative Austrian work and tasteful machine-made
imitations.[100] Machine embroidery from Switzerland was cheaper,
and often more stylish, than the local product. Irish manufacturers
of cambric continued to send their linen to Switzerland to be
embroidered.[101] English lace factories reached their peak in 1907,
employing over 40,000 workers.[102] World markets were becoming restricted. 'McKinley's' tariff of 1891 increased American
duties on knitted goods, and in 1909 a prohibitive tariff on lace
was introduced in the United States. The industry's dependency
on overseas markets made it especially vulnerable.

It is not necessary to argue that the promotion of home industries was encouraged by British governments and other villains
(such as John Redmond!) to ensure that Ireland remained indus-
trially underdeveloped, to note that it was at odds with the
mechanizing tendencies in other countries.[103] The mechanization
of industries such as embroidery, lacemaking, and knitting in
other countries destroyed Irish cottage industries. As George
Fletcher of the DATI noted in 1914: 'The spinning wheel gave
place to the "spinning jenny", the handloom to the powerloom,
the knitting needles to the "Automatic", and now the "tambour"
is yielding to the Swiss Embroidery Machine.'[104] The numbers of

[98] DATI, *5th Annual General Report, 1904–1905* (Cd. 2929), HC 1906, xxiii. 60,
and RCCI, *Final Report*, xlii. 99.
[99] Anderson, 'Notes on the Irish Lace and Crochet Industry', 57; and *Lace and
Embroidery Review*, 8/1 (Apr. 1912), 34.
[100] DATI, *11th Annual General Report*, xii. 139, report by Miss L. Anderson, instructress of home industries.   [101] Ibid. 104.
[102] Board of Trade, *Working Party Reports: Lace* (1947), 13.
[103] Col. F. T. Warburton, 'Home Industries versus Machine Industries', *IH*, 30
Aug. 1913: 715, and Irish Technical Instruction Association, *Annual Congress,
Killarney, 1914* (Cork, 1915), 61.
[104] George Fletcher, 'The Problem of Small Industries: Machine Embroidery',
DATI Journal, 14/4 (July 1914), 695.

outworkers in the sprigging industry declined by 50 per cent
between 1903 and 1913 because of improvements in machinery
and the popularity of machine-made coloured shirts.[105] There were
four outworkers for every factory worker in 1860, but this ratio
had been halved by 1908.[106] Cottage production was too slow.
Mechanized industries produced a standardized product at
greater speed. Only the finest work was given to hand-sewers:
the average worker could not compete with the machine.[107]

Reformers were concerned with the issue of mechanization
and its relationship to the problems of marketing:

But in watching an industry of such a type [home industry] carefully
one finds that after twelve months or so he can see no further progress
being made. The sales are kept up, but there is no increase, and the
industry remains too small to be run economically. On inquiry one finds
that while the people in the district are very sympathetic, it is quite
impossible to secure a larger market. For instance, if they come to Dublin
seeking to obtain custom, the large houses will say, 'We shall be very
glad to give you an order for so many thousand dozens, prepared according to this sample, and we must have them delivered in such a
time', and the small industry finds it impossible to meet these conditions. Having only a few workers, it is impossible to complete the
orders in time, though they have a market for the goods. They cannot
buy the plant needful for the execution of such an order, and altogether
they fail to hold the general market.[108]

Communities most desperate for home industries lacked the
capital for their successful development. Even during periods
when demand for their products was high, supply could not
increase because of the lack of credit.[109]

It was not only a question of capital. Associations of rural
reformers were torn by debates on the advisability of introducing
simple mechanical aids into the Irish home. On one side were
those who argued that home industries could not compete without some mechanical innovations. Economic considerations were
paramount in their arguments. Minor mechanical aids would

---

[105] *Ireland of To-Day*, 332.
[106] Philip Ollerenshaw, 'Industry, 1820–1914', in Liam Kennedy and Philip
Ollerenshaw (eds.), *An Economic History of Ulster, 1820–1940* (Manchester, 1985),
85.   [107] DATI, *12th Annual General Report*, xii. 185.
[108] Fletcher, 'The Department in Relation to Rural Industries', 667–8, address
at the 11th meeting of the Council of Agriculture on 17 May 1907.
[109] DATI, *Report of the Committee on Agricultural Credit*, xiii. 333.

prepare the peasant community for large-scale industrialization, which would create a prosperous peasantry. On the other side were those who stressed the non-economic purposes of home industries. They argued that mechanization would not benefit the rural household: it would retard housework. Other justifications for this stance included the notion of preserving the Irish *craft* of embroidery or lacemaking. These promoters reminded listeners of the history of Irish home industries, calling for a preservation of the old traditions irrespective of economic viability.[110] The non-economic arguments generally prevailed.

In the few instances where mechanization was achieved within the home, female employment decreased. For instance, the mechanical carding-machine temporarily boosted the male-dominated weaving industry, but it threatened to eradicate female employment in carding.[111] It was claimed that knitting-machines would improve female home employment, but, without the subsidies and loans provided by the CDB, few could afford them.[112] Knitting-machines forced Irish homeworkers to compete even more directly with large factories. If they had any effect, it was to accelerate declining wages and female unemployment.

The main problem was that the *Irish* market for home industries was small. Few people in Ireland could afford luxurious lace, and even these households preferred foreign luxury goods.[113] Imported lace was cheaper than the Irish variety.[114] When the fast tourist steamers of the Cunard and White Star lines ceased calling at Queenstown, the southern lace market was drastically reduced.[115] Irish cottage lace was exported, and distance from the market became a major problem given the poor (though improving) Irish infrastructure.

The Irish promoters struggled with marketing. The Irish Lace Depot, established by Ben Lindsay and then taken over by the

[110] For a lengthy example of such debates, see Irish Technical Instruction Association, *Annual Congress, 1914*, 62 ff.; and Katherine Roche, 'The Lady Teachers' Own Page', *Irish School Weekly*, 15 Nov. 1913: 266.

[111] RCCI, *Appendix to the 10th Report*, xlii. 60, evidence by Christopher O'Connor of Letterard in Clifden, representing the United Irish League.

[112] 'The Sisters of Mercy', 'Enniscorthy Shirt-Making Firm', *IH*, 3 Mar. 1900: 137; 'Industries: Training for a Lace Teacher', ibid. 20 Sept. 1902: 744, and CDB, *20th Report*, xvii. 29.   [113] 'O'S', *United Irishman*, 5 Apr. 1902: 6.

[114] RCCI, *Appendix to the 8th Report*, xli. 127, evidence by Ven. Archdeacon David O'Leary of Kenmare and the Vicar-General of the diocese of Kerry.

[115] DATI, *14th Annual General Report, 1913–1914* (Cd. 7839), HC 1914–16, vi. 138.

bustling Countess of Aberdeen, distributed the products of the CDB and DATI classes. A small number of middle-class rural women might be able to sell their products through urban groups such as the Wife and Maid Club of the *Irish Weekly Independent*; but all others relied on the efforts of inefficient shopkeepers or of stumbling local patrons, and on the erratic marketing arrangements of government departments and co-operative societies. Local marketing arrangements were the major problem. Particularly in the northern sprigging industry, the agents were usually shopkeepers, who received a commission of about 10 per cent. This commission scarcely covered the labour involved in collecting, sending, and accounting for the products. Rather, the shopkeeper's return was in the form of custom in his or her shop and the receipt of general approbation.[116] Most critics blame the failure of home industries on trucking by local shopkeepers, which drove down wages. However, it was hardly in the economic or social interest of the shopkeeper to engage in this sort of activity. The incidence of trucking has been exaggerated.[117] The problem was one of non-specialization. Shopkeepers were inefficient. So long as they maintained a steady flow of incoming work, the quality of products was irrelevant. Indeed, it was in their interest to encourage unskilled women to work at the industry. Delays in collecting and sending were habitual.

Home industries were susceptible to sudden swings in trade. In 1891 a seller of lace from county Armagh explained: 'The lace trade is most fluctuating and though we have more orders than we can execute in one season, we may have almost nothing to do in the next, and stock accumulates to a very large extent; then, I regret to say, none but the experts can get constant employment.'[118] The market for lace was precariously dependent on rapidly changing tastes. Between 1897 and 1898, sales of Ardara homespun plummeted by 35 per cent without warning.[119] The death of King Edward precipitated a decline in sales of white

---

[116] Contracts and letters between the Coleraine Woollen Manufacturing Company and Edmund F. McCambridge, general merchant of Ballycastle and agent, *c.*1903, PRONI D1376/5/6.

[117] *Report from the Select Committee on Home Work*, 42, evidence by W. J. D. Walker.

[118] Donaldson, 'Irish Lace', 96; 'Special Commissioner of the *Daily Express*', *Mr Balfour's Tours in Connemara and Donegal* (n.d.), 59, quoting Revd F. Lague of Kilcar (county Donegal).

[119] CDB, *8th Report, 1899* (C. 9375), HC 1899, lxxvii. 24.

lace work in England. The promotional work of the Gaelic League in the United States caused a brief boom.[120] Sales were dependent on private orders rather than on a wide base of demand.[121] A maker of cosy-covers described how she would earn 8s. a week for a few months, then would be lucky to earn 3s. a week, and would have to supplement her wages by taking in washing and by charring.[122] Low earnings drove women to produce as much as possible in the shortest period of time. In depressed years, their labour was wasted. In better years, prices were rapidly driven down by overproduction. The market could not absorb the large-scale production of low-quality, poorly designed lace.

The third main threat to home industries came from within the communities. They were not stable enough to sustain home industries. Industrial reformers hoped that the classes would stop, or at least reduce, female emigration. This did not occur. Instead, home industries were continually weakened by emigration. The Reverend Mother of the Sisters of Poor Clare complained that their lace classes had stagnated because all the skilled workers had emigrated.[123] In one year, half of the women in the Carna lace class emigrated.[124] Home industries actually encouraged emigration by increasing the sense of independence in young women and by raising expectations of remunerative employment that could not be fulfilled for more than short bursts.[125]

The level of technical education was low. Education for the industries consisted of a crash course by an itinerant instructress, or a hotchpotch series of practical lessons by an amateur practitioner,

---

[120] Waldon Fawcett, 'Making and Marketing Hand-Made Lace in Ireland', *Lace and Embroidery Review*, 8/4 (July 1912), 57.

[121] DATI, *6th Annual General Report, 1905–1906* (Cd. 3543), HC 1907, xvii. 66.

[122] 'Report of Inspectors re. Sweating in Making-Up and Embroidery Trades', Woman no. 47.

[123] RCL, *The Agricultural Labourer*, iv. *Ireland, II, Reports by Mr W. P. O'Brien* (C. 6894-xix), HC 1893–4, xxxvii/1: 29; and Blackburn, 'Thoughts on Home Industries', 5.

[124] RCCI, *Appendix to the 10th Report*, xlii. 53, evidence by W. J. D. Walker. Similar evidence is provided by Revd Michael McHugh of Carna, ibid. 49 (147).

[125] George H. Berkeley, 'Home Work and Small Industries in Italy', *New Ireland Review*, 30/2 (Oct. 1908), 65; Sir Henry Doran, 'Self-Help Among the Western "Congests" ', in W. G. Fitzgerald (ed.), *The Voice of Ireland* (Dublin, 1924), 335; 'K', 'In the Kingdom of Thomond', *IH*, 20 Feb. 1904: 153; 'O'S', 6; and Horace Plunkett, *The Problem of Congestion in Ireland* (Dublin, 1907), 38.

often in philanthropic guise.[126] Attempting to resolve this problem by employing instructresses to work with the classes did not improve the popularity of the local industries: nationalists were affronted by the employment of instructresses and specialized workers from England, Scotland, and Wales; the geographical dispersal of the classes meant that the teachers could spend only short periods in each area; and the teachers were alienated from the communities.[127] Lacemaking was a skilled employment requiring about three years' training.[128] Roving instructresses did not have the time to teach women to make high-quality products, and workers were not skilled enough to experiment. Design inflexibility reduced the value of their product.

The isolation of many of the communities hindered the successful establishment of home industries. Roads were poor and transport facilities were unreliable. A severe rainstorm might delay orders for weeks. Women rarely had any contact with workers in other communities.[129] They had little idea of the needs of the market and rarely had access to new designs. It was scarcely surprising that Irish workers were berated for lacking 'individual initiative', which was deemed vital for successful industrial production.[130] Isolation discouraged any attempts to innovate. Workers were reluctant to exchange the designs they had learned from their mother or grandmother for new designs.[131] The absence of a centralized organization qualified to give advice

[126] 'Technical Education in Ireland', *Irish Textile Journal*, 15 Feb. 1893: 22–4, condensed report from the *Northern Whig* of a meeting of the Technical Education Instruction Association in Dublin; 'National Schools in Ireland', *Irish Technical Journal*, 15 Sept. 1895: 118; 'Technical Education', 64; and Arthur Smith, 'Agricultural Education in Ireland', *New Ireland Review* (May 1905), 155.

[127] Irish Technical Instruction Association, *Annual Congress, 1914*, reply by A. O'Shaughnesy to J. F. Crowley's paper on the woollen industry, 76; and Cork Archives Institute U189, 'Minutes of the Meeting of the Technical Instruction Committee, Thursday, 4 Aug. 1904', 62. The Department, for example, had a rule that Irish instructresses could not be employed in their home county.

[128] 'Over-Production in Lace', *IH*, 11 July 1903: 562.

[129] The advantages of a geographical concentration of skilled home industries is discussed in Board of Trade, *Working Party Reports: Hosiery* (1946), 7.

[130] *The Irish Year-Book, 1908* (Dublin, 1908), 207.

[131] DATI, *5th Annual General Report*, xxiii. 61; 'Irish Lace Makers', *Kings' County Chronicle*, 9 Sept. 1886: 4; 'Revival of Irish Lace Making', *Irish Textile Journal*, 15 Jan. 1897: 157; 'Wanted a New Industry', *IH*, 26 Mar. 1898: 279; 'Castlebellinham', ibid. 28 Mar. 1903: 259; 'Irish Crochet', ibid. 13 Jan. 1905: 23; and Lindsay, *Irish Lace*, 25.

increased their reluctance. Change was resisted.[132] Despite hopeful comments to the contrary, Irish lace design continued to consist of 'a distorted harp, a few caricatured shamrocks, and an Irish deerhound with a round tower beside him as though it were his kennel'.[133] Overproduction of the same designs led to periodic lack of demand and falling wages. The result was poor-quality work, lagging behind market demands. The women's columnist for *Ireland's Own* gave the most damning criticism of Irish home products that she could imagine when she claimed that 'no-one but a nigger would fancy them'.[134] Admittedly, English and American women often looked wryly at Irish products.

The isolation of the communities, the agricultural cycle of production and demands on female members in the household led many rural reformers to complain, with some justification, that Irish homeworkers lacked the necessary traits for a successful modern industry. Workers did not place the 'proper' value on time. They were unpunctual. They worked irregularly. Orders were delayed.[135] The Countess of Arran accused her Irish workers of lacking 'energy and enterprise'.[136] Irish women failed home industries.

THE PURPOSE OF HOME INDUSTRIES

The promoters of home industries had little difficulty in accepting the economic failure of their schemes. The low priority given to female employment opportunities may be a reason for their nonchalance, but this sort of response begs the question.

We can edge towards an explanation for the reformer's nonchalance by looking at the relationship between home industries and agricultural labour. Home industries were promoted to

---

[132] Stephen B. Roche, 'Iveragh Industries, Limited', *New Ireland Review* (Oct. 1899), 98–102, for an example of resistance by Iveragh home-spinners.

[133] May Curran, *United Irishman*, 19 Nov. 1904: 6, who is quoting an unnamed 'foreign writer'; and Alan S. Cole, *A Renascence of the Irish Art of Lace Making* (1888), 36–7.

[134] Helen Hawthorn, 'Dress, Gossip and Cookery', *Ireland's Own*, 17 June 1903: 12.

[135] CDB, *10th Report, 1901* (Cd. 681), HC 1901, lx. 44, and *14th Report, 1905* (Cd. 2757), HC 1906, xcvii. 33.   [136] *Irish Textile Journal*, 15 Feb. 1894: 21.

supplement agricultural work, providing some occupation for female members of small farming households. It was assumed that women would be *unable* to devote all their time to the industries. Besides the performance of housework, women on small farms had to help with planting and harvesting. Thus, the output of lace, crochet, and embroidery dropped in the spring and autumn, when agricultural labour demand peaked.[137] Miss Mary A. Dolan, manageress of the Belleek lace class, explained to Ireland Brothers: 'Sorry for the delay on hurried goods. I could not get them from the workers. They workers [*sic*] aren't doing half as much work as they used to owing to have [*sic*] to work out in the fields this year.'[138] Promoters had no difficulty with this, claiming that what was important was remunerative occupation for women during the parts of the year when their labour was not required on the farm.[139]

Less easy to understand is the reason why some parents objected to their daughters learning skills such as lacemaking and embroidery. The reason that they gave was that 'they never knew a lace school started which did not make the girls useless'.[140] Home industries reduced the casual female agricultural workforce. A Ballinrea landowner (county Cork) grumbled that girls would not work for him during peak seasons because farm work spoiled their hands for lacemaking.[141] There were two sides to the problem. Women found it difficult to make good lace if their hands were hardened by years of farm work.[142] Once they had learned this skill, they were reluctant to spoil their hands by resuming farm work. During the early years of the home industries movement, when wages were higher than those received from farm labouring, women withdrew from agricultural work.

[137] CDB, *16th Report, 1907* (Cd. 3767), HC 1908, xxiii. 27. The attendance statistics entered in the daily Report-Book of Industrial Instruction by the mistress at the Carclinty National Primary School confirms women's low attendance at needlework classes (both absolutely and relative to attendance at other classes) during Apr. to June and in Aug.: PRONI SCH 548/8C/1.

[138] Belleek Needlework Industry, Correspondence, letter dated 21 May 1908, PRONI D2149/7.

[139] Coyne (ed.), *Ireland: Industrial and Agricultural*, 173, and NLI R39, 'Commission on Technical Education, Typescript of Evidence, 1927', evidence by Revd Father Conefrey of Moyne (county Cavan), no pagination, 1st page of his evidence. [140] 'Keilam', 'The Power of the Purse', 44.

[141] RCCI, *Appendix to the 8th Report*, xli. 189, Capt. Richard W. Cooper, farmer of Ballinrea (county Cork). [142] Micks, *An Account of the CDB*, 67.

During periods of slump, they were reluctant to resume farm labour, hoping instead for another industrial boom. Until 1906, the booms came sufficiently often to encourage this practice. In times of depression, they were more likely to increase the quantity and quality of housework than to resume agricultural work. Where cottage industries were established, women moved out of the fields and into the homes. On farms where male family labour was insufficient and where the household economy could not afford to employ outside labour (or where such labour was unavailable), women in the household were given the lightest agricultural tasks in an attempt to protect their hands and to safeguard what their hands were coming to symbolize; gentle, mothering appendages, in contrast to the hard, practical hands admired in menfolk.

The relationship between home industries and housework goes deeper. Rural reformers used home industries as a halfway house between female employment in agriculture and full-time unwaged labour within the home. For instance, the DATI confessed that it was not concerned with the failure of home industries:

The want of success that has attended the efforts to establish lace industries was to be expected, and need not be regretted. The centres where female labour is in excess of home and farm demands had been previously provided with expert [domestic economy] instructresses of trained ability, and in agricultural districts it is much more important that future wives and mothers should be afforded facilities for becoming good housewives, vegetable gardeners and poultry-rearers.[143]

The Department made it compulsory for women attending their home industry classes to attend an equal number of classes in domestic economy.[144] Father Finlay, Horace Plunkett, and Miss O'Conor Eccles (the author of an Irish domestic economy textbook) transformed one of the most successful lace classes into a centre of domestic instruction.[145] Horace Plunkett warned the CDB against spending too much energy and capital on promoting home

[143] DATI, *12th Annual General Report*, xii. 123–4, report by Mr McGann, inspector in western central districts.
[144] DATI, *4th Annual General Report*, xxi. 6–7.
[145] The St Macartan's Co-operative Lace Industry was one of the few remunerative lace classes, with 200 workers: 'Dromore', *IH*, 30 July 1904: 632, and 'Co-operation and the Improvement of the Home: Sir Horace Plunkett Visits Dromore', ibid. 22 Oct. 1904: 892.

industries: 'the limitations of the home industry must always be kept in view and care taken—with regard at least to women workers—that they are also trained to look properly after the interests and economies of the home.'[146] The CDB did not need reminding. It was also concerned that women would become excessively distracted by home industries:

Another point that has to be noted is that these industries sometimes tend to a certain extent, though in a less degree than do the factory industries in English towns, to diminish the usefulness of girls at home, by causing overmuch attention to be directed to the industry, because of the money value of such work. Hence it is important to see that lacemaking classes should be supplemented by a course of domestic economy.[147]

School classes in needlework were increasingly promoted as instruction in housework rather than as industrial instruction.[148] The committee of ladies led by Alice Spring Rice who visited schools in the Limerick district to provide extra needlework instruction for girls were motivated by domestic aims. The inspector for the area commented: 'The Committee do not, I believe, think it practicable to start cottage or home industries. Their primary object is to make the girls good housewives.'[149] The encouragement of housework was the primary consideration of all reformers promoting home industries.[150]

---

[146] Plunkett, *Problem of Congestion*, 41.   [147] RCCI, *Final Report*, xlii. 98–9.

[148] Katherine E. Duffy, 'Some Thoughts on the Curriculum of Secondary Schools', *Irish Educational Review*, 3/2 (Nov. 1909), 80; *Appendix to the 56th Report of the Commissioners of National Education, 1889* (C. 6074-i), HC 1890, xxx. 8; *72nd Report of the Commissioners of National Education, 1905–1906* (Cd. 3154), HC 1906, xxix. 18; Katherine Roche, 'The Lady Teachers' Own Page', *Irish School Weekly*, 20 Dec. 1913: 424; 'Miss Prendergast on the Decadence of Needlework in the Schools', ibid. 25 Nov. 1905: 60; and NLI, 'Minutes of the Proceedings of the Commissioners of National Education at their Meeting, Tuesday, 9 July 1912', 275, where Miss Prendergast, in charge of needlework, resigned and proposed that the departments of needlework and cookery be amalgamated.

[149] *Appendix to the 66th Report of the Commissioners of National Education, 1899–1900*, I (Cd. 286), HC 1900, xxiii. 58–9, report on the Limerick DED by G. Bateman.

[150] DATI, *7th Annual General Report, 1906–1907* (Cd. 4148), H. C. 1908, xiv. 72; 'DATI, Council of Agriculture, 11th Meeting, Proceedings', 80–5; Cork Archives Institute U189, 'Minutes of the Meeting of the Technical Instruction Committee, Thursday 19 Apr. 1906', 167; 'Home Industries', 470; and RCCI, *Appendix to the 7th Report*, xl. 122–3, evidence by Revd Philip O'Doherty of Cumber-Claudy (counties Londonderry and Tyrone).

PART TWO:

SUBSISTENCE ENTREPRENEURS

5

Household Agriculture

The farming labour force of the family was primarily made
up of adult males.[1]

IT is difficult to deal with the involvement of women in peasant
farming. The problems intrinsic to all analyses of female labour
are exacerbated by the paucity of statistical data on family farms.
The census proves to be useless: it completely ignores the contribution of female members of the household to the farm, while
assuming maximum levels of labour input from all adult male
members of the household. Every census between 1881 and 1911
described farmers' sons, grandsons, brothers, and nephews over
15 years of age, as being 'employed in fields and pastures' if they
had not been given another occupation. Corresponding female
relatives were referred to the 'unoccupied' category.[2] To exclude
farmers' wives, daughters, sisters, granddaughters, and nieces
from the agricultural tables of the census, while including farmers'
husbands, sons, brothers, grandsons, and nephews, seriously mis-
represents the structure of the unwaged agricultural labour force.

It is not surprising that census enumerators and agricultural
specialists excluded women. The organization of agriculture into
small, family-operated farms makes the collection of accurate
statistics difficult. There are other problems. Female employment
in agriculture tended to be less secure and more seasonal than
male employment.[3] A woman working in the fields during the

---

[1] Richard Breen, 'Farm Servanthood in Ireland, 1900–1940', *EHR*, 2nd ser. 36
(1983), 96.

[2] *Census of Ireland, 1901*, ii. *General Report* (Cd. 1190), HC 1902, cxxix. 24. See
also *Census of Ireland, 1881: General Report* (C. 3365), HC 1882, lxxvi. 22; *Census of
Ireland, 1891*, ii. *General Report* (C. 6780), HC 1892, xc. 24; and *Census of Ireland,
1911: General Report* (Cd. 6663), HC 1912–13, cxviii. xxix.

[3] DATI, *Report of the Departmental Committee on Food Production in Ireland* (Cd.
8158), HC 1914–16, v. 78; RCCI, *The Agricultural Labourer*, iv. *Ireland, II, Reports
by Mr W. P. O'Brien* (C. 6894-xix), HC 1893–4, xxxvii. 29. See also ibid. iv/IV,
Report by Mr Arthur Wilson Fox (C. 6894-xxi), HC 1893, xxxvii. 91, on Castlereagh,
and Board of Trade, *Earnings of Agricultural Labourers: Second Report by Mr Wilson
Fox* (Cd. 2376), HC 1905, xcvii. 118.

harvest would be less likely to classify herself as a labourer in the census than a seasonal male labourer. Individual classifications were problematic. What occupation would be given to a female landholder who earned her living through growing potatoes, raising poultry, and making lace? If the census was conducted in April, how would a woman who helped to bring in the harvest on the family farm classify herself?

Agricultural data collected by the DATI offer more promising estimates of family farm labour than the census. These statistics are examined first. The sample of eight DEDs is also useful.

In June 1912 the enumerators of agricultural statistics collected information on the number of persons 'actively engaged in agriculture' on the first day of that month. They divided the statistics by age, sex, and farm size, and noted whether workers were members of farmers' families, other permanent labourers, or persons temporarily employed.[4] How accurate are these figures? The 1912 statistic for the number of male farmers and farmers' relatives was 12 per cent lower than the 1911 census statistic, while the 1912 figure for paid labourers was almost 9 per cent higher than the 1911 census statistic. Although the differential is significant, it is not outrageous. The 1912 count refers to only one day of the year, while the census asks people to state their occupation more generally. Account has to be taken of the different criteria for classification. For instance, the 1911 census asked 'heads of families' to give themselves an occupation, while in 1912 the local constabulary were asked to count the number of persons actually engaged in agriculture in their area. Many of the men working as 'labourers' on 1 June 1912 owned land and would have described themselves as 'farmers' for the purpose of the census in 1911. Given the total neglect of female relatives in the census, the 1912 data are essential in quantifying the unwaged female agricultural population. The 1911 census tables recorded 54,700 female farmers and no female farmers' relatives. In 1912, 223,900 female farmers and farmers' relatives were actually engaged in agriculture. Women working casually in agriculture were much more likely to be classified in the 1912 data. Table 5.1 summarizes the number of men and women working on their own farm, and Tables 5.2 and 5.3 give a breakdown of the non-farmers working in agriculture. The majority of female and male

[4] DIC, *Agricultural Statistics, 1847–1926: Report and Tables* (Dublin, 1928), 154–60.

Table 5.1. Number of men and women working on their own farm, 1 June 1912 (000s)

Farm acreage	Men		Women	
	Under 18	Over 18	Under 18	Over 18
0–1 acre	2.0	18.9	1.3	8.5
1–5 acres	3.3	28.1	2.3	10.6
5–15 acres	18.0	116.6	10.6	39.2
15–30 acres	22.1	136.8	12.8	46.2
30–50 acres	13.1	86.8	8.1	31.7
50–100 acres	10.5	70.7	6.7	28.5
100–200 acres	3.6	25.9	2.6	10.8
200 + acres	1.1	8.4	0.8	3.4
TOTAL	73.7	492.2	45.2	178.9

Source: DIC, *Agricultural Statistics, 1847–1926: Report and Tables* (Dublin, 1928), 160. Statistics refer to Ireland and Northern Ireland.

agricultural workers laboured on the family farm. In 1912, over 85 per cent of all female agricultural labourers over the age of 18 worked for their own family, compared with 67 per cent of adult male workers. On farms under thirty acres—70 per cent of all farms in Ireland—practically all female agricultural workers worked for their family. Owners of larger farms were more likely to hire non-relatives. Just over 44 per cent of the younger members of the family working on small family farms on 1 June 1912 were female. Owners of small farms were more likely to hire men than the owners of larger ones. Age, not farm size, was a more important criterion in the employment of female members of the family and of other permanent labourers.

The 1912 data can be used to estimate the relative values of male and female farm labour.[5] According to Table 5.4, a high

[5] Combining the 1912 data with wage data, I have assumed that permanent labourers received the maximum winter wage and that temporary labourers received half the maximum summer wage. In designating a value to the work of family members, I assumed that full- or part-time employment of family members on farms occurred in the same ratio as for their peers in the paid agricultural labour force. Then I divided males and females (differentiating them by adult or child status) into permanent or temporary workers and assigned to them their respective wages. The effect of these procedures is to underestimate the labour of family workers compared to paid workers.

Table 5.2. Employment in agriculture, 1 June 1912 (%)

Farm acreage	Men				Women			
	Under 18	Over 18	All ages		Under 18	Over 18	All ages
0–30 acres							
Family member	84.90	82.78	82.99		89.53	95.20	93.98
Permanent labourer	7.22	5.97	6.10		4.27	2.13	2.61
Temporary employee	7.87	11.25	10.90		6.10	2.67	3.41
30 + acres							
Family member	54.36	72.66	56.78		76.27	70.62	75.10
Permanent labourer	29.63	17.72	28.05		14.17	17.68	14.90
Temporary employee	16.01	9.61	15.16		9.55	11.69	9.99
All farms							
Family member	77.92	68.73	69.81		80.91	86.36	85.20
Permanent labourer	13.21	17.66	17.14		10.44	7.75	8.32
Temporary employee	8.86	13.60	13.05		8.65	5.88	6.47

Source: DIC, *Agricultural Statistics, 1847–1926: Report and Tables,* 160. Statistics refer to Ireland and Northern Ireland.

Table 5.3. Female employment in agriculture, 1 June 1912 (%)

Farm acreage	Under 18	Over 18	All ages
0–30 acres			
Family member	44.02	25.94	28.33
Permanent labourer	31.09	9.79	13.01
Temporary employee	36.61	6.75	9.84
30 + acres			
Family member	31.36	27.73	28.37
Permanent labourer	31.93	11.56	13.72
Temporary employee	36.39	14.02	16.49
All farms			
Family member	37.93	26.65	28.35
Permanent labourer	31.73	11.27	13.60
Temporary employee	37.47	11.12	13.85

Source: DIC, *Agricultural Statistics, 1847–1926: Report and Tables*, 160.
Statistics refer to Ireland and Northern Ireland.

proportion of labour value on the farm came from family labour, especially in the poorer western counties of Mayo, Leitrim, Galway, Roscommon, Kerry, Clare, and Donegal (column 1). Familial labour was proportionately less important in the counties of Dublin, Kildare, and Meath. Looking only at adult family labour, approximately 18 per cent was female labour (column 4). This proportion was highest in the Munster counties and in Wexford and Carlow, where over one-quarter of the labour value was created by female family labour. Looking at those under the age of 18, the labour value of girls was almost one-third of that for boys. Female children were relatively more important in the south and in the northern counties of Armagh, Londonderry, and Antrim (column 5). Child labour was more interchangeable in terms of the skills required for performance of the labour and in terms of time restraints.

FARM ACTIVITIES OF WOMEN

What types of agricultural work were these women performing? Women laid potatoes, spread manure, collected stones for drains,

Table 5.4. Farm 'wages' as % of total 'wages', 1912

County	'Wages' earned by				
	Family members	Female family members	Male family members	Adult women	Female children
Carlow	61.2	15.5	45.7	24.2	35.4
Dublin	26.4	1.7	24.7	5.9	12.0
Kildare	46.3	4.9	41.4	9.7	25.3
Kilkenny	66.6	16.3	50.3	22.7	38.3
Kings'	67.4	12.5	54.9	16.8	38.7
Longford	75.3	11.7	63.6	13.9	33.1
Louth	55.6	7.4	48.2	12.3	23.6
Meath	47.5	5.3	42.2	10.2	25.1
Queens'	65.5	15.2	50.3	21.9	35.0
Westmeath	67.0	8.4	58.6	11.6	25.8
Wexford	57.0	15.7	41.3	26.0	41.8
Wicklow	53.5	8.1	45.4	13.3	35.4
Clare	80.1	16.4	63.7	19.4	30.2
Cork	69.5	19.7	49.8	27.1	39.3
Kerry	81.9	27.7	54.2	32.8	41.3
Limerick	68.5	21.5	47.0	30.4	42.7
Tipperary	67.0	18.4	48.6	26.2	42.3
Waterford	67.2	20.2	47.0	28.9	45.1
Antrim	67.2	12.1	55.1	16.2	34.6
Armagh	74.2	17.5	56.7	22.1	35.1
Cavan	78.0	7.2	70.8	7.9	22.6
Donegal	80.1	10.4	69.7	11.8	24.0
Down	64.9	10.1	54.8	14.3	30.5
Fermanagh	72.3	8.6	63.7	11.0	22.0
Derry	68.4	12.3	56.1	16.4	34.9
Monaghan	76.4	13.2	63.2	16.0	28.2
Tyrone	71.8	13.5	58.3	17.5	31.7
Galway	85.3	19.2	66.1	20.8	32.6
Leitrim	87.1	12.3	74.8	12.7	25.6
Mayo	91.8	21.4	70.4	21.2	33.3
Roscommon	84.5	9.7	74.8	10.8	18.5
Sligo	69.8	9.6	60.2	13.1	19.7

Source: DIC, *Agricultural Statistics, 1847–1926: Report and Tables* 160, and the wage returns in the DATI Annual General Reports (British parliamentary papers).

fed the cows in busy times, hand-raked the meadows, prepared turf, and bound corn. They rarely herded or sold cattle.[6] Women occasionally ploughed, although they more commonly performed spadework.[7]

Female labour was essential to the peasant farm economy. In the poorer, congested districts, attendance at lace, crochet, and domestic classes declined when women were needed to work on the family farm, increasing again in the slack months.[8] Even on the wealthier Ulster farms in the 1890s, female familial labour was crucial: 'Land is for the most part easily worked and fertile in these settlements, and it is the custom for the people to work it "amongst themselves".'[9] Women performed most agricultural tasks during planting and harvesting, but throughout the year specific tasks on the farm were seen as 'women's work': women earned money for the household through feeding pigs, raising poultry, and dairying. In each of these areas, important changes occurred between 1890 and 1914. Chapter 3 looked at female participation in dairying on the farms of other people. The same arguments apply to the work of female family members in milking cows, churning butter, and marketing the produce. Chapter 6 looks at poultry-rearing in particular. The aim of this chapter, therefore, is to examine what evidence is available on the broad trend of female labour on the family farm.

THE CHANGE

Contemporaries noted that 'there is a growing indisposition on the part of females to field labour, except on their own holdings'.[10] Unfortunately, the only statistical data on the extent to which women continued to work on family farms are confined to the Republic of Ireland in 1912 and 1926. These data are summarized

[6] 'Observer', 'Migratory Labour and Women's Work on the Farm', *IH*, 5 Feb. 1910: 110.

[7] *The Agricultural Labourer*, iv/II, *Reports by Mr W. P. O'Brien*, xxxvii: 114, on the Poor Law Union of Mountmelick (Queens' County).

[8] CDB, *16th Report, 1907* (Cd. 3767), HC 1908, xxiii. 27, and DATI, *11th Annual General Report, 1910–1911* (Cd. 6107), HC 1912–13, xii. 38.

[9] 'A Guardian of the Poor', *The Irish Peasant* (1892), 51.

[10] RCL, *The Agricultural Labourer*, iv. *Ireland*, I, *Reports by Mr R. McCrea* (C. 6894-xviii), HC 1893–4, xxxvii/1: 8, summary report.

Table 5.5. Family labour on farms, Saorstát Éireann, 1912 and 1926 (% change)

Farm acreage	Under 18		Over 18	
	Men	Women	Men	Women
1–5 acres	−61.3	−69.5	−44.7	−34.2
5–15 acres	−50.6	−61.8	−12.0	−19.5
15–30 acres	−49.9	−63.3	0.8	−23.7
30–50 acres	−45.0	−62.4	13.5	−20.4
50–100 acres	−51.2	−67.4	10.8	−27.0
100–200 acres	−49.3	−67.2	14.4	−23.4
200 + acres	−50.4	−70.3	12.8	−19.7

Source: DIC, *Agricultural Statistics, 1847–1926: Report and Tables*, 160.

in Table 5.5. Between 1912 and 1926, there was a faster decline in the number of male family members on farms, under five acres. This is partly because of higher productivity on the smallest farms and partly because of expanding employment opportunities for rural men, causing them to move out of agricultural production even faster than women. On farms over five acres, the numbers of adult women workers declined between 1912 and 1926 by approximately 22 per cent, while the numbers of male family labourers on these farms increased by approximately 10 per cent. Children (especially if they were female) rapidly ceased working for their families.

LABOUR DEMAND

Another way to analyse labour demand on farms is to regard the farm household as an integral unit of labour, and to differentiate labour demand within this unit. The size of the household varied with the size of the farm; larger farms supported more people than smaller farms, where surplus labour left as early as possible. Thus, in 1901 nearly three-quarters of the households on farms of between one and five acres contained less than five members, compared with 30 per cent of households on farms of

Table 5.6. Average number of adult men and women per farm, 1901 and 1911

Farm acreage	1901[a]		1911[b]	
	Men	Women	Men	Women
1–5 acres	1.6	1.8	1.5	1.4
5–15 acres	1.8	1.7	1.6	1.6
15–30 acres	1.8	1.7	1.6	1.7
30–50 acres	2.1	1.8	2.2	2.0
50–100 acres	2.4	2.1	2.5	2.2
100 + acres	3.1	2.8	3.0	1.2

Note: This analysis excludes households with less than 1 acre of land and composed only of men or women. The term 'adult' refers to people between the ages of 15 and 65.

[a] n (no. in sample) = 380 men and 387 women.
[b] n = 406 men and 429 women.

Source: Manuscript census returns for 6 DEDs, NAI, 1901 and 1911; Valuation Books at the Valuation Office, Dublin (nearest year to 1911).

between thirty and fifty acres. By 1911, mean household size on farms had increased, with just over 60 per cent of households on land between one and five acres containing less than five members, compared with 36 per cent of households on land between thirty and fifty acres.

These comments are interesting when men and women are differentiated. Table 5.6 shows the number of adult men and women in each household, according to farm size. In general, farming households contained more men than women, although this was not always true on small farms. For farms of between one and fifteen acres, potential female labour declined. On farms of between fifteen and thirty acres, the numbers of women remained stable, whereas they increased on farms of between thirty and a hundred acres and declined on the largest farms. To what extent were these adjustments a result of the changing 'mix' between unwaged family labour and paid labour? Was the rapid decline in the number of women on farms of over one hundred acres caused by the reduced demand for the *paid* labour of female

Table 5.7. Domestic service and farm acreage, 1901 and 1911 (%)

Farm acreage	Households with domestic servants	
	1901[a]	1911[b]
1–5 acres	0.0	5.0
5–15 acres	5.0	4.5
15–30 acres	6.9	4.8
30–50 acres	9.3	13.6
50–100 acres	18.2	35.7
100 + acres	48.1	50.0

[a] n (no. in sample) = 621.
[b] n = 597.

Source: Manuscript census returns for 6 DEDs, NAI, 1901 and 1911;
Valuation Books at the Valuation Office, Dublin (nearest year to 1911).

domestic and farm servants? After all, demand for male labour on these farms declined only slightly during the same period. Is there any evidence that male farm servants were replacing female farm servants? As we saw in Chapter 2, the changes cannot be attributed to an increase in the number of households with paid domestic servants. Farms of over one hundred acres were more likely to have paid female domestic servants. It was only farms of between five and thirty acres that were less liable to have domestic servants (see Table 5.7). An important decline occurred in the number of female farm servants, and this would have reduced the amount of female labour on farms, particularly on large farms (see Table 2.3).

Demand for the labour of female members of the family also diminished. Thus, in 1901 every farm contained, on average, 1.5 female members of the family between the ages of 15 and 65. This had dropped to 1.4 within the decade. However, looking at these changes by farm size, a differential emerges. Female family labour declined fastest on farms of between one and five acres. In 1901, the average number of such women on farms of between one and five acres was 1.8, dropping to 1.2 in 1911. What is most striking is that, on farms of between fifteen and

Table 5.8. Female family employment and farm acreage, 1901 and 1911 (%)

Farm acreage	'Occupied' family members	
	1901[a]	1911[b]
1–5 acres	21.3	12.9
5–15 acres	27.9	17.6
15–30 acres	23.2	15.0
30–50 acres	17.6	11.8
50–100 acres	17.0	7.9
100 + acres	17.4	12.5

  [a] n (no. in sample) = 415.
  [b] n = 437.

Source: Manuscript census returns for 6 DEDs, NAI, 1901 and 1911; Valuation Books at the Valuation Office, Dublin (nearest year to 1911).

thirty acres (that is, over one-quarter of all the holdings in the sample), the available labour force of female familial members increased from 1.1 persons to 1.4 persons.

Family members from small farms were more likely to find alternative forms of employment. For the small family, such income was more necessary to household stability. In 1901, between one-fifth and one-quarter of adult female family members on farms of less than thirty acres were given an occupation in the census, compared with only 17 per cent of women on farms of over thirty acres. By 1911 the pattern is much more mixed, as women living on all farms were less liable to be employed (see Table 5.8).

A number of forces may have been reducing demand for female labour on the farm. What was the role of ideology in lowering the demand for female labour in the fields? How influential were changes in farm size? What part did the shift from tillage to pasturage play? Was mechanization significant? What was the impact of relative wage differentials? Alternative demands on female labour led to a contraction of the supply available for agricultural production. The rest of the chapter examines these features, attempting not only to explain the decline of female family labour, but also to supplement the discussion on the decline of paid female labourers (see Chapter 2).

CHANGING TASTES AND EDUCATIONAL INVESTMENT IN CHILDREN

Changing attitudes towards female labour in agriculture were reflected in the notion that 'modern' women were weaker than men: 'The women them times were different ta fot they are now. They was never ashamed to take their turn doin' an honesht day's work, where there was a wage ta be earned, an' they could do handy jobs that a lot o' the chraythurs these times 'id get weak at, if their men washtnt knockin' around.'[11] There was general disapproval of women—particularly mothers—working in the fields. Poverty might drive a woman to perform heavy agricultural labour, 'leaving her children to the tender care of Providence', causing commentators to moan: 'If children are allowed to drift without proper care, and if mothers are maimed and distorted with hard and heavy work, how is the country going to prosper or have a healthy and vigorous manhood?'[12] Women of the small-farming and labouring classes no longer wanted to feed pigs, as they had done in the past. A pig-farmer from Dundalk in county Louth complained that 'the standard of living and ideas of the farmers' daughters are too high and they will not do this work. This has a retarding effect, and the result is that more direct labour has to be depended on.'[13] 'Connemara Girl' tried to explain why men in Connemara worked their women so hard:

The only explanation I can offer is the temperaments of the men of Connemara, owing to the hardships they are obliged to endure, have

---

[11] IFC MS 485, Bean ui Cealliaz, aged 75, from parish of Coill Uairar (county Sligo), 120, spelling and punctuation as in original (1938). See also *The Agricultural Labourer*, iv/IV, *Report by Mr Arthur Wilson Fox*, xxxvii. 19, 57, 91, 109, and 125–6.

[12] 'Ireland's Eye', 'The Lot of the Farm Woman', *Irish Worker*, 31 May 1913: 1.

[13] DATI, *Departmental Committee on the Irish Pig-Breeding Industry* (Cd. 8004), HC 1914–16, vi. 69, evidence by T. J. Byrne of Rosnakegh, Dundalk (county Louth), member of the Council of Agriculture, a tillage farmer with pigs. See also ibid. 54, where P. Maher (from Ivy Hall, Templemore, county Tipperary, a farmer and breeder of pigs) noted that female farm servants refused to feed pigs.

become soured, and consequently have lost the chivalrous feelings they ought to bear towards the women. As for the women, they accept the hardships of life and the additional hardships given them by the men with a cheerfulness and willingness to oblige that is the characteristic of all women.[14]

After describing the agricultural work of women in the west, the editor of the *Irish Homestead* noted that: 'In Connemara one can see the most beautiful young girls in Ireland. One rarely sees a beautiful woman over forty there.'[15] There was a plethora of statements noting that the life of a small farmer was one of continuous hard work, with many privations and little leisure.[16] 'Women are not intended for manual labour, and yet how many of them work more than the men, especially among the small farmers. This is one of the evils we want to remedy. If money can be made by light and pleasant work there will be something to pay the skilled labourer with.'[17]

The employment of children was becoming less acceptable. This, in turn, affected female labour. Farm service was probably the most important occupation for children in rural Ireland. The wages earned by children hired out between the ages of 10 and 14 were important to the family economy.[18] The Royal Commission on Agricultural Labourers noted that 'under ordinary circumstances, the lot of the married labourer, until his family are able to go to service, must be one of hardship, but after some of them are employed, his condition rapidly improves.'[19] However, as wage differentials between children and adults narrowed (as shown below), the employment of children became relatively

[14] 'Connemara Girl', 'The Revolt of Women', *IH*, 19 Mar. 1910: 232, original grammar.
[15] 'Those Left Behind', ibid. 5 Feb. 1910: 103. The editor was responding to a letter from 'Observer', who argued that the system of migratory labour in Connaught was responsible for the hardship of women on small holdings: 'Migratory Labour and Women's Work on the Farm', 110.
[16] 'H. G. B.', 'How the State Spoils the Broth', ibid. 27 Mar. 1909: 247–8.
[17] 'United Irishwomen', ibid. 28 May 1910: 452, copy of the paper read at the meeting to discuss the formation of the UI, held at Ballynadara, Enniscorthy (county Wexford), by unidentified woman.
[18] RCCI, *Appendix to the 7th Report* (Cd. 3785), HC 1908, xl. 85, evidence by Revd Thomas McCann of Kildress (county Tyrone).
[19] *The Agricultural Labourer*, iv/I, *Reports by Mr R. McCrea*, xxxvii/1: 12, 34, and 51, reports on Ardee (counties Louth and Meath) and Clones (county Monaghan), and ibid. ii/II, *Reports by W. P. O'Brien*, xxxvii/1: 20, on Kanturk (county Cork).

less attractive to employers. Furthermore, the age at which
parental investment in children could be realized was receding.
Children stayed at school longer.[20] Local government boards set
up school attendance committees to examine the extent of child
employment and to enforce school attendance legislation.[21]
Compulsory education made things more difficult for married
women, because it meant that older children were no longer
available to look after the younger children. Dependent children
limited the opportunities for mothers to seek employment, even
during harvesting. In this way, educational investment in children limited the employment role of women.

OWNERSHIP OF LAND

David Fitzpatrick uses an 'increasing integration of farm workers within the farming class' to explain the declining numbers of
male agricultural labourers.[22] Opportunities to own land increased (see the Introduction). However, there is no evidence to
suggest that similar opportunities were available to *female* farm
workers. Women did not benefit directly from land redistri-
bution schemes. Increased access to land for *male* agricultural
labourers may have enabled the wives, daughters and sisters of
these upwardly mobile labourers to stop working in the fields of
other farmers, but not on their own holding.

FARM SIZE AND FARM TYPE

Since economies of scale on larger holdings meant that fewer
labourers were required, we would expect to find employment in
agriculture falling as Irish farms grew larger. Table 5.9 shows the

[20] This was discussed in the Introduction.
[21] See e.g. PRONI LA16/7AA/1, the minutes of the Ballymoney Rural District
School Attendance Committee, which in 1901 repeatedly bemoaned the fact that
large numbers of girls under the age of 14 were not attending school because of
employment, and RCCI, *Appendix to the 7th Report*, xl. 85, evidence by Revd Thomas
McCann of Kildress (county Tyrone).
[22] David Fitzpatrick, 'The Disappearance of the Irish Agricultural Labourer,
1841–1912', *Irish Economic and Social History*, 7 (1980), 78.

Table 5.9. Farm labouring and farm acreage, 1912

Farm acreage	Number of labourers employed			
	Leinster	Munster	Ulster	Connaught
0–1 acre				
Men	1.00	0.80	0.48	0.56
Women	0.03	0.03	0.07	0.07
1–5 acres				
Men	4.80	4.22	2.34	1.58
Women	0.31	0.55	0.23	0.10
5–15 acres				
Men	8.05	5.27	3.72	1.25
Women	0.43	1.08	0.34	0.12
15–30 acres				
Men	17.00	9.38	11.12 ˙	2.56
Women	1.37	2.33	0.99	0.18
30–50 acres				
Men	33.05	18.89	30.74	8.18
Women	2.82	5.19	2.63	0.61
50–100 acres				
Men	70.00	42.89	68.55	22.06
Women	6.78	12.15	7.44	1.38
100–200 acres				
Men	150.20	97.64	134.46	59.57
Women	13.80	23.27	12.75	4.22
200–500 acres				
Men	338.40	196.07	233.44	110.91
Women	29.20	34.86	14.56	6.89
500 + acres				
Men	1097.20	678.26	428.57	348.30
Women	49.50	70.08	18.41	18.18

Note: Only those labourers over the age of 18 were included; 100 farms were examined.

Source: DIC, *Agricultural Statistics, 1847–1926: Report and Tables* 160.

number of permanent labourers on holdings of certain sizes. As the farm size increases, so too does the total number of labourers, but the number of labourers *per acre* decreases. Data from 1912 shows that, although female workers were less likely than male workers to be employed on farms of all sizes, they were even less likely to be employed on large farms. As farm sizes in Ireland increased, one would expect female labourers (within a given area) to move out of paid agricultural employment more rapidly than their male counterparts. This did not occur. The proposition was tested by assuming that the same proportion of male or female labourers recorded for each size of farm in 1912 was employed twenty years earlier, in 1892.[23] Males and females were tested separately. Provincial and age variations were examined for each sex. The formula was tested for permanent paid labourers, temporary labourers, and unwaged family labourers.

Table 5.10 shows that changes in average farm size cannot explain changing labour patterns. Only in Connaught could we predict lower employment on farms from changes in farm size between 1892 and 1912. These changes might have resulted in a 4–8 per cent decline in *both* male and female employment on farms between 1892 and 1912. In all other provinces, slight and insignificant (with the exception, perhaps, of Munster) *increases* in labouring employment might have been expected.

Further, the argument that the movement from tillage to pasturage resulted in reduced female participation in agriculture is only partially sustainable. If we correlate the number of milch cows, cattle, and poultry per one hundred acres and the amount of crops planted per one hundred acres by the number of adult women working as 'permanent labourers' in 1912, we get the figures shown in Table 5.11. High numbers of milch cows on farms of all sizes encouraged the employment of women. Similarly, crop production on farms of over thirty acres, would lead to the employment of women. High numbers of poultry and a high proportion of land in crops did not favour female employment on small farms. And, on farms of over fifteen acres, cattle numbers also resulted in lower proportions of female workers.

---

[23] 1912 was the only year for which employment data by size of farm were available.

Table 5.10. Farm employment (labourers and family members), 1892 and 1912

Province	Men under 18		Men over 18		Women under 18		Women over 18	
	1912	1892	1912	1892	1912	1892	1912	1892
Permanent labourers								
Leinster	3,191	3,141	46,563	45,813	1,288	1,272	3,859	3,806
Munster	3,859	3,732	35,494	34,391	2,635	2,541	8,350	8,062
Olster	4,446	4,365	35,423	34,769	1,572	1,545	3,249	3,191
Connaught	1,007	1,051	8,966	9,712	317	333	600	643
Temporary labourers								
Leinster	2,192	2,132	25,135	24,443	1,479	1,456	4,798	4,716
Munster	1,946	1,849	22,258	21,081	1,257	1,191	3,886	3,746
Olster	2,881	2,857	33,284	33,002	1,614	1,604	2,871	2,835
Connaught	1,368	1,367	17,795	17,637	466	461	631	634
Family members								
Leinster	10,189	9,833	86,319	83,499	6,214	6,173	27,772	26,760
Munster	17,092	16,134	122,124	114,344	13,246	12,509	66,429	61,911
Olster	22,255	22,250	162,018	161,728	12,060	12,070	45,452	45,501
Connaught	24,187	23,170	121,761	116,712	13,535	12,967	39,155	37,534

Source: DIC, *Agricultural Statistics, 1847–1926: Report and Tables*, 160.

Table 5.11. Correlation coefficients: Female farm employment and output per 100 acres, 1912

Farm acreage	Crops	Milch cows	Cattle	Poultry
5–15 acres	−0.0150	0.4709	0.2720	−0.0895
15–30 acres	−0.0814	0.5597	−0.1088	−0.1396
30–50 acres	0.1689	0.7371	−0.1149	0.0361
50–100 acres	0.3347	0.6742	−0.2160	0.1929

Source: DIC, *Agricultural Statistics, 1847–1926: Report and Tables*, 160, and the annual statistics published by the DATI (British parliamentary papers).

TECHNOLOGY

The introduction of horses and equipment may have marginally reduced women's role in agriculture.[24] Machinery affected female employment in a number of ways. First, it reduced the total number of labourers required to work on farms.[25] Second, women were excluded from training for the equipment, which was seen as 'masculine'. Chapter 3 pointed out how women were excluded from creamery technology.[26] Tillage implements such as drill ploughs, cultivators, and harrows appeared predominantly in the north, while hay-rakes, reapers, and mowers were used in the provinces of Leinster and Munster. Connaught had very few of these machines or implements.[27] This mechanical argument can be tested by examining a farm activity that men and women performed together, but in which separate tasks were allotted to each sex—for instance, reaping and binding. Men reaped and mowed, followed by women who bound the grain. Increasingly, machines came to be used for these processes. A number of reaping and mowing machines would be required for each binding machine. Statistics exist for the number of binders, reapers, and

[24] For a discussion of the role of farm equipment on female labour, see Maureen M. Mackintosh, 'Domestic Labour and the Household', in Sandra Burman, *Fit Work for Women* (1979), 179.

[25] RCL, *The Agricultural Labourer*, iv. Ireland, III, *Reports by Mr Roger C. Richards* (C. 6894-xx), HC 1893–4, xxxvii/1: 44.

[26] 'To the Girls of the House', *IH*, 16 Mar. 1895: 26.

[27] DATI, *Agricultural Statistics, Ireland, 1908–1909: Report and Tables Relating to Irish Agricultural Labourers* (Cd. 4919), HC 1909, cii. 17–18.

mowers in Ireland in 1908, 1912, and 1917. The number of binders increased from 7,620 to 9,394 and then to 14,296 in these three years. The number of reapers and mowers increased from 79,603 to 91,766 and then to 108,006. Thus, while reapers and mowers increased by 36 per cent in nine years, the number of binders increased by 88 per cent. Another example would be women's role during the 'little harvest'—that is, the harvest on the family's small farm. Women used reaping hooks and men used scythes.[28] As scythes took over from reaping hooks as the most efficient method of harvesting, women might have been expected to move out of this sector of farm employment.

SEASONAL MIGRATORY LABOUR

As seasonal employment for men declined, so did female labour on farms. Women worked intensively in the fields during those times, and in those areas, where the male members of the household left for seasonal employment in England, Scotland, or elsewhere in Ireland. Although most seasonal migrants from Achill were female, in Ireland as a whole the majority were male. For example, between 1902 and 1907 over 1,000 women left each year for seasonal employment, compared with between 17,000 (1903) and 25,000 (1906) men.[29] While so many men were away in England and Scotland, the care of the holdings was left entirely to women and children. The barrister and writer Michael J. F. McCarthy commented:

I have often been struck in harvest time at seeing mere children cutting corn in the little fields; some of the boys so young that a farmer in the south of Ireland would be afraid to entrust them with the use of a scythe, and the girls who followed the youthful mowers so small that they should have been at school. A gentleman who lives in the locality informed me one day that the fathers and elder brothers of some children at whom we were looking, were at that time, in England, to his knowledge, with packs on their backs.[30]

---

[28] IFC MS 107, Patrick Martin of Ballymitty (county Wexford), talking to Tomas O Ciardha on 5 Apr. 1935: 36.

[29] From the DATI's reports and tables on Irish agricultural labourers, published in the British parliamentary papers, 1903–10.

[30] Michael J. F. McCarthy, *Priests and People in Ireland* (Dublin, 1903), 22.

In Ballymena during the 1890s it was not uncommon for men to work in factories some distance away while the women and children remained at home to work in the household's fields.[31] In certain coastal areas of Donegal, women tended the farms while men fished.[32] The Royal Commission on Agricultural Labour (1893–4) pointed to a decline in the number of male seasonal migrants, caused partly by the introduction of machinery on English farms from the 1860s. As fewer men were needed for seasonal work in the fields of Scotland and England, this type of replacement labour by women also declined.

DECLINE OF TRADITIONAL AREAS OF FEMALE LABOUR

With the collapse of some areas of family agriculture in which female labour predominated, we would expect a decline of female labour. Poultry-rearing is examined in detail in the next chapter. The other example is the care of pigs. For small farmers and labouring families, the pig had a traditional place of importance in the household economy. Nineteenth-century descriptions of Ireland rarely failed to mention the 'gintleman that pays the rint'.

But almost certainly the pig will be there [by the fire] with the family, waiting for his share of the rough meal cooking on the fire. For the pig represents the future means of existence of the family for several months. On the little money which it will fetch at the next fair the father, mother, children, and the old parents will exist until next season.[33]

Women were responsible for the rearing of pigs. After the turn of the century, there was a movement of women away from this form of agricultural labour.[34] Although the statistics on the total

---

[31] *The Agricultural Labourer*, iv/I, *Reports by Mr R. McCrea*, xxxvii/1: 86, report on Ballymena (county Antrim).

[32] Local Government Board for Ireland, *Copies of a Report from the Local Government Board, 1883, with Regard to Distress in Ireland* (.92), HC 1883, lix. 5, report by H. J. MacFarlane, Local Government Board Inspector for Donegal.

[33] H. Saint-Thomas, *Paddy's Dream and John Bull's Nightmare*, trans. Emile Hatzfeld (*c*.1886), 231. See also RCCI, *Appendix to the 9th Report* (Cd. 3845), HC 1908, xli. 201, evidence by A. C. Larminie.

[34] DATI, *Departmental Committee on the Pig-Breeding Industry*, vi: 3.

number of pigs in Ireland show a series of peaks and troughs with only a slight decline, fewer small farmers and labourers reared pigs after 1911.[35] Certainly, the low pre-war price of pork and the high cost of suckling-pigs, coupled with the decline of tillage and the cost of animal foodstuffs in the shops, must have discouraged small farming households from investing in a pig. The decline might also be blamed on sanitary restrictions in towns and on the lack of a suitable pigsty in many of the cottages built for agricultural labourers by rural district committees.

WAGE RELATIVITIES AND HOUSEWORK

Wage data tell us more about labour supply and demand than any other single source. This section examines trends in wages for men and women, and then looks at the implications of these changes for the employment of each sex. Wage data for agricultural labourers exist for both men and women for the years 1890 to 1906.[36] Female wages were lowest in the summer, when women received about one-third as much as their male counterparts in most parts of the country. Winter female wages were just over half the size of men's. In Cork, Kerry, Limerick, and Tipperary less significant seasonal changes in agricultural demand meant that female wages changed very little in summer and winter. High wages were received in areas where the supply of labour was reduced by competition from other industries and in those areas most affected by seasonal swings in labour demand. Thus, summer wages were highest in the eastern counties and in the northern counties of Antrim and Down.

[35] Statistics taken from the agricultural reports and tables released by the DATI and published annually in the British parliamentary papers.

[36] Between 1890 and 1906 the wage data were given in the annual reports and tables released by the DATI. After 1906, wage data were given in the annual reports on migratory labourers, but, since only male wages were given, they are not useful for this analysis. The following analysis uses the statistics on the maximum summer and winter wages of agricultural labourers in each constabulary district to calculate the average rate for the county. The footnotes to the wage rates make it clear that these wages apply not only to harvest or strictly agricultural labourers, but also to what this chapter calls 'farm servants'. For instance, dairymaids, charwomen, and domestic servants are mentioned as some of the occupations of these women. For a comment on problems with these statistics, see Fitzpatrick, 'The Disappearance of the Irish Labourer', 80–1.

The most striking change in wage rates is the narrowing differential between male and female wages. Occasionally, the wages of young girls even exceeded those of young boys. This occurred with the summer wages of girls in Queens' County and county Cork in 1890, and in Kings' County in 1906. Female wages in 1890 were particularly poor in Fermanagh and Leitrim, where women received less than half as much as men. By 1906, women generally received more than half the male rate, although this was not the case in Antrim, Cavan, Roscommon, Galway, Leitrim, Donegal, and Sligo. Adult female wages were closest to male wages in Westmeath and Wexford in 1890, where they were three-quarters the size of male wages, and in Kings' and Tipperary in 1906, where they received two-thirds as much as men. In most counties the summer wages of female agricultural labourers increased between 1890 and 1906. The only exceptions were female labourers in Kildare, Kilkenny, and Roscommon. Significantly, both summer and winter female wages increased faster than the wages of their adult male counterparts. The summer wages of women and girls rose by 29 per cent between 1890 and 1906, while their winter wages increased by 18 per cent. The mean increase for adult males was 19 per cent in summer and 17 per cent in winter. This rise in female wages suggests that women were withdrawing voluntarily from waged work, with a consequent increase in wages for female-specific work.

Only the wages of young boys increased faster than those of adult women. In terms of rates of *change*, female wages were closer to the wages of young male labourers than to those of adult male labourers. The wages of women and girls were closer together than the wages of adult and young boys. The first effect of the shortage of female labour was that boys were hired to perform work previously given to women.[37] Young men could replace women in certain agricultural jobs without loss of manliness. By the turn of the century, escalating *relative* wages for young boys led to the movement to employ men. With the narrowing wage differential between men and women, men became relatively cheaper. Employers traded wages against expected output; since men were expected to be stronger and more productive,

[37] *The Agricultural Labourer*, iv/IV, *Reports by Mr Arthur Wilson Fox*, xxxvii. 81, on Westport (county Mayo), concern with the replacement of women by boys in the weeding and cutting of thistles on Lord John Browne's estate.

narrowing differences between male and female wages resulted in the substitution of male labourers for female.

Part of what seems at first to be productivity differentials concerns certain 'costs' involved in employing women rather than men. These costs were related to the economic responsibilities of women in the household. The requirements of housework meant that employers allowed (and expected) women to work shorter hours than men. The morning duties of women—such as the care of poultry and the preparation of breakfast for the household—required half an hour of daylight. Similarly, children had to be woken and sent to school, or dispersed to relatives and friends. Men in Bailieborough (county Cavan) and Ballyshannon (county Donegal) started work in summer at 6 a.m.; their wives at 7 a.m.[38] In Balrothery (county Dublin) female labourers arrived at work one and a half hours after their male relatives.[39] In Roscrea (county Tipperary) men and women started work at the same hour of the morning, except when men had to work before dawn. Then the women would begin half an hour later.[40] What this suggests is that housework played a crucial role in predicting the labour-force participation rates of women, whether the women were married or unmarried. To take an example of household agriculture mentioned earlier, pig-rearing was a time-consuming job that got in the way of housework. Irish households customarily fed their pigs with cooked meal and potatoes. The cost of preparing pig-food was huge, particularly as the boiling was generally done in the kitchen.[41]

There are but twenty-four hours in one short day, and how can a woman feed, clothe, educate her children, and minister to her husband's needs, to say nothing of her own, if she has to labour on the farm and feed farm stock as well? Who can blame her if she neglects to cook proper food, to provide sufficient clothes, or to make her home what it ought to be? She has not time to think of her responsibilities, or, if she has, she is too tired to meet them.[42]

---

[38] Ibid. iv/III, *Reports by Mr Roger C. Richards*, xxxvii/1: 65, on Bailieborough (county Cavan) and ibid. iv/I, *Reports by Mr R. McCrea*, xxxvii/1: 35, on Ballyshannon (county Donegal).

[39] Ibid. iv/III, *Reports by Mr Roger C. Richards*, xxxvii/1: 48.

[40] Ibid. 37 (301).

[41] James M. Adams, 'Pig Feeding with Uncooked Meal', *DATI Journal*, 13/2 (Jan. 1913), 346.

[42] Ellice Pilkington, 'The Irish Countrywoman', *IH*, 9 Apr. 1910: 294.

As was argued in Chapter 2 when we examined the reasons for the decline in domestic service, the time demands of housework are central in explaining why women reduced the amount of work that they did on the family farm.

The gradual movement of women out of many types of farm work was not regretted. Mrs W. J. Starkie had this to say about the changes: 'With regard to women's work in the country districts, it will become, I think, daily more interesting and more important, for a revolution has taken place, though quietly, in the ideals of farming, which will give women a place of increasing importance in her own domain.'[43] Shifts in agricultural practices, increased educational investment in children, combined with swings in wages which made it relatively more productive to employ boys or men, resulted in the slow movement of women out of the fields—in both the waged and unwaged spheres. For the mothers, wives, sisters, and daughters of farmers, the demands of household labour were increasing. The most pertinent 'slip' was made by Sir Horace Plunkett in his address to the Federation of Women's Institutes. For a paper entitled 'How I feed my pig', Plunkett suggested deleting the word 'pig' and inserting the word 'baby'.[44] The revised title would have been more appropriate to women's concerns.

---

[43] Mrs W. J. Starkie, 'Women's Work in Rural Districts', *Irish Education Review*, 9 (June 1912), 515.   [44] *United Irishwomen*, Dec. 1925: 1.

6

Poultry-Rearing

> I heard that there were no hens in Ireland at one time, and
> when the Danes invaded the country they brought them
> with them from Denmark. They brought them to do harm
> to the Irish people. The hens would go up on the roofs of
> the houses and start scraping and they'd scrape the covers
> off the houses and let in the wind and rain. The Danes were
> doing awful things till Brian Boru made war on them and
> defeated them at Clontarf. . . . The Irish people found that
> the hens weren't going to do all the rascality that the Danes
> intended. And the Irish people kept the hens.[1]

THUS, folklore explains how poultry came to Ireland. During the
period examined in this chapter, rearing poultry for sale was one
of the most important occupations of the farm woman. Indeed,
despite the impassioned debates and controversial decisions
concerning the poultry industry from the 1890s, one thing was
agreed: for better or (more commonly) for worse, the poultry
industry was dominated by women. In the words of the vice-
president of the DATI, T. W. Russell, 'women have a distinct
ability in this direction'.[2] Successful poultry-rearing demanded
'minute personal care and supervision . . . exactly the requisite
which the wife and family of the cottager can bestow'.[3] Women
were more successful poultry-rearers than men, allegedly because
they understood the temperamental character of the fowl and
were therefore 'more careful about the little details'.[4] With the
exception of the exportation of eggs and fowl, practically the

---

[1] James Arguel of Galbroke, aged 91, speaks to P. J. Gaynor of Bailieborough
(county Cavan), Dec. 1952, IFC MS 1310: 606. For a similar story, see P. J. Gaynor
of Bailieborough (county Cavan) speaking to a number of people in counties
Meath and Cavan, Jan. 1953, IFC MS 1321: 326–32.

[2] DATI, *Conference on the Poultry Industry, Dublin, May 1911* (Dublin, 1911), 76.

[3] H. Villiers Stuart, *Prices of Farm Products in Ireland from Year to Year for Thirty-
Six Years* (Dublin, 1886), 15–16. See also Thomas Barrington, 'A Review of Irish
Agricultural Prices', *Journal of the Statistical and Social Inquiry Society of Ireland*, 14
(1926–7), 252–3.   [4] *Ark*, 6/54 (Mar. 1914), 12.

whole industry was in the hands of women. As reformers were to discover, poultry-rearing was a woman's industry, one which they found it 'impossible to induce Irishmen' to adopt.[5] This chapter is a study in discrimination. It examines poultry-rearing in Ireland, illustrating how institutional policies attempted to change the nature of the industry for farm women. Institutionalized discrimination was effective in the dairy industry; the poultry story is more complex.

THE POULTRY INDUSTRY

Poultry were reared on small arable farms. In 1912 the average number of poultry on holdings of less than one acre was 2,833, compared with 735 on holdings of between one and five acres. On holdings of more than 200 acres, the average number of poultry was under 28.[6] Geographically, poultry-rearing was particularly important in the central counties of Ulster and in the southernmost counties. The main product was eggs, but table poultry were a feature in the south and south-east (especially Wexford).

For women of the labouring and small-farmer class, poultry-keeping enabled them to contribute substantially to the household economy. The poor depended on the sale of poultry products for the bare necessities of life.[7] Poultry was 'the chief source of income to many a poor woman who depends upon her egg money for many little purchases which could never be procured from the husband's hire'.[8] The Royal Commission on Congestion commented that 'a very considerable part of the income of farmers, particularly of small farmers, cottagers and labourers is derived from the sale of eggs and fowl.'[9] Women in county Wexford were noted for rearing fowls, and 'the close attention obviously given by the labourers' wives here to this branch of domestic industry has proved an important element in

[5] RCCI, *Appendix to the 4th Report* (Cd. 3509), HC 1907, xxxvi, app. 4: 186.

[6] DIC, *Agricultural Statistics, 1847–1926: Report and Tables* (Dublin, 1928), 140–2.

[7] RCCI, *Appendix to 7th Report* (Cd. 3785), HC 1908, xl. 119, evidence by P. G. Dalliager, secretary of Tyrone County Council.

[8] E. Anderson, 'Irish Poultry and Poultry Rearing', *IH*, 4 Sept. 1897: 529.

[9] RCCI, *Appendix to the 4th Report*, xxxvi, app. 4: 186.

the additions they are able to make to their small resources.'[10] Similarly, at Naas (county Kildare), although fixing a precise money value on poultry-rearing proved difficult, 'there can be no doubt that they contribute very materially to better the general condition of the class.'[11] Roger C. Richards claimed that in Bailieborough (county Cavan) wives made as much cash in one day by selling eggs as their husbands made in a week.[12] Wives of bibulous men testified to the importance of eggs in the household budget.[13] The farm near the border of Meath and Kildare which won first prize in the Small Farm Competition held by the County Committee of Agriculture earned £12 a year from 200 fowl.[14] Taking the earnings of this farm into account, the DATI may have been exaggerating when it claimed in 1911 that women on small farms in certain areas earned between £20 and £60 a year by raising poultry. However, there can be little doubt that the receipts from eggs paid the rent and provided the groceries in many households.[15] In north Longford the money commonly received from poultry on a twelve-acre farm would buy a quarter-pound of tea, two pounds of sugar, a four-pound loaf of bread, and an ounce of tobacco each week.[16]

It often happened that a poor person ran short of money and wanted it badly to buy groceries for the house and they'd put a few hens in a

[10] RCL, *The Agricultural Labourer*, iv. *Ireland*, II, *Reports by Mr W. P. O'Brien* (C. 6894-xix), HC 1893–4, xxxvii. 74, on the Poor Law Union of Wexford (county Wexford).

[11] Ibid. 44, on the Poor Law Union of Naas (counties Kildare and Wicklow).

[12] RCL, *The Agricultural Labourer*, iv. *Ireland*, III, *Reports by Mr Roger C. Richards* (C. 6894-xx), HC 1893–4, xxxvii/1: 64–8, on the Poor Law Union of Bailieborough (county Cavan).

[13] PRONI T3249/1, W. A. Greer, 'Eighteen Years, 1896–1914' (unpublished autobiography), 19–20.

[14] T. Wade, 'A Prize-Winning Small Farm', *New Ireland Review*, 30 (1908), 151.

[15] DATI, *Conference on the Poultry Industry*, 47. See also J. S. Gordon, 'The History of the Development of Instruction in Connection with the Poultry Industry in Ireland', *DATI Journal*, 13/1 (Oct. 1912), 52–3. For statistics on the economic importance of poultry in the household economy, see NLI, DATI, 'Minutes of the Council of Agriculture, 19th meeting, Tuesday, 30 May 1911, Report of Proceedings', 65, and DATI, 'Minutes of the Council of Agriculture, 27th Meeting, Tuesday, 4 May 1915, Report of Proceedings', 6.

[16] Hugh Corrigan, aged 60 years, of Drumlish (county Longford), speaking to James Delaney of Longford about 'Life on a Farm of Twelve Acres in North Longford Fifty Years Ago', IFC MS 1458: 436; and Simon Smith of Carngarve, speaking to P. J. Gaynor of Bailieborough (county Cavan), Jan. 1953, IFC MS 317: 317.

basket and bring them to the town and sell them to a fowl buyer. That often happened in a day that wasn't a market day at all. There are farmer's wives and farmer's daughters and they make as much selling fowl as buys most of the groceries for the household.[17]

Folklore notes that egg money brought luck when invested in expensive agricultural items such as horses.[18] The importance of poultry as a source of income can also be seen during those times, and in those areas, where disease struck the industry, throwing many families into extreme poverty.[19] In those areas where farmers forbade women to raise poultry (fearing that cattle would not eat grass soiled with poultry droppings, or that poultry would be 'destructive to tillage'), families struggled to make a living on small plots.[20] It was hardly surprising that poultry-rearing was hailed as the one 'healthy and remunerative' employment for rural women, who were chronically short of paid work.[21]

REFORMING THE INDUSTRY

Because of the obvious importance of poultry to the rural community, various institutions had set out to rationalize the poultry

[17] Michael Gargan of Tierworker, speaking to P. J. Gaynor of Bailieborough (county Cavan), IFC MS 1321: 319. See also ibid. 318, discussions by Margaret Argue of Galbolie (county Cavan).

[18] Letter in the Ulster Folk and Transport Museum from Mrs Robert Pailsey (born Lucinda Macartney), near Clones. She lived her childhood at Scotstown and Clabby, then lived near Clogher and Fivemiletown (county Tyrone). She worked as a household help and farm labourer and was 44 years old. The letter was written on 15 Feb. 1957 and is inserted in the box containing the questionnaire on hiring-fairs. For reference to this belief, as well as for other folklore regarding the production and sale of eggs, see the interviews by P. J. Gaynor of Bailieborough (county Cavan) of various women and men, in IFC MS 1321: 310–97.

[19] J. A. Fox, *Reports on the Condition of the Peasantry of the County of Mayo during the Famine Crisis of 1880* (Dublin, 1881), 20–1. For other evidence of financial difficulties in areas where fowl could not be reared, see *The Agricultural Labourer*, iv/II, *Report by Mr W. P. O'Brien*, xxxvii/1: 117; Trinity College, Dublin, MS Library, 'Confidential Report [Baseline Reports], CDB, County of Donegal—Union of Inishowen, Report of Major Gaskell, Inspector, District of North Inishowen', 3; and Miss L. Reynolds, 'Report on the Cushendall Co-operative Poultry Society', 7–25 Sept. 1908, NAI 1088/312/1.

[20] RCCI, *Appendix to 6th Report* (Cd. 3748), HC 1908, xxxix. 31, evidence by John George Guilty of Drumcliffe, a shopkeeper, small farmer, and member of the North Sligo Divisional Executive of the United Irish League.

[21] DATI, *Conference on the Poultry Industry*, 47.

business by the last decade of the nineteenth century. No one had any illusions about the difficulties of the task. The IAOS noted the 'technical' ignorance of women who raised poultry— accusing them ('into whose hands this part of the farming opera- tions naturally fell') of being out of touch with modern farming methods:

The hens roamed at large over the estate or picked up their living along the 'long pasture'. Winter egg production was as unusual as winter dairying. An expert would have found great difficulty in identifying the constituent breeds of the ordinary Irish fowl; its chief characteristic was a rich and unproductive old age. The marketing arrangements were crude and inefficient. Eggs were collected from the fields and hedges as the necessities of the moment, the visits of the egg collector, and the energies of the owner directed. No attempt was made to keep them clean or sizeable, no attempt to ensure a really fresh product. The egg collector was among the most virulent of the middleman class. . . . If there were no egg collector, the shopkeeper at the crossroads played his role with equal distinction. Eventually the eggs found their way to the market; dirty, ungraded and badly packed.[22]

Not only was the industry in a deplorable state, but the very nature of poultry farming was antagonistic to the imposition of structural reforms. One activist in Kilkenny summed up these difficulties:

It is the industry of very many scattered individuals, persons of small means, and of little influence frequently, with no bond uniting them, removed as a rule from the centres of population, often in remote parts away from railway stations, out of touch with the great markets, de- pendent on interested parties for their knowledge of prices, and hence too often the victim of the private buyer and barterer.[23]

It would be difficult to effect change within a group that was politically marginal, geographically scattered, and female, as well as divided regarding the value of any reform. Intervention, how- ever, was seen as imperative. The CDB, the co-operative societies, and the DATI poured money and other resources into attempts to increase the quality and quantity of eggs and poultry produced in cottages throughout the country. In conception, the schemes were ingenious; in execution, the enthusiasm engendered by the

[22] Lionel Smith-Gordon and Lawrence C. Staples, *Rural Reconstruction in Ire- land* (1917), 174–5.
[23] DATI, *Conference on the Poultry Industry*, 129.

schemes seemed to promise success. The following pages provide a detailed analysis of the schemes. Success was unforthcoming. Explanations for this are complex.

The CDB instigated a poultry-improvement scheme in 1892. Attempting to persuade rural women that poultry-rearing was more than just a way of paying the shopkeeper, the Board set about distributing new breeds of cockerels and pullets and providing a market for eggs in remote areas.[24] Providing live poultry, however, soon proved 'both too liberal and too expensive', so they began distributing eggs instead.[25] Soon after 1896, half a million eggs (most of the Black Minorca, Indian Runner, and Plymouth Rock breeds) had been distributed in the setting season, and a female poultry expert had travelled extensively around the congested districts advising women on poultry-rearing.[26]

In 1897 independent societies for poultry were started by the IAOS. Marketing preoccupied these societies. In some areas they collected the eggs, but more commonly they demanded their delivery to the creameries, where clean, fresh eggs would be bought by weight (rather than by the dozen or the score) and then packed in wool-wood into non-returnable cases. Although IAOS publications generally state that capital for the societies was provided by shares of £1 (payable either in eggs or by instalments of cash), local societies, mindful that potential co-operators were poor women, generally sold their shares for 5s. The price of shares was a problem for dairy societies that wanted to include eggs and poultry in their co-operative. Dairy farmers could afford £1 shares, unlike women raising a few chickens. When the Sessagh O'Neill Co-operative Dairy Society (county Donegal) wanted to deal in eggs, R. A. Anderson advised their local secretary that 'the majority of people who have eggs to sell belong to a poorer class than the average farmer and one pound shares might have a detrimental effect on them.'[27] Lists of shareholders show that most women only paid the 2s. 6d. required

[24] RCCI, *Appendix to the 2nd Report* (Cd. 3319), HC 1907, xxxv. 74, evidence by John A. Pomeroy, agent of the Marquis of Conyngham's estate (county Donegal).
[25] William P. Coyne (ed.), *Ireland: Industrial and Agricultural* (Dublin, 1902), 266.
[26] Sir Henry Doran, 'Self-Help Among the Western "Congests": A Review of Thirty Years of Official Labour', in William G. Fitzgerald (ed.), *The Voice of Ireland* (Dublin, 1924), 330–9.
[27] Letter dated 6 Feb. 1903, in Co-operative Societies Collection, NAI 1088/826/1.

for the honour of selling their eggs through the society, and never paid for a complete share.[28] Loans could be received through the society. The management of each society was vested in a committee elected by the shareholders. In turn, the committee would appoint a manager. Profits went to the shareholders. Interest, at a rate not exceeding 5 per cent on paid-up capital, was the first charge on the net profits, after which the residue of the profit was allocated to the members in proportion to their trade with the society. Only a few societies dealt exclusively in eggs. By 1915 there were thirteen active co-operative poultry societies, with a membership of 4,000 and a turnover of £85,000.[29] The creameries set up by the IAOS also collected, graded, packed, and marketed eggs for their members; some even dressed poultry.

The IAOS appointed Henry de Courcy, an experienced poultry farmer and a graduate of the Reading University Extension College, as its 'poultry expert'. It also invited a Danish poultry expert, Viggo Scharz, to come to Ireland to advise on packing and grading methods. Unlike the other organizations involved in improving poultry during this period, the IAOS appointed these instructors reluctantly, declaring that technical instruction was not the proper function of a co-operative society. With the setting up of the DATI, its educational activities ceased.[30]

The most successful co-operative societies were those which sent round collectors—thus performing one of the functions of the traditional itinerant egg-buyers. The North Kilkenny Co-operative Poultry Society, which operated over a radius of 380 square miles in northern Kilkenny and parts of Queens' County, employed two vans that travelled about forty miles daily visiting twenty centres.[31] Thomas Booth of Collumbrone collected eggs for the Augher Co-operative Agricultural and Dairy Society

[28] For an example, see Registry of Friendly Societies, Dublin, 353 R Cork, Newmarket Co-operative Poultry Society, list of shareholders, 1915.

[29] Ministry for Reconstruction, *Summaries of Evidence Taken before the Agricultural Policy Sub-Committee Appointed in August, 1916* (Cd. 9080), HC 1918, v. 93, evidence by R. A. Anderson, secretary of the IAOS. Smith-Gordon and Staples, *Rural Reconstruction*, 174–5, claimed that there were 'eleven active societies' and that the 7 societies for which statistics exist showed a turnover of £85,000.

[30] IAOS, *Annual General Report, 1898* (Dublin, 1899), 53, app. D, comments by R. A. Anderson at the third conference of delegates from the co-operative dairy and agricultural societies.

[31] DATI, *Conference on the Poultry Industry*, 129–30, comments by the Very Revd Canon Barry.

(county Tyrone). He was paid a rate that varied seasonally. Payment also depended on the delivery of clean and fresh eggs.[32] Collectors, however, substantially reduced profit margins. For instance, in 1907 the isolated Cushendall Co-operative Poultry Society (county Antrim) was forced to pay only 6*d*. a dozen for eggs—a price well below that offered by 'egglers'—because of its collecting costs. In September of that year it purchased £76 worth of eggs, out of which it paid the collector 9 per cent.[33] Furthermore, this collector, reproached by the managers of the co-operative society for being 'extremely slow', was very popular. Management complained that members 'seem more attached to the carter than to the society, and last year they were willing to give their eggs to him when he temporarily left the Society's service'.[34]

Management was also a problem. The shortage of experienced managers for these poultry societies forced the IAOS to provide a seven-week crash course in management during the winter of 1902.[35] The expansion of training for the poultry industry had to wait for the intervention of the DATI.

The DATI aimed to provide capital to farmers and farmers' wives, enabling them to build up their poultry business. From 1902 the poultry scheme was presented to the county committees.[36] While the Department took charge of all the general costs (such as the training of teachers, the appointing and payment of inspectresses, giving expert advice, solving marketing problems, and conducting scientific experiments), the county councillors provided overall management of the scheme and appointed committees to deal with day-to-day affairs. With the exception of Antrim, all counties set up egg centres, which hatched high-quality eggs to be sold at low prices to farmers. Only 'authorized' breeds could be raised in egg distribution centres. The

---

[32] Papers of the Augher Co-operative Agricultural and Dairy Society (county Tyrone), PRONI D3057/AB/4.

[33] Report by Richard Noble during his visit to Cushendall, 10–14 Sept. 1907, NAI 1088/312/1. Note that a departmental memorandum sent to (and at the request of) Miss McDonnell and R. Noble on 2 Oct. 1907 regarding the average cost of collection in 5 other poultry societies gave an estimate of 3$^1/2$*d*.

[34] Report by Richard Noble during his visit to Cushendall, 10–14 Sept. 1907, NAI 1088/312/1.

[35] IAOS, *Annual General Report, 1902* (Dublin, 1903), 22: the courses were held in Dunboe (county Londonderry) and Dervock (county Antrim).

[36] In 1901 they experimented with this scheme in one county.

manager of the centre had to supply locals with at least seventy settings of eggs each season at 1s. per dozen, for which the Department paid a premium of £5.[37] In 1906 three-quarters of the managers of egg distribution centres were women.[38] These centres tried to introduce fresh blood into poultry breeds, reduce disease, provide eggs, increase egg quality and size, and give advice to individual rearers. Although the Department singled out the congested districts as needing egg distribution centres more urgently than anywhere else, the schemes covered a much wider area. In 1911–12 almost 400 egg distribution centres were scattered over every county in Ireland.[39] At the turn of the century, 24,000 dozen eggs were being distributed annually. By 1914 this had risen to over 86,000 dozen eggs.[40] In addition, nearly 400 hen and duck centres, 660 pure-bred turkey centres, 383 geese centres, and a school for the training of poultry-fatteners had been established.[41]

In conjunction with the distribution centres, a novel way of instructing people in poultry farming was started in county Tyrone. The 'portable poultry farm' was equipped with two pens of fowl, modern fowl-houses and runs, one pen of ducks, the means for the artificial incubation and rearing of young chickens, and a small fattening-plant. The farm would be set up at an egg distribution centre or on other land for six weeks, classes would be held, and then the farm would be moved on.[42] The county committee at Antrim adopted a quite different scheme. Instead of egg distribution centres or 'portable farms', they established a twenty-two-acre poultry farm at Cullybackey, keeping over 1,000 birds. From this farm, young chickens and eggs

[37] Before 1905, a manager had to provide 60 settings: DATI, *Report of the Departmental Commission of Inquiry into the Provisions of the Agricultural and Technical Instruction (Ireland) Act, 1899* (Cd. 3572), HC 1907, xvii. 149, 'Memorandum on Certain Agricultural Questions Prepared at the Request of the Chairman by the Hon. John Dryden and Referred to in the Report as Mr Dryden's Report'.

[38] In fact, there was a great deal of variety between counties. In Galway and Sligo there were no male managers, whereas in Kerry 65% of the managers were male: RCCI, *Appendix to 4th Report*, xxxvi. 211–12, app. 4, 'Documents Put in by Professor J. R. Campbell'.

[39] DATI, *12th Annual General Report, 1911–1912* (Cd. 6647), HC 1912–13, xii, 48.

[40] DATI, *7th Annual General Report, 1906–1907* (Cd. 4148), HC 1908, xiv. 29, and DATI, *12th Annual General Report*, xii. 48.

[41] DATI, *18th Annual General Report, 1917–18* (Cmd. 106), HC 1919, ix. 32.

[42] RCCI, *Appendix to the 7th Report*, xl. 119, evidence by P. G. Dalliager, secretary of Tyrone County Council.

were distributed (often by post) at moderate prices to people throughout the county. They encouraged women to visit the farm for advice and practical instruction.[43]

Itinerant poultry instructresses, financed by the DATI, lectured on poultry-keeping, visited poultry runs, gave advice, and conducted classes on fattening, killing, plucking, trussing, and preparing fowl for the market, and on grading, testing, and packing eggs. These poultry instructresses 'galloped over the country teaching hens how to lay'.[44] They gave lectures both on a daily basis and (particularly after 1912) in the form of tutorial classes lasting from ten to twenty days. Initially, only four counties appointed instructresses in poultry-keeping, but by 1911 all counties employed them. Rules governing instructresses were strict: they could not work in their home county, they could not be paid more than £2 a week in addition to travelling allowances, and their contracts automatically terminated at marriage.[45] They were bound to avoid discussing the pertinent issue of organization—joint stock or co-operative.[46] In 1911–12, thirty-six instructresses visited 15,905 private poultry runs and held 1,600 classes on poultry-keeping.[47] Most instructresses lectured between October and March and visited farms between April and September. Every farm had to be visited at least once.[48]

What type of woman became an instructress? Miss Mary J. Brody was born in 1894 in Doon, Borris-in-Ossory (Queens' County). According to the 1911 census, she came from a Catholic farming family. Her mother, a widow with four children, was the 'head of the family' in 1911 and, at 56 years of age, called herself a farmer. Mary was the youngest sibling, although a 5-year-old grandchild also lived in the household. Their house was classified as second class, but they had eight outhouses,

[43] DATI, *4th Annual General Report, 1903–1904* (Cd. 2509), HC 1905, xxi. 34.

[44] DATI, *Conference on the Poultry Industry*, 122, comment by R. A. Anderson.

[45] The County Donegal Committee of Agriculture and Technical Instruction tried to force the Department to change the residential rule. Eventually, the economic sanctions applied by the Department forced the committee to end the deadlock while registering a strong protest against the Department's 'despotism'. See 'Department of Agriculture and Donegal: The "No Natives Need Apply" Order', *Frontier Sentinel*, 22 Oct. 1904: 7, and DATI, *Conference on the Poultry Industry*, 201, 'Appendix: Scheme No. 11: Instruction in Poultry-Keeping, 1910–1911'. [46] *Leader*, 7 Mar. 1908: 41.

[47] DATI, *12th Annual General Report*, xxii. 48.

[48] RCCI, *Appendix to the 7th Report*, xl. 119, comment by P. G. Dalliager.

including a stable, a cow-house, a calf-house, a dairy, a piggery, a boiling-room, a turf-shed, and a fowl-house. Mary Brody trained at the Munster Institute for eighteen months, then, at the age of 22, she was employed by the Department. She was well paid, receiving £100 a year, a sum which included the cost of maintenance, required one month's notice to quit, and was entitled to an annual vacation of twenty-four weekdays.[49] With promotion, her annual salary might have increased to just over £122, but promotion was unlikely if she did not qualify to teach dairying as well as poultry-rearing.[50]

The demand for itinerant instructresses like Mary Brody required the establishment or extension of colleges to train women in farm work. The organizers rapidly discovered the shortage of qualified Irish teachers in poultry-keeping. When they first advertised for teachers, they received 300 applications. However, only three applicants had any training or experience, and only one passed the qualifying examination.[51] At first, it seemed as though men would receive priority in such advanced training. When the act of 1899 transferred responsibility of the Albert Agricultural College from the Commissioners of National Education to the DATI, the agricultural courses for women were abandoned.[52] However, with financial help from the DATI, communities of nuns and private individuals set up small schools to train women in poultry-keeping, dairying, and domestic work. The Department awarded grants to set up the schools, paid the teachers' salaries, and contributed towards the costs of pupils.[53]

The Munster Institute classes in poultry-keeping, dairying, and rural domestic economy for women continued. Each pupil had to take a preliminary course in all three subjects. After six months, a limited number of girls were allowed to specialize. Pupils wanting to become poultry instructresses would complete the

[49] Record of Service of itinerant poultry teacher, Miss Mary J. Brophy, NAI, DATI Papers, AG1 A1400/16, and 1911 manuscript census returns for Queens' 19/9, no. 5, NAI.

[50] NAI, DATI Papers, AG1 A37366.

[51] Miss L. Murphy, 'Women's Sphere in the Poultry Industry', *DATI Journal*, 19 (May 1919), 294–5.

[52] See DATI, *Report of the Committee of Inquiry into the Agricultural and Technical Instruction Act, 1899*, xvii. 22.

[53] Daniel Hoctor, *The Department's Story: A History of the Department of Agriculture* (Dublin, 1971), 62.

full course in eighteen to twenty-four months. Until 1905, when this scheme of training women in advanced poultry-keeping became operative, a pass certificate in poultry-keeping from the Reading College Poultry School at Theale was accepted as a qualifying certificate. However, the short course held at Theale was too costly for the average female student from Ireland, and the training that women received there was too theoretical for hopeful Irish instructresses. It was not surprising that there was strenuous competition for places at the Munster Institute. Applicants often had to wait over a year between the acceptance of their application and a vacancy at the college.[54] In 1908 the Ulster Dairy School at Loughry (county Tyrone) accepted its first pupils. This was similar to the Munster Institute, teaching poultry-keeping, dairying, cooking, laundry work, sewing and cottage gardening to farm women. Between 1905 and 1913, however, the Munster Institute was the only training-centre in Ireland for instructresses in poultry-keeping and dairying.[55]

Women who had been trained as instructresses could be employed by the county committees as instructresses in poultry-keeping. A few obtained positions as poultry-keepers on model farms or at egg distribution centres. Some were employed in private houses, and some as servants. Others emigrated.[56] Repeatedly, commentators on the agricultural schemes expressed the fear that the education that the women received would simply provide them with the skills—and the confidence—to emigrate, denying Irish agriculture of their help.

As well as the educational schemes mentioned above, the DATI turned its attention to the marketing aspects of the poultry industry. Numerous conferences were held and experiments conducted in an attempt to improve access to egg markets, particularly in Britain. As a part of this campaign, displays of Irish poultry products appeared at nearly every grocery and agricultural exhibition in both Ireland and Britain.

---

[54] DATI, *7th Annual General Report*, xiv. 21–2.

[55] After 1913, the Ulster Dairy School began to provide similar training for women.

[56] RCCI, *Appendix to 4th Report*, xxxvi. 53, 'Documents Put in by Professor J. R. Campbell in Connection with the Evidence Given by him before the Commission'.

WOMEN AND MEN

Despite comprehensive planning and management, the schemes proved problematical. From the start, the organizers worried about the dominance of women, both on their poultry training-courses and in the poultry farming community at large. All three societies believed that none of the schemes would ultimately succeed unless *men* were induced to make poultry-rearing the 'serious business of their lives'. Without men, 'maximum expansion of the industry cannot be secured'.[57] Part of the ambivalence towards female poultry-keepers resulted from simple misunderstandings about the agricultural practices of female poultry farmers. Relations between poultry societies and the women raising poultry were often tense.

The fact that this industry is largely in the hands of the women has endowed it with particular problems of its own. They have considered it their perquisite and resented the introduction of the societies, whose members are usually men, thus putting an end to a source of 'pin' money. Thus far, experience would indicate that Irishwomen are far less co-operative than Irishmen. The sex, largely on account of the nature of its life hitherto, has generally shown a lack of associative qualities. Trade-unionism makes slow progress among them, for the same reasons which make them poor co-operators. The allurement of the glittering pan of the pedlar or of the halfpenny more per dozen he willingly offers for a time in order to put an end to the co-operative society is often too much. The bargain is made with the result that the society starves and disappears.[58]

The reformers felt that improvement of the poultry industry depended on replacing female poultry-keepers with male poultry-keepers. This would be difficult. Generally, male farmers disliked poultry—men were more likely to be caught 'casting missiles with evil intent at some particularly offending hen' than pandering to each individual hen's needs.[59] The few men who were

[57] DIC, *Commission of Inquiry on Post-Emergency Agricultural Policy, Second Interim Report: Poultry Productions* (Dublin, 1951), 7.

[58] Smith-Gordon and Staples, *Rural Reconstruction*, 174–8. See the comment by R. A. Anderson in DATI, *Conference on the Poultry Industry*, 125. This tension contributed to the general failure of the poultry societies to attract women: see the minutes of UI and The Irish Countrywoman's Association, 14 Jan. 1914: 85.

[59] DATI, *Conference on the Poultry Industry*, 56, paper by Percy A. Francis, superintending poultry instructor for the Department.

interested in poultry-rearing were more concerned with large-scale table-poultry farming than with eggs.[60] However, the Department still hoped that one day the poultry industry in Ireland would be raised 'to the worthy position it occupies in so many other countries where farmers and their sons—and not only wives and daughters—find in poultry-keeping an interesting and profitable occupation'.[61]

Attempts were made to encourage men to take poultry more seriously. Agricultural journals stressed the success of male poultry farmers. One man wrote that 'he no longer looks on it [poultry farming] as a woman's job', but simply as 'one of the biggest jobs ever tackled'.[62] Mothers were encouraged to instruct their young sons in poultry-rearing.[63] The IAOS offered special courses for men to train as managers of poultry societies.[64] From 1907 the DATI made arrangements with certain co-operative poultry societies to pay travel expenses, training fees, and subsistence costs to young men who were training as managers of poultry societies.[65] Even this scheme failed to entice young men into the industry. J. A. Tuckey of the Munster Institute reasoned that men had to be introduced at the level of instructors rather than of managers:

If some of the Instructors in Ireland were male Instructors—that is, if we got a few men to take up the work instead of leaving it entirely to the ladies, we might do something to remove the prejudice and the ignorance which exists amongst farmers on this subject. It is a very common thing for men to think that poultry are altogether beneath their dignity; that they do well enough for women, but that a man was only wasting his time in dealing with such a small matter. I think possibly the appointment of a few men as Instructors might counteract that feeling, and

---

[60] Miss L. Murphy, 'Women's Sphere in the Poultry Industry', 293. The dominance of men in specialized and large-scale poultry farming can be seen in the 1926 census for the Republic of Ireland, which provides a category for people involved in the 'professional' egg and poultry industry. Women constituted only 17% of this category in 1926 (10% in 1936), and were much less likely to be 'employed on own account' (27% of all men in the poultry industry were 'employed on own account', compared with 16% of women in 1926).

[61] DATI, *4th Annual General Report*, xxi. 33.

[62] *Ark*, 6/72 (Sept. 1915), 9.   [63] Ibid. 7/69 (June 1915), 9.

[64] 'The Training of Managers for Poultry Societies', *IH*, 23 Aug. 1902: 660.

[65] DATI, *8th Annual General Report, 1907–1908* (Cd. 4430), HC 1908, xxii. 63. See also Michael Kirwan, *Irish Cottage Industries: How Best to Develop Them* (Cork, 1909), 9–10 (University College of Cork Archives, MP 418).

might impress on farmers that the subject was well worthy of the consideration of men.[66]

But such attempts also failed, despite offering male instructors over £100 per annum.[67] Representatives of the DATI admitted that the few male instructors whom they had managed to recruit had been 'a ghastly failure'.[68] In 1901 the Department lamented: 'Of the 23 Instructors at work last year [1901], 20 were women and 3 young men. Notwithstanding the liberal salaries offered, it has been found impossible to induce young men to take up the development of poultry-keeping with enthusiasm.'[69] The Department was lucky to have enticed even three men into the business in 1901—by 1908 there were none.[70]

These attempts to move men into the poultry business should not be exaggerated. The usual poultry farmers—women—had to be encouraged meanwhile. Organizations such as the IAOS discovered the folly of ignoring the women in its poultry societies. It admitted that, at the start of the co-operative attempt to reform poultry-raising, it had been 'stupid enough to ignore the women and to attempt to secure an egg supply to a society composed of "mere men"'. It rapidly discovered that this was a mistake, noticing that the huckster had thrived by disregarding the men and making 'his terms with the women'.[71] Irish women had extensive experience in poultry-rearing; men did not. Not surprisingly, the women on the poultry committees were credited with keeping the societies afloat.[72]

The IAOS was more willing than other organizations publicly to acknowledge the importance of women in poultry reorganization. The *Irish Homestead* advised 'women who have to earn their own livelihood':

Perhaps one of the most interesting of all country pursuits is that of poultry keeping. There seems to be a fascination about it to those who

---

[66] DATI, *Conference on the Poultry Industry*, 62, comment by J. A. Tucker of the Munster Institute.   [67] Ibid. 11.

[68] Ibid. 71, comment by Canon Young of Monaghan County Council of Agriculture.

[69] DIC, *Commission of Inquiry on Post-Emergency Agricultural Policy: Poultry Productions*, 7.   [70] DATI, *Conference on the Poultry Industry*, 11.

[71] Ibid. 125, comment by R. A. Anderson.

[72] Ibid. 11–12, comment by R. H. Prior-Wandesforde, chairman of the North Kilkenny Co-operative Poultry Society.

take it up. It is easy work as well as interesting. And that it is profitable hardly needs to be proved. . . . Beyond a doubt there is money in poultry for the woman or girl who undertakes to keep them with industry and care. In poultry rearing you have a profession.[73]

It must be pointed out, however, that the IAOS had particularly strong reasons for encouraging female poultry farmers. It was being attacked for the way in which its creameries pushed women and girls out of employment, and defended itself against such attacks by declaring that its encouragement of the poultry industry provided the female members of the farming community with an alternative, and more remunerative, occupation. At a meeting of tenant farmers to consider establishing a co-operative dairy in Tralee, R. A. Anderson (secretary of the IAOS), argued: 'They might be told that their wives and daughters would become demoralised from having nothing to do if creameries were started, but there was nothing to prevent them creating a tremendous trade in eggs and fowl, at which their wives and daughters could be much more profitably employed.'[74]

The co-operators' unease with promoting women as poultry-keepers is clear. On the one hand, they aggressively asserted that poultry-keeping was a serious agricultural industry, requiring the active labour and management of *men*. On the other, they promoted poultry farming as an integral part of *housework* as opposed to farm work. Their propaganda argued that girls must be taught 'how to feed poultry and make shirts'.[75] Yet they could also say:

We have sometimes heard it said that the education of our girls at our primary and intermediary schools is on mistaken lines, that they are . . . afflicting themselves with the hardships of piano-playing when they ought to be learning how to rear poultry. We have the greatest respect for the arts of the dairy and the poultry yard . . . but we cannot help expressing our sympathy with the art needlework and the piano in moderation.[76]

In practice, the individual co-operative societies differed widely in the extent to which they accepted female poultry-keepers as

[73] *IH*, 12 Oct. 1895: 515–16.   [74] 'Among the Societies', ibid. 9 Mar. 1895: 6.
[75] 'Women's Work in Irish Homes', ibid. 24 Aug. 1895: 405.
[76] 'The Fireside', ibid. 9 Mar. 1895: 13.

active members of the society. No women were present at a meeting of the Burriscarra (county Mayo) Agricultural Society, although women were important organizers in the society.[77] The committees of the co-operative poultry societies of Shanagolden and Foyne (county Limerick), Sessiagh O'Neill (Donegal), Rath-keale (Limerick), Borris (Carlow), Athlone (Westmeath), and north Kilkenny were composed only of men. The committees of the Cushendall Co-operative Poultry Society, the Forth Co-operative Poultry Society, the Dervoy and District Co-operative Poultry Society, and the Erne Co-operative Poultry Federation—including one person who signed the rules with his mark—were also men.[78] The Kinvara and Tynagh societies were largely composed of women. In north Carlow one of the three officers was a female. In 1914 the Clonbrock and Castlegar Co-operative Poultry Society could boast that, although the manager, the treasurer, and the secretary were male, three out of the remaining four officers were female.[79] In 1910 Miss Barbara MacDonnell of Monavert was secretary of the Cushendall Co-operative Poultry Society.[80] The committee of the Irish Poultry Keepers' Co-operative Society, based in Templeogue (county Dublin), was evenly divided between men and women.[81]

A similar situation is seen if we examine the proportion of female shareholders (see Table 6.1). The percentage of female shareholders varies widely. The explanation for the low percentage of women in the Athlone society is that it was primarily a collecting body. Five male collectors moved through the country, buying eggs from women who were not members. The society was a large one (six other societies were affiliated), but with a very small individual membership. In the three societies for which we have data for two years (Newmarket, Borris, and Athlone), the proportion of female members can be seen to be declining.

Employment in the societies also favoured men, but not exclusively. In addition to a full-time male secretary, the Athlone

[77] Ibid. 23 Apr. 1898: 351, and 30 July 1898: 646.
[78] See their 'Rules', NAI 1088/428/1–3, 1088/323/3, 1088/406/1, and 1088/312/2.
[79] Registry of Friendly Societies, Dublin, file nos. 883, 471, 659, 705, 1187, 808, 311, and 795.
[80] Co-operative Societies Collection, NAI 1088/312/1–2.
[81] *Rules of the Irish Poultry Keepers' Co-operative Society, Limited* (Dublin, c.1901), 33.

Table 6.1. Female shareholders in co-operative poultry societies, 1915–1919

Co-operative poultry society	County	Year	No. of members	% of women
Newmarket	Cork	1915	41	73.2
Newmarket	Cork	1918	42	69.0
Clonbrock, Castlegar	Galway	1916	348	62.6
Rathkeale	Limerick	1928	276	33.7
Borris	Carlow	1916	380	33.1
Borris	Carlow	1919	379	19.8
Athlone	Westmeath	1916	29	6.7
Athlone	Westmeath	1919	29	3.4

Source: Lists of shareholders held in the Registry of Friendly Societies, Dublin. All lists that contained both first name and surname were used.

Co-operative Poultry and Farm Produce Society would employ two or three men to work in its store in the spring. From July until shortly after Christmas it employed one storeman. Throughout the year, five male collectors moved around the county. Women were only employed for one week at Christmas to pluck turkeys. Ten to twenty women would be hired to do this. Similarly, the Forth Co-operative Poultry Society only employed women to pluck fowl for 1*d.* a bird.[82] The societies at Newmarket, Shanagolden and Foyne, and Sessiagh O'Neill employed between two and four men, and no women. The Rathkeale society employed two men and two women in 1913, but within four years it had five men and no women on its staff. Overall, the number and proportion of women employed by these societies declined rapidly between the years 1913–19. But, whatever the ambivalence as to women's role as managers, committee members, or employees, one thing was clear: they could not be excluded at a grass-roots level.

---

[82] Forth Co-operative Poultry Society, report by the manager of the fattening-station at Tagoat, 31 Jan. 1907, NAI 1088/428/1–3. Feathers could be a remunerative field for poultry societies.

EFFECT OF THE SCHEMES

Men failed to be enticed by poultry-rearing, so the schemes came to depend on the organizational talents of poultry reformers and farm women. The schemes were harshly criticized. The DATI was accused of supplying fowl only to affluent farmers, and thus effecting no general improvement of stock.[83] Critics claimed that poor cottagers rarely benefited. In Cork in 1909, only four out of the sixty egg distribution centres were held by cottagers. Cottagers could not even afford to buy settings of eggs from the centres.[84] The chief agriculturalist employed by the CDB, Thomas Porter, told the Royal Commission on Congestion that the schemes were unsuccessful in the long term, and 'in not more than five per cent of the poultry in the congested districts is there now any trace of the work of the Board in the shape of an improvement'.[85]

Admittedly, their task was difficult. Local pressure meant that county committees were constrained when deciding what breed of fowl to encourage in their centres.[86] In some areas, women simply refused to go along with schemes claiming to improve their efficiency.[87] In other areas, drunken men expressed their hostility during lectures by a poultry instructress.[88] R. A. Anderson spoke about the continued existence of 'many localities where the hen of other days, untainted by any cross or foreign breeds, may still be found living the simple life, and where the housewife has refused to listen to the voice of the instructress or organizer'.[89] The new breeds were 'aristocratic birds accustomed to more luxurious methods of living'.[90] Although the new breeds of fowl laid bigger eggs, the increased profits did not cover the

---

[83] RCCI, *Appendix to 7th Report*, xl, 84–5, evidence by Revd Thomas McCann of Kildress (county Tyrone).   [84] Kirwan, *Irish Cottage Industries*, 9–10.

[85] RCCI, *Appendix to 3rd Report* (Cd. 3414), HC 1907, xxxv. 38, evidence by Thomas Porter, chief agriculturalist employed by the CDB.

[86] 'Old Woman', 'What Poultry Breeds Should be Encouraged', *IH*, 14 Feb. 1914: 126.

[87] 'Spectator', 'Things in General', ibid. 12 Nov. 1904: 956; 'Spectator', 'Things in General', ibid. 19 Nov. 1904: 977; and Edna L. Walter, *The Fascination of Ireland* (1913), 29–30.

[88] 'Poultry Keeping in Longford', *IH*, 21 Mar. 1908: 226, at lectures in Longford by Miss Hogan.

[89] DATI, *Conference on the Poultry Industry*, 122.

[90] 'Poultry Keeping in Congested Districts', *IH*, 17 Nov. 1906: 933.

costs of feeding these larger fowl. Instead of using the new fowl for breeding purposes, the women preferred to sell the improved breeds and earn a little extra money to spend on household necessities.[91]

Co-operative attempts to improve poultry-rearing faced special organizational resistance. Women disliked sending their eggs to the creameries, even if they were paid more for them. When they sold eggs to the creameries, the money was added to the milk account and was paid in a lump sum to the husband, father, or brother when he collected the family's monthly account; if the woman sold the eggs at a market or to the higgler, she was able to control the money herself.[92] No one doubted that egg money was more profitably spent when controlled by farm women rather than by farm men.[93] Since payment by the creameries was made in a monthly lump sum, the advantages of a small but regular flow of money into the household should not be minimized.

Despite the rhetoric of co-operation, the abrupt introduction of some co-operative societies helps to explain their inefficacy. A society was doomed if it failed to win the support of the priest or of local politicians.[94] Within a few weeks, the manager sent to work for the Cushendall Co-operative Poultry Society (county Antrim) had made himself so politically unpopular that he had to be placed under police protection. At the earliest opportunity, he abandoned the open shop and jumped on the mail cart bound for Belfast.[95] The women selling the eggs were much more attached to the sociable carter, a member of their community, than they were to the society.[96] The person who started the Cushendall Co-operative Poultry Society, Barbara M. McDonnell, wrote to R. A. Anderson on 28 August 1908, informing him that the society was collapsing and that it might be closed: 'I fear it was a mistake to try co-operation among people so ignorant and behind

---

[91] RCCI, *Appendix to 3rd Report*, xxxv. 38, evidence by Thomas Porter.

[92] DATI, *Report of the Departmental Committee on Food Production* (Cd. 8158), HC 1914–16, v. 8, evidence by Sydney Smith, the Department's marketing representative in Great Britain.

[93] 'Poultry', *Ark*, 6/71 (Aug. 1915), 7. See also ibid. 3/4 (Mar. 1913), 7, and 3/51 (Dec. 1913), 13.

[94] See NAI 1088/312/1–2, for the failure of the Cushendall Co-Operative Poultry Society to win the support of these powerful groups in 1910.

[95] Letter from Miss B. MacDonnell to Mr Adams, 15 Feb. 1908, NAI 1088/312/1.

[96] Letter from Miss B. McDonnell to R. A. Anderson, 28 Aug. 1908, ibid.

the rest of the world as ours here are—they are not ready for it and *will* not understand that it is not a joint stock company or private enterprise—but their own.' Typically, Horace Plunkett lacked empathy with his audience. Plunkett visited the Cushendall Co-operative Poultry Society on 25 March 1908, and spoke to the people in this insular mountain community suffering the effects of a poor harvest and a fowl epidemic about international trade competition.[97]

Societies frequently faced powerful trade opposition within the community. Higglers 'spare nothing to tempt the people to leave the society'.[98] Shopkeepers applied sanctions by refusing to buy butter or to give credit to women who traded with co-operatives.[99] Where women resisted poultry schemes, a direct offensive aimed at pressuring them to sell their eggs to the co-operative was launched. For instance, in districts where 'egglers' or 'gombeeners' were a particularly powerful threat to the societies, the co-operative poultry societies paid an inflated price for the eggs in order to compete with the equally inflated prices offered by the local dealers.[100] Attempting to break the opposition of the shopkeepers in 1907, the Cushendall Co-operative Poultry Society paid shopkeepers who handed eggs to the collector $1/2d.$ for each pound of eggs. This raised the costs of egg collection unrealistically as henwives, shopkeepers, collectors, packers, and members all took large shares of the takings.[101] Propaganda included placards with the crude messages, 'Every egg sold to the higgler is an egg nearer the workhouse', and 'Every egg you sell to the higgler you will eat six months later in the emigrant ship.'[102]

Crucially, the organizers had misjudged the significance of the higgler. The financial exploitation of women by some village egg-collectors or grocers could be immense:

The current market price of the day, as registered in the daily papers, was 10d. and 11d. per dozen; the price fixed by the egg collector was 6d. per dozen. The 6d. was not, however, given in coin; its value in tea and sugar was delivered instead. Two ounces of tea and one pound of sugar

[97] Report by Mr J. C. Adams, 25 Mar. 1908, ibid.
[98] Miss L. Reynolds, 'Report on the Cushendall Co-operative Poultry Society'.
[99] Ibid.   [100] National Council, *Irish Year-Book, 1908* (Dublin, 1908), 206.
[101] Report by Richard Noble, 1–2 Aug. 1907, NAI 1088/312/1.
[102] 'Battle for Irish Eggs', *IH*, 7 Apr. 1906: 262.

was the equivalent substitutes for the 6*d*. These commodities, valued at current retail prices, were worth about 2³/₄*d*. or at the most 3*d*. So that, for 10*d*. or 11*d*. worth of eggs, the dealer gave 3*d*. worth of commodities, and on these had, moreover, the usual retailers' profits.[103]

But other egg-collectors did not make as much profit. The agricultural inspector for the DATI, Thomas A. Porter, claimed that the shopkeepers who took eggs did not make a 'great profit' on the transaction, but did it to retain customers.[104] What the reformers recognized only dimly was the important role that these higglers played in the lives of houseworkers:

The housewife, however, appreciates the saving of time and trouble afforded either by selling to the higgler who comes to her door, and not only purchases her eggs, but supplies the necessary groceries, or by selling to the neighbouring shopkeeper, from whom she obtains household supplies. When these systems prevail she will usually accept a lower price than is obtainable in the wholesale markets. Against the small loss thus incurred there is usually a very considerable saving of time, and, in addition, the avoidance of the risk of breaking or chipping eggs when taking them to market. It would therefore appear that both the higgler and the shopkeeper who takes eggs are useful persons to the poultry-keeper in those districts in which there is no other organised system of egg collection.[105]

The houseworker who sold or exchanged her eggs with the local shopkeeper or higgler was acknowledging the economic value of her time and energies within the home.

Finally, the attitude of IAOS officials and outside managers betrayed their alienation from the very people with whom they were trying to co-operate. Miss L. Reynolds, visiting the Cushendall Co-operative Poultry Society between 7 and 25 September 1908, noted that higglers retained their hold over their customers by periodically offering them ¹/₂*d*. to 1*d*. more than the society. She concluded that uneducated women were easily tempted:

[103] T. A. Finlay, 'The Economics of Carna', *New Ireland Review* (Apr. 1898), 72.

[104] DATI, *Conference on the Poultry Industry*, 167. See also 'Cross Roads', 'One Expert [Higgler] on Another', *IH*, 16 Sept. 1905: 696.

[105] DATI, *Conference on the Poultry Industry*, 168. See also the discussion on egglers in IFC MS 1321: 400–2, interviews by P. J. Gaynor of Bailieborough (county Cavan) of various people from Bailieborough, Killan, Shercock, Kingscourt, Muff, Moybolgue, Mullagh, Killinkere, Coss, Knockbrid Virginia, Ballyjamesduff, Mount Nugent, and Kilnaleck in county Cavan, and Tierworker, Kilmainhamwood, and Moynalty in county Meath, recorded in Jan. 1953. The egglers were spoken of favourably, and their business was described as being efficient.

They do not see how this action tends to their own eventual loss. They are in intelligence like children and must be treated accordingly. If a child at school does not learn the first or second year, the effort to teach on the part of the school master is not given up. He goes on teaching and eventually the lesson is learnt. We must go on teaching and our lesson—co-operation—will be learnt.[106]

Even if the henwife agreed to deposit her eggs at the poultry society or creamery, other difficulties became apparent. Marketing problems were experienced at every level:

We have seen a good many complaints about rotten eggs from our societies lately. This is too bad. Farmers' wives, we are informed by the secretary of a poultry society, have been keeping over their eggs on account of the low prices, hoping with the optimism which curiously springs up about the wrong way of doing things in Ireland, that prices would rise, and that buyers were fools in England. . . . Women are pro-verbially more penny wise and pound foolish than men. Whether this is true or not we won't say, but it lies with them to disprove it by not keeping back their eggs and palming them off later on as fresh when prices rise.[107]

These types of marketing problems were exactly the same as those expressed by the earlier export marketers of eggs: the shippers. Mr. Caulfield, the principal speaker at a conference of western shippers in Claremorris (county Mayo) in November 1897, de-clared that the blame for the English complaints lay with the 'mischief' that was wrought by county shopkeepers and farmers' wives who were incapable of providing them with fresh eggs.[108] As the DATI noted in response to threats by the Liverpool and Glasgow egg merchants that they would cease to buy Irish eggs if they were not fresh, clean, and properly packed, improvements in quality were unlikely, since no guarantee of higher prices for fresh, clean eggs could be given to the henwives.[109]

Amidst an outpouring of criticism, the occasional person (usu-ally an official of one of the reforming organizations) was willing to praise the schemes:

The result of our poultry instructress's work is apparent all over the country. No one can fail to notice the remarkable improvement that has

---

[106] Miss L. Reynolds, 'Report on the Cushendall Co-operative Poultry Society'.
[107] 'Elections not Near—Poultry Societies, Notice!', *IH*, 14 Oct. 1905: 751–2.
[108] 'Notes of the Week', ibid. 20 Nov. 1897, 776.
[109] Coyne (ed.), *Ireland: Industrial and Agricultural*, 226–7.

taken place in the quality of the various fowls reared by the farmers and the cottiers both for egg laying and table purposes. The puny nondescript breeds that prevailed a few years since have now given place generally to some of the very best breeds that the world can produce. The poultry exhibits at Nenagh and Thurles Shows surpassed anything of the kind held in former years in any provincial town, both for number and quality.[110]

The increased price of eggs was noted. For example, a poultry society was established in county Tyrone in March 1902. In 1900 the average price of eggs per dozen in one market town in Tyrone was 9.47*d*. By 1905 this had increased from 12.2*d*. The average price of a pair of dead poultry had increased from 2*s*. 6*d*. to 3*s*. Over Ireland as a whole, the price of ten dozen eggs had risen from 7*s*. 3*d*. in 1881 to 9*s*. by 1911.[111] However, it would be foolish to ascribe these increases in prices to the reforms. The profits from rearing poultry had been climbing well before the instigation of the poultry schemes. Forty years before such schemes had even been thought about, profits from poultry products had escalated with the doubling of the price of eggs and the declining price of grain such as Indian corn and wheat.[112] The latter change may have been extremely important, since the profit margins on poultry production were largely determined by the price of foodstuffs.[113] The rise in the price of eggs in the early years of the new century was a world-wide phenomenon.[114] Noticeably, however, the returns of the poultry societies do not show outstanding profits. Adding together the profits and losses of the twenty-six poultry societies of the IAOS in 1901, the profit came to over £174 and the loss to over £78. Most poultry societies made a loss that year.[115] Detailed examination of the accounts of seven poultry societies confirms this impression. Poultry societies expanded only after 1917. Before this date they stagnated, or

[110] DATI, *Minutes of Evidence Taken before the Departmental Committee of Inquiry* (Cd. 3574), HC 1907, xviii. 341, evidence by Revd B. Crowe, chairman of the North Tipperary Committee of Agriculture.
[111] Ibid. 427 (493), evidence by Percy G. Dalliager.
[112] Stuart, *Prices of Farm Products*, 15–16.
[113] DIC, *Commission of Inquiry on Post-Emergency Agricultural Policy: Poultry Productions*, 4.
[114] DATI, *Conference on the Poultry Industry*, 146–7, comment by Mr W. T. Parker of Bristol.
[115] 'Returns of Home Industries for 1901', *IH*, 17 Jan. 1903: 50–1.

they grew only very slowly in response to increased member-ship. If they attempted to implement their wider goal of improv-ing the technology of poultry farming (as opposed to simply working as a marketing organization) their success was limited. Only one of the societies examined sold 'agricultural require-ments'. This part of their operations was small and fluctuated with the success of egg production.

The quantity and value of the eggs imported into Ireland did not decrease during this period, and both began to increase after 1915. For instance, in 1904 McLean and Company imported Russian, Canadian, and Danish eggs into Belfast through Robert Telford of Glasgow.[116] The importation of dead poultry peaked in 1908 and did not really decline until the beginning of the war. Although egg and poultry exports from Ireland increased slowly after 1905, there was no real acceleration until after 1917.[117] From 1905, a higher proportion of all poultry imported into Great Britain came from Ireland, but the expansion in egg imports into Great Britain did not occur until the crisis of 1914.

A series of statistics quoted by Raymond Crotty helps to per-petuate the view that the volume and quality of egg production increased from 1891.[118] Crotty noted that the number of poultry rose from 15.3 million in 1891 to 24.3 million in 1907. However, this increase was caused by a change in the method of collecting the statistics. Making allowance for the statistical revision of 1906–7 reveals no unexpected acceleration in the number of poultry.[119] Claims that the schemes were responsible for producing heavier eggs may be questioned once we notice that the weight of eggs had been increasing steadily before the schemes started. [120] The

---

[116] Papers of McClean and Co., PRONI D1326/13/30.

[117] 1905 is the earliest date for which export statistics are available.

[118] DATI, *Report of the Committee of Inquiry into the Agricultural and Technical Instruction Act, 1899*, xvii. 51–2, for examples of such praise from all over the country. See also RCCI, *Appendix to the 7th Report*, xl. 19, evidence by W. R. Bell, clerk of Newry Union, secretary of Newry Rural District Council 1 and 2, mem-ber of the County Armagh County Committee, and honorary secretary of the Newry Agricultural Society.

[119] Raymond D. Crotty, *Irish Agricultural Production* (Cork, 1966), 61. DATI, *Agricultural Statistics of Ireland with Detailed Report, 1909* (Cd. 5382), HC 1910, cviii. 17, stressed that the increase in poultry numbers between 1906 and 1907 was due to a more complete record being made of young birds.

[120] 'Poultry Show', *Kings' County Chronicle*, 3 Jan. 1895: 3, gives the average annual weights of eggs at the poultry show held in Mullingar (county Westmeath).

average fowl continued to lay few eggs. Even as late as the 1950s, the average for the whole country was less than 110 eggs for each bird each year.[121] In the congested districts of Mayo, Galway, Roscommon and Sligo, nondescript old fowl were laying as many eggs as this in 1892.[122] Even the poultry competing for prizes from the DATI failed to show consistent production increases each year.[123] Production was so low that the alleged advertisement, 'Poultry for Sale—5 hens and a cock, all laying, apply', was amusing rather than libellous.[124] Furthermore, the societies failed to alter seasonal differences in poultry production. Eggs continued to be scarce between September and June, when prices were high, while flooding the market between February and August.[125]

Poultry organizations claimed that their efforts had led to substantial improvements in marketing arrangements. At the 1911 conference on the poultry industry in the United Kingdom, held in Dublin in May, Ireland was shown to hold first place among countries supplying eggs and poultry to Great Britain. The value of Ireland's exports of eggs and poultry to Great Britain in 1910 and 1911 amounted to £4 million a year (an increase of almost £1 million over 1904).[126] Even this triumph is undermined, however, when we hear the claim of shippers and other local traders that the poor marketing facilities of earlier years had been exaggerated by the new organizers. For example, the shipper Geo.

[121] DIC, *Commission of Inquiry on Post-Emergency Agricultural Policy: Poultry Productions*, 4.

[122] Trinity College, Dublin, MS Library, 'CDB Base-Line Reports, Confidential, General Report by Mr [Henry] Doran on the Counties of Mayo, Galway, Roscommon, and Sligo', app. A, 'Appendix to the General Report of Mr Doran, Dated 30 April 1892', 9.

[123] The average egg production of 13 breeds of pullets competing for the prizes is contained in annual reports in the *DATI* Journal (from 1908).

[124] 'Notes of the Week', *IH*, 18 Sept. 1897: 567.

[125] DIC, *Commission of Inquiry on Post-Emergency Agricultural Policy: Poultry Productions*, 5. See also John Busteed, *Agricultural Bulletin No. 2: A Statistical Analysis of Irish Egg Production, Prices and Trade* (Cork, 1926), 3; Percy A. Francis, superintending poultry instructor for the Department, in DATI, *Conference on the Poultry Industry*, 60; and 'R. N.', 'The Expensiveness of the Easier Way', *IH*, 24 Feb. 1906: 146.

[126] The value of poultry supplied by Ireland to Great Britain in those years exceeded that of all other countries in Europe combined: DATI, *11th Annual General Report, 1910–1911* (Cd. 6107), HC 1912–13, xii. 79. For the 1904 data, see RCCI, *Appendix to 4th Report*, xxxvi. 186, app. 4, 'Documents Put in by Professor J. R. Campbell'.

Steedman of Coleraine gave his reaction to the criticisms levelled at him when the poultry movements began:

It was rather amusing, to say the least of, to hear the opinions of the farmers on the subject and the criticism the shippers had to listen to; in fact, it appeared as though the doom of the shipper was an accomplished fact, and the man who had been buying eggs at 2*d*. and 3*d*. per dozen too cheaply for years back were to be wiped out, and the farmers were to do the business themselves, and receive this extra 2*d*. and 3*d*. per dozen right away. They have now had a trial of the new system, but the extra payment, as far as some districts are concerned, is still a thing of the future, for the co-operative movement, in places, is simply a diversion of the shipping from the original buyers to a new class without a corresponding increase to the producer, except in those cases where the eggs are over 16 lbs. to the hhd., and even then the shippers paid higher prices to the suppliers of large eggs long before the movement was contemplated.[127]

Profits made through improved marketing benefited middlemen and the larger poultry farmers rather than the farm woman: 'Someone was gaining, but the producer was not gaining.'[128] Complaints from England about poor packaging resulting in breakages, and stale eggs continued to flow into the Department.[129] In the 1920s eggs were still more likely to be sold through higglers or to be exchanged in the country shops than to go through any of the more formal marketing networks.[130]

By attempting to change and control the poultry work of farm women, the various schemes tended to transfer managerial power to male members of the family or to male organizers in poultry societies. Certain improvements did help henwives. For example, the risks of destitution from disease among poultry populations decreased, providing increased security for women keeping fowl. But the improvements and the expansion in poultry numbers that were urged on women by the organizations were ineffective because of the nature of farmhouse poultry-keeping. For farm women, poultry-keeping was a side-job, important—even vital—

---

[127] DATI, *Conference on the Poultry Industry*, 135.

[128] RCCI, *Appendix to 3rd Report*, xxxv. 38, evidence by Thomas Porter.

[129] DATI Papers. See e.g. NAI AG1 G1431/14 and G744/15.

[130] Horace Plunkett Foundation, *Agricultural Co-operation in Ireland: A Survey* (1931), 391.

to the household economy in the earlier years, but still a secondary concern. There was simply no time available in the day to cope with increased poultry numbers or to spend on improved poultry care. Before the intervention of poultry societies, 'a score of hins was aqual to one cow' [*sic*], since hens scratched around for their own living, while a cow meant trouble and expense for Irish countrywomen.[131] The reforming organizations tended to dismiss the labour costs of women in the home. Co-operative societies gave up fattening and cramming because it was too labour-intensive, and thus too expensive, but then they recommended that the industry should be carried out in homes where there was 'practically no cost as regards labour'.[132] The organizers acknowledged (and, in the case of the IAOS, hoped) that the reformed poultry industry would mean more work for the farm wife. In contrast to the lighthearted way in which the agricultural community used to speak about poultry-rearing, the second decade of the twentieth century saw the appearance of a series of one-line sayings on the hard work entailed in poultry-keeping in agricultural papers:

Like the housewife, the henwife's work is never done.[133]

The working hours of the poultry-woman extend from early to late; there are no holidays.[134]

Good luck and lazy poultrywomen are strangers.[135]

For the promoters of poultry schemes, it was a common-sense principle that poultry-rearing required poultry houses. Poultry houses, however, increased labour costs:

There is no necessity for us to consider whether the use of houses is essential or not, for it is taken as an axiom that without them no profitable results can be obtained. . . . Every house should be raked over each day, the litter dug over each week, the ends of the perches dipped in paraffin to kill the insect life, and thoroughly cleaned and whitewashed each quarter. This is a most important consideration, and unless the places are kept perfectly clean good results can never be obtained.[136]

---

[131] DATI, *Conference on the Poultry Industry*, 121.   [132] Ibid. 134.
[133] 'Poultry as a Lucrative Branch of Farming', *IH*, 18 Apr. 1896: 104.
[134] *Ark*, 3/48 (Sept. 1913), 12.   [135] Ibid. 3/47 (Aug. 1913), 14.
[136] 'How to Make Poultry Pay', *Kings' County Chronicle*, 2 Jan. 1913: 4.

Poultry women were expected to work. At seven o'clock the fowl had to be released from their roosting-houses. They were then fed from troughs in the yards. Farm women had to prepare the food, carefully differentiating between the different types of fowl. After breakfast, the troughs were cleaned and filled with fresh water. Coops were scrubbed. At noon the fowl were given a smaller feed of green stuff or corn. Then the eggs had to be collected and the evening meal prepared. In addition, the fowl-houses required scouring once a week. Insect-destroyers were applied every month. Houses were limewashed quarterly.[137] If farm women complained about the extra work entailed in re-formed poultry-keeping, the organizations advised:

One objection sometimes raised to increasing the poultry production of the farm is that it will add to the care and labour of the farmer's wife, sometimes already overburdened for want of sufficient and efficient help; but this ought not to be. If poultry-keeping pays at all it should be a recognized branch of farm labour; and while the mistress of the house could superintend, all such work as feeding, watering, and keeping the houses in order should be the work of farm labourers or servants. The poultry business should not be conducted merely for pleasure or pastime, but as a branch of farm industry likely to bring in more profit, considering the investment, than any other farm product.[138]

Given the economics of small farming, such a proposal was unhelpful. The extra burden of improved poultry farming would have to be borne by the family of the farmer, or not at all. While the proportion of households with fowl-pens increased from 30 to 49 per cent between 1901 and 1911 in the eight DEDs in our sample, the proportion of households with fowl-pens *and* either a domestic servant or a farm servant declined from 31 to 27 per cent. Arguments about the improvement of poultry farming suited the political aspirations of a vulnerable co-operative movement under fire for reducing female employment in rural areas.

More general changes within the agricultural community also affected the poultry-rearing work of farm women. While the labour required in poultry-rearing increased, poultry became a proportionally less crucial element in the family budget as the

---

[137] 'Homestead Poultry Expert', 'Poultry: November Work in the Poultry Yard. Not the Business for an Invalid', *IH*, 17 Nov. 1906: 938.
[138] *Ark*, 2/51 (Dec. 1913), 13.

twentieth century progressed. Farmers experienced an expansion in profits from cattle. Housing improvements in rural areas
meant the transfer of chickens from inside homes, where the
farm woman could easily care for them while cooking the family
meal or looking after children, to outside chicken-runs. Schemes
to disseminate portable poultry houses throughout the small-
farmer community had as their *raison d'être* the removal of
chickens as far as possible from the 'tainted farmyard where the
poultry have probably been thickly kept for years past' to distant
fields.[139] Chickens were thus moved out of the farmyard and into
the fields, where they formed a part of crop rotation schemes:
out of terrain convenient for female workers and into distinctly
male territory. Higglers gradually stopped collecting eggs from
door-to-door. Shops slowly ceased to exchange food and other
household necessities for eggs. Instead, women had to deliver
the eggs to the co-operative societies, creameries, or egg centres—
or entrust the delivery to their menfolk. What the organizations
attempting to promote poultry-raising in Ireland saw as best for
the poultry industry was not what the farm women perceived as
best for them.

[139] DATI, *Conference on the Poultry Industry*, 60, and DATI, *Portable Poultry Houses*
(DATI Leaflet 50, rev., n.d.), 1.

PART THREE:

HOUSEWORKERS

7

From the Beginning: Housework

A woman's work is never done let her do her best and try.
From morning until bedtime I'm sure you can't deny . . .
So men don't grumble at your wife for I'm sure there's none of you
Can tell the daily labour that a woman has to do.[1]

THE home is a site of labour. For women, household labour was
(and continues to be) a central form of work. Unsurprisingly,
changes in the actual or expected quantity or quality of goods
and services provided by the houseworker substantially altered
the labour process. In rural Ireland between 1890 and 1914,
changes in housework raised the economic value of domestic
production, resulting in a shift from paid employment and familial
farm labour to unwaged domestic work. All areas of housework
underwent revolutionary processes. These innovations were noted
by the Revd Joseph Guinan in 1915, when he revisited his first
parish in Rathmore. On entering the parlour/drawing-room of
the parochial house, he discovered that, during his twenty years'
absence, the hearthstone fireplace and turf-barrel had been replaced by a grate and a coal-box, and a piano stood in the place
of the old chest of drawers.[2] Improved living standards and
other domestic reforms altered the labour of houseworkers.[3]

NUMBERS OF HOUSEWORKERS

Most houseworkers were women. In 1926 (the only year for which
any Irish census asked for the number of people 'engaged in

---

[1] 'The Labouring Woman', in James N. Healy (ed.), *The Mercier Book of Old Irish Street Ballads* (Cork, 1969), iv. 109–10.
[2] Revd Joseph Guinan, 'Rathmore Re-Visited', *Irish Monthly* (1915), 419.
[3] The argument that increased prosperity leads to more housework has also been used by Sally McMurry, *Families and Farmhouses in Nineteenth-Century America: Vernacular Design and Social Change* (Oxford, 1988), 88–9. However, she contends that the impetus was a 'scrambling to meet new standards of housekeeping, gentility and childrearing' (standards taken unchanged from the middle-class urban populace).

domestic duties') the 550,147 female houseworkers in the Republic outnumbered the 1,593 male houseworkers. In most areas, between 37 and 39 per cent of all women over 12 years old were 'engaged in home duties'.[4] Rural women were more likely to be classed as houseworkers than urban women, and 90 per cent of all *married* women claimed to be houseworkers. There were higher proportions of *unmarried* women as houseworkers in the province of Connaught and in the counties of Donegal, Meath, Kings' (or Offaly), Longford, and Cavan than elsewhere. Where paid employment opportunities were higher—in the cities and in county Dublin—fewer unmarried women depended for their livelihood on the performance of unwaged domestic work. *Widowed* women were less likely to claim unwaged domestic work as their occupation in Connaught and in the western counties, and much more likely to describe themselves as houseworkers in the south-east and in the cities (especially the county boroughs of Dublin and Cork).

There are two ways of estimating the number of houseworkers in Ireland *before* 1926. The simplest is to assume that all those adult women not entered as having an occupation in the census were in fact houseworkers. Using published census data, the number of houseworkers over the age of 20 increased by 11 per cent between 1891 and 1911, and, defining all 'unoccupied' adult women in the eight DEDs as houseworkers, not only did the number of houseworkers increase, but households became more likely to require the labour of two or more houseworkers (see Table 7.1). This method of estimating the number of houseworkers ignores the fact that employed women tended to do a substantial amount of housework.[5]

The second method provides a less conservative estimate of the number of houseworkers by acknowledging that 'occupied' women also performed some housework. We can assume that (1) only women between the ages of 20 and 65 performed housework; (2) women not entered as having an occupation in the

---

[4] This understates the number of full-time houseworkers. When more than 1 person in a family of 6 or less was described as being 'engaged in home duties', census enumerators only counted 1 person, and the other person/s was given no occupation: *Census of Population, 1926*, ii. *Occupations of Males and Females in Each Province, County, County Borough, Urban and Rural District* (Dublin, 1926), 13.

[5] 'Working Women's Column', *Irish Worker*, 2 Nov. 1912: 2, discusses this aspect.

Table 7.1. Houseworkers per household, 1901 and 1911 (%)

Number of houseworkers per household	1901[a]	1911[b]
1	65.9	63.8
2	25.7	26.9
3 +	8.4	9.3

[a] n (no. in sample) = 784.
[b] n = 758.

Source: Manuscript census returns for 8 DEDs, NAI, 1901 and 1911; Valuation Books at the Valuation Office, Dublin (nearest year to 1911).

census were full-time houseworkers; (3) every 'unoccupied' woman who did full-time housework relieved an 'occupied' woman from such tasks; (4) an 'occupied' woman who did not have an 'unoccupied' woman to substitute for her labour performed half the housework of an 'unoccupied' woman; and (5) the presence of a domestic servant in the household supplemented rather than replaced for the work of at least one other houseworker.[6] Under these assumptions, a clear transition from paid domestic work to unwaged domestic work can be seen (see Tables 7.2 and 7.3). In 1861, nearly 29 per cent of the women doing housework were being paid. This percentage increased slightly to over 30 per cent in 1871 and 1881, before dropping dramatically in 1891 to 18 per cent. In 1901, nearly 16 per cent of the women doing housework were paid workers, declining further to nearly 12 per cent by 1911. The number of 'full-time equivalent' unwaged houseworkers increased from 993,000 to 1,082,000 between 1891 and 1911. Concentrating on the two full-time groups, in 1891 there was one paid domestic servant to every

[6] My second definition of houseworkers is similar to that used by E. Lindhal, Einar Dahlgren, and Karin Kock, *Wages, Cost of Living and National Income in Sweden, 1800–1930*, iii. *National Income of Sweden, 1861–1930*, I and II (1933), when they calculated the national income for Sweden. This book contains a defence of these assumptions. For a survey of the empirical literature showing that the presence or absence of servants does not reduce the amount of time that the mistress spends on housework, see Heidi I. Hartmann, *Capitalism and Women's Work in the Home, 1900–1980* (Ann Arbor, Mich., 1975), 249–53.

Table 7.2. Estimated number of unwaged houseworkers and waged domestic servants, 1861–1911 (000s)

Year	Full-time houseworkers	Full-time equivalent houseworkers	Paid domestic servants
1861	394.7	769.1	309.0
1871	504.8	695.5	356.7
1881	748.7	846.5	392.1
1891	798.1	993.1	220.7
1901	818.5	1030.7	193.3
1911	819.1	1081.5	144.9

Source: Censuses of Ireland, 1861–1911.

Table 7.3. Estimated number of unwaged houseworkers and waged domestic servants per capita, 1861–1911

Year	Full-time houseworkers	Full-time equivalent houseworkers	Paid domestic servants
1861	14.7	7.5	18.8
1871	10.7	7.8	15.2
1881	6.9	6.1	13.2
1891	5.9	4.7	21.3
1901	5.4	4.3	23.1
1911	5.3	4.0	30.3

Source: Censuses of Ireland, 1861–1911.

twenty-one people in the population; by 1911 there was one paid domestic servant to every thirty people in the population. In 1891 each full-time houseworker catered for the needs of six people, compared with only five people twenty years later.

Obviously, households were affected in different ways. Using the more conservative method of estimating the number of house-workers, where did the demand for unwaged domestic female labour increase fastest? The data source restricts us to a ten-year period, but we can see that the demand for unwaged domestic labour increased more rapidly on the larger farms. On average, farms of less than thirty acres required the same number of 'unoccupied' women in 1901 as they had in 1911. In both years they needed just over one 'unoccupied' woman. The change occurred on farms of over thirty acres. By 1911, farms of this size, which had absorbed the labour of one and a half women (on average), were now requiring nearly two women. Farmers living on larger holdings were much more likely to have access to the labour of three or more houseworkers than farmers on smaller holdings. While three-quarters of families with a holding of between one and five acres had only one houseworker, half the families with farms of over fifty acres had at least two houseworkers. *Unmarried* women also had to make their labour-force decisions in a household context. The labour of the wife was insufficient. The production of other women within the house has to be considered.[7]

The conventional response to the link between wealth (measured here by farm acreage) and the number of 'unoccupied' women within households involves reference to Veblen's notion of 'conspicuous consumption'.[8] This response is based on a misguided notion of what actually constitutes 'consumption'. Households did not consume unprocessed products from the farm or shop. Potatoes were washed, cabbages were cut. Consumption did not start when the cow was slaughtered. Consumption was eating a meal, not preparing it.[9] Increased consumption required increased production. This has been clearly expressed by John Kenneth Galbraith in his *Economics and Public Purpose*. While Galbraith argues correctly that increased consumption requires greater inputs of time, he sees the force driving women to perform housework as social virtue rather than economic reward.[10]

What explains the increased numbers of houseworkers? The forces pushing women out of paid employment have already been discussed. In communities experiencing a contraction of employment, women were impelled to maximize their possible

[7] This contrasts with Jacob Mincer's view that only the labour of *married* women has to be explained differently from that of men.

[8] Thorstein Veblen, *The Theory of the Leisure Class* (New York, 1934).

[9] 'Labour' is any activity that could be performed by a 'third person' without any reduction in its utility function. This definition is crucial if we are to distinguish between leisure (or consumption) and labour.

[10] Steffan Burenstam Linder, *The Harried Leisure Class* (New York, 1970), and John Kenneth Galbraith, *Economics and the Public Purpose* (Boston, 1973).

economic contribution by focusing their energies on familial domestic work. But there were also forces *drawing* women into housework. There was simply more housework to do. The theme was repeated: 'In the home there is no limit to the possibilities for employment.'[11] Economic growth released capital (as well as labour) for investment in the household sector. The following section examines some areas in which this investment occurred, concentrating on housing, diet, standards of cleanliness, and child care.[12]

HOUSING

The house was the workplace. Improvements in rural housing radically affected labour requirements. In the nineteenth century Irish houses were reputed to be the worst in the United Kingdom. In overcrowded cabins where animals slept with humans, poor women cogently argued that house-cleaning meant loss of manure reserves; but reformers were unsympathetic.[13] The general standard of many houses was extremely poor: 'Floors of mud; roofs of rotten thatch; one wretched chamber often doing duty as a kitchen by day, and as a bedroom, pigsty and stable by night; one bed, or a truss of straw having often to accommodate the whole family of all ages and both sexes.'[14]

However, housing was improving. As was mentioned at the

[11] 'For Wife and Maid', *Irish Weekly Independent*, 19 Apr. 1906: 10.

[12] These factors cannot be estimated in a statistically sophisticated manner, given the limitations of the data.

[13] RCL, *The Agricultural Labourer*, iv. Ireland, III, *Reports by Mr Roger C. Richards* (C. 6894-xx), HC 1893–4, xxxvii/1: 38. See also the comment by Richard Newman Somerville, a borough engineer of Galway, in *3rd Report of Her Majesty's Commissioners for Inquiring into the Housing of the Working Classes* (C. 4547-i), HC 1884–5, xxxi. 86, and H. Villiers Stuart, *Observations and Statistics Concerning the Question of Irish Agricultural Labourers* (1884), 4–5.

[14] Ibid. 2–3. See also 'The Position and Prospects of Ireland in 1845', *Union Magazine* (Mar. 1845), 1–4; Thomas Campbell Foster, *Letters on the Condition of the People of Ireland* (1846), 199–202 and 294–5; James Caird, *The Plantation Scheme; or, The West of Ireland as a Field for Investment* (1850), 53; James Godkin, *Ireland and her Churches* (1867), 274–5; Peter MacLagan, *Land Culture and Land Tenure in Ireland* (Dublin, 1869), 34; *Reports from Poor Law Inspectors on the Wages of Agricultural Labourers in Ireland* (C. 35), HC 1870, xiv. 11–13; 'A Scot', *Ireland as it Is and as it Might Be* (Dundee, 1879), 8–9 on Limerick; James M. Tuke, *A Visit to Donegal and Connemara in the Spring of 1880* (1880), 14–15 on Carrick; and *The Agricultural Labourer*, iv/III, *Reports by Mr Roger C. Richards*, xxxvii/1: 66.

Table 7.4. Rural houses and housing 'classes', 1861–1911 (%)

Year	'Class' of house			
	First	Second	Third	Fourth
1861	3.1	32.7	54.0	10.3
1871	3.6	35.2	42.2	19.0
1881	4.8	41.7	48.1	5.3
1891	5.8	49.3	42.4	2.9
1901	6.4	55.8	36.3	1.5
1911	7.2	64.2	27.8	0.8

Source: Censuses of Ireland, 1861–1911.

end of Chapter 1, data on the 'class' of inhabited housing in rural and urban areas were collected for each decade between 1841 and 1911. Houses were divided into four categories, according to the number of rooms, the number of windows, and the materials from which the house was built. Fourth-class houses were small mud huts. Third-class houses had windows and between one and four rooms; they were made of sturdier materials. Second-class houses were often good farmhouses, having five to nine rooms and windows. First-class houses were generally 'gentlemen's houses'. To what extent do these categories represent real differences in housing? In Ballinrobe Rural District 2 in 1901, 90 per cent of the houses reported by the medical officer as being 'unsanitary' were in classes three or four.[15] In six DEDs in 1901 and 1911, all of the houses in the fourth class and 90 per cent of the houses in the third class were valued at less than £1. Nearly three-quarters of the houses in the second class were valued at between £1 and £2, and half of the houses in the first class were valued at over £3.[16] Tables 7.4 and 7.5, therefore, do provide some

[15] NAI MS 12328–9 'Minute-Book of the Medical Officer of Health, Report on Unsanitary Dwellings, Ballinrobe No. 2 RDC, 1901': 25 were examined.

[16] From an analysis of the 6 DEDs that were matched with the valuation records at the Valuation Office in Dublin. For a more general discussion of housing improvements, including a discussion of the growing size of houses, the social desirability of privacy within homes, and the development of the parlour, see Alan Gailey, 'Changes in Irish Rural Housing, 1600–1900', in Patrick O'Flanagan, Paul Ferguson, and Kevin Whelan (eds.), *Rural Ireland, 1600–1900: Modernisation and Change* (Cork, 1987), 86–103.

Table 7.5. Housing characteristics, 1901 and 1911 (%)

Housing characteristics	1901[a]	1911[b]
Roof made of non-perishable materials	36.4	45.5
Walls made of non-perishable materials	91.6	94.9
Number of windows		
0	1.4	0.8
1–2	37.8	32.7
3–4	50.6	53.5
5–6	6.4	8.2
7+	3.8	4.8
Number of rooms		
1	3.5	2.8
2	74.5	72.3
3	12.5	13.4
4+	9.5	11.4

[a] n (no. in sample) = 976.
[b] n = 912.

Source: Manuscript census returns for 8 DEDs, NAI, 1901 and 1911.

indication of improvements in rural housing. In 1891, nearly half of all rural houses were third or fourth class, but twenty years later nearly three-quarters were first or second class. Between 1901 and 1911, sturdy roofs and walls became more prevalent in the eight DEDs; houses were larger and were more likely to have windows.

Better housing has been seen by reformers in many different countries as one of the most effective instruments of social change.[17] Acts of Parliament in 1856, 1860, 1870, 1872, and 1881 aimed to encourage Irish landlords and Poor Law authorities to improve the housing of their labourers. By and large, they were ineffectual. After 1883, local authorities in Ireland had been empowered to provide dwellings and gardens for labourers, but at the end of the decade the attention of the House of Commons was again called to the failure of the labourers' acts in Ireland.[18]

[17] For a discussion, see Clifford E. Clark, 'Domestic Architecture as an Index to Social History', *Journal of Interdisciplinary History*, 7/1 (Summer 1976), 33–56.
[18] 'The Labourers' Cottage Failure', *Kings' County Chronicle*, 15 Mar. 1888: 4. See also 'The Labourers' Cottages', ibid. 19 June 1890: 1.

Up until 1892 the labourers' acts had been acted upon only in Leinster and Munster, where nearly 12,000 cottages had been built. Less than ninety cottages had been built in either Ulster or Connaught. Amendments to the labourers' acts in the 1890s resulted in a spate of building. The new councillors elected under the 1898 Local Government Act proved to be enthusiastic about housing issues. Under the Labourers' Act of 1906 the powers of local authorities were extended, and £4.5 million was set aside as loans to rural authorities for housing operations.[19] The act empowered local councils to provide all manual workers earning less than 15s. a week with cottages. The average agricultural wage in Ireland was 11s. Local councils began seriously to invest in housing.[20] In 1894, over 10,000 houses were built under labourers' acts. The number rose to over 13,000 houses in 1898, 15,000 in 1902, 20,600 in 1906, 29,000 in 1910, and then jumped to 43,700 in 1914. By then, a quarter of a million people had been rehoused.[21]

Other state bodies invested heavily in housing. The CDB claimed that their schemes to improve houses represented their most 'productive' work.[22] Housing was central to four schemes: the Parish Committee Scheme, the House Improvement Scheme, the Migrant Scheme, and the Estates Scheme. In total, from their instigation to 31 March 1909, these four schemes were responsible for the execution of nearly 40,000 works and paid out £225,000.[23] The Housing Improvement Scheme applied only to estates purchased by the Board. Householders would receive a repayable advance and a free grant to build or substantially improve dwelling-houses and outhouses. The 'advance' would be included in the sale price of the holding and would be repaid with the price of the land by half-yearly annuities.[24] Generally, the building was done by the landholder under the supervision of CDB officials. If members of the household could not carry

[19] These loans were repayable in 68½ years by annual instalments of 3.25%, covering principal and interest.
[20] PRONI LA 44/12e/4, Larne District Council, discussions about the proposed labourers' cottages, 1911.
[21] Statistics taken from the annual reports of the Local Government (Ireland) Board, as published in the British parliamentary papers. This government-sponsored housing scheme was unique in the United Kingdom until 1919.
[22] CDB, *18th Report, 1909* (Cd. 4927), HC 1909, xvi. 11–12.
[23] Ibid. 11–12.
[24] These loans were given at a rate of 3½% a year, over 68½ years.

out the work, the Board might approve a second loan, repayable in fifty half-yearly instalments. Loans in either case never exceeded £25. Parish Committee Schemes provided capital for the erection or substantial improvement of dwelling-houses and outhouses, drainage and fencing, the repair or construction of roads, and the reclamation of wasteland. Grants of £1,500 in its first year of operation (1897) had reached £10,700 by 1907. The value of the labour was generally four or five times the amount of the grant, which was usually used for buying materials.[25] In county Donegal these grants were replaced by a system of prizes for occupiers who improved or built dwellings.[26] Between 1900 and 1908, nearly 8,000 dwelling-houses were built or substantially improved under the scheme, and over 10,000 outhouses for cattle were erected.[27] No grants or prizes were given to occupiers whose land and house valuation exceeded £7. The scheme was discontinued in 1908.

What did reformers expect from improved housing? Housing was a moral and social question. Its political content was understated. At the very least, reformers hoped that improved houses would mean improved housework.[28] Human surroundings either 'elevate or degrade'.[29] If Ireland was to contain a 'moral, sober, intelligent, healthy and industrious people', they must have improved homes.[30] The idealization of the labourers' cottages, attractively managed by women, reached exalted heights with Bishop Browne of Cloyne declaring in his 1911 Lenten pastoral:

I have seen many of these new cottages, outside and inside. It is a pleasure to visit them. The outside walls fresh with whitest limewash, the windows kept regularly painted, the woodbine and the clematis winding round the door, an indication of the development of taste; inside the house, the floor is brushed and unspotted, the walls are decorated with suitable prints, the simple household furniture is neatly kept and arranged, and the mother of the home, the proud queen in her own

---

[25] RCCI, *Final Report* (Cd. 4097), HC 1908, xlii. 31.

[26] The resident magistrates had control in Donegal.

[27] CDB, *18th Report*, xvi. 23.

[28] *The Agricultural Labourer*, iv/III, *Reports by Mr Roger C. Richards*, xxxvii/1: 40, on Roscrea (county Galway).

[29] 'Working Women's Column', *Irish Worker*, 19 Aug. 1911: 2, and Miss Mary Fogarty, 'Influence of Home on Life', *Irish Education Review*, 3/10 (July 1910), 604.

[30] 'The Provision of Labourers' Cottages in Ireland', *Irish Builder*, 26/587 (1 June 1884), 155–6, and Miss Eibhlain MacNeill of the Coisde Gnotha, 'The Place of Women in the Irish Revival', *Irish Peasant*, 6 Jan. 1906: 3.

little realm, is surrounded by healthy, happy children. It is a blessed change, hopeful of the future of our country.[31]

Improved houses would (and were expected to) increase female workloads. The public—men and women—discussed the planning and construction of these houses extensively. Housing had to meet the requirements of prospective residents. Ideas of 're-spectability' were integrated into the designs, as, for example, in the Lisburn Union, where cottages were built with a closed panelled front door (complete with knocker) and with varnished sheeting on the ceiling.[32] Equally, labourers' wives demanded that their labour requirements were met, and they complained bitterly if they were ignored.[33] Some of the new labourers' cottages were too small to accommodate the large households—they were 'bird baskets'—and housewives complained about smoking chimneys, damp walls, the 'want of rendering in the slating', the absence of a loft, the coldness of the houses, and kitchen grates which were too narrow for pots.[34] Problems with the hearth were the most serious, and the extreme measures that district councils were often forced to take had profound effects on the labour of houseworkers. For instance, the Newtownards Rural District Council (county Down) built forty-three cottages along the shore between Ballywalter and Mill Isle and in Portavogie. Since the back-draughts of these cottages would not draw, the council was forced to put small 'Plantress' stoves into each house; they then had to teach the women how to use the stoves.[35]

[31] Bishop Browne of Cloyne's Lenten pastoral, quoted by T. P. Gill, in 'The Management of a Cottage Garden', *DATI Journal*, 12/1 (Oct. 1911), 14. He went on to warn his listeners that the forces of evil were never completely conquered, drawing an analogy between uncleanliness and sin.

[32] Francis Joseph Biggar, *Labourers' Cottages for Ireland* (Dublin, 1907), 5.

[33] RCL, *The Agricultural Labourer*, iv. *Ireland*, II, *Reports by Mr W. P. O'Brien* (C. 6894-xix), HC 1893–4, xxxvii. 65, on Cashel.

[34] Ibid. 65 (197). See also Mrs Cloudesley Brereton before the Institute of Civil Engineers, quoted in *Irish Citizen*, 11 Apr. 1914: 1; 'L. de K. K.', 'The Homestead and its In-Dwellers', *IH*, 15 Apr. 1905: 301; *The Agricultural Labourer*, iv / II, *Reports by Mr W. P. O'Brien*, xxxvii: 44, 85, 105, and 126, on Lismore, Kilmallock, Carlow, and Naas; *Irish Peasant*, 4 Apr. 1906: 5; and Revd J. M. Robinson, *Facts From Ireland* (Dublin, 1910), 125. For a particularly interesting account by Mrs McBride of Loughries, whose fireplace was constructed in such a way that she could not hang a pot on the fire, see PRONI LA 61/3c/1, Newtownards Rural District Council, 1909–11, Reports of the Committees of Public Health, Water Supply, Finance, and Lighting, meeting of 12 Mar. 1910.

[35] PRONI LA 61/3c/1, Newtownards Rural District Council, 1909–11, Committee Reports, meeting of 29 Jan. 1910, report by Walter K. Walker of Bloomfield on the cottages built by the council.

Even the floors in these improved houses were seen as relevant in discussions about housework. For instance, disagreements in the 1880s between the Local Government Board and the Commissioners for the Select Committee on Agricultural Labourers centred upon the type of floors laid in the new cottages. No one doubted that the floors must be sealed: unsealed floors were cleaned too infrequently. The commissioners recommended concrete floors, allowing women to slosh them down with water. The Local Government Board opposed concrete floors on the grounds that women found them difficult and time-consuming to clean. They recommended timber or tile floors, because they were easily cleaned and quick to dry.[36] Later reformers followed in this tradition. Subsequent plans for the labourers' cottages listed one of the seven 'essential requirements' as being 'strong smooth floors which can be thoroughly cleaned by washing, with boarding in bedrooms'.[37] Floors were being sealed in older houses as well. Dr Brendan MacCarthy, medical inspector under the Local Government Board for the north-western quarter of Ireland, noted that, although earth floors were still 'fairly common', their numbers were declining rapidly, as 'public opinion was being formed against the use of these floors to a very remarkable extent'.[38] Sealed floors showed dirt more clearly. They created housework.

CLEANLINESS

Housing reform cannot be separated from attempts to disseminate notions of cleanliness. At the same time as 'Brigid' of the *Irish Homestead* was jesting that the word 'tidiness' was a grating Anglo-Saxon word, she was heavily engaged in the campaign to appropriate the word into Irish culture.[39] Women were encouraged to

[36] *Report from the Select Committee on Agricultural Labourers (Ireland)* (.32), HC 1884, vii. 32–3.
[37] 'Memorandum in Relation to the Model Plans and General Specification for Labourers' Cottages Issued by the Local Government for Ireland', 24 June 1907.
[38] *Commission of Inquiry into the Conditions of Employment and Other Making-Up Trades in the North of Ireland: Report and Evidence* (Cd. 6509), HC 1912–13, xxxiv. 161. For further discussion on the sealing of floors, see Gailey, 'Changes in Irish Rural Housing', 86–103.   [39] 'Brigid', 'Tidiness', *IH*, 17 Jan. 1903: 53.

sweep regularly rather than to wait for the annual spring-clean
or even a weekly clean:

A wonderful housewife is Mrs O'More,
Every Saturday morning you'll see
A whirlwind of dust from window and door,—
Such a thorough sweeper is she.
No whirlwind of dust from window or door
Of her neighbour across the way;
That's because the neighbour of Mrs O'More
Sweeps a little up every day.[40]

The *purpose* of cleaning changed. Sweeping the floor became less
of a ritual linked with visiting fairies and festivals and more
of a 'scientific' dirt-control movement to combat disease. In the
nineteenth century, before going to bed, an Irish peasant woman
might sweep the hearth and arrange chairs in front of it for the
comfort of the dead.[41] In the twentieth century the younger generation watched their elders perform these functions. John
O'Donaghue, born in an Irish cottage in 1900, remembered seeing his grandmother sweep the fireplace before going to bed,
especially on stormy nights, because, she said, 'the dead might
be coming in for shelter. If they find the place untidy ... they
might talk about it among the neighbouring pookies because the
dead have endless time for gossip.'[42] Good fairies were still said
to visit only clean houses,[43] but it was more important for visiting good neighbours to be impressed.

Rising standards in house-cleaning had significant implications
for the building of new cottages. The president of United Irishwomen, Mrs Harold Lett, protested about the number of labourers' cottages in county Wexford that had been built over half a
mile from water supplies, and demanded that the planners think
more about houseworkers: 'Try and put yourself for a moment
in the position of some of these labourers' wives, and imagine
yourself trudging half a mile up a hill carrying in one hand a can
of water and with an infant tucked under the other arm, while

---

[40] 'Homely Wrinkles', *Ark*, 6/71 (Aug. 1915), 6. See also 'Brigid', 'A Woman's
Work Is Never Done, II', *IH*, 4 Jan. 1902: 11.
[41] Stephen Gwynn, *To-Day and To-Morrow in Ireland* (Dublin, 1903), 102.
[42] Quoted in Caroline Davidson, *A Woman's Work Is Never Done* (1982), 73.
[43] Conrad M. Arensburg, *The Irish Countryman: An Anthropological Study* (1937),
188.

one or two mites hang onto your skirts.' She pointed out that an 'ordinary family' would require about nine gallons of water a day, with an extra nine gallons on wash day. By washing once every nine days, she would be required to use an average of ten gallons a day. If a woman could carry two gallons of water at a time (weighing about twenty-four pounds in a can), then labourers' wives who lived half a mile from a water supply would have to walk at least five miles a day for water.[44]

One way of examining changes in housing is through the sanitary officers' reports. The problem with this method is that sanitary officers celebrated broadening legislative powers by rooting out offenders of housing laws.[45] Thus, between 1909 and 1911, Dr R. Henry, medical officer for the Newtownards Rural District Council, was concerned that people in his district had earth floors, fowl in the privies (or no privy at all), windows that would not open, and unplastered walls.[46] In 1910 the sanitary officer in the Ballycastle Rural District constructed a long list of houses that had no privies, dripped with dampness, were overcrowded (and thus morally suspect), possessed permanently closed windows and hingeless doors, or had rotting roofs and walls.[47] In spite of these criticisms, the long-term trend in sanitary offences was one of steady decline. Most offences never reached the courts, but of those that did between 1892 and 1911, the number decreased fourfold.[48] Furthermore, the type of sanitary problem changed (see Table 7.6). At least in the Ballymoney Union, problems with drainage and cesspools were reported less frequently. The practice of keeping livestock inside the house

[44] Paper read by Mrs Harold Lett (president of the UI) at the first AGM of the UI, 15 Nov. 1911: see the minutes and papers of the Irish Countrywoman's Association. The UI sent a deputation to the Local Government Board regarding the water supply to the labourers' cottages on 10 Jan. 1912: Local Government Board for Ireland, *Annual Report, 1912* (Cd. 6339), HC 1912–13, xxxvii. 47. For other complaints about distance from water supplies, see 'Working Terrier', 'Man, the Blatherer', *IH*, 19 Feb. 1910: 151.

[45] For a summary of these laws, see Mary E. Daly, *Dublin: The Deposed Capital. A Social and Economic History, 1860–1914* (Cork, 1984), 255–64.

[46] PRONI LA 61/3c/1, Newtownards Rural District Council, 1909–11, Committee Reports.

[47] The officer was applying for labourers' cottages to be built: see PRONI LA 11/12b/1, Ballycastle Rural District Council, Sanitary Officer's certificates for Nov. 1910.

[48] *Judicial Statistics, Ireland, 1911*, i (Cd. 6419), HC 1912–13, cx. 28–9.

Table 7.6. Complaints by sanitary officers in Ballymoney Poor Law
Union, 1875–1877 and 1905–1907 (%)

Complaint relating to	1875–7[a]	1905–7[b]
Cesspools and drainage	65.8	34.0
Animals in house	23.9	5.0
Filthy house	5.4	14.9
Roof	2.9	7.8
Water supply	0.8	7.8
Lack of privy	0.8	26.3
Overcrowding	0.4	0.0
Walls and floors	0.0	3.5
House used to slaughter animals	0.0	0.7

[a] n (no. in sample) = 243.
[b] n = 141.

Source: Ballymoney Poor Law Union, Executive Sanitary Officer's
Report and Report-Book, 1875–1940, PRONI LA 16/9d/1.

declined, a trend which was commented on by sanitary and
medical inspectors throughout the country.[49] The new reasons for
complaining about house sanitation concerned issues of waste
disposal and general uncleanliness.

Reforming organizations attempted to stimulate clean behaviour directly. Private organizations such as the Faughanvale
Gardening Society (county Londonderry) and the Irish Peasantry
Society generously rewarded tidy and 'healthy' householders.[50]
Since sanitary officers could not deal with the widespread problem
of domestic sanitation, the CDB (under the Parish Committee
Scheme) awarded money to householders who removed animals
from inside houses or who cleared away manure heaps. These
prizes were derogatorily called 'parish doles', given to people

---

[49] *Commission of Inquiry into Conditions of Employment in the North of Ireland:
Report and Evidence*, xxxiv. 161. Similar evidence was given in the report of Sir
Acheson MacCullagh, public health inspector for Kerry, Galway, Limerick,
Roscommon, Mayo, and Clare, in Local Government Board for Ireland, *Annual
Report, 1912*, xxxvii. 56.
[50] Vice-Regal Commission on Irish Milk Supplies, *Appendix to the Final Report*
(Cd. 7134), HC 1914, xxxvi. 53, evidence by Mrs Steele Hanna, hon. sec. of the
Eglinton branch of the WNHA in county Londonderry.

'for what they should obviously do of their own accord'.[51] The Board justified their actions on the grounds that the history of poverty in the congested districts had led to 'habits that would never have been formed under happier conditions'.[52] From 1901 the DATI also awarded prizes to 'ideal' cottagers, sending out teams of judges to examine the cleanliness and the general orderliness of houses and their grounds, the cultivation of the garden, the general management of livestock (with particular attention given to poultry), and the provision for manure. As the *Irish Homestead* advised, to win a prize, wooden floors had to be white from scrubbing.[53] Similar criteria applied to the competitions for small farms, but, in addition to home cleanliness, cropping practices and the care of land were also examined. Between 3,000 and 5,000 householders entered the competition annually, and nearly £54,000 was given in prizes under the schemes.[54]

HOUSEHOLD GOODS

The material environment of the home vitally affected housework. The improving economy saw increased investment in household goods. Some reformers saw this movement as essential to general 'development'. A regular columnist for the women's page in the *Irish Homestead* commented:

Honest Tommy Traddles felt himself compelled to defer his marriage with the dearest girl in the world (prepared to wait for him twenty years if necessary), when he counted what the plenishings [*sic*] would cost— the sheets and pillowcases and tablecloths, and the gridirons and saucepans and salamanders. Of course, you may talk about artificial wants! but nobody has been able to trace a beginning of what we call civilization; and the more people give up in this respect the more they degenerate.[55]

Others claimed that household equipment would reduce the 'drudgery' of housework.[56] Modern research shows, however, that the average amount of time spent on housework does not decrease

[51] RCCI, *Final Report*, xlii. 31–3.   [52] Ibid.

[53] 'Queries and Replies: The Best Kept Cottage', *IH*, 10 Oct. 1903: 829.

[54] Data taken from the annual reports of the DATI, published in the British parliamentary papers.

[55] 'L. de K. K.', 'The Homestead and its In-Dwellers', *IH*, 29 Apr. 1905: 348.

[56] 'Homely Wrinkles', *Ark*, May 1915: 6. See also, 'Editorial: Our Monthly Chat', *Ark*, Oct. 1915: 1; Elizabeth Bloxham, 'Training our Housekeepers', in Fitzgerald (ed.), *Voice of Ireland*, 169; and 'Lines of Progress', *IH*, 26 Mar. 1910: 251.

Table 7.7. Value of imports of household goods, 1904–1914

Year	Value (£000s)	Index[a]
1904	1,068.3	100.0
1905	1,164.0	108.9
1906	1,258.0	117.7
1907	1,276.5	119.5
1908	1,291.4	120.9
1909	1,307.5	122.4
1910	1,439.6	134.7
1911	1,491.4	139.6
1912	1,606.4	150.4
1913	1,603.9	150.1
1914	1,852.4	173.4

Note: A detailed trade series for Ireland only begins in 1904. Household goods include: candles, lamps, electroplated ware, mats and matting, washboards, bedsteads, brushes and brooms, chinaware, clocks, ranges and ovens (including parts), pots, pans, and buckets, cutlery, polishes, carpets, mattresses, picture-frames, and furniture.

[a] 1904 = 100.

Source: Annual Irish trade statistics (British parliamentary papers).

with technological sophistication.[57] In Ireland investment in household goods substantially *increased* the amount of work that women performed in the home, both by altering expectations of the goods and services that houseworkers should provide and by increasing the time spent on maintaining the new products.

One indicator of increased investment in the home can be found in the importation of household goods, which increased by 50 per cent in the nine years between 1904 and 1913, and by a further 23 per cent in the years 1913 to 1914. The figures in Table 7.7 refer only to imported household goods, ignoring the proportion of these products that was produced locally. The fact that *exports* of these household goods increased even more rapidly than imports suggests that there was a real increase in the demand for

[57] Summaries of this literature are given by Christine Bose, 'Technology and Changes in the Division of Labour in the American Home', *Women's Studies International Quarterly*, 2 (1979), 295–304; Alexander Szalai, *The Use of Time* (Paris, 1972); and Kathryn E. Walker and Margaret E. Woods, *Time Use* (Washington, DC, 1976), 32.

such items, rather than simply the substitution of Irish-made goods by imported goods.[58]

The three types of household goods which most affected domestic labour were furniture, floor-coverings, and kitchen implements. Retail sales of furniture boomed from the 1890s. Local production seems to have been buoyant: exports of furniture increased from nearly 30,000 cwt. in 1904 to over 56,000 in 1914. The CDB established classes in 'manual instruction' to teach boys and men how to make their own furniture.[59] Furniture required daily arrangement and maintenance. The introduction of a kitchen table changed patterns of food consumption: extra labour was required to set the table, to bring food from the cooking area to the table, and finally to clear the table. Widespread dissemination of special furniture for the parlour meant more work for a broader class of women. Chests of drawers required folded clothes; and elaborate drawing-room tables required careful arrangement of crockery.

More people were buying floor-coverings. Between 1904 and 1911, the value of imports of carpets and matting increased by 36 per cent. In houses with dirt floors and resident animals, the process of cleaning was irrelevant to the household.[60] With the removal of animals to outhouses and the subsequent sealing of floors, a new form of household labour was created with investment in carpets, rugs, and linoleum. A new ideology came hand-in-hand with investment. Women were warned that dirty carpets spread disease: carpets had to be cleaned regularly.[61]

Implements were important in cookery: 'there's little use in talking about improving the cookery in her [Ireland's] small households, without first improving their facilities for cooking', asserted 'L. de K. K.' of the *Irish Homestead*.[62] Sales of minor

[58] The value of exports of these household goods steadily increased from £197,000 in 1904 to £445,600 in 1914. For a separate discussion on the expansion in household furniture in rural areas, see 'United Irishwomen', *IH*, 24 Nov. 1911: 946–7, speech by Mrs Harold Lett at the first AGM of the UI, 15 Nov. 1911.

[59] W. L. Micks, *An Account of the Constitution, Administration, and Dissolution of The CDB from 1891 to 1923* (Dublin, 1925), 93–4, and 'United Irishwomen', 946–7.

[60] The best discussion can be found in Leonore Davidoff, 'The Rationalization of Housework', in Diana L. Barker and Sheila Allen (eds.), *Dependence and Exploitation in Work and Marriage* (1976).

[61] 'For Wife and Maid', *Irish Weekly Independent*, 14 Dec. 1905: 10.

[62] 'L. de K. K.', 'The Homestead and its In-Dwellers', *IH*, 29 Apr. 1905: 348.

cooking equipment—such as spatulas, mixing- and serving-spoons, and a variety of pots and bowls—undoubtedly increased. In 1913 Maguire and Gatchell, a Dublin company established just after the famine, noted their rapidly increasing trade in cooking apparatus over the previous couple of decades.[63] Larger consumer goods were less influential. Most women continued to cook over an open hearth fire. As late as 1944, only 40 per cent of households cooked over a range; another 40 per cent cooked over an open hearth fire, and the remaining 20 per cent over an open grate. Since most of the ranges had been installed after 1920, we must assume that the open hearth fire and grate were the most common way of cooking in the period before World War I.[64] All the same, stoves were popularly advertised. Coal and anthracite stoves were marketed as efficient and durable; oil stoves dispensed with 'the kitchen fire and cookery'; gas stoves were clean; and electric stoves were 'absolutely safe'.[65] It was unlikely that many of these stoves reached ordinary rural homes.[66] However, the widespread dissemination of information about these new technologies created a demand in poorer rural households that could not be fulfilled. In 1886, for instance, free classes in Cork on how to cook on gas stoves attracted only a small number of women, but by the turn of the century girls attending cooking classes were demanding to be taught how to cook on ranges (which they did not possess in their own houses) rather than in the customary pot-oven.[67] In her study of Irish embroidery and lacemaking Elizabeth Boyle encapsulated the attitude of rural women when she discussed the activities of Miss Florence

[63] *Illustrated Record: Maguire and Gatchell, Ltd., Dublin, September 1913* (Dublin, 1913), 118–57 and 229–56.

[64] John M. Mogey, *Rural Life in Northern Ireland* (1947), 208–9. For a broader description of household equipment, see Estyn E. Evans, *Irish Heritage: The Landscape, the People and their Work* (Dundalk, 1942), 57–78.

[65] 'The Tortoise' slow-combustion stove, in *Daily Express*, 1 Dec. 1885: 1; kitchen ranges, in *Cork Constitution*, 18 Jan. 1886: 1, and 24 Feb. 1886: 4; fire kitchen ranges, in *Warder*, 6 Aug. 1894: 4, and 5 Jan. 1895: 8; Frank Rippingille's oil cooking stove, ibid. 12 Sept. 1896: 1; the 'Frugal' cooking range, in *Dublin Trade and Labour Journal*, May 1909: 2; anthracite coal stove, in *Irish Weekly Independent*, 5 Nov. 1910: 6; 'Salamandre' stove, ibid. 12 Nov. 1910: 12; gas stove, ibid. 30 July 1910: 9; and electric cooking, in *Leader*, 21 May 1910: 331.

[66] The number of stove and kitchen-range warehouses listed in *Thom's Directory* (1890, 1895, 1900, 1905, 1910, 1915) remained at 7 throughout the period.

[67] *Cork Constitution*, 3 May 1886: 1, classes by Miss E. Thorne, held at the Assembly Rooms, Cork, between 5–8 May.

Irwin, a domestic economy instructress who travelled through rural districts selling cheap kitchen utensils:

Miss Irwin's aim on her jaunting-car rounds was to sell cheap items to farmers' wives who were not by local standards poor, but were remote from shops and would produce the family wash basin when she asked at demonstrations for a bowl in which to mix a few ounces of flour and fat. Unfortunately the policy of the Department was to teach rural girls in poorer districts the use of homely articles they knew such as these very pot ovens, rather than modern toys like turf or coal-burning ranges. The decision was taken in order to counter emigration but it was not popular, and girls in one centre asked for schools with the two 'Rs': residence (so they need not walk long distances) and ranges.[68]

Domestic instructresses realized that stoves meant more work for the houseworker. Ranges in this period cooked unevenly. Most had to be cleaned daily with black lead, and the grate had to be emptied of ash every day. More important, their use led to increased specialization in the process of cooking, and encouraged a movement to the production of time-consuming baked foods.[69]

FUEL

Fuel collection was essential. Turf was the most important fuel in Ireland. As late as 1920, over 60 per cent of Irish households burned only turf.[70] The housework involved in a turf fire consisted of obtaining and preparing the fuel. Obtaining the fuel was a job for the entire household, involving cutting the peat, transporting it to the spreading-field, spreading it over the field to allow its water content to fall, then stacking, and, finally, transporting the peat to the house. Once the peat was inside, little housework was required, since peat fires were easily laid and kindled, and needed less attention than wood or coal fires, where bellows had to be used. Baking coal was difficult, for coals

---

[68] Elizabeth Boyle, *The Irish Flowerers* (Belfast, 1971), 124.

[69] Davidson, *A Woman's Work Is Never Done*, 60–3, and Alison Ravetz, 'The Victorian Coal Kitchen and its Reformers', *Victorian Studies*, 11/4 (June 1968), 435–60. For contemporary comment, see 'Cooking', *Leinster Star*, 14 Mar. 1885: 4, and D. Edgar Flinn, *Our Dress and our Food in Relation to Health* (Dublin, 1886), 45, lectures given to the Dublin Ladies' Sanitary Association at Kingstown (county Dublin).

[70] Department of Scientific and Industrial Research (Great Britain), Fuel Research Board, *Special Report Number 2: The Peat Resources of Ireland. A Lecture Given before the Dublin Society on 5th March, 1919, by Professor Pierce F. Purcell* (1920), 12.

placed on the lid of the pot-oven would go out, unlike peat.[71] For houseworkers, the advantages of peat over other fuel sources were sufficiently great to make households in the 'congested districts' reluctant to move to the superior land offered to them by the CDB if that land was some distance from peat reserves.[72] However, coal was used by wealthier and urban households; poorer households used it only when landlords refused them access to turf, when heavy rain prevented the turf from drying, or when there was a shortage of labour to cut turf. Ireland had few coal deposits, so most had to be imported and taken inland by rail, thus virtually excluding dependency on coal for households in the west and north-west. Electricity could be afforded only by the wealthy. The Dublin Electrical Works was opened in Fleet Street in 1892. In 1904 there were only 650 consumers, mostly business premises in the centre of Dublin.[73] Electricity was much more expensive in Dublin than in England at the turn of the century.[74] For those who did not have access to peat and who could not afford coal, the alternatives were straw, wood, and cow-dung. In the case of fuel, therefore, the use of peat dominated for most classes of rural dweller. With the same labour-intensive types of fuel, houseworkers now had to cook more elaborate meals.

DIET

Diet had been changing rapidly since the famine.[75] Assuming that the increased imports of food products meant increased consumption of these goods, rather than the substitution of imports for home production, we can get some measure of dietary

[71] Bloxham, 'Training our Housekeepers', 169.

[72] RCCI, *Appendix to the 5th Report* (Cd. 3630), HC 1907, xxxvi. 182–3, evidence of John Fitzgibbon, representing the United Irish League, member of the Central Council, chairman of Roscommon County Council, member of the Land League and the National League.

[73] Electricity Supply Board, *Report by the ESB Investigation Committee* (Dublin, 1972).

[74] The average cost of production per unit in 1898 was 3.8*d.* in Ireland and 3.5*d.* in England. The average price was 6.5*d.* in Ireland and 4.5*d.* in England: 'The Practical Application of Electricity', *Warder*, 9 Apr. 1898: 3.

[75] James Godkin, *Land-War in Ireland: A History for the Times* (1870), 320, and report by Richard Hamilton, in *Reports from Poor Law Inspectors on the Wages of Agricultural Labourers in Ireland* (C. 35), HC 1870, xiv. 19. For the best discussion of long-term changes in diet, see Louis M. Cullen, *The Emergence of Modern Ireland 1600–1900* (1981), 140–92. The widespread improvement in diet since the 1890s is also noted by Cullen, *Life in Ireland* (1968), 157.

diversification. If we compare import levels in 1904 and 1911, sugar (and sugar manufactures), tea, and cheese imports increased by between 6 and 10 per cent; imports of fruit and vegetables increased by almost 20 per cent; imports of spices and condensed milk increased by between 40 and 50 per cent; and imports of luxury items such as chocolate increased by 132 per cent.

Contemporaries noted higher levels of protein intake by rural households. In 1914 James Stewart of Strabane testified that agricultural labourers who never used butter in the 1880s were now using at least one pound a week. This was a sign that people were 'better off'.[76] Farming households ate more of their own eggs.[77] Between 1904 and 1913, estimated egg production increased by 32 per cent, while exports of eggs increased by only 16 per cent.[78] Agricultural statistics show increased vegetable and fruit cultivation.[79]

We can also get some idea of changes in dietary expectations by looking at the food of farm labourers. Labourers had to be fed better if farmers were to be able to attract them.[80] One large farmer in Cashel in the 1890s complained that, whereas labourers used to be fed only potatoes and milk for breakfast and dinner, and oaten stirabout for supper, they now demanded eggs for breakfast, meat for dinner four or five days a week, and butter and 'very often' tea for supper on the other days.[81] The manager of the Armaghbrague National School, J. McMurdie, wrote to the Reverend Fletcher de Cobain: 'John Griley left here this morning, he said he would stop no longer on the meat he was getting, that it was not sufficient for a working man. He wanted some eggs to [*sic*] his breakfast and beef for dinner and without butter he said he would not stay.'[82] For both employers expected to feed their workers and houseworkers cooking for the household, meat

[76] Vice-Regal Commission on Irish Milk Supplies, *Appendix to the Final Report*, xxxvi. 80, evidence by James Stewart from Strabane, and 'Poultry-Keeping More Important Now to Ireland than the Butter Industry', *IH*, 11 Feb. 1911: 105.

[77] 'Poultry-Keeping More Important Now to Ireland than the Butter Industry', 105.   [78] Assuming an annual laying capacity of 96 eggs.

[79] RCCI, *Appendix to the 7th Report* (Cd. 3785), HC 1908, xl. 82, evidence by Patrick Treanor of Pomeroy, and DATI, *6th Annual General Report, 1905–1906* (Cd. 3543), HC 1907, xvii. 48.   [80] RCCI, *Appendix to the 7th Report*, xl. 115.

[81] *The Agricultural Labourer*, iv/II, *Reports by Mr W. P. O'Brien*, xxxvii. 63, on Cashel.

[82] Letter from J. McMurdie, manager of the Armaghbrague National School, in the Revd Fletcher de Cobain papers, NLI MS 17740(3).

became a larger part of the diet, perhaps because of its declining relative cost. Out of eighty-eight centres in the United Kingdom with a population of over 100,000, Belfast and Doblin were the only two where meat prices declined between 1905 and 1912.[83] As incomes increased, so did meat consumption. Meat required more time to cook and a more extensive array of cooking equipment.

As diet diversified, the degree of specialized knowledge required by houseworkers increased. Cooking was no longer a job that could be 'properly' performed by everyone in the household; rather, a degree of elementary training was required. Long preparation time gives status to food. The provision of a more varied diet had higher time costs, in terms of preparation and administration. Thus, the fall in the consumption of home-cured bacon was made up by the increase in the consumption of American bacon, bought in shops.[84] There was general agreement that women were buying more freely—and buying a better class of goods.[85] This process of shopping involved labour. With widening expectations of home production and services, priorities of domestic labour shifted. Improved access to commercial establishments changed labour from the production of goods in the household with the use of primary materials, to labour involved in gaining access to goods that were already partially or completely processed.[86]

LABOUR AND CONSUMPTION

The labour involved in food does not stop with the purchase of processed or unprocessed food and the preparation of that food. The ritual of consumption entailed work for the houseworker:

[83] Board of Trade (Dept. of Labour Statistics,) *16th Abstract of Labour Statistics* (Cd. 7131), HC 1914, lxxx. 152.

[84] Cullen, *The Emergence of Modern Ireland*, 147–9, 153, and 158.

[85] RCCI, *Appendix to the 2nd Report* (Cd. 3319), HC 1907, xxxv. 218, evidence by James Boyle, shopkeeper at Carrick; 'H. B.', *Letters from Ireland* (Dublin, 1902), 62; George Fletcher, 'Home Life and Training for Home Life', in *Irish Rural Life and Industry* (Dublin, 1907), 47; Cullen, *Life in Ireland*, 156; and Samuel Clark, *Social Origins of the Irish Land War* (Princeton, NJ, 1979), 136. For a delightful poem on this theme, see *Ark*, Apr. 1914: 5.

[86] For a discussion of the role of co-operative retail outlets and 'gombeen-men', see George William Russell, *Templecrone: A Record of Co-operative Effort* (Dublin, 1915).

In the family life each meal time should be looked forward to as a time of pleasure—a rest and refreshment for the mind and body. The woman of the household should set the example of always sitting down to the table neatly dressed, and of having the room, whether it be the kitchen or any other room, where the meals are served in perfect order, and the table should be as temptingly set out as possible . . . all jarring subjects of conversation should be put aside.[87]

Hospitality was labour. Women were responsible for feeding all the members of the household, including the increasing number of male farm servants. The work involved in 'entertaining' can be illustrated by the memoirs of R. A. Anderson, the co-operative adviser. Anderson revelled in the 'unrestrained hospitality' of the homes that he visited on his travels. After one 'gargantuan feast' of ham, geese, duck, mutton (one leg boiled and the other leg roasted), chickens, cabbage, and potatoes, the 'host' turned to his wife and two daughters, who had waited on them during the meal, and commanded them to bring the whiskey and sugar tumblers, and 'be *continually* bringing hot water!'[88] We must assume that it was only after the men had finished consuming that the wife and daughter were allowed to begin. It was the responsibility of the wife or the 'most senior woman' in the household to 'manage' consumption. Just after her marriage, a young wife was given instructions by her mother-in-law on how to feed her husband: 'Mrs Scott [mother-in-law] told me he could not eat much food or coarse food, so it was necessary to give him whatever he liked in every way.'[89] The comment that 'the home is, or ought to be, the woman's kingdom, and that she must rule it wisely, she must serve it well', can be interpreted at different levels.[90]

CLOTHING

Changes in clothing during this period can be seen in the differentiation between the shawl and the fashionable hat. Both sexes increasingly bought their clothes from drapers or travelling

[87] 'Household Hints', *IH*, 4 Mar. 1899: 173.
[88] R. A. Anderson, *With Plunkett in Ireland: The Co-op Organiser's Story* (orig. publ. 1935; Dublin, 1983), 26–7, emphasis in original. Another revealing comment is made by Nora Connolly O'Brien, *Portrait of a Rebel Father* (Dublin, 1935), 29.
[89] PRONI D1884/6/1, papers of Mrs C. Scott.
[90] 'Household Hints', 173.

dealers, and they were prepared to spend large sums on Sunday clothing.[91] Rural journals of the 1880s had encouraged girls to make their own clothing, but by the twentieth century girls were sternly warned against this practice.[92] Certainly, there was a booming trade in ready-made clothes. Sales of 'ready-mades' from the company of Young and Anderson increased by 151 per cent between 1888 and 1913, while haberdashery and other simple goods increased by less than 20 per cent.[93]

People not only had more clothes, they also washed them more frequently, thus increasing the time devoted to laundry (the most disliked of all household chores).[94] The irritation with this chore stemmed from the labour involved in carrying the water.[95] Piped water to individual houses was rare. As late as 1944, the Northern Ireland Housing Survey reported that 87 per cent of all rural houses lacked both piped water and a toilet.[96] Women in households with easy access to a water supply were expected to do more washing and cleaning, and they were less likely to receive help from other members of the household in carting the water. Significantly, the market alternative to home laundry was never developed.[97] Women's columns and domestic education courses argued against laundries on the grounds that the machines tore the clothes and that communal washing spread disease.[98] Most women would have been forced to do their own laundry,

[91] Desmond Murphy, 'Derry and North-West Ulster, 1790–1914', Ph.D. thesis (Dublin, 1978), 435; Michael MacDonagh, 'In the Bye-Ways of Rural Ireland, I', *Nineteenth Century*, July 1900: 79–80; Fletcher, 'Home Life and Training for Home Life', 47; and *Report from the Select Committee on Distress from Want of Employment* (.321), HC 1896: 90, evidence by Anthony J. Staunton, general merchant and farmer, Poor Law Guardian, chairman of the Swinford Union, county Mayo.

[92] 'Extracts from a Country Girl's Diary', *Irish Farming World*, 18 Dec. 1891: 816, and 'L. de K. K.', 'The Homestead and its In-Dwellers', *IH*, 30 June 1906: 540.

[93] PRONI D3641/c/1, Young and Anderson Ltd., wholesale drapers, Belfast, business records.

[94] For a summary of the immense work involved in laundry, and the attitudes of women to laundry work during this period, see Ruth Cowan, *More Work for Mother* (New York, 1983); Davidson, *A Women's Work Is Never Done*, 7–23; Susan Strasser, *Never Done: A History of American Housework* (New York, 1982), 85–124; and S. Minwel Tribbott, 'Laundering in the Welsh Home', *Folklife*, 19 (1981), 36–57.

[95] *3rd Report of Her Majesty's Commissioners for Inquiring into the Housing of the Working Classes*, xxxi. 91.

[96] Northern Ireland Housing Survey, 1944, quoted in Mogey, *Rural Life in Northern Ireland*, 208.

[97] Hartmann, *Capitalism and Women's Work in the Home*, 270–320.

[98] 'Moira', 'Washing: General Directions', *IH*, 12 Nov. 1904: 954.

since laundry facilities (usually at the local convent) were sparse.[99] Sympathetically, the women's pages in newspapers admonished women not to overstrain themselves:

The woman who will overwork on washday and take the rest of the week to recuperate is not an economist but a spendthrift. She who uses up her strength in a day's housecleaning, who strains her muscles with heavy lifting, and is afterwards compelled to keep to her bed, perhaps for a week, nursing a twisted back, does herself and her family a serious harm.[100]

The proposed remedy was ingenious: instead of concentrating a week's, a fortnight's, or a month's washing into one day, women should wash small amounts every day. This 'solution' was guaranteed to increase female labour in the home.

CHILDREN

Much less time was spent on child care than on cleaning and cooking. In part, this was a function of environment. Children in the countryside were supervised less.[101] The labour of child care was undergoing change, however. Child care was an important part of housework. An infertile marriage rebounded on the wife. To have a large number of children made sense on these small farms, even though only one son was needed to take over the farm and to ensure the attachment of the name to the land. Additional children drew on the family purse most heavily when both parents were at their peak-producing period.[102] Emigrant children were the most secure form of investment for old age. The 'correct' care of children was a source of status within both the community and the household. Changing attitudes towards children were reflected in the growing importance of toys. We do not have data on the domestic manufacture of toys, but imports

[99] 'Firin', 'The Rural Districts', ibid. 10 Oct. 1903: 834; Tobar Gurrha, 'It Seems to me: Wanted, a Mary the Wash', ibid. 15 Feb. 1902: 134; and Inter–Departmental Committee on Physical Deterioration, *Appendix to the Report*, iii (Cd. 2186), HC 1904, xxxii. 59, appendix to the evidence of Miss Anderson.

[100] 'For Wife and Maid', *Irish Weekly Independent*, 7 Oct. 1911: 9.

[101] Hartmann, *Capitalism and Women's Work in the Home*, 254, argues that it is urbanization and industrialization that increase the time costs of child care.

[102] Both agricultural productivity and domestic productivity peak between the ages of 35 and 39: Reuben Gronau, 'Home Production: A Forgotten Industry', *Review of Economics and Statistics*, 62 (1980), 408.

of toys and other fancy goods increased from 11,890 cwt. in 1904 to 18,249 cwt. in 1911, an increase of 54 per cent in seven years. A boom in the domestic production of toys is suggested by the increased exportation of toys from only 99 cwt. in 1904 to 701 cwt. by 1911, a sevenfold increase.

Family size and the age of children helped to determine the amount of time spent on housework.[103] Demographers disagree about fertility trends. Brendan M. Walsh argued that marital fertility declined slightly between 1871 and 1911.[104] However, according to R. E. Kennedy, the number of legitimate births per 1,000 married women aged between 15 and 44 increased from 284 in 1881 to 305 in 1911. Marital fertility increased by 1 per cent between 1881 and 1891, by 2 per cent in the next decade, and by 4.4 per cent between 1900 and 1911.[105] The most convincing fertility estimates have been worked out by David Fitzpatrick. Using estimates based on census survivors, Fitzpatrick's index of marital fertility decreases steadily, from 796 in the decade 1871–81 to 743 in the decade 1901–11.[106] In the eight DEDs, however, households were slightly larger.[107] Women living on smaller farms

[103] F. L. Campbell, 'Family in Growth and Variation in Family Role Structure', *Journal of Marriage and Family*, 32 (1970), 45–53; Reuben Gronau, 'The Effects of Children on the Housewife's Value of Time', *JPE* 81/2 (Mar.–Apr. 1973), 168–99; Gronau, 'Home Production', 408–14; Hartmann, *Capitalism and Women's Work in the Home*, 236; Jacob Mincer and Solomon W. Polacek, 'Family Investment in Human Capital: Earnings of Women', *JPE* 82/2 (Mar.–Apr. 1974), 76–108; J. A. Sweet, *Women in the Labour Force* (New York, 1973); Joann Vanek, 'Time Spent in Housework', in Amsden, Alice H. (ed.), *The Economics of Women and Work* (Harmondsworth, 1980), 82–90; and Walker and Woods, *Time Use*.

[104] Brendan M. Walsh, 'Marriage Rates and Population Pressure: Ireland, 1871–1911', *EHR*, 2nd ser. 13 (1970), 148–62.

[105] Robert E. Kennedy, *The Irish: Emigration, Marriage and Fertility* (Berkeley, Calif., 1973), 176.

[106] Statistics kindly provided by David Fitzpatrick. His index of marital fertility gives the ratio of the number of births in each intercensal decade to the number expected from the same age distribution of married Hutterite women (1921–30), multiplied by 1,000. The number of births was estimated from the number of censal survivors aged 2–9 at the end of each decade, plus appropriate proportions of decadal deaths at ages 0, 1, 2, 3, 4, and 5–9, and also of quinquennial emigrants at ages 0, 1–5, and 5–9. He assumes that, within each category, the number of vital events was constant for each year of age and during each year of the period. The resultant estimates for births were converted to decadal estimates using the ratio of registered births for the decade to registered births for the first 8 years.

[107] In the 8 DEDs, 55.9% of unemployed adult women lived in households with more than 5 members in 1901, compared with 56.4% in 1911.

Table 7.8. Average intervals between siblings (aged up to 15), 1901 and 1911

Years between children	% distribution in households	
	1901[a]	1911[b]
1	20.4	26.9
2	50.1	45.3
3	17.9	17.9
4	6.7	5.5
5	2.3	2.9
6	1.5	0.9
6 +	1.1	0.6

[a] n (no. in sample) = 896.
[b] n = 797.

Source: Manuscript census returns for 8 DEDs, NAI, 1901 and 1911.

were increasingly likely to find themselves with more children to take care of during this period. While families living on holdings of between thirty and fifty acres in 1901 contained one more child under the age of 15 than families living on holdings of between one and five acres, by 1911 the differential had narrowed, with the average number of children under 15 decreasing on the larger farms and increasing on the smaller farms. Children were spaced more closely together, increasing the dependency period as well as potentially (though not actually) shortening the extent of full-time child care (see Table 7.8). Children were dependent for longer. This change can be seen even in the ten years between 1901 and 1911. Taking boys aged between 12 and 15, nearly one-third were either entered as having an occupation in 1901, or were said to be occupied on the farm as a 'relative'. By 1911, this had decreased to less than one-quarter of all boys. Most of the change was caused by boys remaining at school for longer.[108] The movement of women into the household allowed more time to be devoted to child-rearing.

---

[108] All 8 DEDs were examined. Girls were left out so that the issue of unemployment specific to *females* would not distort the trends. There were 178 boys aged between 12 and 15 in 1901, compared with 150 boys in 1911.

MEN AND HOUSEWORK

The way in which this extra work in the domestic sphere was distributed requires further analysis. Children might well have been expected to do less housework as their dependency within the household increased with their extra schooling and with the dissemination of an ideology acknowledging the vulnerability of children. Similarly, elderly people did not increase the amount of domestic work that they performed within the household. Certainly, people were living longer and they were likely to spend their final years in their own, or their children's, home (even allowing a wide margin for error with regard to qualifying for the pension!). In 1901 every ninth household contained at least one person over the age of 75. By 1911 every sixth household contained an elderly person.[109] However, just as a new ethos was increasing the standards of care that children required, a similar ethos was developing towards the elderly. The provision of a pension provided old people with an incentive to 'retire', while simultaneously reducing the pressure on them to compensate for their 'dependency' by performing domestic labour.

What about men? Did they take a larger share of the housework? Economists today sometimes claim that the employment of women outside the household increases the amount of housework performed by men.[110] Did the opposite happen when women moved out of paid employment? Exhortations regarding the primacy of *female* labour in child care were common. For instance, the *Ark* published the following warning: ' "Adam", said

[109] The analysis was based on the 8 DEDs. In 1901, 987 households contained 113 persons over 75, and in 1911, 924 households contained 156 persons over 75.

[110] For evidence of increased male participation in households containing employed women, see Lois Wladis Hoffman, 'The Decision to Work', in F. I. Nye and Lois Wladis Hoffman (eds.), *The Employed Mother in America* (Chicago, 1963), and Stephen J. Bahr, 'Effects on Power and the Division of Labour in the Family', in Lois Wladis Hoffman and F. I. Nye (eds.), *Working Mothers* (San Francisco, 1975), 167–85. According to the following authors, the change has been greatly exaggerated: Richard A. Berk and Sarah Fenstermaker Berk, *Labor and Leisure at Home* (Beverly Hills, Calif., 1979); L. L. Holmstrom, *The Two-Career Family* (Cambridge, Mass., 1972); Kathryn E. Walker, 'Time Used by Husbands for Household Work', *Family Economic Review* (June 1970), 8–11; Kathryn E. Walker and William H. Gauger, *The Dollar Value of Household Work* (New York, 1973); and Walker and Woods, *Time Use*, 36.

Eve, "you can take care of the baby now, while I go to the club". Then it was that Adam began raising Cain."[111]

For the reformers, the only role that men were expected to play in the domestic revolution was in encouraging their wives and daughters. Men who attended the meeting to establish a local branch of United Irishwomen were reported as 'giving a sympathetic chorus of approval when the speakers touched on more attention to be given to food and cooking'. The only other time that men raised their voices was when they protested at their exclusion from managerial committees. The men argued that 'they would work it best'.[112] Mrs W. J. Fennell, a subscriber to the Public Health Committee, rebuked men for their indifference to home affairs: 'She thought if men when they go home from their work expressed the pleasure that their wives' efforts in connection with their home give them it would be a great encouragement, in place of jokingly wondering how they put in their time.' Even here, however, the responsibility placed on men was revoked by the statement: 'it rests chiefly with the women to secure the encouragement so persuasively pleaded for by Mrs Fennell.'[113]

But we cannot dismiss men from housework so easily. Young boys might be expected to do more housework than older men. James Cousins, born in Belfast in 1872, spoke about his childhood chores of lighting the kitchen fire and sweeping the floor.[114] 'Noa' of the *Ark* expected men to bring in the fuel, as she nagged in her column: 'Peter, did you fetch some coal this morning before starting out for the field? Why not? Do you think a woman can make bread, pie and cake, boil potatoes, and get a good meal, without coal? Don't grumble because you have so much else to do.'[115] In Nora Tynan O'Mahoney's short story entitled 'Old Friends and True' a male lodger performs a considerable portion of the child care and casual kitchen work.[116] Old men in the Aran

[111] 'Homely Wrinkles', *Ark*, Jan. 1914: 7.
[112] 'Pages for the United Irishwomen', *IH*, 28 Oct. 1911: 859.
[113] 'Topics of the Times', *Irish Weekly Independent*, 11 Jan. 1906: 4. In 1905 the Public Health Committee was at the height of its campaign for neater and cleaner houses.
[114] James H. Cousins and Margaret E. Cousins, *We Two Together* (Madras, 1950), 7.
[115] 'Notes by Noa', *Ark*, 3/33 (June 1912), 3. For similar comments, see 'Notes by Noa', ibid. 3/46 (July 1913), 3.
[116] Nora Tynan O'Mahoney, 'Old Friends and True', *Irish Weekly Independent*, 2 Dec. 1911: 7.

Islands rocked babies in their cradles.[117] Reminiscing about his youth, 86-year-old Richard Denihan of county Limerick said: 'The nursing of children was naturally left to the woman except when the woman would hand the child to the man of the house to mind it for a while if she wanted to do something about the house. 'Twas very unusual to see a man baking or washing.'[118] More commonly, fathers began to assume 'airs of proprietorship' when the child reached 12 years of age.[119] Men might help with the shopping, particularly of bulk goods.[120] Certain culinary traditions included men. Men were involved in the food process at its earliest stage, such as slaughtering pigs, digging potatoes, or providing grain for bread-making. Male visitors were expected to 'give the meat a spin' when meat was cooked on spits, and men took part in preparing meats for 'special' occasions, such as cooking the goose at Christmas.[121]

Contemporary justifications for the sexual division of household labour included the distribution of skills and strength. Thus, women fed pigs because 'they were better at doing that than the men'; whereas men fed cattle. If there was a 'spare' man in the household, he would do the churning, since 'it was too heavy a work for women . . . but if there was only one man in the house, the woman would keep at it.'[122] This sexual division of labour was not simply one of men taking care of 'house' (outdoor work such as carpentry and whitewashing), and women taking care of 'home' (indoor or 'clean' work). The women's columns and domestic instruction books took it for granted that women would be repairing creaky hinges, cupboard-handles, broken plasterwork, and rough wooden doors.[123] 'Heavy' forms of housework

[117] John M. Synge, *The Aran Islands* (Leipzig, 1926), 48.
[118] IFC MS 1210: 179, Richard Denihan, aged 86, of Barony Seanaid (county Limerick) talking to Colm O Danacain in Jan. 1951.
[119] 'United Irishwomen in Conference', *IH*, 8 Oct. 1910: 832. See also Richard Denihan talking to Colm O Danacain, IFC MS 1210: 179.
[120] John Cullen, aged 71, a labourer from Bailieborough (county Cavan), speaking to folklore collector P. J. Gaynor in Jan. 1948, IFC MS 1024: 381–2, and *United Irishman*, 12 July 1902: 5.
[121] Dr Patrick J. Quinn from Mourne (county Down) DED, manuscript essay 'Recollections', in the UFTM questionnaire, 'The Hearth, its Equipment and Traditions', 3, and W. A. Greer, '18 Years, 1896–1914', written between Jan. and July 1967, PRONI T3249/1.
[122] IFC MS 1024: 375, John Cullen speaking to P. J. Gaynor. 375.
[123] 'For Wife and Maid', *Irish Weekly Independent*, 27 May 1911: 9.

were more likely to be seen as male responsibilities, but there were as many definitions of 'heaviness' as there were household tasks.[124]

In 1958 the Irish Folklore Commission sent out a questionnaire entitled 'The Social Aspects of Work'. Question 6 read: 'What part, if any, did men take in housework? Did men ever cook or wash dishes? Did men sweep, clean, or whitewash the house?' of the thirty-seven people, mainly from the counties of Tipperary, Clare, Cork, and Galway, who responded, 15 per cent claimed that men did no housework. Patrick Finn of Loughrea (county Galway) commented that a man who did more than whitewashing 'would inspire some local raftery'. Over half of them said that the sole form of housework performed by men was whitewashing.[125] The only other jobs that men might perform were sweeping the yard, cleaning the chimney, and churning. Three respondents said that single men might be forced to cook.[126] Men only washed, cooked, and cleaned inside the house when there was no other adult women in the household:

Men that lived alone had to do all that class of work [housework] themselves. Some of them could bake and cook and wash as good as any woman. Some men could do their own knitting, and there were men that could sew as well as any woman. They could patch their clothes, and there were men that could make up butter as good as a woman would do it—they'd make it better than some women. There was many an unfortunate man that his wife died and left him with a family of small children, and that poor fellow had to wash and clean the children and cook and mend for them, and do all the work about the house and try to do his own work along with that. You'd see two or three old brothers living together, and no woman in the house, and one of them would have to do the baking and cooking and mending and washing and all the work that a woman would do about a house. In some cases like that they'd get in a woman once in a while to do the washing or any mending that was a wanting to be done.[127]

---

[124] Charlotte O'Conor-Eccles instructed men to carry water and turf in order to 'free' women for all the other housework: *Simple Advice to be Followed by All who Desire the Good of Ireland, and Especially by Gaelic Leaguers* (Dublin, 1905), 6. The very heavy job of washing clothes was relegated to women, while repairing cupboard-handles was often performed by men.

[125] Women also whitewashed the outside and inside of houses: IFC MS 1024: 379, John Cullen speaking to P. J. Gaynor.

[126] IFC MS 1828, 'The Social Aspects of Work', 1958; and MS 1523, 1669, 1670, and 1829.   [127] IFC MS 1024: 380–1, John Cullen speaking to P. J. Gaynor.

Men who were suddenly left without a female houseworker found the transition difficult. Some of them hired women (generally elderly women) to 'keep house' for them;[128] others simply failed to perform other functions satisfactorily. In May 1901 and in October 1912 Samuel H. Kingston, principal of Tullywest National School, struggled unsuccessfully to get to his classes on time. In 1901 his excuse was being without a servant girl for two weeks. He was married by 1912, but his wife's sickness perpetuated the problem.[129]

If men had usually only performed housework when a female worker was unavailable, we would expect an increase in the number of male houseworkers. In the eight DEDs, 5 per cent of all households in 1901 had no resident female relative or domestic servant. This had increased to 7 per cent by 1911. Much of this change was due to the decline in the number of female domestic servants in households with no female relative. Thus, nearly 15 per cent of households with no female relative had a resident domestic servant in 1901, compared with nearly 8 per cent in 1911. What is interesting, therefore, is the marginalization of men from ideologies of housework.[130]

Nevertheless, housework remained a predominantly female occupation. Taking male-headed households in the eight DEDs, Table 7.9 shows that even households without a wife usually had another woman present to perform the tasks required.[131] Of course, these were very good reasons why women wished men to do *less* housework. Especially as alternative sources of employment for women were contracting, male participation in housework jeopardized their chief source of power. Similarly,

---

[128] 'A Guardian of the Poor', *Irish Peasant* (1892), 9.

[129] PRONI SCH 192/9/2, Tullywest National School, Inspector's Observation Book, 25 May 1901 and 2 Oct. 1912. The inspector on both occasions was W. Macmillan, and the principal was Samuel H. Kingston. For a humorous story of what happens when a wife or female servant is absent, see 'Tullyneil', 'Cooking', in *At Home in Tyrone. Sketches and Short Stories* (Belfast, 1945), 15–23.

[130] The relatively high proportion of all-male households in Ireland contrasts with contemporary rural societies, where rigid sexual divisions of labour in the domestic sphere meant that households without at least 1 healthy woman could not survive.

[131] See e.g. the comment by Peig Sayers that her sister could not get married until the brother brought a wife into the house to help with the housework: Peig Sayers, *Peig: The Autobiography of Peig Sayers of the Great Blasket Island* (Dublin, 1974), 24.

Table 7.9. Women as houseworkers, and their relationship to the 'head' of the household, 1901 and 1911 (%)

Characteristics of household	Distribution of houseworkers within households	
	1901[a]	1911[b]
Female-headed household	1.3	1.6
1 man only in household	4.3	5.6
No women in household, more than 1 man	1.0	1.5
Wife in household	72.0	71.2
Unmarried daughter (adult) in household	6.7	5.3
Married daughter (adult) in household	1.1	1.0
Granddaughter (adult) in household	0.5	0.3
Unmarried sister (adult) in household	7.4	8.1
Married sister or sister-in-law in household	0.5	0.4
Niece or cousin in household	0.7	0.8
Daughter-in-law in household	0.9	2.0
Mother in household	1.6	0.7
Aunt in household	0.4	0.4
Domestic servant in household	1.6	1.1

[a] n (no. in sample) = 744.
[b] n = 712.

Source: Manuscript census returns for 8 DEDs, NAI, 1901 and 1911.

women increasingly performed housework without the help of domestic servants. By 1910 the *Irish Weekly Independent* could say that man's ideal woman 'must be a splendid Housekeeper and not require any servants'.[132] Advertisers quickly exploited this shift in their market by claiming that their products were 'just as good as' a domestic servant, or even by declaring that their products *were* domestic servants.[133] Housework came to be regarded as the work performed, without payment, by female members of the

---

[132] 'For Wife and Mother', *Irish Weekly Independent*, 12 Feb. 1910: 9.
[133] See e.g. the advertisement for 'STOBIE', in *Irish Peasant*, 6 Dec. 1905: 4: 'If Mothers of Young Families Only Knew its Virtues as a Household Servant They Would Never be Without It . . . *Stobie* will Destroy Every Living Thing in a Child's Head in One Hour.' See also *Irish Weekly Independent*, 30 Apr. 1910: 9.

household. Even in the small proportion of households without potential female houseworkers, the labour was regarded as fundamentally feminine.

Housework was a form of necessary labour; unsurprisingly, domestic production was crucial in determining an individual woman's choice of work. Analysis of the changes in the material culture of housework allows us to minimize the importance of strictly 'ideological' factors, which develop more slowly than material changes and may remain out of step. As the gap narrowed between female productivity in the household and their potential productivity in the waged and subsistence labour markets, women moved out of these markets and into the household. This chapter has traced increases in household production through changes in the demand for domestic labour. Although this shift was particularly important in rural areas, where houseworkers produced a larger proportion of goods for household consumption from raw materials, the time required to prepare processed foods for consumption was significant even for urban houseworkers.[134] Houseworkers were not only better prepared for domestic work in terms of education and health, but the time that they spent on housework was liable to be greater, with increased female unemployment, changing technologies of housework, and alterations in family structure. Their output of goods and services increased in line with labour and capital investment in the home. It was not only *social* status and levels of conspicuous displays of consumption which were enhanced by increased labour in the home.[135] Improvements in basic economic status were more crucial. While houseworkers saved labour in some areas (such as making clothes), they increased their labour in other areas (such as shopping for clothes and washing clothes). Rising living standards resulted in an increase of household labour for lower classes of women. Women found that there was more work for them to do inside the home.

[134] Bill Reimer, 'Women as Farm Labor', *Rural Sociology*, 51/2 (1986), 143–55.
[135] Veblen, *Theory of the Leisure Class*, 126.

8

Education for the Home

She [Mrs Moore] walked in, an' she sat down there in the chair. She was asking about the child an' this thing an' that thing, but in the end she began telling me, about a meeting they had in the church, the minister's wife was lecturing she said, an' telling the women what to do. They should have a nice 'clane' house an' a good fire before their husbands when they'd come into their meals, a nice meal before 'em an' a smiling face, to make 'em cheerful and happy. Yerra, I don't know how many more things she said but in the end when I was sick out of her [*sic*] an' I couldn't be listening to her any longer. 'Tis easy for the minister's wife to talk, says I, if she were here trying to boil a pot o' praties often with a wet green bush, an' a child 'longside her crying with the hunger. I wander [*sic*] what sort of face she'd have on when her husband would come to his dinner. She had to laugh at me.[1]

HOUSEWORK has always required training. However, in certain periods the training that females received at home came to be deemed inadequate, and organizations arose to supplement it. From the 1880s, the poor domestic skills of Irishwomen began to attract comment as one of the more serious causes of distress in rural Ireland.[2] By the 1890s, these calls had become increasingly vocal.[3] Education in housework came to be seen as a way of

---

[1] IFC MS 843: 91–2, story told by Paddy Murphy about a couple with 7 children who lived on a farm 'seventy years ago'. The tale was recounted by Mickey Crowley of Carrigroe (county Cork), between Aug. and Oct. 1942. Crowley was 95 years old at the time of recording.

[2] *Report of the Select Committee on Industries (Ireland)* (.288), HC 1884–5, ix. 370–1 and 298, evidence by William H. Keating (small proprietor, shareholder, and Irish agent in an English manufacturing and warehouse company), and evidence by Lt.-Col. James O'Hara (chairman of the Town and Harbour Commission of Galway, auditor of the Poor Law Board for Mayo, Galway, and a greater part of Clare, and chairman of the Jute Spinning Company in Galway).

[3] RCL, *The Agricultural Labourer*, iv. *Ireland*, II, *Reports by Mr W. P. O'Brien* (C. 6894-xix), HC 1893–4, xxxvii/1: 75, on the Poor Law Union of Wexford (county Wexford); and 'The Reasons for United Irishwomen', *IH*, 26 Oct. 1912: 864. See also Irish Technical Instruction Association, *15th Congress: Dublin, June 4th, 5th*

stimulating a revolution in the unwaged domestic sphere. The organizations devoting capital to educational schemes in domestic labour shared a vision of a prosperous countryside which could only be realized by the increased and improved expenditure of unwaged labour in the home.

DOMESTIC EDUCATION CLASSES

In response to the preoccupation with domestic standards of living, private and public organizations developed schemes designed to teach housework to Irishwomen. The principal organizations concerned with domestic education were (in ascending order of significance) the Women's National Health Association (WNHA), United Irishwomen (UI), the IAOS, the CDB, the DATI, and the Board of National Education.[4]

The WNHA was inaugurated on 13 March 1907. Although an attack of rheumatic fever prevented her from attending the inaugural meeting, the Countess of Aberdeen (wife of the Lord-Lieutenant of Ireland), was responsible for the establishment and growth of this organization. The Association was urban-based and dependent on the fund-raising abilities of its powerful patrons. The WNHA undertook to rouse the women of Ireland into bearing responsibility for the health of the country. The need for an organization that looked beyond tuberculosis was reflected in the Countess of Aberdeen's original rejection of the name 'Anti-Consumption Society' for the broader title of 'National Health Society'. Imitating the Americans, the Association used caravans to deliver information about tuberculosis. However, since the key to the prevention of tuberculosis lay in improved methods of housework (both in the menial form of dusting, sweeping, and

and 6th, 1919 (Athlone, 1919), 79. In educated Dublin circles, the stress on domestic education was translated into a demand for the teaching of domestic economy in universities, thus obscuring the more central argument concerning the admittance and place of women in Irish universities: see *Dublin Journal of Medical Science*, 1 Sept. 1911 (132/477), 166; articles and papers on women in universities by Hanna Sheehy Skeffington and Mary Hayden, in NLI MS 22262; letters from Hanna Sheehy Skeffington to Mary Hayden, in NLI MS 24009; and Mary Hayden's paper, 'Not Worth Mentioning', in NLI MS 24010.

[4] These are the main institutions in the rural areas. Other organizations involved in this work include the urban-based Irish Co-operative Women's Guild.

scrubbing and in the more elevated form of child care), domestic education featured prominently in the itinerant programmes. The first caravan, *Eire*, visited 370 rural centres and performed for around 74,000 people, with the slogan 'Our Enemies are Bad Air, Bad Food, Bad Drink and Dirt. Our Friends are Pure Air, Pure Food, Pure Milk and Cleanliness', brightly painted on its sides.[5] By 1911 it had active branches in every county. Colourful and musical promotional strategies, coupled with easily assimilated educational programmes, assured its popularity in entertainment-starved rural communities.

In addition to itinerant classes, from 1908 it established baby clubs, where mothers were taught child care.[6] For young girls, local branches supported 'Girl Guides of Good Health'.[7] An examination of the rules to which these Girl Guides subscribed illustrates the connection between the tuberculosis campaign and education in housework. The girls swore to practise all the laws of health. They learned about dietary requirements and how to keep food free from contamination. In addition, when reciting the rules, girls promised to learn how to prepare meals in an appetizing manner, to study first aid, and to take every opportunity to care for young children and the sick. They swore to learn how to keep houses ventilated and in a 'sanitary condition'. They were taught how to make and repair clothes. Finally, WNHA girls promised to masticate their food well, to breathe through their noses, to keep their backs straight, and to repudiate tight stays and high-heeled shoes.[8] The range of activities carried out by the WNHA may be illustrated by looking at its Wexford branch. This branch employed a district nurse (with the financial help of the Samitarian Fund), set up weekly entertainment in the town hall, offered generous financial prizes for the winner of the 'Best Kept Cottage' competition, introduced schemes whereby young mothers were visited by matrons who initiated them into the rites of mothercraft, started a small lending library,

---

[5] See the photograph in Countess of Aberdeen, *Ireland's Crusade against Tuberculosis*, iii (Dublin, 1909), 120.

[6] Countess of Aberdeen, *The Work of the WNHA of Ireland* (Dublin, c.1910).

[7] The WNHA suggested setting up a male equivalent to the Girl Guides of Good Health. Boys would be taught how to help keep the house tidy, and 'would undertake not to smoke cigarettes until they are twenty-one': WNHA, *Organisation of Local Branches* (Dublin, c.1910), 13.

[8] Sir Robert Matheson, *A Review of the Anti-Tuberculosis Campaign in Ireland* (Dublin, 1908), 17–18.

and bribed young girls to attend classes of visiting speakers with promises of gifts. The concerns of the WNHA were summarized in a letter written by E. S. McManus, president of the Killeaden branch, on 10 April 1911:

We, the Members of this Branch, a body of nearly 100 women and girls, realise we are banded together to fight the great enemy, Consumption, the Dragon with many heads, and to meet this foe we muster suitable forces in opposition. Cleanliness against Dirt, Cheerfulness and Good Comradeship against wretchedness and depression of Poverty. Beauty of surroundings against squalor and disorderliness; wholesome variety of food (we are particularly strong on this point) against the usual unvarying soda-cake, potatoes, and cow-cabbage diet . . . we mean to cook many simple dishes, the ingredients of which are within our reach in nearly all the surrounding village shops; Irish-stews, suet rolls, to be eaten with golden syrup, and cakes of cornflour, and mutton, and chicken broth for our sick. . . . At the General Branch meetings our leaders sound trumpet calls to the girls of the 16 villages we number to make their homes and surroundings as neat and beautiful as any in the world. . . . As regards cleanliness, the path has been a delicate one to tread. At our meetings we speak boldly to the women of coming house to house visitation.[9]

Given the skill with which the WNHA drew 18,000 persons into its membership by 1910, it was doubtful whether Ireland needed any other women's organization.[10] However, the first UI opened a branch in Bree (county Wexford), and then rapidly expanded into the other counties of Leinster as well as into the counties of Waterford, Cork, Limerick, Clare, Galway, Mayo, Sligo, Donegal, Tyrone, Antrim, and Cavan. Associated branches in London, Montreal, and Chicago raised funds. The primary goals of the UI and the WNHA coincided, but, while the WNHA represented the Anglo-Irish élite, the UI was drawn from aspiring, middle-class Irishwomen. The UI scorned the despotism of 'the Countess'. It believed that the efficiency of the WNHA had been irredeemably hurt by its politics.[11] Each UI branch was independent, leaving the central body as an 'organizing organization'.[12]

---

[9] Countess of Aberdeen, *Work of the WNHA*, 9–10, letter by E. S. McManus (president of the Killeaden branch of United Irishwomen), 10 Apr. 1911.

[10] 'Harvest', 'Women's National Health Association', *IH*, 11 June 1910: 488.

[11] 'One of the United Irishwomen', 'United Irishwomen', ibid. 20 Aug. 1910: 694, and John Brennan, 'United Irishwomen', *Bean na-Éireann*, 21 (*c*.1910), 7.

[12] 'New Life for Irish Women', *IH*, 1 Apr. 1911: 245–6.

United Irishwomen claimed that the feminine consciousness
that expressed itself in England by agitating for the vote would
express itself in Ireland by improving conditions of life for rural
women.[13] Whatever tenuous connections it might claim with the
British women's movement, the UI was organized, used, and
supported by a bastion of male bureaucracy—the IAOS. Although
local UI groups refused to allow men on their committees, they
welcomed them in the powerful, and non-responsible, role of
'associates'.[14] Within the co-operative movement, UI carried out
the third portion of Plunkett's maxim: 'Better Farming, Better
Business, Better Living'. It taught cooking, promoted temperance, disseminated co-operative principles, organized charity,
ensured that women received proper representation on local
boards—and obtained legal assistance or redress when required—
and secured competent sanitary officers. Commentators represented the typical United Irishwoman as triumphantly extending
'her interests beyond the home' in reformatory zeal, but failed to
note that this extension occurred only in areas uncontentiously
regarded as women's proper sphere in the first place.[15] Indeed,
the UI keenly encouraged those women whom it saw as 'outside the home' to return. It crusaded against female agricultural
labourers.[16] Equally, it wanted to move men out of what it saw
as women's sphere:

The Irish Peasantry Society of London provide, we are told, £25 to this
Union for prizes for the best kept labourer's cottage, and a similar sum
to two adjourning Unions. This fund is administered by men, and, with
all due deference to the sterner sex, we wonder what they think they
know about how the interior of a cottage should be kept. Probably they
know less than nothing. Women should protest against men coming in
to mismanage what is obviously women's work.[17]

[13] 'The United Irishwomen: What they Are and What they Want to Do', *United
Irishwomen*, 1 (1 May 1912), 1.
[14] 'Pages for the Irish Countrywoman', *IH*, 28 Oct. 1911: 859. For information
on the links between the UI and the IAOS, see the correspondence between
Horace Plunkett and Lord Monteagle, in Monteagle Papers, NLI MS 13414.
[15] 'United Irishwomen', *IH*, 28 May 1910: 441.
[16] Ibid. 452, paper read at a United Irishwomen's meeting in Ballynadara
(Enniscorthy); it does not say who read the paper, although it was the main one
presented. The author wanted these women to be replaced by male labourers,
paid out of the money that women earned through cottage industries and saved
by being full-time houseworkers. See also Darrell Figgis, *Irishmen of Today: AE
(George W. Russell). A Study of a Man and a Nation* (Dublin, 1916), 90.
[17] 'United Irishwomen', *IH*, 28 May 1910: 451.

World War I heralded the decline of the UI. It was not to be revived until the 1930s, under the name 'Irish Countrywoman's'. In 1914 its governing body dropped plans for a library, dissolved the goat club, closed the milk depots, ceased the provision of cocoa for schoolchildren, and applied itself wholly to war work.[18] Its funds had always been very limited. It received one grant from the IAOS, the services of two temporary instructresses from the CDB, and, for the rest, depended on the affiliation fees of its branches—a tiny sum—and on the generosity of subscribers.[19] By 1915 a grant of £1,500 from the Pembroke Trust Fund had run out and the revenue of the Home-Brightening Committee was depleted. Minor financial encouragement in 1914 from the CDB, the Spiddal Gaelic College, and the London branch could not halt the disintegration.

Despite rhetorical avowals of independence, the UI worked under the IAOS. The success of women's co-operation in the UI was seen as demonstrating the success of the entire co-operative movement.[20] This drawing-together of women 'without regard to class, politics, or religion' was vital if Ireland's difficulties were to be solved.[21] As most members of the UI had fathers and brothers within the IAOS, their naïve confidence in their elevated place in the co-operative movement, and thus in the future 'improved' Ireland, was pardonable.[22] However, the attitude of co-operative men towards the UI was ambivalent. Interrupting a statement by George Russell that the emerging UI would give Irish women 'an opportunity of justifying their existence', the Hon. A. Broderick noted: 'the existence of Russell himself was justification for the existence of women'. After prolonged applause and 'hear, hears!', Broderick argued that a woman's greatest need was to be trained herself before she could train others.[23]

These words, 'before a woman could adequately help she must be adequately trained', provided the justification for the IAOS to intervene in the domestic sphere.[24] At its grandest, the IAOS planned to establish centralized cooking halls and kitchens, which,

---

[18] 'United Irishwomen', ibid. 3 July 1915: 444, and 'The United Irishwomen', ibid. 24 Apr. 1915: 273.
[19] St J. Whitty, 'Constructive Criticism of the United Irishwomen', *Better Business Journal*, 1/3 (Apr. 1916), 263–4.
[20] 'United Irishwomen in Conference', *IH*, 10 Sept. 1910: 752–3.
[21] Ibid. 752.   [22] 'New Life for Irishwomen', ibid. 1 Apr. 1911: 245–6.
[23] 'IAOS Annual Meeting, 1910', ibid. 3 Dec. 1910: 1004–5.   [24] Ibid.

using its estimate of one hall for every thirty to forty families, would have entailed the building of around 2,700 such sites.[25] More economically, it encouraged the teaching of cookery in local co-operative societies, particularly in societies set up to promote home industries. Ironically, it attempted to undercut the monetary basis of female home industries: these were justified even if they *lost* money, because home industries raised standards of housework.[26]

The work of these private organizations was supported by the Roman Catholic Church. A number of prominent priests attempted to change the dietary habits of the people. For example, in 1904 the Bishop of Ross, a Tipperary-born man who worked in Ennis (county Clare) and Cork, confessed that, while the priesthood did not generally think it was their job to educate the people in such matters, he exercised his power at confirmations by preaching the importance of providing children with milk and special 'management'. He modestly claimed to have had 'some success'.[27]

The largest investments in domestic education were made by state organizations. The CDB pioneered itinerant classes in 1898, and, within three years, it was holding ninety courses in housework (each lasting four months) within the 'congested districts'. All together, 5,000 women were trained in these classes.[28] The popularity of the classes was confirmed by the long waiting-lists and overcrowded classes.[29] The Board considered itinerant classes in housework to be imperative if the 'congested districts'

[25] 'Centralising the Cookery', ibid. 27 Mar. 1909: 243.

[26] 'Co-operation and the Improvement of the Home: Sir Horace Plunkett Visits Dromore', ibid. 22 Oct. 1904: 892; 'Dromore', ibid. 30 July 1904: 632; 'The Economic Problem and Domestic Life', ibid. 3 June 1905: 438; and 'Co-operation and the Home', ibid. 30 July 1904: 622–3.

[27] Inter-Departmental Committee on Physical Deterioration, *Minutes of Evidence*, iii (Cd. 2210), HC 1904, xxxii: 412, evidence by the Bishop of Ross. For other evidence of the influence of priests in changing the diet of their constituents, see RCCI, *Appendix to the 10th Report* (Cd. 4007), HC 1908, xlii: 15, evidence by Revd John Flatley, representing Clare Island and the diocese of Tuam, and the minutes of a UI meeting, 17 July 1913: 14 (held by the Irish Countrywoman's Association). For a humorous story about a priest's domestic teaching, see Harold Begbie, *The Lady Next Door* (1912), 68–9.

[28] CDB, *9th Report 1900* (Cd. 239), HC 1900, lxvii: 39–40.

[29] 'Irish Work and Irish Workers', *Irish Peasant*, 9 Dec. 1905: 7; CDB, *10th Report, 1901* (Cd. 681), HC 1901, lx: 45; CDB, *11th Report, 1902* (Cd. 1192), HC 1902, lxxxiii: 39; and CDB, *22nd Report, 1913–1914* (Cd. 7865), HC 1914–16, xxiv: 20.

were to avoid becoming the choleraic cousin of a developing Ireland.[30] As its only unwaged scheme, the classes in domestic economy were an anomaly and caused tension between the DATI and the CDB.[31] Despite territorial disputes between these organizations, the CDB extended its domestic education schemes until 1923, when the entire Board was dissolved. A typical course was held in a small Donegal community, Glencolumbkill, where fifty out of a total of seventy women who attended classes in 1906 received certificates of proficiency after four months. Attendance was high. The girls were taught basic cookery, such as making tea and coffee, bread-baking, cooking meat and vegetables, and invalid cookery. Lessons in laundry included instruction in the washing and drying of different types of materials, starching and stiffening, ironing and folding. One-third of the course was devoted to general housekeeping. The girls were instructed in bed-making, table-setting, and the correct cleaning of everything, from the fire grate to the human body.[32] Although the course stressed economical use of everyday utensils, the organizers clearly wanted to raise expectations of housework by introducing novel methods, dietary variety, and new home-made utensils.[33] It was alleged that local standards of housework had improved dramatically as a result of the course. [34]

Fired by the obvious popularity and alleged effectiveness of the Board's itinerant schemes in the congested districts, the DATI assigned itinerant domestic instructresses to educate rural houseworkers in the rest of Ireland. Each year, between 7,000 and 15,000 women attended the locally managed schemes in rural domestic economy. Although this was not the only way in which the Department taught housekeeping, the impact of the itinerant instructresses in rural areas was paramount. The itinerant schemes were particularly popular in the southern counties of Carlow, Kilkenny, Tipperary, and Kerry, where the Department had problems training a sufficient number of instructresses to meet

---

[30] Patrick O'Donnell, writing on 'Practical Primary Education in Congested Districts', in RCCI, *Final Report* (Cd. 4097), HC 1908, xlii: 206–7.

[31] CDB, *19th Report, 1909–1911* (Cd. 5712), HC 1911, xiii: 36–7.

[32] CDB, *9th Report*, lxviii, app. 37: 104.

[33] William P. Coyne (ed.), *Ireland: Industrial and Agricultural* (Dublin, 1902), 270.

[34] RCCI, *Appendix to the 2nd Report* (Cd. 3319), HC 1907, xxxv: 143, evidence by the Very Revd Canon Sweeney.

the demand.[35] Local committees often had to wait a year or more before an instructress was free to come to the area.[36] In January 1914, at the same time as a crochet class in Fermoy (county Cork) had to close because of small enrolments and attendances, the domestic economy class had to be extended from six weeks to ten weeks because of high demand.[37] Bureaucrats in the Department's treasury frequently refused to pay the full grant applied for by the technical committees, on the grounds that the number of students exceeded the maximum of twenty per course.[38]

The Department affirmed the centrality of these classes to the rural economy, arguing that instruction in poultry-keeping, horticulture, home industries, and manual work must remain secondary to that in cooking, laundry work, and home-sewing.[39] It introduced compulsory instruction in cookery in all its agricultural and industrial courses for women.[40] It conducted annual courses for teachers in domestic economy, and gave £1,000 (on average) each year to secondary schools throughout Ireland for cooking equipment. In addition, it established rural domestic economy schools and provided scholarships to facilitate the enrolment of poor students. The Department also assumed control of existing schools for domestic economy, such as the Killarney School of Housewifery. 'Bean-an-Tigue' schools were established in rural centres, often in the home of a religious community. To qualify as a rural centre, a farm had to contain at least twenty-five statute acres, with suitable accommodation for farmyard animals, a small dairy, and a kitchen garden. Although the kitchen had to have at least two open hearths, it did not need a range. Students were to be taught only those dishes which could be made from locally grown products on an open hearth and using

---

[35] 'Wanted: Technical Instructresses', *IH*, 22 Nov. 1902: 923–94.

[36] 'Itinerant Instruction in Domestic Economy', *DATI Journal*, 10/3 (Apr. 1910), 467.

[37] Cork Archives Institute U189: 83, minutes of the meeting of the County Cork Joint Technical Instruction Committee, Thursday, 15 Jan. 1914.

[38] Ibid. 46.

[39] DATI, *4th Annual General Report, 1903–1904* (Cd. 2509), HC 1905, xxi: 5–6.

[40] 'Munster Dairy and Agricultural School', *Irish Farming World*, 23 Oct. 1891: 692, and DATI, 'Council of Agriculture, 11th Meeting, Friday, 17 May 1907, Report of Proceedings', discussion by George Fletcher, 85 (in NLI).

common utensils.[41] As the Convent of St Louis Rural Domestic Economy School at Ramsgrange (county Waterford) advertised: 'This school is not intended for girls who propose emigrating or devoting themselves to domestic service. [It is] *THE* school for FARMER'S DAUGHTERS.'[42]

Finally, after a large public organization such as the DATI had demonstrated the extent of demand for domestic training, domestic economy was formally encouraged by the official education boards. Before official steps were taken in the 1890s, cookery and laundry had frequently appeared on the curriculum of rural schools, particularly of convent schools. By the end of the nineteenth century, pressure on the Commissioners of National Education had made it impossible for them to ignore the issue any longer. Following the lead of the DATI, the Board of National Education began by employing itinerant teachers.[43] In 1905 it gave permission for National schoolchildren to attend DATI classes in domestic economy in lieu of training by their National schoolteacher.[44] Where large numbers of children attended the scheme at a technical school, the Board of Education reimbursed the technical school authorities at a rate of 7s. 6d. per pupil.[45] By 1900, cookery and laundry had become a recognized, and examined, part of the curriculum. Pressure began to be exerted on all schools with female teachers to introduce these subjects. Burgeoning classes necessitated alterations in the syllabus of female teacher training-colleges. In 1908 the committee appointed to examine the provision of cookery and laundry instruction in teacher training-colleges decided that eighty hours would be devoted to cookery, and twenty to laundry—less time would be devoted to English, drawing, elementary science, and vocal music.[46]

---

[41] NAI AG1 A13317/16, DATI Papers, assorted papers from 1907, including a letter to Prof. Campbell from E. Gallagher of the Athenry Agricultural Station (county Galway), 19 Jan. 1907, about the proposed rural domestic economy school in the Convent of Mercy, Clifden.

[42] *Irish Weekly Independent*, 3 Dec. 1910: 45, emphasis in original.

[43] *63rd Report of the Commissioners of National Education, 1896–1897* (C. 8600), HC 1897, xxvii: 34.

[44] NLI, 'Minutes of the Proceedings of the Commissioners of National Education at their Meeting on Tuesday, 29 August 1905', 392.

[45] *77th Report of the Commissioners of National Education, 1910–1911* (Cd. 5903), HC 1911, xxi: 11.

[46] NLI, 'Minutes of the Proceedings of the Commissioners of National Education at their Meeting on Tuesday, 20 October 1908', 405.

Teachers opposed the compulsory classes in cooking and laundry in schools. A few argued that such subjects were outside the scope of a primary school and should be left to technical schools: the function of the National teacher was 'to educate, to develop the mind and to train the senses', not to teach skills that could be learned later in life.[47] The more prevalent argument drew attention to the implications of the scheme for competition between male and female teachers. With compulsory teaching of needlework, and plans to add similar classes in cookery for a further two hours a week, women teachers would have to teach an extra five hours a week.[48] Since the inspection system meant that teachers' wages depended on favourable reports from inspectors of the 'mainstream' subjects, such considerations were important. By 1909, teachers in all counties had adopted resolutions against the compulsory teaching of domestic economy.[49]

Their opposition was ignored. There was a rapid increase in the number of schools teaching domestic economy. By 1914, nearly half of all schools (including all-male schools) taught domestic economy. Educating schoolgirls in cookery and laundry met with general approval. Even teachers were unanimous that Irish girls had to be taught housekeeping at *some* time.[50] Cookery was popular amongst the parents, and there was widespread agreement that the classes increased female enrolment and attendance at school.[51] Hampered in some areas by the lack of the necessary

[47] Catherine A. Mahon, 'Report of Deputation to Education Office: Cookery and Laundry, and Other Organisational Matters', *Irish School Weekly*, 27 Mar. 1909: 182, deputation to Starkie and W. P. Headen; *Appendix to the 76th Report of the Commissioners of National Education, 1909–1910*, i (Cd. 5491), HC 1911, xxi: 124, report on the Portarlington Circuit; and 'Queens' County Association: Eloquent Address by Miss Mahon and Mr Mansfield', *Irish School Weekly*, 27 Mar. 1909: 165.

[48] 'Queens' County Association', 165. See also 'Suffrage Meeting in Birr', *Kings' County Chronicle*, 1 Feb. 1912: 4.

[49] 'Educational News of the Week', *Irish School Weekly*, 3 Apr. 1909: 204.

[50] Alice Spring Rice (of Foynes, county Limerick), 'Housekeeping Instruction in National Schools', *IH*, 26 Mar. 1898: 281.

[51] See e.g. the autobiography of Frances Moffett, *I Also Am of Ireland* (1985), 50, where she quotes from a letter that she wrote between 1912 and 1914 saying how much the female students looked forward to cookery day. See the inspector's reports from the circuits of Waterford and Cork 1, as well as the specialized reports by Miss Prendergast (on industrial instruction) and Miss Catherine M. Shuley (on cookery and laundry), in *Appendix to the 76th Report of the Commissioners of National Education*, i, xxi: 134, 148, 174–5, and 186; J. P. Dalton's report

fittings and appliances in single-roomed schoolhouses, cookery lessons were nevertheless introduced gradually and consistently.[52] Convent schools, in particular, eagerly adopted the Board's scheme for teaching domestic economy, even before the introduction of the compulsory classes for older students, but it was secular teachers who flocked to the courses run by the DATI to train them to teach cookery and laundry.[53] There was a dramatic increase in the number of classes after 1908. This is hardly surprising, since in 1907 the Commissioners of National Education had received Treasury sanction for the payment of a special fee of 5s. a head for girls attending courses in cookery and laundry, ostensibly to cover equipment and materials. Payment of this fee allowed a girl to attend classes for a maximum of one or two years. From 1908, therefore, the less generously endowed schools in the west quickly introduced domestic instruction. Department grants to secondary schools teaching such subjects increased after 1905, rivalling the assistance given to manual instruction classes after 1908, and generated an increase in domestic economy classes. Naturally, progress was slow, and, even with the help of generous grants, equipment remained primitive in some areas. For instance, in the school year 1912–13 the teacher for Kingscourt

on the Galway Circuit, in *Appendix to the 75th Report of the Commissioners of National Education, 1908–1909*, i (Cd. 5062), HC 1910, xxv. 78; and T. P. O'Connor's report on the Cork Circuit 2, in *Appendix to the 78th Report of the Commissioners on National Education, 1911–1912*, i (Cd. 7061), HC 1914, xxvii: 133.

[52] *71st Report of the Commissioners of National Education, 1904–1905* (Cd. 2567), HC 1905, xxviii: 2–4; report by J. B. Skeffington of the Waterford District, in *Appendix to the 66th Report of the Commissioners of National Education, 1899–1900*, i (Cd. 286), HC 1900, xxiii: 138; report by Miss M. Fitzgerald, head of cookery and laundry work, in *Appendix to the 72nd Report of the Commissioners of National Education, 1905–1906*, i (Cd. 3185), HC 1906, xxix: 188 and 191; and the speech by Mrs Nugent T. Everard, in *Verbatim Report of the 16th All-Ireland Industrial Conference, October 4th and 5th, 1910* (Cork, 1910), 118; and *71st Report of the Commissioners of National Education*, xxviii: 2 and 6.

[53] 'National Schools in Ireland', *Irish Textile Journal*, 15 Sept. 1895: 118–19; *Appendix to the 70th Report of the Commissioners of National Education, 1903*, i (C. 2373), HC 1905, xxvii: 206; NLI, 'Minutes of the Proceedings of the Commissioners of National Education at their Meeting on Tuesday, 29th December 1908', 526; *Intermediate Education (Ireland): Report of Messrs F. H. Dale and T. A. Stephens on Intermediate Education* (C. 2546), HC 1905, xxviii: 56; and Miss Fitzgerald, 'General Report on Cookery and Laundry Work, 1904', in *Appendix to the 71st Report of the Commissioners of National Education, 1904*, i (Cd. 2654), HC 1905, xxviii: 124–5. In 1901, of the 806 teachers instructed by Miss Fitzgerald's team of organizers in 60 centres, 66% were secular teachers: see *Appendix to the 68th Report of the Commissioners of National Education, 1901*, i (Cd. 997), HC 1902, xxx: 153.

and Bailieborough (county Cavan), Miss Acheson Smyth, reported that cookery equipment was deficient in nearly half of the eighty-five schools in her area.[54] By 1910, female teachers were offered an extra incentive to teach cookery and laundry: the Board of Education began to withhold salary increments from female teachers who had failed to teach domestic economy 'without sufficient reason'.[55]

OBJECTIVES OF EDUCATIONAL SCHEMES

The motivation for this investment in domestic education was varied. At the turn of the century, educated men and women in Ireland had begun panicking about the health of its poor. The WNHA was formed out of this scare, and justified its intervention in the domestic sphere by drawing attention to Ireland's high infant mortality and tuberculosis rate.[56] Improved housework provided the key to improving the health of the people.[57] The WNHA was the principal agency promoting domestic economy for health reasons, but all other reformers shared their concern. Local schools could claim a fee for their work in domestic economy if instruction were also given in hygiene—a policy justified by appeal to statistics that showed a 'startling increase in the ravages of consumption during recent years'.[58] The IAOS claimed that their domestic economy classes would provide a cure for the 'hollow-eyed, dyspeptic remnant of a once stalwart people'.[59] They claimed a connection between an improper diet, consumption, and insanity.[60] The tubercle was 'a sort of burglar who crawls around in dark and dusty corners, and it is our

[54] *Appendix to the 77th Report of the Commissioners of National Education, 1910–1911*, i (Cd. 6042), HC 1912–13, xxiv: 154, quoted by Miss Catherine M. Shuley.

[55] This debate is found throughout NLI, 'Minutes of the Proceedings of the Commissioners of National Education': see e.g. the meeting on 18 Mar. 1909: 171.

[56] F. B. Smith, *The Retreat of Tuberculosis, 1850–1950* (1988), 6.

[57] Countess of Aberdeen, 'Health and Happiness in the Homes of Ireland', in William G. Fitzgerald (ed.), *The Voice of Ireland*, (Dublin, 1924), 437.

[58] *72nd Report of the Commissioners of National Education, 1905–1906* (Cd. 3154), HC 1906, xxix. 18.

[59] 'A School for Making Homes', *IH*, 19 Sept. 1908: 758.

[60] 'The Food Puzzle', ibid. 21 Oct. 1911: 829–30, and 'Fireless Cookery', ibid. 28 Oct. 1911: 849.

business to see there are no such corners left for him'.[61] Even as late as 1919, the Irish Technical Instruction Association affirmed that compulsory training in housework was essential if child mortality and consumption were to be lowered.[62] National pride was seen by some reformers as being injured by the poor health of the rural Irish. Hypersensitive reformers of the educated, urban élite recoiled under the supposedly scornful looks from foreigners when discussing the standard of Irish domestic life. These reformers argued that the government must do something about this humiliating image, 'so that we can be thoroughly respected abroad'.[63] National respectability depended on differentiating the education of the 'offenders' from the rest of the community. Educationally, therefore, females were targeted.[64] Generations of economic poverty and political abuse had damaged the domestic skills of Irishwomen.[65] No one questioned that it was the role of *women* to raise domestic standards.

These arguments about the health, national respectability, and even the 'place' of women were prominent in the propaganda of the period, but their purpose masked more potent driving forces.[66] George Fletcher told participants at the 1913 congress of the Irish Technical Instruction Association that 'We need to recognise more

[61] 'Young Fogey', 'Some Old Chat: Dust and Darkness', ibid. 17 Nov. 1906: 945–6.

[62] Miss K. E. Warren (of Kingstown), 'Training for Home Life', in Irish Technical Instruction Association, *15th Congress*, 82. See also Revd R. M. Gwynn, 'Education and Citizenship: The Measure of the Stature of the Fulness of Christ', in *Ireland's Hope: A Call to Service* (Belfast, 1913), 105, and the report of the UI meeting in Ballynadara (Enniscorthy), in 'United Irishwomen', *IH*, 28 May 1910: 451.

[63] Kathleen Ferguson, 'The Peasant's Home: How Pat and Mary Started Housekeeping', *IH*, 6 Feb. 1904: 116.

[64] Katherine Roche, 'The Lady Teacher's Own Page', *Irish School Weekly*, 11 Mar. 1911: 296; *Appendix to the 78th Report of the Commissioners of National Education*, i, xxvii: 85, report by J. P. Dalton on Portarlington Circuit; Eileen Byne, 'The Education of Women', *Irish School Monthly*, 3/10 (June 1903), 331; 'Fresh Aid for Rural Reformers', *IH*, 3 Dec. 1910: 992, comment by Miss Broderick of the UI; Louise Kenny, 'A New Irish School of Housewifery', ibid., 25 Mar. 1905: 241.

[65] Mrs A. E. Lett (of Ballynadara, Enniscorthy), 'Irish Mothers', *IH*, 1 Mar. 1913: 173, and 'Home Life in Ireland: A Challenge to Irish Women', ibid. 1 June 1907: 428.

[66] For more direct statements about the 'place of women', see 'The Economic Problem and Domestic Life', ibid. 3 June 1905: 438, on the domestic education scheme in Dromore (county Tyrone); and Menlough (county Galway); and T. P. Gill, 'Newry Technical School: Re-opening of Second Session', *Irish Technical Journal*, 2/22 (Dec. 1904), 150.

clearly that the services of a woman in the home have as real a money value . . . The housewife who saves by her economies is as true a wage-earner as the man who provides the income.'[67] He warned against stimulation of home industries such as sprigging, claiming that these industries might lead to 'a neglect of the ordinary duties of the home, the performance of which, though it does not directly increase the family income, makes for prosperity by diminishing unnecessary expenditure and raising the standard of home comfort'.[68] In 1905 the chairman of the Carlow Technical Committee advised men to marry girls trained in domestic economy, because these girls 'would be far more valuable to their homes than girls who had got no such training but happened to have a few pounds more than the former in the way of a dowry'.[69] Bad housekeeping was one of the most important sources of 'economic impotence and its attendant evils in the emigration of the more vigorous of our young men and women and the thriftlessness and lethargy of many of those who are left':

To men and women alike, a home in the real sense, which includes spiritual and material elements in happy fusion, is the surest incentive to industry, and to those virtues attendant on industry—providence, temperance, and domestic peace—which plays so large a part in the evolution of 'the economic man'. . . . No sounder economic work can be done therefore than that which elevates the homes of the people and helps them to make the most of their means of subsistence.

Co-operators were cautioned against worrying about the loss of female employment with the introduction of creameries: the diversion of women from dairying to full-time housework would yield a bountiful economic harvest.[70] National school inspectors linked the need for instruction in domestic economy with improved living standards. As the inspector of the Galway circuit

[67] George Fletcher, 'Domestic Economy: The Family Budget', *DATI Journal*, 13/4 (July 1913), 736.

[68] George Fletcher, 'Rural Industry and Training for Home Life', in *Irish Rural Life and Industry* (Dublin, 1907), 48.

[69] 'Items of News', *IH*, 9 Sept. 1905: 672. The chairman was the Very Revd Dr Foley, speaking in Aug. 1905. The Irish stress on *production* contrasts with the American stress on teaching management of *consumption*: see Susan M. Strasser, 'The Business of Housekeeping: The Ideology of the Household at the Turn of the Twentieth Century', *Insurgent Sociologist*, 8/2 (Autumn 1978), 149.

[70] 'Co-operation and the Home', 622–3.

commented, the urgent need to reform 'the systems of living that have established themselves within recent years in the homes of our rural population' justified compulsory education in housework in all National schools.[71] 'Noa' of the *Ark* reminded her male readers that 'A woman's strength is the most valuable asset the farm has. Remember this next washday, and turn the washer and wringer.'[72] As contemporaries stressed, 'we could never *afford* to lower the ideal of home'.[73]

ATTENDANCE AT THE CLASSES

The economic importance of domestic education schemes can be understood by looking at the geography of the classes. The popularity of the courses instigated by the National and intermediate school boards and the various government and co-operative societies provides a way of analysing geographical demand for domestic skills. This demand was strongest in the areas that assigned a higher value to female labour in the home than to female labour in the paid or familial farming spheres. In National schools, domestic economy classes began in the south, particularly in counties Wexford and Limerick and in the central counties on either side of the Munster–Leinster border. Increasingly they spread both east and west of this line, especially into the grassland areas of north Leinster. They were not common in Ulster until 1909. Introduction of the classes was slowest in Donegal, Leitrim, and Wicklow.

To what class of women did these promises of economic betterment by housework appeal? There were accusations that conversion to new notions of housework was occurring only within the middling ranks of the rural population.[74] Certainly, women in the highest socio-economic categories were no longer expected to improve their domestic skills in any public fashion. Mrs Starkie,

---

[71] *Appendix to the 75th Report of the Commissioners of National Education,* i, xxv: 78, comment by J. P. Dalton in his report on the Galway Circuit. He argued that domestic science *must* be closely tied with cookery and laundry.

[72] 'Notes by Noa', *Ark,* 3/47 (Aug. 1913), 3.

[73] 'Woman's Work in Irish Homes', *IH,* 24 Aug. 1895: 405.

[74] See the comments by Mr H. de F. Montgomery regarding the classes in county Tyrone, in DATI, 'The Agricultural Board, Minutes of Proceedings, Confidential, 39th Meeting', 23 Apr. 1907: 152 (in NLI).

wife of a Commissioner for National Education and author of at least one article on domestic education, was not expected to learn any such skill herself. Her daughter commented:

My mother thought it fitting as the wife of my father to take an interest in the domestic training side of the education, and she, who could not sew herself, used to examine carefully specimens of needlework; she, who in those days had no knowledge of cooking, used to question the girls closely on the dishes they were cooking and on the methods of preparation.[75]

Background detail exists on the girls who attended the itinerant schemes run by the DATI. Between 1902 and 1919, statistics show the occupations of those taking advantage of the Department's itinerant (non-agricultural) courses for women.[76] These courses were largely in domestic economy, cookery, laundry, and house-keeping. Table 8.1 compares the occupations of women who attended the DATI classes with the stated occupations of women aged 15–24 in the 1901 and 1911 censuses. The table must be interpreted cautiously. The extent to which the courses were attended by farm women is of limited significance, since the census statistics exclude the wives or daughters of farmers. Similarly, it is difficult to draw any firm conclusion from the under-representation of domestic servants. The courses tended to be held in remote rural areas with a smaller proportion of domestic servants than for Ireland as a whole. In spite of these reservations, the low proportion of domestic servants is suggestive. Shopkeepers, saleswomen, and teachers were over-represented in the classes; textile workers were under-represented. As the period progressed, the proportion of saleswomen, shopkeepers, dressmakers, and milliners decreased, while that for 'unoccupied' women and teachers increased. The percentage of civil servants and cashiers remained very low, but slowly increased. Attendance by women in the lace, crochet, and embroidery trades increased in the early years of the century, only to decline again before 1919. The percentage of women from farming occupations peaked during 1909 (at 49 per cent) and always remained over one-quarter. Those attending from school or college reached 17

---

[75] Enid Starkie, *A Lady's Child* (1941).
[76] The statistics are only comparable from 1903.

Table 8.1. Female employment and attendance at DATI itinerant courses, 1903 and 1911 (%)

Occupation	Census[a] 1901	Scheme[b] 1903	Census 1911	Scheme 1911
Domestic servants	17.8	8.6	15.0	8.3
Printers	0.0	0.0	0.0	0.3
Dressmakers, milliners	10.1	3.3	7.0	1.6
Textile workers	0.0	1.3	0.0	0.9
Other factory workers	6.8	1.9	7.2	1.5
Lacemakers etc.	0.0	0.0	0.0	1.9
Shopkeepers, saleswomen	2.1	8.3	1.8	5.2
Clerks, civil servants	0.8	0.5	1.5	0.7
Teachers	1.1	2.6	1.2	4.1
Farmers	0.5	25.0	0.2	37.1
Other	5.3	25.1	6.1	23.7
'Unoccupied'	55.5	23.4	60.0	14.7

Note: As stated in the text, the census figures refer to 'occupied' women aged between 15 and 24.

[a] n (no. in sample) = 464,694 for 1901; 392,996 for 1911.

[b] n = 13,276 for 1903; 10,635 for 1911.

Source: Annual reports of the DATI for Ireland (British parliamentary papers); censuses of Ireland, 1901 and 1911.

per cent in 1905, but declined steadily after that date with the deterioration of relations between the Department and the Board of Education. The obligation on teachers to attend classes held in school premises after hours, as well as to have some knowledge of the subjects on the curriculum, may account for the high number of teachers taking advantage of the schemes. Since between one-quarter and one-third of all female teachers left the profession each year to marry, some of them may have used the classes as preparation for their marriage and subsequent retirement.[77] Much of the demand for the Department's domestic economy classes came from daughters of farmers and shopkeepers.

---

[77] Taken from the reports of the Commissioners of National Education, 1879–1916, in NLI.

Regional influences can be seen by looking at other courses. Waringstown Girls School was in Lurgan County District 2 (county Down). The school was located in an area in which female employment exceeded the average level, not because of a demand for domestic servants (indeed, female employment in domestic service was lower in this district than in the county as a whole), but because of a demand for female labour in the linen and flax industries.[78] However, it was also an area of rapidly increasing female unemployment. The number of females employed in the flax and linen industries here halved between 1891 and 1911. Total female unemployment in this district had increased by 11 per cent. It was in this context that the evening classes in domestic education attracted women. Of the thirty-two who attended the evening course in 1905, twenty were, or had been, employed in the flax and linen industry;[79] four women said that they were houseworkers; there were two shop assistants, one maidservant, one ironer, one teacher, and one bookkeeper; two women gave no occupation. All the students were aged between 15 and 23 and, given the average age of marriage, were probably single. The level of education was generally low: 44 per cent of the girls had not completed their third year at school. This class can be contrasted with the DATI's schools of rural domestic economy in Westport, Clifden, Claremorris, Swinford, and Portumna. Of the 118 successful applicants in 1916, eighty-eight came from farming households or from upwardly mobile households combining retailing with farming; nearly all of them gave their own occupation as housework combined with farming; only four were domestic servants. These women also tended to be younger than the girls attending the evening classes in domestic economy.

IMPACT OF THE CLASSES

As with many educational schemes, it was easy to exaggerate the impact of these classes. A story was told of a poor woman who

[78] In Ulster in 1901 domestic servants comprised 5% of the total female population and 19% of the total occupied female population. The corresponding figures for women over the age of 20 in Lurgan County District 2 were 2% and 3%.

[79] It is difficult to know whether the occupations stated were actual or desired occupations, but, looking at the ages of the women, those without occupations and those who claimed that they worked in the house or were housekeepers were the youngest; veiners, ware-room girls, stitchers, weavers, and teachers were older. This suggests that actual employment was being stated.

was sitting on the steps of a hall in a provincial town where a WNHA lecture was being delivered: 'Another women approached her, who asked, "And what are they talking about in there?" "Sure" replied the former, "they're tellin' us to be clane, and ain't we are clane as we can be?"'[80] Contemporary analyses for the effect of schemes were generally partisan. Much of the dissatisfaction with the courses arose out of the shortage of capital. Criticism of the classes by Alice Spring Rice, for example, was aimed at improving the funding for the schemes, not eliminating them.[81] Educationalists frequently argued that the classes were inefficient because they were compulsory only for girls in the higher standards of schools: this was an argument for extension, not abolition.[82] Keeping the lessons relevant to the lives of poor rural women was a constant concern.[83] Some complained that the courses were too short, that the girls had scarcely begun learning before the teacher left.[84] Trenchant criticism was received about the 'British' content of some of the recipes (this was most insidiously represented in recipes calling for the use of lard).[85]

At the other extreme, some reformers imagined stupendous changes following itinerant classes:

If you revisit some village in the wilds of Donegal or Connemara, that you knew a few years ago, you would probably notice changes. Houses and cabins are cleaner and better kept, windows are made to open, the manure heap is less evident to eyes and nose, the porridge-pot disputes the monopoly of the hob with the little black 'taypot', and the miller has a tale to tell of busier meal mills. If you comment on these changes, you will probably learn that the health caravan has passed that way, and the doctor, 'that had the Irish', and the lady that had the wonderful way with the cooking, had told of what came of keeping out the fresh air and letting in the pig and poultry, of having the manure heap by the front

[80] Matheson, *The Anti-Tuberculosis Campaign in Ireland*, 8.

[81] Rice, 'Housekeeping Instruction in National Schools', 281. For a similar argument, see Mary Power Lalor, 'Housekeeping Instruction in Ireland', *IH*, 7 May 1898: 396.

[82] Mr Dewar of Dungannon, reporting on Crosscavanagh schools (county Tyrone), 'The Irish National Schools: Industrial Education', *Irish Textile Journal*, 15 Mar. 1894: 34–6.

[83] RCCI, *Appendix to the 10th Report*, xlii: 64–5, evidence by Joseph Kelly, schoolmaster in Cashel.

[84] Kathleen Ferguson, 'On the Teaching of Domestic Economy in Ireland', *Irish Educational Review*, 1/5 (Feb. 1908), 294.

[85] Alice Stonach, *What Women Are Doing for Ireland: The Work of the WNHA* (1912), 3–4.

door, and giving the children tea and white bread instead of oatmeal and milk.[86]

Less enthusiastic responses are more convincing. Clergymen praised the effect of the schemes on the domestic labour of women in their districts. For example, the Reverend Canon McFadden applauded the cookery classes run by the CDB:

We priests have a habit of visiting our parishes twice a year to hold 'stations'. We take breakfast in these houses and I notice the change. They can give you potatoes whole, potatoes mashed, potatoes in chips, and they can give you boiled eggs, and scrambled eggs—it is simply marvellous. I say the result is simply marvellous, and with the desire to put the priest in good humour, they generally get one of those instructed girls to look after the breakfast.[87]

Educational critics were positive about the effect of the classes on their rural communities.[88] Improvement could be judged by simple signs, such as open windows.[89]

UNWAGED HOUSEWORK AND EMIGRATION

The relevance of these classes to the discussion of female labour is that, in theory and in practice, they aimed at providing Irish women with a rationale for remaining in Ireland to provide (without payment) the 'improved' goods and services to support a 'developing' rural economy. One of the key objectives in these attempts to enhance the standard of housework was to ensure that the labour remained unwaged. Demand for domestic servants

[86] Miss Mary Fogarty, 'Influence of Home on Life', *Irish Educational Review*, 3/10 (July 1910), 604.

[87] RCCI, *Appendix to the 2nd Report*, xxxv: 92, evidence by the Very Revd Canon McFadden. For similar reports by local clergy, see the letter from a clergyman in county Leitrim, in CDB, *11th Report*, lxxxiii: 39; Revd John Doherty, in RCCI, *Appendix to the 2nd Report*, xxxv: 48–9; and Revd Michael McHugh of Carna, in RCCI, *Appendix to the 10th Report*, xlii: 51.

[88] 'A Mere Woman', 'Women's Work in the Technical Schools', *Leader*, 25 June 1910: 400.

[89] John Dryden, 'Memorandum on Certain Agricultural Questions, Prepared at the Request of the Chairman, by the Hon. John Dryden, and Referred to in the Report as Mr Dryden's Memorandum', in DATI, *Report of the Departmental Committee of Inquiry into the Provisions of the Agricultural and Technical Instruction (Ireland) Act, 1899* (Cd. 3572), HC 1907, xvii. 154–5.

was declining. Women who attended the classes in domestic economy did not intend to become domestic servants. They tended to hail from classes that repudiated domestic service as a respectable occupation. A cooking instructress in 1909 said that, out of the hundreds of girls she had taught, only two had shown interest in becoming cooks.[90] Furthermore, the demand for domestic science schools that specialized explicitly in training domestic servants was far less than the demand for the itinerant domestic courses. A number of schools were set up specifically for domestic servants. Lady Castlerosse established one in Killarney in 1900.[91] Then there was the Dublin School of Cookery, Laundrymaking, and Dressmaking in Kildare Street (renamed the Irish Training School of Domestic Economy); the Dublin School of Domestic Training in Charlemont Street; the Belfast School of Domestic Training in Clanchatten House; and the Carrigart Housekeeping School, all of which catered for women requiring training in paid domestic service. Although domestic economy classes were introduced in the early years in those wealthier counties with a high proportion of women in paid domestic occupations, by 1911 there was no relationship between the two variables.[92] For those girls able to secure employment as domestic servants after completing a course in cookery or laundry, there was an increasing likelihood that they would leave their employment on marriage and assume the responsibilities of enlightened housework within their own household. For women settling in Ireland, there were good reasons to prolong their schooling or to attend classes out of school hours, so that they would get adequate training in housework.[93] Attendance at

[90] 'Irishwoman', 'Why Has Not the Irishwoman Evolved Some Elementary Knowledge of Cookery?', *IH*, 3 Apr. 1909: 267.

[91] C. Dease, 'Domestic Service as a Profession', *New Ireland Review*, June 1903: 221–4; Miss A. Ryan of Mullingar, 'Training for Domestic Service', in Irish Technical Instruction Association, *15th Congress*, 83, and *Report of the Department of Education, 1924–1925, and the Financial and Administrative Years 1924/25/26* (Dublin, 1926), 67; DATI, *Programme of the Killarney School of Housewifery: Session 1913–1914* (Killarney, 1913), 3–5; CDB, *18th Report, 1909* (Cd. 4927), HC 1909, xvi: 21; and DATI, *3rd Annual General Report, 1902–1903* (Cd. 1919), HC 1904, xvi: 88.

[92] In the 32 counties, the proportion of women involved in paid domestic occupations regressed on the proportion of women attending domestic economy classes: in 1901 the correlation was +0.6248 (t-statistic 10.42), and in 1911 it was −0.0015 (t-statistic 1.87).

[93] CDB, *16th Report, 1907* (Cd. 3767), HC 1908, xxiii: 28.

the courses was an attempt to maintain or to improve their own or their family's standard of living in an economy that offered them fewer employment opportunities. They hoped to improve their status as unwaged houseworkers by training.

From the start, the organizers of the schemes stressed that they were not training women to become domestic servants. The itinerant instructresses taught housekeeping as it would be experienced by women in their own homes, rather than in the homes of women with servants.[94] They were more likely to teach the girls to cook on turf fires than on stoves.[95] Explicitly, the policy was to 'train housewives, and not domestic servants, nor future teachers of domestic economy'.[96]

The organizers of the CDB's schemes were the least reluctant to send women into domestic service. They frequently remarked that their certificates of proficiency in domestic economy might enable the women who completed their courses to get higher wages as servants.[97] However, with declining opportunities in paid domestic service and with diminishing emigration, the more likely beneficiaries of the classes were the girls remaining in their own homes. The course outlines and suggestions given each week by Nora Nectar and (later) M. E. Graham in the *Irish School Weekly* were basic, involving a great deal of dusting, cleaning, and scrubbing.[98] The textbook, *Cookery for School Girls: Ten Elementary Lessons*, starts with the question 'Why we cook our foods', and concludes with 'The best way to boil an egg'.[99] The utensils required for the classes were minimal. 'Essential' utensils consisted of merely one frying-pan, three saucepans, two pot-ovens, one kettle, and two iron tripods, at a total cost of £1 5s. Other optional utensils could be purchased for £1 10s.[100]

Furthermore, these classes were not simply being used by the girls as a way of attaining the necessary skills for emigration. David Fitzpatrick's article on the connections between emigration

---

[94] DATI, *2nd Annual General Report, 1901–1902* (Cd. 1314), HC 1902, ii: 75.

[95] See the minutes of the UI for a letter to the DATI, 11 Dec. 1913: 73 (held by the Irish Countrywoman's Association).

[96] DATI, *3rd Annual General Report*, xvi: 68.

[97] CDB, *21st Report, 1912–1913* (Cd. 7312), HC 1914, xvi: 30–1.

[98] See the *Irish School Weekly* from 14 Nov. 1908.

[99] May Ross McDonald, *Cookery for School Girls: Ten Elementary Lessons* (Dublin, c.1900), price 3d.

[100] 'The Month's Work', *Irish School Monthly*, 1/2 (Oct. 1900), 57–8.

and education can be easily defended in general terms.[101] There is little doubt that increased schooling helped to make emigration a more feasible option, and also that many young Irish people were encouraged to improve their education for such a purpose. However, there is some evidence to suggest that girls who attended classes in domestic economy may have been more likely to settle in Ireland. It was in the economic interest of women who did not intend to emigrate to stay at school to attend domestic classes.[102] Certainly, promoters of domestic economy *believed* that educating girls to be good houseworkers would stop, or at least reduce, emigration.[103] For instance, the cessation of female emigration from Dromore was attributed to the domestic economy classes.[104] Girls planning to emigrate were more likely to take industrial courses than cooking. Classes in domestic industries such as lacemaking and crochet raised the earning potential of women intending to emigrate in search of respectable paid employment. Industrial classes brought in the cash required by potential emigrants. In a letter to Professor Campbell in 1907, E. Gallagher argued that the girls in Swinford and Carna who wanted to emigrate were unlikely to attend courses in domestic economy, which held out little money-earning potential in desirable occupations. Emigrants demanded industrial courses.[105] There were examples of entire lace classes emigrating, but no analogous examples of domestic education classes.[106] The market for domestic servants in both the United States and Britain was declining rapidly. Particularly after 1910, female emigrants were more likely to be going to work in commercial and industrial establishments.[107] Furthermore, black women in America and

---

[101] David Fitzpatrick, '"A Share of the Honeycomb": Education, Emigration and Irishwomen', *Continuity and Change*, 1/2 (1986), 217–34.

[102] *Appendix to the 78th Report of the Commissioners of National Education*, i, xxvii: 455, T. P. O'Connor's report on the Cork Circuit 2.

[103] See 'An Irish MP', 'Industrial Development in Ireland', *Irish Industrial Journal*, 9 Nov. 1912: 786

[104] 'Irish Clergy and Irish Civilization', *IH*, 7 Oct. 1905: 733.

[105] NAI AG1 A13317/16, DATI Papers, concerned with the proposed rural domestic economy school in Swinford and Carna.

[106] e.g. the Ballyjamesduff Convent National School lace class see: *Appendix to the 59th Report of the Commissioners of National Education, 1892* (C. 7124-i), HC 1893–4, xxvii: 166.

[107] Donna L. Van Raaphorst, *Union Maids Not Wanted* (New York, 1988), 37–40.

other immigrant groups in Britain had begun to take over domestic service jobs from the Irish.[108]

Statistically, the connection between emigration and domestic education is tenuous. In part, the relationship depends on the method used to calculate the regional distribution of emigration. If the number of women in a particular county in 1901 (or 1911) is divided by the number of women emigrating from that county (according to the Registrar-General's statistics) in the decade 1891–1901 (or 1901–11), some indication of differentials of emigration can be calculated. Taking 1901 as an example, correlating emigration between 1891 and 1901 with the percentage of all schools with domestic economy classes, shows that the higher the number of classes, the *lower* the rate of emigration, suggesting that counties with a low emigration rate were the first to introduce domestic economy classes. The correlation was weak. The opposite relationship was stronger by 1911, when the figures suggest that the greater the number of classes, the higher the rate of female emigration.[109] Using statistics on cohort depletion for both sexes, the effect of emigration was even more slight—and negative—for the years 1901 and 1911.[110] As the classes were more established by this time, this could be interpreted to mean that they encouraged emigration, or that they were introduced in areas with high emigration to stem the tide. Weight is lent to the second interpretation by looking at the change in emigration. David Fitzpatrick's county statistics on the emigration of women aged between 20 and 25 provide the data to compute the change in the emigration of yourg females between 1876 and 1895, and between 1896 and 1914.[111] The statistics in Table 8.2 show clearly that rapidly declining emigration was prevalent in areas with domestic economy classes, whereas rapidly increasing emigration occurred in the counties with the lowest concentration of domestic economy classes. Looking at the top quartile, the eight counties with the largest proportion of schools teaching domestic economy, six of these counties experienced an extremely rapid increase in the emigration of women between the ages of 20 and

[108] Ibid. 40–5.
[109] The correlation in 1901 was −0.18 (t-statistic 4.35), and in 1911 it was +0.3513 (24.52).
[110] The correlation in 1901 was −0.3893 (4.42), and −0.0520 (11.90) in 1911.
[111] Personal communication of unpublished data by David Fitzpatrick.

Table 8.2. Female emigration rates and domestic economy classes, 1914

	Changes in emigration rates	
	1876–95	1896–1914
Top quartile		
Antrim	−116	100
Cork	250	−328
Kerry	548	−192
Clare	185	−42
Mayo	301	−328
Sligo	77	−106
Roscommon	250	−310
Longford	31	144
Bottom quartile		
Armagh	45	144
Donegal	63	162
Monaghan	112	78
Wicklow	−54	68
Cavan	56	100
Kings'	8	64
Louth	31	87
Down	−52	214

Note: Figures refer to women aged between 20 and 25 only.

Source: Annual reports on domestic education published by the Department of Education for Ireland (British parliamentary papers). The emigration data were kindly provided by David Fitzpatrick.

25 in 1876–95 (before the classes), a trend that was reversed after the introduction of the domestic classes in 1896–1914. This contrasts with the eight counties with the lowest proportions of domestic economy classes. In all of these cases, level of emigration were much higher between 1896 and 1914 than they had been in the earlier period. In two of the counties (Wicklow and Down), levels of emigration which had been slowing down between 1876 and 1895 actually began accelerating between 1896 and 1914.

Domestic classes proved popular because they attempted to secure a place within Irish society for girls and women who decided to remain in a country that offered them a narrowing range of economic activities. In communities experiencing a contraction of employment in textiles or in domestic service, women chose to maximize their economic contribution by funnelling energies into familial domestic work. Education in housework was one expression of this maximization process. An auxiliary role of the classes was the changing of tastes and expectations. In the words of Miss Reynolds, a domestic education instructress for the UI, her job was to 'lay before them that we in Ireland are very backward indeed'.[112] Given the economic importance of housework, the dynamics of Irish development could be threatened should the problems of being a 'farm wife' prove a disincentive to new entrants. Standards of housework could be raised by education, and it was precisely these 'standards' that were essential to the stimulation and sustainment of economic growth.

[112] 'United Irishwomen', *IH*, 25 Nov. 1911: 950, speech by Miss Reynolds at the AGM of the UI.

Conclusion: Housework and the Well-Being of Women in Ireland, 1890–1914

LITTLE GIRL [*aged 8*]. If I am married shall I have to marry
a man like papa?
MOTHER. Yes, I suppose so, my child.
LITTLE GIRL. And if I don't marry, shall I be an old maid
like Aunt Julia?
MOTHER. Yes.
LITTLE GIRL. Well, it's very hard on women.[1]

THIS book deals with the questions that are customarily asked
by labour historians about employment, the factors leading to
changes in female work, and the effects of those changes on
women. In Ireland between 1890 and 1914 the position of women
within the paid labour markets deteriorated. Married women
were increasingly dependent on their husband's wage. Economic
opportunities for unmarried women collapsed. Even forms of
paid employment for women shifted into the home. Thus, reforming organizations invested in home industries rather than in
factory production. Rural women entered the fields only during
times of peak agricultural demand, if at all. Unwaged domestic
production became more important.

This book also examines current concerns about economic
growth and the impact of public and private investment in agricultural and social reform. The effect of improvements in living
standards differed for men and women. The pattern of growth
and development did improve female well-being: women were
better fed, housed, and educated in 1911 than in 1891. Women did
not always gain a smaller share of the gratifications of affluence.
For instance, housing for female 'heads' of families improved

---

[1] *IH*, 9 July 1898: 584.

more rapidly than it did for male 'heads'. In other areas, however, economic growth exacerbated inequality within the household, making women worse off *in relation to men* than they had been in 1891. Economic progress brought new aspirations. The demand for domestic labour intensified. At the same time, rising living standards provided the means to fulfil those aspirations in a way that would *benefit* the household rather than penalize it; that is, in a way that strengthened existing power structures within the home as well as maintained power between a particular household and its neighbours. The dynamic relationship between housework and rising living standards was complex. Improving living standards stimulated housework, which, in turn, raised living standards. Similarly, the collapse of certain employment sectors conventionally reserved for women stimulated a shift of female labour into the home, which, in turn, encouraged the further substitution of men for women in the employment market. This coincidence of sectoral shifts in the employment market, investment in the rural economy, and an increase in the labour and capital requirements of the household was crucial.

The costs of the movement into full-time unwaged domestic work were substantial. However, it would be wrong to deny that many women found housework fulfilling. The intensification of the two 'spheres of labour' was part of an attempt by women of this period to minimize the risk of poverty. The costs and benefits of the movement to full-time unwaged housework will now be examined in turn.

THE COSTS OF UNWAGED DOMESTIC LABOUR

The problem set out in the Introduction remains: how to identify the beneficiaries of economic growth. There are few indicators of the distribution of benefits. Economists working in Third World countries stress that discrimination against women *increases* as households become wealthier: the unequal distribution of goods within households can only take place if there are surpluses. Landowning usually encourages the primacy of sons (as opposed to daughters). The most common types of inequality are those relating to food and housing. Diet improved in Ireland at the end of the nineteenth century; but children, the elderly, and women received less food than men of 'working' ages. When there was meat, it was generally reserved for the 'breadwinner' of the family.[2] Even in the workhouses and hospitals, men were given more meat, potatoes, and bread.[3] Female labourers were excluded from the attempts by reforming organizations to improve the housing of rural Irish workers. Houses for agricultural labourers were generally given to male heads of families. Local councils even debated whether women could really be classed as 'labourers'.[4] Disproportionate numbers of houses were given to families containing young male labourers, on the grounds that, if men could be persuaded to remain in Ireland, young women would 'naturally' remain behind also, attracted by increasing marriage opportunities. Current owners of the relatively scarce factor of production—land—benefited from these changes to a much greater extent than other groups.

One of the principal ways in which the position of women deteriorated was through the narrowing of their employment opportunities and the concurrent reduction of female access to cash resources. The direct impact of agricultural growth on women depended on their access to income-earning opportunities. This is not to ignore the indirect impact of agricultural growth, which may improve the *household's* economic position. In the dairy industry, capital was transferred to male heads of families. Women expressed concern about the way in which control over the household's income affected household consumption. Many women no longer received the money from the sale of butter or eggs: 'her lord taking this regularly to the nearest bank to deposit'.[5] The increased seasonality of work for the female members of small farming families and for female labourers limited their independent access to an income to particular times of the year. By focusing on the needs of male 'heads', the institutional reforms resulted in women losing their right to the independent

[2] Sir Charles A. Cameron, *Reminiscences* (Dublin, 1913), 169. Cameron was the chief medical officer for Dublin Corporation.
[3] The diets of male and female paupers can be found in many reports and commissions of inquiries into the Poor Law. No comment was ever made which implied that the different diets were unacceptable. For many examples, see Royal Commission on the Poor Laws and Relief of Distress, Appendix, xxviii (Cd. 4974), HC 1910, liv. 357 and 355.
[4] 'Is a Woman a Labourer?', *Kings' County Chronicle*, 17 Feb. 1898: 1.
[5] *United Irishman*, 12 July 1902: 5.

control of the products of their own labour. By not earning cash themselves, women became more dependent on the generosity or 'love' of the male earner.

Before that I went out to day [sic], my wife she said, says she,
Be very careful of your pay, and bring it home to me,
You know you're wanting a Sunday hat and the children wanting shoes,
So bring me home yez overtime and not go on the booze.
Says I, my darling that I will, I'll bring yez ivery cent,
For your [sic] the girl knows the way that money should be spent
But I'm absent minded and the warning soon forgot,
I got a drop, and now of course I mean to spend the lot.[6]

The increased female dependency occasioned by the movement of women out of the waged market should not be exaggerated. Wages *may* increase female independence, widen their number of choices, and provide access to status outside the family. The extent to which this did actually occur is doubtful, however, as female employment options in rural areas were customarily based on the social standing of the male 'head', and opportunities to move beyond this depended on geographical mobility rather than on the labour market.

The most significant change was the movement of women into full-time housework. Although statements such as 'For the labourer, who is abroad from early morning to nightfall, a wife is a necessity', were common, male dependence on female domestic labour did not require any transfer of power.[7] Indeed, male dependency itself drew some of its acceptability from the increased status that it gave to men.[8] There was no strict relationship between the economic value of the labour performed by an individual and the social status bestowed on that individual, especially when the labour was unwaged. Furthermore, the stress on housework carried certain threats with it. Domestic violence centred increasingly on accusations of poor housework. Assaults were admitted by husbands ('he said it [aggravated assault on his mother] was too little for her'), but excused because the woman

[6] 'Working Overtime', music sheets (no date), in National Library Australia.
[7] Charlotte G. O'Brien, 'The Irish "Poor Man"', *Nineteenth Century* (Dec. 1880), 877.
[8] In the same way that the dependency of a female householder on the services of a domestic servant increases the status of the female householder.

was not performing her duties adequately ('as she had no sup-per ready for him').[9] 'Grania' of the *Irish Homestead* was not at all surprised that men 'drink and beat their wives'; and she wished that they would 'beat them a great deal more, until they served proper meals, and kept the children in order'.[10] Lawyers testified that, only if a woman were a good cook and housekeeper, could she be confident that her husband would not abandon her.[11] The basis of domestic bliss was good housekeeping, and bad house-keeping was criminal:[12]

The truth is, and few women blink it now, women have made a mess of their business, the home. . . . After thousands of years' apprenticeship to their trade they are as ignorant of it as the poor woman who when remonstrated with on her improper feeding of her infant said, 'You needn't teach me how to bring up children, I buried nine of them.' Women have murdered their homes, their health, their children and their husbands for long enough, and have been as thoroughly satisfied with themselves as our friend who had only nine victims. But they are awakening to a conviction of their criminality . . .[13]

Improved housework brought a new sense of guilt and respon-sibility.

Power can be measured by the amount of control that a par-ticular group has over crucial societal resources. One of these resources is children. Housework within marriage involves child-bearing, and the childless wife could be stigmatized by the com-munity.[14] In Ireland, women's reproductive capacities were accorded greater and increasing status, but fewer women were allowed access to the only legitimate means to attain this goal —marriage. In 1891, 17 per cent of women aged 45–55 who remained in Ireland were single, compared with 25 per cent by 1911.

[9] Quoted from the *Evening Mail*, probably 1901, by Michael J. F. McCarthy, *Priests and People in Ireland* (Dublin, 1903), 300.

[10] 'Grania', 'Are Mothers the Ruin of Ireland', *IH*, 15 Feb. 1913: 130. A similar sentiment is expressed by Mrs Frank Pentrill, 'Everyday Thoughts: The Teapot and Kettles', *Irish Monthly* (1882), 526, and Helen Hawthorn, 'The Ideal Girl', *Ireland's Own*, 26 Nov. 1902: 8.

[11] 'Homely Wrinkles', *Ark*, Mar. 1913: 4.

[12] T. B. Cronin, 'Systems of Primary and Secondary Education Relative to In-dustrialisation', *United Irishman*, 18 Nov. 1905: 7.

[13] 'Feeling their Way', *IH*, 4 July 1914: 537.

[14] David Fitzpatrick, 'The Modernisation of the Irish Female', in P. O'Flanagan, P. Ferguson, and K. Whelan (eds.), *Rural Ireland, 1600–1900* (Cork, 1987), 170–1.

Women's role in the new order was not easy. Not only were women supposed to be ideal houseworkers, but they were also responsible for 'making an ideal husband'—and the recipe was complex, ranging from instructions on how to 'feed him well', to exhortations that he must always 'feel that your interest centres chiefly in him'.[15] Mothers had equally onerous obligations: 'Don't forget to live so that your memory will be the tenderest and holiest upon earth to your children.'[16] On the one side, the wife had to act as intermediary between the father and the children, on the other, her power to achieve her goals against the resistance of her children lay with him. Mrs Hogan had to explain to her husband that their son had decided not to return to school:

How to so arrange matters with her husband that Jack's surrender may be prevented is now the poor woman's critical perplexity. Even with his own family Tom Hogan is very distant. His word is law; his command never disobeyed or questioned. Tomorrow evening he is expected home, and being naturally supposed after his retreat to be in the state of grace, and consequently in good humour, he will, Mrs Hogan hopes, be comparatively easily managed.[17]

Women's role as mediator was strictly limited to the domestic sphere. Women were increasingly excluded from nationalist aspirations. For instance, *Sinn Fein* published a column aimed at women, entitled 'Letters to Nora'. The letter on 19 May 1906 began: 'The work is calling, I said. It awaits us in our own homes. We must be clear about that point. No Irishwoman can afford to claim a part in the public duties of patriotism until she has fully satisfied the claims her "home" makes on her.'[18] After this the writer declares that 'Nora' may feel that the burden of housework is too great for her: but she is not afraid of hard work, and, after all, 'it is a step in nation building all the same'.

Unmarried women in the poorest households suffered most in the new order. The prevailing poverty in households that did not benefit from the growth in the rural economy meant that the unmarried woman had to find paid employment to supplement her dowry. Since the size of the dowry determined the size and

---

[15] 'For Wife and Maid', *Irish Weekly Independent*, 14 Dec. 1905: 10.
[16] 'Don'ts for Mothers', *Irish Peasant*, 18 Nov. 1905: 7.
[17] P. Hickey, *The Irish Problem* (1906), 32.
[18] *Sinn Fein*, 19 May 1906: 6.

fertility of the farm on which she would eventually reside, a good dowry was the best way of avoiding poverty in her married life. The best way of doing this was to accumulate a higher dowry by working either in Ireland or—more realistically—in the United States. In Ireland she had to find paid employment in an unfavourable market. In some cases, young unmarried women might do better not to seek employment but, rather, to concentrate on increasing the family's income by substituting as a domestic servant in the familial household; but there was no guarantee that the household would then fulfil its obligations by providing a dowry.

It was this group of women, born into very poor households, never able to marry, and with limited chances of emigrating, who were hardest hit in old age. If they came from a large family, and if the parents refused to make a settlement of the land until their death, they were *less* liable to face destitution in the future. However, the unmarried elderly woman without a kinship network—especially without a network of unmarried brothers or uncles—was vulnerable. In 1901, 68 per cent of women in the Roscrea workhouse were over the age of 60; nearly 80 per cent of women in the Glenties workhouses were elderly. The vulnerability of elderly women was greater if they had remained unmarried. This was the case for 71 and 77 per cent of the women in two Donegal workhouses in 1911. Most of these women claimed to have been domestic servants.[19] However, the economic insecurity of single unmarried women must not be exaggerated. These women were vulnerable whether or not they were restricted to household labour, because the paid labour market was substantially closed to them. The greater value of elderly women, as opposed to elderly men, in the house should also be acknowledged. Men over the age of 65 were more liable to end up in Irish workhouses than women over the age of 65.[20] Women remained productive by performing domestic tasks from which men were increasingly excluded. The greater productive activity

[19] Glenties and Stranorlar workhouses in 1911, and Roscrea workhouse in 1901; manuscript census returns from Donegal 149 and 56 and Tipperary 120 (in NLI).

[20] According to David Fitzpatrick, 6.4% of all unmarried men over the age of 65 in 1911 were in workhouses, compared with 5.2% of elderly women: 'Retirement Arrangements in Rural Ireland: A Study in Family Diplomacy', unpublished paper presented in Chicago (Nov. 1986), table 6.

of the woman did not necessarily confer a higher status on her than on the leisured male. Was status more likely to be attained by an old patriarch smoking by the fire and creating work for other members of the household, or by an elderly woman busily minding children and repairing stockings?

The tendency for women to have less leisure time than men was accentuated when the primary labour involved was housework. The theme was stressed in the papers of the period:

In a home there is no limit to the possibilities for occupation, and when leisure time does come it brings with it the opportunity for assisting those less fortunate.[21]

A man often works much harder than a woman whilst at work, but through all his labour runs the consciousness that it has a finish. The busy wife and mother has no such consciousness to sustain her in her manifold duties and worries . . . and when utterly too tired and worn out to do another hands turn, [she] turns to the family mending basket as a source of recreation.[22]

The two facts noticeable in connection with womenkind in rural districts are: Their recreation is nonexistent and their work is never done. . . . That mythological gentleman who was perpetually employed in rolling a stone into a place where it would not stay is the prototype of the modern country girl; at least he has no counterpart nearly so accurate in our time—the only thing differentiating the daily routine of brushing, sweeping, cooking and cleaning from the eternal stone-rolling process being the zest for usefulness.[23]

The houseworker did not know any real sabbatical rest—after mass, her duties resumed.[24] Housework was a continual process: no sooner was the house cleaned than it was dirty.

THE BENEFITS OF UNWAGED DOMESTIC LABOUR

The changes in female labour that have been described in this book were not always experienced negatively by women. For the

[21] 'For Wife and Maid', *Irish Weekly Independent*, 19 Apr. 1906: 10.
[22] Ibid. 27 Oct. 1906: 10. See also ibid. 3 Sept. 1910: 9, and 'Working Women's Column', *Irish Worker*, 19 Aug. 1911: 2.
[23] *United Irishman*, 12 Nov. 1904: 3.
[24] Ibid. 3; 'Working Women's Column', *Irish Worker*, 19 Aug. 1911: 2, and 'The Country Girl', *United Irishman*, 12 Nov. 1904: 3.

women who made the decision to leave paid employment, or never to engage in it, housework offered a chance to increase their status and to improve the quality of their lives. Anything that alleviated poverty was in the interests of women. There was no necessary trade-off between household living standards (met by increased division of labour) and women's status (allegedly declining as women moved out of the two other labour markets). At the least, during periods when the paid and agricultural labour markets were unfavourable to women, attempts to work outside the home as well as within it might have increased poverty for the individual woman as well as for the household. It might have made more sense for the man to increase his share of paid employment and for the woman to have withdrawn completely from the paid markets. By concentrating on domestic production, a woman could increase her own consumption as well as that of the household, strengthen moral ties of dependency and independence, and increase her own power over and above its potential in the paid workforce and in the familial farming market, where she was subject to the dictates of the 'head' of the family. The increasing movement of women into full-time housework was a sensible strategy for reducing the risk of poverty and for maximizing possible control over their own lives and the lives of their family. This was true for rural parts of Ireland because of the rapid changes in the domestic sphere.

It is useful to distinguish here between production within the household (that is, cooking, cleaning, making clothes, and so on) and reproduction (that is, child-bearing and child-rearing). While productive housework was a short-term expedient for maintaining a certain standard of living, children were the long-term strategy that a woman might have chosen. As such, children were more important for female members of the household than for male members. Since women tended to marry younger, they tended to outlive their husbands. With the general improvement in diet, health care, and living standards, women were less liable to die giving birth.[25] They were more liable to be dependent on the future resources of their children, whether those children were male or female. Particularly in the period before old-age

---

[25] For annual maternal mortality rates, see *48th Detailed Annual Report of the Registrar-General, 1911* (Cd. 6313), HC 1912–13, xiv. xxxv.

pensions, reproductive housework was crucial. The effect of the increased dependency of children (partly a result of declining employment opportunities for the young, and partly due to increased pressure for regular school attendance) was to reduce their immediate value while, simultaneously, increasing their long-term value. Children also cemented the economic contract between the couple. A woman's rights to the property of her husband's farm were not clearly established until the birth of children had assured the succession to the farm through her husband's line. Thus, there was an acute loss of economic power and security if a woman remained childless. Once she had children, the wife's position was stronger, since, if widowed, she was allowed to hold the land in trust for her husband's heirs. If she were childless and made a widow, the collateral kin of her husband could oust her from the farm, returning the cash equivalent of the dowry. *Male* children in particular were an immensely important long-term investment for married women. A mother might try to provide for her old age by marrying her son to a woman with a good dowry. As women's life expectancy improved, and the marrying age of both men and women retreated, it became increasingly likely that it would be the widow (rather than the married couple or the widower) who would benefit from the dowry brought by the son's wife.

Elderly widowed women benefited from the emphasis on domestic work. Their labour was liable to be much more useful to the household than the labour of elderly widowed men. Widowed men over the age of 65 were more liable to end up in a workhouse than widowed women over 65.[26] The land inheritance system favoured widows with children; it assured them of a place in the household. If the widow handed the land over to a son, certain customary rights provided important economic resources.[27] The provision of pensions to old people created incentives to 'retire', while simultaneously reducing pressure on the parents to compensate for their 'dependency' by performing domestic labour. In Ireland the old-age pension was seen as a

---

[26] In 1911, 4.5% of widowed men over the age of 65 were in workhouses, compared with 2.0% of widowed women: see Fitzpatrick, 'Retirement Arrangements in Rural Ireland', table 6.

[27] e.g. the widowed mother (not the daughter-in-law) controlled the poultry.

significant sum of money. It allowed elderly women (whether married or not) some freedom from the constraints of family.

When the affairs of house or land
Go clean against her will,
She boasts: 'I have my Pension
And I'm independent still.'[28]

Not all women married. Over one-quarter of all women in Ireland remained single; yet, even these women were affected by the economic demands of increased housework. In part, this was due to the particularly late transfer of land in many Irish communities (especially in the west), which resulted in a unmarried men and women living together in one household all their lives, with sisters or aunts assuming the role of houseworkers. Young unmarried women might choose to perform unwaged housework as long as there was a chance of marrying. If marriage was no longer a probable outcome, their best option was to emigrate. Every year 20,000 women, mostly women between the ages of 18 and 26, emigrated. Their labour as houseworkers would pay off in America or Australia. The wealth of the parental household and her ranking in the line of siblings determined whether a daughter even attempted to find a position for herself in the Irish marriage market.

Even if an unmarried woman chose not to emigrate, her risk of poverty decreased dramatically during the period under study. Older unmarried women were less liable to be residing in a workhouse. More significantly, the risk of ending up in the workhouse had declined faster for them than for unmarried men. For instance, 6.1 per cent of unmarried women aged over 55 were residing in a workhouse on census day in 1891, compared with 7.5 per cent of unmarried men aged over 55. By 1911, this percentage had fallen to 3.6, while the percentage for elderly men had only fallen to 5.7.

The transfer of women to full-time housework did not necessarily increase the risk (*vis-à-vis* men) of 'dependency' in another person's home. If we define 'dependent' persons as relatives (but not the 'head' of the family) over the age of 40, then both men and women in the eight DEDs were more liable to be 'dependent'

---

[28] 'The Mother that Didn't Die', in Jack Lane and Brendan Clifford (eds.), *Ned Buckley's Poems* (Aubane, 1987), 23. Buckley was a Duhallow poet, 1880–1954.

members of the household between 1901 and 1911. The percentage of 'dependent' women increased from 14.8 per cent in 1901
to 16.6 in 1911. However, the percentage of 'dependent' men
increased much faster, from 12.3 per cent in 1901 to 16.5 in 1911.
Both men and women over the age of 40 were liable to find
themselves in households headed by a relative to whom they
were not married, and the respective positions of men and women
came to resemble each other. Put in another way, the chances
for a man over the age of 40 to establish his own household
decreased faster than the chances for a woman over the age of
40. Whether through emigration or marriage, women were more
liable to escape.[29]

The alternative options to housework for unmarried women
were unattractive. Young unmarried women risked paying a high
cost for engaging in paid employment: they risked celibacy. Paid
work increased the time costs of finding a husband. Employment
lowered their status both as potential wives and as productive
workers. Unmarried rural women preferred non-agricultural
forms of employment—that is, employment that widened opportunities for marriage by providing male contacts outside the local parish, or by allowing more freedom than was permissible
when a woman resided with her employers. The unmarried
woman who decided to take up paid employment, would find
that her opportunities were poor. Women were discriminated
against, especially in the context of the newly reformed types of
work catered for by the all-male agricultural colleges. Legislative
changes restricted the employment of women. Economic reorganization and reform reduced the options of rural women in
what had traditionally been female jobs.

Even for unmarried women, housework had certain benefits.
In agricultural communities where work was physically demanding, monotonous, and heavily dependent on such factors
as the weather, women (and men) might have preferred to work
inside.[30] The fact that domestic work was unpaid did not necessarily make it less satisfying. The move into the home allowed

[29] The total number of 'dependent' women and men over the age of 40 in
households in the 8 DEDs were 728 and 697 (respectively) in 1901, and 716 and
747 (respectively) in 1911.

[30] 'Observer', 'Those Left Behind', *IH*, 5 Feb. 1910: 103, and a series of letters,
ibid. 110–11.

women to expand into other areas of life, outside the strictly economic realm. Given the conventional assumptions within Irish society, housework enabled women to adopt a more creative and productive role within the domestic environment than they could have done in the paid employment market. Not all households allowed women a creative function, but it would be foolish to assume that there was creativity in monotonous jobs for a subsistence wage.

Women's strategies of well-being through work also raised more general issues. It is usually the case that, once women are limited to the domestic labour market, tension between reproduction and domestic production tends to threaten their welfare. This is especially true when the productive aspects of the home are removed, leaving women with only their *long-term* strategy for avoiding poverty (that is, reproduction). Before the First World War at least, this did not happen in Ireland. Reproductive labour remained—as it had been—a crucial determinant of welfare: if anything, the value of women's reproductive labour increased as emigrant remittances became an established practice. But it was that hidden investment in the future of the household which was crucial.

This book has argued that the coincidence of declining demand for female labour in jobs customarily reserved for women and the increasing potential for productive labour within the home encouraged the transfer of Irish women from paid employment (or work on the family farm) to unpaid production in the home. The changes in rural Irish society between 1890 and 1914 led to the development of a non-market household sector which demanded skilled labour—this demand was met by women.

THE COMPARATIVE DIMENSION: HOUSEWORK IN BRITAIN

It may be appropriate to consider the implications of this study for the social history of housework in other countries. Housework is a neglected field in British history, so no authoritative statements of a comparative kind can be made. It is clear, however, that many of the changes in Ireland have parallels in Britain. In both countries, women moved progressively out of paid employment and into full-time unpaid housewifery. This shift occurred amidst rapid alterations in domestic production and reproduction.[31] Investment in working-class and lower middle-class housing is one example.[32] In working-class Britain the parlour became the symbol of the housewife's power and control over her family. The parlour was a confirmation of the housewife's pre-eminent role in the management of resources, and symbolized her success in budgeting a limited income to allow for this 'surplus'. In addition, the dietary changes noted in Ireland from the 1890s onwards were replicated in Britain.[33] The 'discovery' and popularization of nutritional science in the early years of the twentieth century gave prestige to British housewives. Food was not merely a way of alleviating hunger: it could protect the family from scurvy, anaemia, gross dental decay, rickets, and a host of other ailments.[34] Domestic labour was important and dynamic, and women in Britain were as keen as their counterparts in Ireland to concentrate their labour in that sphere.

This interpretation of housework as a potentially positive feature of women's lives in this period goes against the implications of the influential work of Ann Oakley. She would maintain that, from the 1950s, housewives led isolated lives, performing monotonous jobs without remuneration or recognition.[35] This book suggests that, whatever the truth of her statements for contemporary society, her analysis is less helpful with respect to agricultural societies in general and to pre-war Britain and Ireland in particular. Rather, the labour that women performed within the household became more varied. There was a chorus of praise and admiration for the labour of the housewife in Britain from the late nineteenth century. This domestic rhetoric was not simply an attempt by the upper classes to manipulate

[31] For a more detailed description of these changes, see Caroline Davidson, *A Woman's Work Is Never Done* (1982); Alison Ravetz, 'The Victorian Coal Kitchen and its Reformers', *Victorian Studies*, 11/4 (1968); and Christina Hardyment, *From Mangle to Microwave* (1988).

[32] D. Read (ed.), *Edwardian England* (1982).

[33] D. J. Oddy, 'Working-Class Diets in Late Nineteenth-Century Britain', *EHR*, 2nd ser. 23 (1970), 314–23; J. C. Drummond and Anne Wilbraham, *The Englishman's Food* (1957); *British Cookery: A Complete Guide to Culinary Practice in the British Isles*, rev. edn. (1977); and Molly Harrison, *The Kitchen in History* (1972).

[34] Maisie Steven, *The Good Scots Diet: What Happened to it?* (Aberdeen, 1985), 103–5.   [35] Ann Oakley, *Woman's Work* (New York, 1974).

poorer women, nor was it solely due to patriarchal 'heads' of families recognizing the gains to be made by keeping women in their place. The domestic rhetoric in part described the rational choices that some women had made. By the turn of the century, more women had decided that they were in a position to invest a higher proportion of their work-time within the household, and, for many of these women, this investment was worth making.

As in Ireland, one of the ways in which British women attempted to take control of the domestic sphere and change it to suit their own needs was through education. Private organizations, school boards, and local government authorities in Britain established classes in cooking, laundry work, and housewifery for schoolgirls and adult women from the end of the nineteenth century. For example, 7,000 schoolgirls in England had attended a sufficient number of cookery lessons in 1883 to earn them the cooking grant. Within twelve years this had jumped to over 146,000 girls a year. By 1910, nearly 490,000 girls were attending domestic education classes each year.[36] Historians such as Dena Attar, Anna Davin, Carol Dyhouse, June Purvis, and Annmarie Turnbull represent this education as part of an attempt by the middle classes to disseminate a particular form of domestic ideology amongst working-class girls. They argue that domestic education was intended to ensure that women knew their 'place' in society.[37] Clearly, many of the classes were interventionalist. For instance, teachers of domestic subjects in Staffordshire and Warwickshire were proud of their success in 'targeting' certain working-class homes.[38] Also, these writers claim, domestic classes

[36] *Board of Education, General Report on the Teaching of Domestic Subjects* (1912), 38, and Fanny L. Calder, 'The Training of Teachers in Cookery', *Journal of Education*, 1 Dec. 1894: 712. Calder was hon. sec. for the National Union for the Technical Education of Women in Domestic Science, and hon. sec for the Liverpool Training School of Cookery and Technical College for Women.

[37] Dena Attar, *Wasting Girls' Time: The History and Politics of Home Economics* (1990); Anna Davin, '"Mind that you Do as you Are Told": Reading Books for Board School Children, 1870–1902', *Feminist Review*, 3 (1979); Carol Dyhouse, *Girls Growing up in Late Victorian and Edwardian England* (1981); June Purvis, 'Domestic Subjects since 1870', in Ivor Goodson (ed.), *Social Histories of the Secondary Curriculum* (1985); and Annmarie Turnbull, 'Learning her Womanly Work: The Elementary School Curriculum, 1870–1914', in Felicity Hunt (ed.), *Lessons for Life: The Schooling of Girls and Women, 1850–1950* (1987).

[38] Board of Education, *General Report on the Teaching of Domestic Subjects*, 22.

aimed to invest young girls with desirable traits such as docility. In the words of Miss Edith C. Wilson, assistant secretary and tutor in the Owens College Department for Women, in 1888: 'the wisest ideal to put before girls is not one of self-development, but of serviceableness.'[39]

To leave the analysis at this point, however, is insufficient. The passive acceptance of a middle-class ideology of domesticity does not explain the popularity of domestic education. School reports noted that the demand for domestic education from students and their parents exceeded the supply of teachers.[40] Frequently, girls stayed at school for an extra year in order to receive training in housewifery.[41] Girls would walk long distances to attend the classes, and teachers were besieged with applications to admit older girls and women.[42] As in Ireland, girls and women who attended the classes in Britain were actively seeking to improve their status within the home by reducing the 'menial' elements of housework and by emphasizing the more specialized and skilled forms of domestic labour.

One of the noticeable features of the British domestic education classes was the way in which they were used to exclude men from domestic management. Housework became more specialized and skilled: as the housewife took over these skills, the male 'head' of the family was gradually excluded. Thus, the bargaining power of women was enhanced. This exclusion of men was not only based on the biological or psychological differences between men and women, but also on the need of women to ensure their underlying eminence within the household. Thus, while none of the mainstream domestic classes included men,

---

[39] Miss Edith C. Wilson, 'A Survey of the Present State of the Education of Women', *Journal of Education*, 1 Sept. 1888: 426, paper read on the 9 May 1888 to the Schoolmistresses' Association in Manchester.

[40] See the reports in the Public Record Office in London [hereafter PRO Kew] ED 164–3, ED 77–8, ED 96–198.

[41] Board of Education, *Report of the Consultative Committee on Practical Work in Secondary Schools* (Cd. 6849), HC 1913, xx. 302 (608), evidence by Miss S. A. Burstall, headmistress of the Manchester High School, on 9 Dec. 1909; and Miss Rowland, 'Wales (with Monmouthshire) Domestic Subjects in Public Elementary Schools Annual Report 1911–1912', PRO Kew ED 92–10.

[42] Board of Education, *General Report on the Teaching of Domestic Subjects*, 10, 32, and 36, and Rowland, 'Wales (with Monmouthshire) Domestic Subjects'.

classes in cookery for men who worked on ships and boats caused no comment.[43] Men were able to learn domestic skills, but only in contexts that did not threaten the dominance of women within the home. A similar motive lay behind the opposition of some working-class mothers to the provision of school meals. In the words of Anna Martin in 1911: 'The women have a vague dread of being superseded and dethroned. Each of them knows perfectly well that the strength of her position in the home lies in the physical dependence of her husband and children upon her and she is suspicious of anything that would tend to undermine this.'[44]

In Britain as in Ireland, discussions about women's power and status were linked to housework. To take one example, the journal *Women and Progress* published an exchange of letters about housework in 1906.[45] On 23 November 1906 J. A. M. Priestley suggested a radical solution to the problem of female status within the home. Priestley noted that the severe shortage of domestic servants had forced many women to become 'household drudges'. The reader was told to remember Jane Welsh Carlyle 'on her knees, scrubbing the kitchen floor of that bleak Scotch farmhouse'. The solution, according to Priestley, was for housework to be made communal: co-operative kitchens would raise dietary standards and would give cooking the status that it required. Washing and child care would be dealt with in a similar fashion. Priestley's vision resulted in a vigorous response from a woman called Kate Jenkins. She noted that Priestley seemed to think that women disliked housework: 'but surely she is in error in supposing that all women, even intellectual women, feel dislike rather than interest in the details of the home. . . . Is not the work of the hands a thing in which thousands of women take pleasure and pride?' Jenkins went on to argue that women experienced

[43] PRO Kew HO 45–9839 1310432, letters between the Shipmasters' Society and the Commission of Council on Education, Apr. 1891; PRO Kew ED 164–3, Committee of Management of the National Training School for Cookery, 16 Feb. 1904: 205–7; ibid. 164–4, Committee of Management of the National Training School for Cookery, 4 Apr. 1911, no page number; and Rowland, 'Wales (with Monmouthshire) Domestic Subjects'.

[44] Anna Martin, *Married Working Women* (1911), 29–30.

[45] Letters in *Women and Progress*, 23 Nov. 1906: 60–1, and 30 Nov. 1906: 78.

pleasure in producing 'a high quality of food', and that domestic competition between neighbours added to the enjoyment of life. Further, Jenkins says, it was unnecessary for Jane Welsh Carlyle to scrub floors: 'linoleum will do, or one day's work with beeswax and turpentine'. According to Jenkins, the way to raise women's status was to improve (through domestic education) the quality of household goods and services.

The benefits of full-time housewifery for working-class women in Britain are similar to those identified in Ireland. It made sense for these women to reject working a double shift—in the factory and in the home—if they could avoid it. In the words of the trade-unionist Mary MacArthur, the ideal that women's place was in the home had 'something to be said for it'.[46] Rising living standards amongst the working classes in Britain from the late nineteenth century could only have occurred in conjunction with the increased investment of female labour within the home, converting income into consumable goods.[47] Thus, the political economist Jane Humphries argues that the increased sexual division of labour was the best way of maximizing the welfare of the working-class family.[48] David Vincent's argument that the rising prosperity of the labouring poor in late nineteenth-century Britain facilitated the emergence of companionable marriages and a more 'humane' form of family life points to the importance of domestic work in improving women's lives.[49] In the words of a proverb popular amongst agricultural labourers in Berkshire: 'There's only fourpence a year difference between what she gets who goes out to work, and what she gets who stays at home; and *she who stays at home wins it.*'[50]

---

[46] Mary R. MacArthur, 'The Woman Trade-Unionist's Point of View', in Marion Phillips (ed.), *Women and the Labour Party* (1917), 18.

[47] For discussion of the contribution of women's housework to consumption standards, see Charles Booth, *London Life and Labour*, i (1889), 199; Helen Bosanquet, *Rich and Poor* (1986); and H. Higgs, 'Workmen's Budgets', *Journal of the Royal Statistical Society*, 56 (June 1893), 255–85.

[48] Jane Humphries, 'Class Struggle and the Resistance of the Working Class Family', *Cambridge Journal of Economics*, 1 (Sept. 1977), 241–58.

[49] David Vincent, 'Love and Death and the Nineteenth-Century Working Class', *Social History*, 5 (1980), 247.

[50] Commission on the Employment of Children, Young Persons and Women in Agriculture (1867), *First Report of the Commissioners, with Appendix*, i (.4068), HC 1967–8, xvii. 17, emphasis in original.

THE STATE AND THE PECULIARITIES OF THE IRISH

Crucial to the changes in Ireland was the role of the state. Government intervention in wages, education, and housing was important in both countries. However, this intervention occurred earlier, and involved more substantial and more direct investment of capital, in Ireland than in Britain. Although, the state in Ireland did reflect and reproduce class relationships (ironically, English urban relationships), individual state élites did have some autonomous power to shape economic and social interests.[51] This was particularly true when (as in Ireland) economic and legitimacy crises threatened the basis of the state. The role of domestic labour becomes more significant for capital in times of crisis.[52] From the 1890s the state in Ireland assumed wider powers of intervention, twisting the meaning of the political sneer that the British government was trying to 'kill Home Rule with kindness'.

Why did the state prefer women to work in the home rather than in the market? Part of the explanation must lie in the recognition that improved forms of housework would improve the performance of the labour force. In the words of 'Ireland's Eye' in 1913: 'If children are allowed to drift without proper care, and if mothers are maimed and distorted with hard and heavy work, how is the country going to prosper or have a healthy and vigorous manhood?'[53] Women's work inside the home was crucial because the value it created was absorbed immediately into the household economy, making it more profitable. If any surplus were created, it was promptly reinvested in productive economic ventures. The efficiency of the labour force was important. Emigration could be reduced by providing men with employment: if men stayed, women also stayed, to marry and bear children. Intensification of efficient housework on the English and urban model would require increased specialization within the home. Finally, the role of women who performed the labour necessary for consumption was accepted as crucial. The expansion of a

[51] A good example of a member of the élite who exerted considerable individual power is Plunkett.

[52] For further discussion, see Jean Gardiner, 'Women's Domestic Labour', *NLR*, 89 (1975), 51.

[53] 'Ireland's Eye', 'The Lot of the Farm Woman', *Irish Worker*, 31 May 1913: 1.

market for commodities, everyone knew, required the energies of women. It was this final reason which galvanized nationalist opinion behind the movement for improved housewifery in Ireland. 'Buy Irish' was a direct call for the reproduction of capital —that is, Irish capital. Ironically, although initial attempts to redirect female labour were British-based, Irish nationalists willingly complied with this aim and used it for politically subversive purposes.

Government had a direct fiscal and political interest in the profitability of all economic sectors of the community—from the agricultural to the household sector. Just as land reform was intended to meet certain social and political ends, and only incidentally concerned with agricultural productivity, domestic reforms were part of a value-laden New Unionist policy.

COUNTERFACTUALS: ALTERNATIVES TO THE UNWAGED FEMALE HOUSEWORKER

Without these changes in the rural and domestic economies, all sectors of the community would have been worse off. However, given the increased time requirements of housework, it was not inevitable that the extra work would be taken up within the unwaged or 'private' sphere. Market alternatives to housework were unsuccessful and undeveloped. For instance, co-operative societies could have established bread-baking societies. The fact that the one such society to be established had a membership of almost 1,000 suggested that it was not lack of a viable market that restricted the establishment of domestically orientated co-operative societies.[54] Similarly, the collection and delivery of water and the washing of clothes remained inside the home and continued to be executed by women in the household rather than by paid laundresses. The number of people classified in the census as being 'engaged in washing and bathing service' actually dropped by one-fifth in the twenty years between 1891 and 1911.

A final alternative outcome would have entailed a reduction

[54] Registry of Friendly Societies, Dublin, 817 R Dublin, Industrial Co-operative Society. Other examples could be consumer societies or co-operative stores such as the Shamrock Co-operative Store Society (papers held at 10 R Cork) and the Dublin Consumers Co-operative Society (papers held at 1235 R. Dublin).

in the sexual division of housework, with men and women dividing the 'new' tasks evenly between them. There were a number of economic reasons why this did not occur, including wage relativities, differential education, and sectoral shifts in desirable skills in other labour markets. The economic and social changes that have been traced in this book were not sufficiently disruptive to change conventional attitudes towards gender roles. Faced with highly unsatisfactory, partial explanations, this book attempts only to describe how, given a society permeated with divisions based on gender, women were designated certain forms of labour. It was women themselves, however, who made that labour into a way of life.

Bibliography

MANUSCRIPT SOURCES

Cork Archives Institute

U210, James Bence Papers: Aghalurky Farm balance sheets (1848–80).

U271, Laim de Roiste: papers and diaries (1902–47).

U280, Evans Papers: memoirs of a childhood spent in Cork, Irish correspondence, and some pamphlets.

U239, Farm labourer's Account-Book: O'Donoghue, Greenfort, Blarney (1879–1901).

U173, D. P. Fitzgerald, Emeritus Professor of Anatomy, UCC: notes on Cork industry.

U60/14, Folklore of the Millstreet area, collected by Fr. Ferris (n.d.).

U170, Hurley Emigrant Letters: 127 letters from Denis and Michael Hurley, natives of Tawnies, Clonakilty, who emigrated to Nevada in 1871 (1871–1935).

U59, Irish Medical Association, Cork branch: minutes and correspondence (1902–17).

U313, Irish Mothers' Pension Society, Dublin: papers.

U251, John Keane: farm account-books, Baltacken, Myvore, Mullingar (1918–35).

U64, Kinsale Convent of Mercy: extracts from the annals of St Joseph's, Kinsale, by Sister Angela Bolsterm (1973).

U274, Kinsale Development Association: papers (1930–40).

U67, Linen manufacture in co. Kerry (18th cent.).

U178, William Litchfield, Ballymaloe, Cloyne: farm accounts (1870–1917).

U323, Hugh Loudon, manager, Provincial Bank of Ireland, Skibbereen: report on the harvest of 1864 and on the condition and prospects of the landowners and the agricultural labouring classes in Skibbereen district, made to Thomas Hewat, Esq., London (1864).

U339, Lucy and O'Connell, farm machinery suppliers, Mallow Rd., Cork: ledgers etc. (1890–1960).

U174, J. Matterson and Sons, Ltd., Limerick: stock-book (1877–87) and dividend-book (1910–19).

U250, James Pomeroy: farm account-book, Knockcahill, Rathcoolem Banteer (1854–1910).

U86, Power Correspondence (1896–1935).

U223, School Inspector's Report-Book for Kanturk National School (1868–98).

U189, Vocational Education Committee Minutes (1903–25), and co. Cork Joint Technical Instruction Committee Minute-Books (1906–25).

Irish Countrywoman's Association, Dublin

Minutes, accounts, correspondence, memoirs, etc. for the UI and the Irish Countrywoman's Association (1901–85).

Irish Folklore Commission, University College, Dublin

The following manuscript books were examined: 22, 25, 28, 30, 38, 42, 43, 53, 54, 70, 77, 79, 107, 117, 132, 145, 172, 203, 227, 254, 259, 266, 289, 404, 407, 437, 460, 462, 485, 580, 600, 618, 691, 732, 737, 744, 782, 828, 840, 843, 975, 1020, 1036, 1057, 1137, 1164, 1177, 1310, 1321, 1340, 1360, 1361, 1371, 1386, 1389, 1391, 1393, 1430, 1480, 1838, 1839, 1845, 1862.

National Library of Ireland: Manuscript Collection

MS 7779, Sir Thomas Aiskew Papers: papers and newscuttings on the Social Science Association and its meetings in Dublin (1860–8).

MS 19782, Sarah Seling Blakeney: manuscript recollections of Sarah Seling Blakeney of Ballyglunin, co. Galway (c.1820–1900).

MS 26148, Joseph Brennan Papers: papers and correspondence (1912–17).

MS 7997, Census of Kilmallock Parish (c.1902).

MS 22951, Robert Craig: letters from Robert Craig to William Ruxton of Bath on the management of the latter's farm at Ardee, co. Louth, together with workmen's accounts etc. (1894–5).

MS 17740, Revd Fletcher, de Cobain Papers: Armaghbrague National School, co. Armagh, letters (1880–97).

MS 9967–9, Alan Denson (selector): letters from George W. Russell, unpubl. collection, 3 vols. (1960).

R630 a15, DATI for Ireland, Agricultural Board: Minutes of proceedings, confidential (1900–21).

MS 22706, W. G. Fallon: papers and typescript of a diary by James M'Colgan of a motoring tour through Ireland in July 1910.

MS 23260–3, 23549–56, FitzMaurice Papers: account-books (1890–1909) and diaries (1888–1915).

MS 9804, Industrial Committee (Connradh na Gaedhilge) Minute-Book (1902–11).

MS 13827, Bishop Michael Logue: papers.

MS 24423, Fionan MacColuim: papers and report of an arbitration meeting called to settle differences between Conradh na Gaeilge and the Irish National Teachers' Association. (23 July 1910).

MS 23350–1, Mahon Papers: farm accounts and rentals of Sir William Vesey Ross Mahon and Sir William Henry Mahon, of Castelegar, co. Galway, 2 vols. (1889–1915).

MS 24529, Amy Mander: account of an industrial and technical exhibition of Irish industries at Foxford, co. Mayo, 4–6 Sept. 1890.

MS 13414, Monteagle Papers: letters to and from Horace Plunkett (1911–   ).

MS 24874, T. C. Murray: reminiscences about his life as a teacher.

MS 23833–24951, Ormonde Papers: rules to be observed by lodgekeeper at Kilkenny Castle (1913), workmen's account-books (1856–1931), farm account books (1883–1932), and personal expenditure account-books (1892–1952).

MS 16910–41, 17910–85, Dr Michael Quane: papers (*c*.17–*c*.20).

MS 21623, Sheehy Skeffington Papers: letters to Francis Sheehy Skeffington (1912).

MS 19878, Studdert Papers: rough domestic account-books of Studdert, Bunratty, co. Clare (1893–5).

MS 580, Trenchard Estate: accounts of labour employed on Mount Trenchard Estate (1882–6).

MS 19825, Thomas Tynan: debtors' ledger of Thomas Tynan, grocer and vintner, of Monsterevin, co. Kildare (*c*.1908–23).

MS 24674–81, Villiers-Stuart Papers: labourers' accounts, Dromana (1885–93).

MS 23562, Widows' Almshouse: rough minute-book of the Governors, Dublin (1852–1906).

MS 33105, Women's Labour League: papers.

National Archives of Ireland (Dublin)

Board of Education Papers.

Census of Ireland, manuscript returns, 1901 and 1911.

DATI Papers.

Co-operative Societies Collection (ICOS files).

IIDA 1091, Irish Industrial Development Society: correspondence files, annual reports, and other records (1904–70).

MS 12328–9, Minute-Book of the Medical Officers of Health: report on unsanitary dwellings, Ballinrobe Rural District Council 2 (1901).

CO 904/120/11, Reports on the state of the country, 1916–17.

IIDA 1091/2/1–2, Edward J. Riordan: 'A Popular Sketch on the

Industrial Movement' (Aug. 1904); 'A Snap-Shot History of the Cork Industrial Development Association' (c.1905).

Public Record Office of Northern Ireland

General Manuscripts

LA8/7AA/1, Antrim Rural District: minutes of School Attendance Committee on expenditure, salaries, employment of children (1900–25).

LA11/12b/1, Ballycastle Rural District Council: correspondence on labourers' cottages (1911–14).

LA16/7AA/1, Ballymoney Rural District Council: minute-book of School Attendance Committee (1900–14).

LA16/9D/1, Ballymoney Union: executive sanitary officer's record- and report-book (1875–1940).

LA75/2F/1, Belleek Rural District Council: minute-book (1914–15).

D1534, William Boyd, Blackstaff Flax Spinning and Weaving Co. Ltd., Belfast: household account-books (1901–11).

D1132/4/15B, Miss F. E. Bushe of Rockdale: diary (1885).

D1422/4/7, Cooper Collection: Doneyloop cookery class (c.1915).

D2936/1–8, Miss Felicitie Ferguson of Newcastle: letters, photograph albums, diaries, family papers, domestic accounts (1859–1965).

T3038/1, Robert Finnegan of Drumarden, Clogher, and Portaferry, co. Down, merchant seaman: biography, manuscript of text furnished in 1915, typed 1921, unpubl. (1868–89).

D3618/D, Vere Henry Lewis Foster: papers, pamphlets, originals of correspondence quoted in pamphlets and other correspondence, and daguerrotype photographs of a female emigrant servant enclosed in Vere Foster's diary of 1864 (1849–c.1890).

D1835, T. M. Green: payments to domestic servants (1889–93), memo-book containing full abstracts of interviews with tenants etc. on purchases of holdings (1907–17).

T3249/1, W. A. Greer: '18 Years, 1896–1914', unpubl. autobiography, written between Jan. and July 1967, covering his young life in East Belfast with relations in Crossgar, Dromore, co. Down (1896–1914).

D517, Irish Protestant National Teachers' Union: minute-book (1911–26).

D3550/3, Killyleagh, Killinchy, Kilmead, and Tullynakill Farming Society: minute-book (1906–21).

D3524/2/1, Killyleagh Women's Guild: papers and booklet (c.1914–18).

T2992/1, R. Kyle Knox: transcript vol. of reminiscences about Coleraine, co. Derry (c.1920).

LA16/12A/1, Labourers' Act: minutes (1878–1902).

LA44, Larne Rural District Council: School Attendance Committee minute-book (1900–25), estimates, reports, and correspondence on labourers' cottages (1910), representations from agricultural labourers about housing (1911–20).

LA49, Lisnaskea Rural District Council: sanitary officer's certificates and reports on sanitary conditions of dwelling-houses (1904–20), circulars and orders from the Local Government Board (c.1870–c.1910), and report of committee appointed to select sites for labourers' cottages and allotments (1908).

D1769/12/4, Miss Anne McCulloch of Mount Oriel, Bangor: testimonial papers, including correspondence, domestic and grocery account-books, etc. (c.1890).

T3580, Frederick B. McGinley: memoirs, on electricity supply industry and as electrical and goods retailer, Belfast (1900–70).

3300/8, Michael McGuigan: typescript account of the spirit grocery businesses in villages and rural areas of Northern Ireland in the 1920s (1977).

D1821/2/2–3, Francis McKee Papers (tea, wine and spirit merchant), Armagh: grocers' cash-Book (1872–96).

D627, H. de F. Montgomery: letters from John Pomeroy, Fivemiletown, co. Tyrone, and James Watt, Northern Bank, Fivemiletown (1880), and family correspondence (1866–82).

LA55/9D/8, Newcastle Rural District Council: sanitary officer's report-book (1905–38).

LA61/3c/1, Newtownards Rural District Council: reports of Public Health, Finance, Water Supply, Law, and Lighting Committees (1909–11).

D1132/9/1, Pomeroy Estate: papers, correspondence, accounts, circulars, etc. on National schools and the agricultural scheme in Pomeroy and the surrounding area (late 19th cent.–1946).

T1848, Sarah Potts, Brookfield, co. Antrim: diary on life as a school-teacher (1852–1957).

2149/9/1, Recipe-Book (c.1912).

D1884, Mrs C. Scott Papers: including papers on WNHA (c.1910–21).

D1791/16, Shop Hours, Act 1904: letters about the act (13 June 1908).

D1813/11/1/1, Patrick Smyth of Coalisland, co. Tyrone, grocer, wine and spirit merchant: correspondence, statement of offers with creditors (c.1899).

D2481/5/4, Stewartstown Red Cross Cookery Book (1918).

D1884/1/1/1–5, WNHA Records (1907–12).

D1812, Women's Working Association, Belfast: working minute-book (1909–16). D1812.

Farm Account-Books

D1132/1, Accounts and correspondence on farming at Pomeroy (*c.*1892–1921).

D2983/1, David J. Alexander: farm account-book, Larrycormick, Moneymore, co. Londonderry (1906–24).

D1096/57, Edward Bird, Trillick, co. Tyrone: account for livestock, including sheep, and loans of money, farm and cattle accounts (1874–99).

D1065/2, James Courley, Saintfield, co. Down: diary extracts on farm management (1883–1902).

T2642/2, Frederick Greer, Lisson, co. Tyrone: note on the feeding of cows, estimates of workers' wages, memos on places he has lived, and part of an account-book and memoirs (1907).

T2992/2, Mr Knox: farm account-book, Secon (1894–1900).

D3323, H. R. Morrison, Moneydig, Kilrea, co. Derry, on the estate of the Marquis of Waterford: farm work account-book (1857–1923).

Papers on Dairy and Poultry Industries

T3132, Ballyrashane Co-operative Agricultural and Dairy Society Ltd., Coleraine (co. Derry), 1897–1924.

D2357, John Bell, poultry dealer, Downpatrick St., Crossgar, co. Down, 1894–1910.

D3506/X/2, Brackey Co-operative Agricultural and Dairy Society Ltd. (n.d.).

D1132/9/3, Co-operative Agricultural and Dairy Societies for Pomeroy and Carrickmore, late 19th and early 20th cents.

D3076, Deerpark Co-operative Agricultural and Dairy Society Ltd., Glenarm, co. Antrim, 1908–55.

D3046/BA/1–2, Derrygonnelly Co-operative Agricultural and Dairy Society Ltd., co. Fermanagh, 1898–1922.

T2737/1, Derrygonnelly Co-operative Creamery Company, Derrygonnell, co. Fermanagh, 1898–1900.

LA36/9C/1, Enniskillen Rural District Committee: register of cowkeepers, dairymen, and purveyors of milk (1912–34).

D1132/10/40b, J. Fait (instructor in dairying): recommendation made after a visit to the creamery at Pomeroy (1907).

D1132/10/40a, Inspectors report of the creamery at Pomeroy (1906).

T3132/3, Mrs Mary Jameson: indenture between Jameson and the Ballyrashane Agricultural and Dairy Society Ltd. (1896).

D3101/CA/1, Killen Co-operative Agricultural and Dairy Society Ltd., Killen, Castlederg, co. Tyrone, 1900–02.

D1280, J. Kilpatrick, poultry and seed specialist, 117–19 Victoria St., Belfast, 1925–38.

LA44/1E/1, Larne Rural District Council: regulations on dairies, cow-sheds, and milk shops (1900).

LA47/9C/4, Lisburn Rural District Council: register of cowkeepers, dairymen (1908–33).

D1077/4/2, Pat McKenna, Desertmartin, egg-dealer, 1916–31.

D1813/1/33, Peter Mackinney, wholesale poultry and fruit merchant, Londonderry, c.1890–1905.

D3059, Moneymore Co-operative Agricultural and Dairy Society Ltd., 1898–1923.

LA55/9C/2, Newcastle Rural District Council: register of cowkeepers, dairymen, and purveyors of milk (1906–34).

D1132/1/53, Notebook on milk and cream etc., 1905.

T2473/3A–G, Col. M. C. Perceval-Price, egg-marketing, Saintfield House, Saintfield, co. Down, c.1890.

LA67/9C/1–2, Strabane Rural District Council 1: register of cowkeepers, dairymen, or purveyors of milk (1910–12 and 1929–34).

D1326/13/30, Robert Telford, Glasgow, and McLean and Co., Belfast, 1904.

Papers on Linen, Clothing, and Sprigging Industries

D792, Account-Books of linen traveller, Belfast, 1899.

D824, A. and S. Henry and Co., linen manufacturers, 1847–1955.

D3582, Barron and Co., cotton and jute bag manufacturers, Belfast, 1896–1936.

T3582, J. Baxter: typescript history of the Baxter, Kyle, Davidson, and Wilson families, co. Antrim and Belfast, c.1780–1980, with remarks by Mr J. Baxter on his life in working-class Belfast with employment in linen trade (1900–70).

D2149, Belleek Needlework Industry, co. Fermanagh: papers (1908–21).

SCH548/6C/1, Carclinty Primary School, Rasharkin, co. Antrim: daily report of industrial instruction (1901–4).

D2149/3/10, Cashelnadrea Lace and Sprigging Association, 1905–6.

D1376/5, Coleraine Woollen Manufacturing Co., 1901–3.

D1905/2/25/4–5, John and Frank Dinsmore of Crebilly House, woollen manufacturers, 1899–1900.

D1191/76B, Edward Gribbon and Sons: handloom winders' book, coleraine (1887–92).

D1326/13/20, Government School of Art, Belfast, 1872–1901.

D1835/23, Robert Gunning, Greenmount, co. Down: flax spinner's testimonial papers (1870).

D1064/52, Hale and Martin, Balnamore, Ballymoney, co. Antrim: linen mill records (1906–11).

D1621, Island Spinning Co., Lisburn, co. Antrim, 1866–1940.

D2346/10/1, McBride and Williamson, cotton and lawn manufacturers and embroiderers, Belfast: bleachers' stock-book (1913–18).

D1195/5/2, 'Theta', essay entitled 'Our Local Industries, Newtownards' (5 Feb. 1885).

D2423, D1941, Ulster Woollen Co. Ltd.: papers (1887–1952).

D1042, John Johnson: wages book of hemstitching factory, Banbridge, co. Down (1899–1900).

D3480/41/1, Reports of inspectors on 'Sweating in Making-Up and Embroidery Trades', probably in co. Tyrone (c.1910).

D2956, D2375, J. N. Richardson: family correspondence and linen business papers (1840–1950).

D2346/3/1, H. M. Robb and Co. Ltd., linen manufacturers, 1909–53.

D2662, Bryson Spencer and Co. Ltd., linen manufacturers, Portadown, co. Armagh, 1907–17.

D1504/9, Strain and Elliot, linen manufacturers, Bedford St., Belfast, 1890–1912.

T3377/1, Tillie and Henderson Ltd., linen merchants and shirt manufacturers, 1907–20.

D837/1/2, Malcolmson Watson and Co., Belfast: goods account-book (1894–9).

D1769/40/2, Woodborn Weaving Co., Carrickfergus: papers to McKean and Brice [sic] Smyth (1892).

D3641, Young and Anderson Ltd., wholesale drapers, Belfast, 1888–1920.

Registry of Friendly Societies, Dublin

Bacon Factory (R821).
Catholic Girls' Insurance (1409).
Co-operative (989).
Consumers Co-operative (1235).
Co-operative Agricultural Societies (677, 830, 836, 924, 1000).
Co-operative Agricultural and Dairy Societies (152, 153, 215, 275, 280, 371, 374, 465, 472, 542, 547, 560, 633, 638, 648, 651, 693, 774, 783).
Co-operative Agricultural and Industrial Societies (190, 916).
Co-operative Beekeepers' Societies (567, 595).
Co-operative Creamery Societies (959, 972, 1097, 1172, 1230).
Co-operative Dairies (109).
Co-operative Development and Transit Society (1082).
Co-operative Farmer's Society (387).
Co-operative Industries (442, 817, 1148).
Co-operative Home Industries Societies (591, 615, 666, 706).
Co-operative Industrial and Agricultural Societies (831, 1349, 1459).

Co-operative Lace Society (216).
Co-operative Poultry Societies (311, 353, 471, 659, 705, 795, 883, 1043, 1187).
Co-operative Poultry and Farm Produce (808).
Co-operative Store (10).
Co-operative Wholesale (1081).
Dun Emer (766, 767).
Handspinners and Weavers (1190).
Irish Agricultural Organization (182).
Irish Homestead (841).
Knitting Co-operative (2980).
United Irishwomen (1230).

Trinity College, Dublin, Manuscript Library

CDB, Confidential base-line reports on the congested districts.
V106–14, Courtown Papers (1867–1914).
MS 2276a–d, Revd Joseph Charles Mansfield: collection of Irish folk-tales and poems, Kenmare, co. Kerry (*c*.1895).
MS 6184, 'Maxims for a Young Person Going to Service: To Be Posted or Hung up in the Pantry or Bedroom' (Dublin, n.d.).
MS 5026–41, Mrs Florence Vere O'Brien: papers (1901–17).

Ulster Folk and Transport Museum Archives

C-1, Agricultural pamphlets, *c*.19–20.
EL-80, Agricultural textbooks and assorted manuscripts.
B-3-6, Mrs Butler: laundry receipts of Mrs Butler of Holywood to Whitehall Hygienic Laundry Co. (1897 and 1910).
T-5-3b, Byers Collection: folklore of the Irish child.
D4, S. A. G. Caldwell: papers on flax, linen, and jute industry in Northern Ireland.
D-3, Children's books and rhymes.
X-5-1, Children's songs collection (Hugh Shield's Oral History Project).
EL-90, Cookery, needlework, and domestic economy books and assorted manuscripts.
B7-1, 2, Cookery notebooks, hand-written.
G4-2-7b, Father Hugh Donnelly, 'Stewartstown', written just before his death in 1981, on his childhood in the first decade of the 20th cent.
C-4, Farm account-books.
J1-45, Folk medicine collection.
Folklore questionnaires on agricultural labourers, bread-making, clothing, handloom weaving, harvest suppers, hearths, hiring-fairs, meat

preserving, migratory labourers, milk, quilting, seasonal variations in diet, social aspects of work.

B-1-17, Dr Harper: valuation and farming accounts.

EL-105, Health books and assorted manuscripts.

B-3-8, City Laundry: laundry receipt notebooks etc.

D-4-10-8, Mrs Susan McAraw, Tattymacall, Lisbellaw, co. Fermanagh: lace and crochet account-books (1900–13).

C-1-22, United Irishwomen Collection.

University College, Cork, Archives

MP 417–717, Cork Industrial Development Association Collection.

U212, Patrick Cunningham, 'The Log of a Labourer' (n.d.), 2 vols., belonging to the late Fr. J. O'Leary.

U155(b), Miss B. Donovan: cash-book in account with J. S. Coppinger (1906–10).

U6, Charlotte Grace O'Brien: correspondence (n.d.).

U155(a), Maurice Ronayne: late 19th-cent. account-book, Midleton, co. Cork.

U203, Red bound vols. (3) of photocopies of broadsheets, Cork (n.d.).

U152, St Georges St. National School, Cork: district inspector's observation book, June 1859–June 1919; correspondence concerning the salary of monitors (June 1859–June 1919).

University College, Dublin, Archives

P31, Elizabeth Bloxham, domestic instructress: papers.

NUWGA/2/3(5), Irish Association of Women Graduates: papers.

P36, McDonnell family, Kilrush, co. Clare and co. Limerick: papers.

P48a, Mary MacSwiney: papers (1872–1942).

P48a/462, Mary MacSwiney: typescript biographical text of Mary MacSwiney by her sister, Mother Argaret MacSwiney, c.1940.

TU4, Waterford Bakers' Union: papers (1826–1908).

CONTEMPORARY PRINTED SOURCES

Official Publications (British Parliamentary Papers)

Appendix to the Report of the Inter-Departmental Committee on Physical Deterioration, iii. *Appendix and General Report* (Cd. 2186), HC 1904, xxxii.

Board of Education, *Report of the Consultative Committee on Practical Work in Secondary Schools* (Cd. 6849), HC 1913, xx.

Board of Trade (Dept. of Labour), *Report by Miss Collett on the Money Wages of Indoor Domestic Servants* (C. 9346), HC 1899, xcii.

—— *Report on Industrial and Agricultural Co-operative Societies in the UK, with Statistical Tables* (Cd. 6045), HC 1912–13, lxxv.

—— *Report on Workmen's Co-operative Societies in the UK, with Statistical Tables* (Cd. 698), HC 1901, lxxiv.

—— *2nd Report by Mr Wilson Fox on the Wages, Earnings, and Conditions of Employment of Agricultural Labourers in the United Kingdom* (Cd. 2376), HC 1905, xcvii.

—— (Dept. of Labour Statistics), *16th Abstract of Labour Statistics of the UK* (Cd. 7131), HC 1914, lxxx.

Census of Ireland, 1861, iv. Reports and Tables Relating to the Religious Professions, Education, and Occupations of the People, II (.3204-iii), HC 1863, lx.

—— *1881. General Report, with Illustrative Maps and Diagrams, Tables and Appendix* (C. 3365), HC 1882, lxxvi.

—— *1891. General Report, with Illustrative Maps and Diagrams, Tables and Appendix* (C. 6780), HC 1892, xc.

—— *1901, ii. General Report, with Illustrative Maps and Diagrams, Tables and Appendix* (Cd. 1190), HC 1902, cxxix.

—— *1911, General Report, with Tables and Appendix* (Cd. 6663), HC 1912–13, cxviii.

Commission of Inquiry into the Conditions of Employment and Other Making-Up Trades in the North of Ireland: Report and Evidence (Cd. 6509), HC 1912–13, xxxiv.

Commission on the Employment of Children, Young Persons and Women in Agriculture (1867), First Report, with Appendix, i (.4068), HC 1967–8, xvii.

Commission of Inquiry into the Housing of the Working Classes, *Minutes of Evidence, Ireland* (C. 4547-i), HC 1884–5, xxxi.

Commissioners of National Education in Ireland, *Appendix to the 56th Report, 1889* (C. 6074-i), HC 1890, xxx.

—— *Appendix to the 59th Report, 1892* (C. 7124-i), HC 1893–4, xxvii.

—— *Appendix to the 62nd Report, 1895* (C. 8185), HC 1896, xxviii.

—— *Appendix to the 66th Report, 1899–1900*, i. *General Report on the State of National Education by Inspectors and Others* (Cd. 286), HC 1900, xxiii.

—— *Appendix to the 68th Report, 1901*, i (Cd. 997), HC 1902, xxx; ii (Cd. 1444), HC 1903, xxi.

—— *Appendix to the 70th Report, 1903*, i (C. 2373), HC 1905, xxvii.

—— *Appendix to the 71st Report, 1904*, i. *General Report on the State of National Education by Inspectors and Others* (Cd. 2654), HC 1905, xxviii.

—— *Appendix to the 72nd Report, 1905–1906*, i (C. 3185), HC 1906, xxix.

—— *Appendix to the 75th Report, 1908–1909*, i. *General Report on the State of National Education by Inspectors and Others* (Cd. 5062), HC 1910, xxv.

Commissioners of National Education in Ireland, *Appendix to the 76th Report, 1909–1910*, i. *General Report on the State of National Education by Inspectors and Others* (Cd. 5491), HC 1911, xxi.

—— *Appendix to the 77th Report, 1910–1911*, i. *General Report on the State of National Education by Inspectors and Others* (Cd. 6042), HC 1912–13, xxiv.

—— *Appendix to the 78th Report, 1911–1912*, i. *General Report on the State of National Education by Inspectors and Others* (Cd. 7061), HC 1914, xxvii.

—— *63rd Report, 1896–1897* (C. 8600), HC 1897, xxviii.

—— *71st Report, 1904–1905* (Cd. 2567), HC 1905, xxviii.

—— *72nd Report, 1905–1906* (Cd. 3154), HC 1906, xxix.

—— *77th Report, 1910–1911* (Cd. 5903), HC 1911, xxi.

Committee on Butter Regulations, *Minutes of Evidence to the Interim Report of the Departmental Committee* (Cd. 1039), HC 1902, xx.

CDB, *1st Report, 1892* (C. 6908), HC 1893–4, lxxi.

—— *8th Report, 1899* (C. 9375), HC 1899, lxxvii.

—— *9th Report, 1900* (Cd. 239), HC 1900, lxviii.

—— *10th Report, 1901* (Cd. 681), HC 1901, lx.

—— *11th Report, 1902* (Cd. 1192), HC 1902, lxxxiii.

—— *14th Report, 1905* (Cd. 2757), HC 1906, xcvii.

—— *16th Report, 1907* (Cd. 3767), HC 1908, xxiii.

—— *18th Report, 1909* (Cd. 4927), HC 1909, xvi.

—— *19th Report, 1909–1911* (Cd. 5712), HC 1911, xiii.

—— *20th Report, 1911–1912* (Cd. 6553), HC 1912–13, xvii.

—— *21st Report, 1912–1913* (Cd. 7312), HC 1914, xvi.

—— *22nd Report, 1913–1914* (Cd. 7865), HC 1914–16, xxiv.

DATI, *Agricultural Statistics, Ireland, 1890, with a Detailed Report on Agriculture* (C. 6518), HC 1890–1, xci.

—— *Agricultural Statistics, Ireland, 1908–1909: Report and Tables Relating to Irish Agricultural Labourers* (Cd. 4919), HC 1909, cii.

—— *Agricultural Statistics, Ireland, 1909, with a Detailed Report on Agriculture* (Cd. 5382), HC 1910, cviii.

—— *Agricultural Statistics, Ireland, 1909–1910: Report and Tables Relating to Irish Agricultural Labourers* (Cd. 5033), HC 1910, cviii.

—— *Agricultural Statistics, Ireland, 1912, with a Detailed Report on Agriculture* (Cd. 6987), HC 1913, lxxvi.

—— *2nd Annual General Report, 1901–1902* (Cd. 1314), HC 1902, ii.

—— *3rd Annual General Report, 1902–1903* (Cd. 1919), HC 1904, xvi.

—— *4th Annual General Report, 1903–1904* (Cd. 2509), HC 1905, xxi.

—— *5th Annual General Report, 1904–1905* (Cd. 2929), HC 1906, xxiii.

—— *6th Annual General Report, 1905–1906* (Cd. 3543), HC 1907, xvii.

—— *7th Annual General Report, 1906–1907* (Cd. 4148), HC 1908, xiv.

—— *8th Annual General Report, 1907–1908* (Cd. 4430), HC 1908, xxii.

—— *10th Annual General Report, 1909–1910* (Cd. 5611), HC 1911, ix.

—— *11th Annual General Report, 1910–1911* (Cd. 6107), HC 1912–13, xii.

—— *12th Annual General Report, 1911–1912* (Cd. 6647), HC 1912–13, xii.

—— *13th Annual General Report, 1912–1913* (Cd. 7298), HC 1914, xii.

—— *14th Annual General Report, 1913–1914* (Cd. 7839), HC 1914–16, vi.

—— *15th Annual General Report, 1914–1915* (Cd. 8299), HC 1916, iv.

—— *18th Annual General Report, 1917–1918* (Cmd. 106), HC 1919, ix.

—— *19th Annual General Report, 1918–1919* (Cmd. 929), HC 1920, ix.

—— *Report of the Departmental Commission of Inquiry into the Provisions of the Agricultural and Technical Instruction (Ireland) Act, 1899* (Cd. 3572), HC 1907, xvii.

—— *Departmental Committee of Inquiry on the DATI: Minutes of Evidence* (Cd. 3574), HC 1907, xviii.

—— *Departmental Committee on Food Production in Ireland: Minutes of Evidence, Minutes of Deliberative Conferences, and Appendix* (Cd. 8158), HC 1914–16, v.

—— *Departmental Committee on the Irish Butter Industry: Minutes of Evidence, Appendix, and Index* (Cd. 5093), HC 1910, viii.

—— *Departmental Committee on the Irish Pig-Breeding Industry: Minutes of Evidence, Appendix, and Index* (Cd. 8004), HC 1914–16, vi.

—— *The Fertilisers and Feeding Stuffs Act, 1906* (Cd. 7846), HC 1914–16, vi.

—— *Report of the Departmental Commission on Agricultural Credit in Ireland* (Cd. 7375), HC 1914, xiii.

—— *Report of the Departmental Commission on the Decline of Dairying in Ireland* (Cmd. 808), HC 1920, ix.

Inter-Departmental Committee on Physical Deterioration, Minutes of Evidence, iii, List of Witnesses and Minutes of Evidence (Cd. 2210), HC 1904, xxxii.

—— *Appendix to the Report, iii* (Cd. 2186), HC 1904, xxii.

Judicial Statistics, Ireland, 1911. i, Criminal Statistics (Cd. 6419), HC 1912–13, cx.

Local Government Board for Ireland, *Annual Report, 1912* (Cd. 6339), HC 1912–13, xxxvii.

—— *Copies of a Report, Dated 25th Day of April, 1883, with Regard to Distress Existing or Apprehended in Certain Parts of Ireland* (.92), HC 1883, lix.

Ministry for Reconstruction, Summaries of Evidence Taken before the Sub-Committee Appointed in August, 1916 to Consider and Report upon the Methods of Effecting an Increase in the Home Growth Food Supplies (Cd. 9080), HC 1918, v.

Registrar-General for Ireland, 48th Annual Report, Containing a General Abstract of the Number of Marriages, Births and Deaths Registered in Ireland, 1911 (Cd. 6313), HC 1912–13, xiv.

Report of the Chief Inspector of Factories and Workshops to Her Majesty's Principal Secretary of State for the Home Department, 1888 (C. 5697), HC 1889, xviii.

Report of Mr F. H. Dale, His Majesty's Inspector of Schools, Board of Education, on Primary Education in Ireland (Cd. 1981), HC 1904, xx.

Report of Mr William F. Bailey, Legal Assistant Commissioner of an Inquiry into the Present Condition of Tenant Purchasers under the Land Purchase Acts (92.), HC 1903, lvii.

Report of the Select Committee on Agricultural Labourers (Ireland), Together with the Proceedings of the Committee and Minutes of Evidence (.32), HC 1884, vii.

Report of the Select Committee on Distress from Want of Employment, Together with Proceedings of the Committee, Minutes of Evidence, Appendix Index (.321), HC 1896, ix.

Report of the Select Committee on Industries (Ireland), Together with the Proceedings of the Committee, Minutes of Evidence, and Appendix (.288), HC 1884–5, ix.

Report of the Select Committee on the Law Relating to the Protection of Young Girls, Together with the Proceedings of the Committee, Minutes of Evidence, and Appendix (.448), HC 1881, ix.

Reports from Poor Law Inspectors on the Wages of Agricultural Labourers in Ireland (C. 35), HC 1870, xiv.

Return Showing, by Counties, the Average Number of Years' Purchase under the Different Land Purchase Acts, 1885 to 1903 (.357), HC 1908, xc.

Return Showing to the Latest Year Available, for Ireland as a Whole 1) The Average Prices from Each Year from 1881 (.181), HC 1921, xli.

Royal Commission on Agriculture, *Minutes of Evidence Taken before Her Majesty's Commissioners Appointed to Enquire into the Subject of the Agricultural Depression, with Appendix*, iii (C. 7400-iii), HC 1894, xvi.

RCCI, *Appendix to the 2nd Report: Minutes of Evidence (Taken in Co. Donegal, 8th to 19th October, 1906), and Documents Relating Thereto* (Cd. 3319), HC 1907, xxxv.

—— *Appendix to 3rd Report: Minutes of Evidence (Taken in London, 3rd to 20th November, 1906), and Documents Relating Thereto* (Cd. 3414), HC 1907, xxxv.

—— *Appendix to the 4th Report: Minutes of Evidence (Taken in London, 14th to 23rd February, 1907), and Documents Relating Thereto* (Cd. 3509), HC 1907, xxxvi.

—— *Appendix to the 5th Report Minutes of Evidence (Taken in London, 12th to 28th March, 1907), and Documents Relating Thereto* (Cd. 3630), HC 1907, xxxvi.

—— *Appendix to the 6th Report: Minutes of Evidence (Taken in Co. Sligo and Co. Leitrim, 17th to 27 April, 1907), and Documents Relating Thereto* (Cd. 3748), HC 1908, xxxix.

—— *Appendix to the 7th Report: Minutes of Evidence (Taken in Ireland, 16th to 11th June, 1907), and Documents Relating Thereto* (Cd. 3785), HC 1908, xl.

—— *Appendix to the 8th Report: Minutes of Evidence (Taken in Kerry and Cork, 3rd to 19th July, 1907), and Documents Relating Thereto* (Cd. 3839), HC 1908, xli.

—— *Appendix to the 9th Report: Minutes of Evidence (Taken in Co. Mayo, 21st August to 3rd September, 1907), and Documents Relating Thereto* (Cd. 3845), HC 1908, xli.

—— *Appendix to the 10th Report: Minutes of Evidence (Taken in Co. Galway and Co. Roscommon, 18th September to 4th October, 1907), and Documents Relating Thereto* (Cd. 4007), HC 1908, xlii.

—— *Final Report* (Cd. 4097), HC 1908, xlii.

—— *20th Report of the CDB for Ireland, 1911–1912* (Cd. 6553), HC 1912–13, xvii.

RCL, *The Agricultural Labourer, iv, Ireland, I–IV, Reports by Mr R. McCrea, Mr W. P. O'Brien, Mr Roger C. Richards and Mr Arthur Wilson Fox upon Certain Selected Districts* (C. 6894-xviii-xxi), HC 1893–4, xxxvi.

—— *The Agricultural Labourer, v, II, Miscellaneous Memorandum, Abstracts and Statistical Tables, by Mr William C. Little, iii E* (C. 6894-xxiv), HC 1893–4, xxxvi/2.

—— *The Employment of Women: Reports by Miss Eliza Orme, Miss Clara E. Collett, Miss Mary E. Abraham, and Miss Margaret H. Irwin on the conditions of Work in Various Industries in England, Wales, Scotland, and Ireland* (C. 6894-xxiii), HC 1893–4, xxxvii/1.

—— *5th and Final Report, ii, Secretary's Report on the Work of the Office: Summaries of Evidence (with Index) and Appendix* (C. 7421-I), HC 1894, xxxv.

Select Committee of the House of Lords on Land Law (Ireland), *First Report, Together with the Proceedings of the Committee, Minutes of Evidence, and Appendix* (.249), HC 1882, xi.

Select Committee on the Cottage Homes Bills, *2nd Special Report, Together with Proceedings of the Committee, Minutes of Evidence, and Appendix* (.271), HC 1899, ix.

Vice-Regal Commission on Irish Milk Supplies, *Appendix to the 1st Report of the Irish Milk Commission, 1911: Minutes of Evidence (Taken in Dublin, Belfast and Newry, 29th November, 1911, to 1st March, 1912, Inclusive), with Evidence* (Cd. 6684), HC 1913, xxix.

—— *Appendix to the Final Report of the Irish Milk Commission, 1911* (Cd. 7134), HC 1914, xxxvi.

Other Contemporary Material

Material published after 1920 will be found in the 'Secondary Sources'
    sections. Entries for annual reports of organizations etc. include de-
    tails of years consulted. Place of publication is London unless stated
    otherwise.
ABERDEEN, COUNTESS OF (comp.), *Guide to the Industrial Village and Blarney
    Columbian Exposition, Chicago (Irish Village Book Store, 1893).*
—— *Ireland at the World Fair* (Irish Village Book Store, 1893).
—— *Why Should We Encourage Irish Industries?* (Irish Village Book Store,
    1893).
—— *Report of the Work of the WNHA of Ireland as it Bears on Tuberculosis
    and with Special Reference to its Itinerant Tuberculosis Exhibition* (Dublin,
    1908).
—— *Ireland's Crusade against Tuberculosis: Being a Series of Miscellaneous
    Lectures Delivered in Connection with the Tuberculosis Exhibition, Together
    with Other Papers Dealing with the Anti-Tuberculosis Campaign and the
    Tuberculosis Prevention (Ireland) Act, 1908, iii* (Dublin, 1909).
—— *The Work of the WNHA of Ireland* (Dublin, c.1910).
*Agricultural Depression in Ireland: The Harvest of 1896, with the Reduction
    in Prices and in Rents since 1881* (Dublin, 1897).
*Agricultural Output of Ireland, 1908: Report and Tables Prepared in Connec-
    tion with the Census of Production Act, 1906* (Dublin, 1912).
All about it; or, The History and Mystery of Common Things (Dublin, 1858).
*An Appeal by a Lancashire Liberal against the Unjust Oppression of the Irish
    Land Act, 1881* (Liverpool, 1882).
An Appeal to the Women of Ireland (n.p., 1919).
AUSTIN, ALFRED, *Spring and Autumn in Ireland* (1800).
BAKER, ERNEST, *Ireland in the Last Fifty Years, 1866–1916* (Oxford, 1917).
BANIM, MARY, *Here and There through Ireland, i, ii* (Dublin, 1891).
BARBOUR, HAROLD, *The Work of the IAOS* (Dublin, 1916).
BARKER, CLARA HELENE, *Wanted: A Young Woman to Do Housework* (New
    York, 1915).
BARNETT, HENRIETTA O. (Mrs Samuel A.), *The Making of the Home: A
    Reading Book of Domestic Economy for the School and the Home* (c.1895).
BAYNE, S. G., *On an Irish Jaunting Car through Donegal and Connemara*
    (1902).
BECKLEY, F. J., *Surveying in the West of Ireland: Being a Reprint of Some
    Papers which Appeared in 'Blackfriars' and 'St Martin's-Le-Grand' Maga-
    zines. For Private Circulation Only* (1891).
BEGBIE, HAROLD, *The Lady Next Door* (1912).
BEHAN, REVD JOHN, *Why Ireland Has No Manufactures: A Lecture Delivered
    in the Hall of the St Nicholas Catholic Abstinence League* (Dublin, 1881).

Belfast Natural History and Philosophy Society, *Report and Proceedings, 1904–1905* (Belfast, 1905), 1904–13.

BIGGAR, FRANCIS JOSEPH, *Labourers' Cottages for Ireland* (Dublin, 1907).

BIGGER, E. COEY, *The Carnegie United Kingdom Trust: Report on the Physical Welfare of Mothers and Children*, iv, *Ireland* (Dublin, 1917).

BLACK, CLEMENTINA, *A New Way of Housekeeping* (1918).

BLACK, WILLIAM, *Shannon Bells: A Novel* (1883).

BLACKBURN, HELEN (ed.), *A Handy Book of Reference for Irishwomen* (1888).

BLACKBURNE, EDWARD, *Cause of the Decadence of the Industries of Ireland: A Retrospect* (Dublin, 1881).

BLACKER, WILLIAM, *An Essay on the Improvement to Be Made in the Cultivation of Small Farms by the Introduction of Green Crops, and House-Feeding the Stock Thereon* (Dublin, 1845).

Board of Agriculture and Fisheries, *Report of Sub-Committee Appointed to Consider the Employment of Women in Agriculture in England and Wales* (1919).

Board of Education, *General Report on the Teaching of Domestic Subjects* (1912).

BODEN-POWELL, SIR GEORGE, *Saving of Ireland: Industrial, Financial, Political* (Edinburgh, 1898).

BOOTH, CHARLES, *London Life and Labour*, i (1889).

BORRER, M. HAMLYN, *The Consumption 'Scare': Reprinted from the Kerry Sentinel, October 6, 1909. Important Letter* (Killarney, 1909).

BRADSHAW, MYRRHA (ed.), *Open Doors for Irishwomen: A Guide to the Professions Open to Educated Women in Ireland* (Dublin, 1907).

BULFIN, WILLIAM, *Rambles in Éireann* (Dublin, 1915).

BUONAIUTI, VERY REVD PROFESSOR ERNESTO, *Impressions of Ireland* (Dublin, 1913).

BURKE, REVD THOMAS N., *Lectures on Faith and Fatherland* (Glasgow, 1871).

BUTLER, LIEUT.-GEN. SIR WILLIAM F., *Why Not as we Once Were?* (Dublin, 1907).

BUTT, ISAAC, *Irish Government and Irish Railways: An Argument for Home Rule* (Dublin, 1872).

BYRNE, MILLS, *Memoirs of Miles Byrne, Edited by his Widow* (Dublin, 1907).

CAIRD, JAMES, *The Plantation Scheme; or, The West of Ireland as a Field for Investment* (1850).

CAIRNES, J. E., *Political Essays* (1873).

CAMERON, SIR CHARLES A., *Reminiscences of Sir Charles Cameron* (Dublin, 1913).

Catholic Association, *Handbook of the Catholic Association* (Dublin, 1903).

CHART, D. A., *Unskilled Labour in Dublin: Its Housing and Living Conditions* (Dublin, 1914).

COFFEY, GEORGE, *Art and Industry: A Lecture (under the Auspices of the Irish*

Industrial League) Given at the Mansion House, December 10, 1888 (Dublin, 1888).

COLE, ALAN S., *Ancient Needlepoint and Pillow Lace, with Notes on the History of Lace-Making and Descriptions of Thirty Examples* (1875).

—— *Two Lectures on the Art of Lace-Making* (Dublin, 1884).

—— *A Renascence of the Irish Art of Lace-Making* (1888).

Commissioners of National Education in Ireland, *Agricultural Class Book; or, How Best to Cultivate a small Farm and Garden: Together with Hints on Domestic Economy* (Dublin, 1848, 1853, 1860, 1867, 1874, 1891).

CDB, *Instructions and Suggestions for the Guidance of Parish Committees* (Dublin, 1911).

—— *Plans for Houses, 1914* (Dublin, 1914).

CONMEE, VERY REVD JOHN STEPHEN, *Old Time in the Barony [of Luainford — a fictitious barony]* (Dublin, 1900).

Cooking Recipes, Contributed by Ladies in Co. Derry (n.p., c.1910).

Cork Industrial Development Association, *Verbatim Report of the First Irish Industrial Conference, Held in the Council Chamber, Cork, November 21st and 22nd, 1905* (Cork, 1905).

Cork Industrial Exhibition, *Cork Industrial Exhibition: Official Catalogue* (Dublin, 1883).

—— *Report of Executive Committee, Awards of Jurors, and Statement of Accounts, 1883* (Cork, 1886).

Cork International Exhibition, 1903: Official Catalogue (Cork, 1903).

CORKEY, WILLIAM, *Memoirs of an Irish Manse* (Belfast, n.d.).

COULTER, HENRY, *The West of Ireland* (Dublin, 1862).

'A COUNTRY CURATE', *Scenes and Sketches in an Irish Parish; or, Priest and People in Doon* (Dublin, 1903).

County Agricultural Instructors, *Agriculture in Ireland* (Dublin, 1907).

Cork, County Borough of, *Technical Instruction Committee Report on a Scheme of Technical Instruction for the County Borough, Dated 12 December 1900* (Cork, 1900).

—— *Report of Special Committee on the Housing of the Working Classes in Cork* (Cork, 1904).

—— *Report on the General Condition of the City Water Supply* (Cork, 1911).

COYNE, WILLIAM P. (ed.), *Ireland: Industrial and Agricultural. Handbook for the Irish Pavilion, Glasgow, International Exhibition, 1901* (Dublin, 1902).

CRAIG, JAMES, *Consumption in Ireland: Its Prevalence and Prevention. An Introductory Address Delivered at the Opening of the Session of 1900–1901 in the Meath Hospital* (Dublin, 1900).

CRAWFORD, W., *Irish Linen and Some Features of its Production* (Dublin, 1910).

CROMPTON, REVD J., *The Irish Bog and How to Get out of it* (1887).

DADD, F., et al., *Irish Pictures: Eighty Sketches Taken on the Spot* (1881).

DALY, J. BOWLES, *Glimpses of Irish Industries* (1889).

DARYL, PHILIPPE, *Ireland's Disease: Notes and Impressions* (1888).

DATI, *Organisation and Policy of the Department* (Dublin, 1903).

—— *Conference on the Poultry Industry, Dublin, May 1911: Report of Proceedings* (Dublin, 1911).

—— *Cookery Notes* (Dublin, 1916).

—— *Programme of the Killarney School of Housewifery: Session 1913–1914* (Killarney, 1913), 1913–21.

—— *Portable Poultry Houses*, Leaflet 50 (DATI, n.d.).

—— *Home Butter-Making*, Leaflet 78 (DATI, n.d.).

DE MOLINARI, G., *French Spectacle in an Irish Case: Letters on the State of Ireland*, trans. L. Colthurst (Dublin, 1881).

DENNIS, ROBERT, *Industrial Ireland: A Practical and Non-Political View of Ireland for the Irish* (1887).

Department of Education (Saorstát Éireann), *Special Reports on Educational Subjects, 1896–1897*, i, ii (1897).

Department of Industry and Commerce (Saorstát Éireann), *Commission of Inquiry into the Resources and Industries of Ireland: Minutes of Evidence*, i, *City Hall, Dublin, 2nd, 3rd and 4th December, 1919: Milk Production and Milk Products, Fisheries* (Dublin, 1919).

Department of Scientific and Industrial Research Board (GB), *Special Report 2: The Peat Resources of Ireland. A Lecture Given before the Dublin Society on 5th March, 1919, by Professor Pierce F. Purcell* (1920).

Directory of Women Teachers and Other Women Engaged in Higher and Secondary Education, 1913: A Reference Book of Secondary Education for Girls (1913).

Domestic Training Institute, *Annual Report, 1906* (Dublin, 1907), 1906–12.

Donegal Christmas Annual, 1883, Containing Stories by Donegal Writers (Londonderry, 1883).

DONELAN, A. M., *Sowing and Reaping: A Tale of Irish Life*, i, ii (1868).

DOYLE, CRISSIE M., *Women in Ancient and Modern Ireland* (Dublin, 1917).

Dublin Industrial Development Association, *Dublin Industrial Development Association, First Annual Report, 1906* (Dublin, 1906), 1906–18.

Lady Dudley's Nursing Scheme, *Lady Dudley's Scheme for the Establishment of District Nurses in the Poorest Parts of Ireland: First Annual Report* (Dublin, 1904), 1903–10.

DUNNE, C. J., *Machinery and the Masses: A Paper Read before the Cork Literary and Scientific Society on 9 November 1905* (Cork, 1905).

DUNNE, J. P. (contributor and collector), *Industrial Ireland: Being a Series of Essays and Poems Connected with the Commercial Interest of Ireland* (Dublin, n.d.).

—— *The Meaning and Need of Mother's Pensions* (Dublin, 1918).

ECKFORD, E. STODDART, and FITZGERALD, M. S., *Household Management: A Book of Domestic Economy and Hygiene* (1915).

EDGEWORTH, MARIA, *Stories of Ireland: Castle Rackrent; The Absentee* (1892).

English Hearths and Irish Homes: Life Scenes from an Editor's Notebook and Social Sketches for Sunny Nooks and Winter Firesides (1868).

FERGUSON, KATHLEEN, *Advanced Lesons on Cookery*, iii (Dublin, n.d.).

—— *Elementary Lessons in Laundry Work: For the Use of Children* (Athlone, 1901).

—— *Hints on Good Manners for the Use of Children* (Athlone, 1901).

—— *Lessons in Cookery and Housewifery for the Use of Children* (Athlone, 1901).

Few Words of Remonstrance and Advice Addressed to the Farming and Labouring Classes of Ireland by a Sincere Friend (Dublin, 1848).

FIGGIS, D., *Irishmen of Today: AE (George Russell). A Study of a Man and a Nation* (Dublin, 1916).

Findlater's Ladies' Housekeeping Book for 1896 (Dublin, 1896).

FITZMAURICE, GEORGE, *The Country Dressmaker* (Dublin, 1914).

FITZ-PATRICK, T. E., *Irish Industrial Enterprise Past and Present: Especially in Connection with the Approaching Exhibition of Native Industries Designed for their Revival and Extension* (Dublin, 1881).

FLINN, D. EDGAR, *Our Dress and our Food in Relation to Health* (Dublin, 1886).

FOSTER, THOMAS CAMPBELL, *Letters on the Condition of the People of Ireland* (1846).

FORSTER, VERE HENRY LEWIS, *Mr Vere Forster's Irish Female Emigration Fund, under the Auspices of All the Clergy of All Denominations in the West of Ireland* (Belfast, 1883).

—— *Second Irish Female Emigration Fund, 1880–1883* (Belfast, 1883).

Fourth Reading Book: Published by Direction of the Commissioners of National Education, Ireland (Dublin, 1889).

FOX, J. A., *Reports on the Condition of the Peasantry of the Co. of Mayo during the Famine Crisis of 1880* (Dublin, 1881).

Friendly Advice to Irish Mothers on Training their Children, 2nd edn. (Armagh, 1842).

FROUDE, JAMES ANTHONY, *Short Stories on Great Subjects* (1871).

GALLAHER, F. M., *Short Lessons in Domestic Science* (Dublin, 1885).

—— *Lessons in Domestic Science* (Dublin, 1899).

GARDINER, MRS STANLEY, *We Two and Shamus* (1913).

GILL, T. P., *Economic Ireland, the War, and Ulster Leadership* (Belfast, 1914).

GILMAN, CHARLOTTE PERKINS, *Women and Economics: The Economic Factor between Men and Women as a Factor in Social Evolution* (Boston, 1896).

—— *The Home: Its Work and Influences* (New York, 1903).

GLAISTER, ELIZABETH, *Needlework* (1880).

GODKIN, JAMES, *Ireland and her Churches* (1867).

—— *Land-War in Ireland: A History for the Times* (1870).

GRAVES, ALFRED PERCEVAL, *Irish Songs and Ballads* (Manchester, 1880).

GREENE, J. BAKER, *Notes on Ireland: Made from Personal Observation of its Political, Social and Economic Condition* (1886).

GREEVES, GEORGIANA ELIZA, *The Linen Fabric: A Poem* (Belfast, 1898).

GRIMSHAW, THOMAS W., *Irish Progress during the Past Ten Years, 1881–1890: Being a Paper Read before the Statistical and Social Inquiry Society of Ireland, Tuesday, 23 June, 1891* (Dublin, 1891).

'GUARDIAN OF THE POOR', *The Irish Peasant: A Sociological Study by a Guardian of the Poor* (1892).

GUY, FRANCIS, *Francis Guy's Illustrated Descriptive and Gossiping Guide to the South of Ireland* (Cork, c.1900).

GWYNN, REV. E. R. M., *Ireland's Hope: A Call to Service* (Belfast, 1913).

GWYNN, STEPHEN, *To-Day and To-Morrow in Ireland: Essays on Irish Subjects* (Dublin, 1903).

—— *The Fair Hills of Ireland* (Dublin, 1914).

'H. B.', *Letters from Ireland* (Dublin, 1902).

HALE, CHARLES W., *Domestic Science*, 2 vols. (1915–22).

HAMILTON, WILLIAM H., *Waifs of Conversation* (Belfast, 1876).

Handbook of Cookery for Irish Workhouses: Compiled from the Manual of Workhouse Cookery, England, the Manual of Military Cooking and Other Authorities. Issued to the Board of Guardians by the Local Government Board for Ireland (Dublin, 1911).

HARLAND, MARION, *Common Sense in the Household: A Manual of Practical Housewifery* (New York, 1890).

HARRIS, ALFRED, *The Revival of Industries in Ireland: Notes Made During a Tour in October, 1887, by Alfred Harris* (Dublin, 1888).

HARRISON, W. JEROME, *The Science of Home Life: A Textbook of Domestic Economy. First Year's Course* (1893).

HART, MRS ERNEST, *The Cottage Industries of Ireland, with an Account of the Work of the Donegal Industrial Fund* (1887).

HASLAM, THOMAS J., *The Rightful Claims of Women: An Address* (Dublin, 1906).

HASSELL, JOSEPH, *Lessons in Domestic Economy* (Glasgow, n.d.).

—— *Lessons in Domestic Economy for Elder Girls* (Collin's School Series, Glasgow, n.d.).

HEDDERMAN, B. N., *Glimpses of my Life in Aran: Some Experiences of a District Nurse in These Remote Islands, Off the West Coast of Ireland* (Bristol, 1917).

HICKEY, P., *The Irish Problem* (1906).

Honest Labour versus School of Scandal: Irish Industrial Facts Addressed to the Taxpayers of the British Empire (Dublin, 1891).

HURLBERT, WILLIAM HENRY, *Ireland under Coercion: The Diary of an American* (Edinburgh, 1889).

306 *Bibliography*

Hussy, S. M., *The Reminiscences of an Irish Land Agent* (1904).

Hutchins, B. L., and Harrison, A., *A History of Factory Legislation* (1911).

IAOS *Annual Report, 1895* (Dublin, 1896), 1896–1921.

—— *First Annual General Conference of Co-operative Societies, and Annual General Meeting of the IAOS, 1896* (Dublin, 1897), 1896–1921.

Industries of Dublin: Historical, Statistical, Biographical. An Account of the Leading Business Men: Commercial Interests, Wealth and Growth (1882).

Instruction in Bee-Keeping for the Use of Irish Bee-Keepers (Dublin, 1905).

Intermediate Education Board for Ireland, *Report of the Examiners, 1911* (Dublin, 1911).

Introduction to Practical Farming: An Elementary Textbook for Use in Irish National Schools, 3rd edn. (Dublin, 1880).

Ireland: Industrial and Agricultural (Dublin, 1902).

Ireland of To-Day, Reprinted with Some Additions from 'The Times' (1913).

Irish Agricultural Wholesale Society, *IAWS* (Dublin, n.d.).

Irish Central Bureau for the Employment of Women, *Report Rep.* 1901–17.

Irish Co-operative Women's Guild, *Rules* (Belfast, 1915).

Irish Home Industries Association, *Irish Home Industries Association* (Dublin, 1887), 1887–1907.

Irish National Education: The O'Neill Memorial School, an Object Lesson in Modern Education (Belfast, 1905).

Irish National Teachers' Organization, Central Executive Committee, *Some Facts and Figures Concerning Irish Primary Education* (Dublin, 1917).

Irish Technical Instruction Association, *Annual Congress, Killarney, 1914* (Cork, 1915).

Irish Wool and what Is Made of it: Half a Century of Home Industry (Lisbellaw, n.d.).

Irish Women Worker's Co-operative Society, *Rules* (Dublin, 1915).

Irish Year-Book, 1908: Issued by the National Council (Sinn Fein) (Dublin, 1908).

James, Humphrey, *Paddy's Woman and Other Stories* (1896).

Joe Jenkins on the Great Crisis: A Labourer's Views on Home Rule (c.1880).

Jones, W. Bence, *The Life's Work in Ireland of a Landlord who Tried to Do his Duty* (1880).

Kane, Sir Robert, *The Industrial Resources of Ireland* (Dublin, 1844).

—— *On the Recent Progress and Present State of Industry in Ireland, and the Dublin International Exhibition of 1865* (1865).

Kelly, Denis (Bishop of Ross), *Women's Share in the Industrial Revival of Ireland* (Dublin, 1905).

Kelly, Richard J., *Some of Ireland's Resources: A Brief View of her Vast Industrial Undeveloped Wealth* (Tuam, 1885).

Kenny, Patrick D., *Economics for Irishmen* (Dublin, 1906).

—— *My Little Farm* (Dublin, 1915).

KINNE, HELEN, and COOLEY, ANNA M., *Shelter and Clothing: A Textbook of the Household Arts* (New York, 1913).

KINNEAR, JOHN BOYD, *Ireland in 1881* (1881).

KIRWAN, MICHAEL, *Irish Cottage Industries: How Best to Develop them* (Cork, 1909).

KRANS, HORATIO SHEAFE, *Irish Life in Irish Fiction* (New York, 1903).

LAING, SAMUEL, *A Visit to Bodyke; or, The Real Meaning of Irish Evictions* (1887).

Larne Rural District, *Regulations Made by the Larne Rural District Council with Respect to Dairies, Cow Sheds, and Milk Shops* (Carrickfergus, 1900).

LE FANU, W. R., *Seventy Years of Irish Life: Being Anedotes and Reminiscences* (1893).

League of Pity Tea Shop, *Cookery Book* (Londonderry, n.d.).

LEAKE, ALBERT H., *The Vocational Education of Girls and Women* (New York, 1918).

LEAKE, ROBERT, *The Tale of an Ulster Tenant by Robert Leake* (Manchester, 1885).

LEHAND, CORNELIUS, *The Industrial Position of Ireland* (Dublin, 1903).

LINDSAY, BEN, *Irish Lace: Its Origin and History* (Dublin, 1886).

Local Goverment Board for Ireland, *Labourers (Ireland) Acts, 1883–1906: Model Plans of Labourers Cottages* (Dublin, 1907).

LOVETT, RICHARD, *Irish Pictures Drawn with Pen and Pencil* (1888).

LYND, ROBERT, *Home Life in Ireland* (1909).

MACARTHUR, MARY R., 'The Woman Trade-Unionist's Point of View', in Phillips, Marion (ed.), *Women and the Labour Party* (1917).

MCCARTHY, MICHAEL J. F., *Five Years in Ireland, 1895–1900* (Dublin, 1901).

—— *Priests and People in Ireland* (Dublin, 1903).

MACDONAGH, MICHAEL, *Irish Life and Character* (1905).

MACDONALD, MAY ROSS, *Cookery for School Girls: Ten Elementary Lessons* (Dublin, c.1900).

MCKENNA, REVD L., *No. 3: The Church and Working Women* (Dublin, 1913–14).

MACLAGAN, PETER, *Land Culture and Land Tenure in Ireland* (Dublin, 1869).

MAGUIRE, J. F., *The Industrial Movement in Ireland, as Illustrated by the National Exhibition of 1852* (Cork, 1852).

MAGUIRE, JOSEPH, *Healthy Dwellings for Labourers, Artisans and the Middle Classes and their Improved Structural Arrangements* (Dublin, 1867).

MAGUIRE and GATCHELL, Ltd., Dublin, *Illustrated Record, September 1913* (Dublin, 1913).

MANN, ROBERT JAMES, *Domestic Economy and Household Science: For Home Education, and for School Mistresses and Pupil Teachers* (1887).

Manual of Needlework for the Use of National Schools (Dublin, 1884).

Manx Lady Tells of Southern Tyranny (Dublin, 1893).

MARSHALL, LESLIE C., *The Practical Flax Spinner* (1885).

MARTIN, ANNA, *Married Working Women* (1911).

MATHESON, SIR ROBERT, *A Review of the Anti-Tuberculosis Campaign in Ireland* (Dublin, 1908).

MATHEW, FRANK, *Ireland Painted by Francis B. S. Walker* (1905).

Memorandum and Specimen of Farm Accounts in Connection with the Farmer's Account Book (Dublin 1918).

Modest Appeal to Irish Householders (Cork, 1905).

MULHALL, MICHAEL G., *The Dictionary of Statistics* (1899).

Munster Dairy School and Agricultural Institute, Cork, *Report of the Governors and Statement of Accounts for 1902* (Cork, 1903), 1903–5.

MURPHY, WILLIAM S., *The Textile Industry*, i (1910).

NAJAN, I. EDWARD, *The Irish People (their Height, Form and Strength)* (Dublin, 1899).

Newbridge Nursing Association, *Eighth Annual Report of the Newbridge Nursing Association (in Affiliation with Queen Victoria's Jubilee Institute for Nurses), March 1903–March 1904* (n.d.), 1903–14.

North East Agricultural Association of Ireland, *Report for 1887, and List of Prizes for 1888* (Belfast, 1888) 1887–1902.

O'BRIEN, ATTIE, *Glimpses of a Hidden Life: Memories of Attie O'Brien* (Dublin, 1887).

O'CONOR-ECCLES, CHARLOTTE, *Domestic Economy Reader for Irish Schools: How Mary Fitzgerald Learned Housekeeping* (Dublin, 1904).

—— *Simple Advice to Be Followed by All who Desire the Good of Ireland, and Especially by Gaelic Leaguers* (Dublin, 1905).

O'CONNOR, MRS T. P., *Herself: Ireland* (1917).

O'DONNELL, THOMAS, *A Trip to Denmark* (Dublin, 1908).

Office of National Education, *Industrial Instruction: Memorandum* (31 July 1889).

O'KANE, REVD MICHAEL M., *Women's Place in the World* (Dublin, 1913).

—— *Paper on the Living Wage and the Family Wage, Society of St Vincent de Paul, Down and Connor, 6th Annual Diocesan Congress, June 17, 1917* (Belfast, 1917).

O'RIORDAN, REVD M., *Catholicity and Progress in Ireland* (1905).

OWEN, CATHERINE, *Progressive Housekeeping: Keeping House without Knowing how, and Knowing how to Keep House Well* (Boston, 1889).

PATERSON, W. H., *Irish Tenants at Home: Tenant Farmers and their Poverty. What we Saw in the West of Ireland* (1881).

PAUL-DUBOIS, L. F., *Contemporary Ireland* (1908).

PETTENGILL, LILLIAN, *Toilers of the Home: The Record of a College Woman's Experience as a Domestic Servant* (New York, 1903).

PIGOTT, RICHARD, *Personal Recollections of an Irish Nationalist Journalist* (Dublin, 1882).

PLUNKETT, HORACE CURZON, *Co-operation for Ireland* (Manchester, 1890).

—— *Co-operation in Ireland: The Best Means of Promoting Both Distributive and Productive Co-operation in the Rural Districts of Ireland. A Paper* (Manchester, 1890).

—— *Ireland in the New Century* (1904).

—— *The Problem of Congestion in Ireland* (Dublin, 1907).

—— *Plain Talks to Irish Farmers* (Dublin, 1910).

—— *The Crisis in Irish Rural Progress: Being Three Letters Reprinted from The 'Times', December, 1911* (1911).

—— PILKINGTON, ELLICE, and RUSSELL, GEORGE, *The United Irishwomen: Their Place, Work and Ideals* (Dublin, 1911).

Practical Housewife: A Complete Encyclopedia of Domestic Economy and Family Medical Guide (c.1890).

Programmes of Instruction in Agriculture in National Schools (Dublin, 1896).

PURDON, C. D., *Sanitary State of the Belfast Factory District* (Belfast, 1877).

Queen's College, Belfast, *QCB, Cookery Book* (Belfast, 1907).

RASHAD, IBRAHIM, *An Egyptian in Ireland* (privately printed for the author, 1920).

Report of the Recess Committee on the Establishment of the DATI for Ireland (Dublin, 1896).

Report of the Scottish Commission on Agriculture in Ireland, 1906, with Comparative Observations and Suggestions (Edinburgh, 1906).

Report from the Select Committee on Home Work, Together with the Proceedings of the Committee, Minutes of Evidence, and Appendix (1908).

Reprints of Reports of Proceedings of the Killyleagh, Killinchy, Kilmood, and Tullynakill Branch of the North-East Farming Society, for the Years 1828, 1829, 1830, 1831, 1832, 1833, 1834, and 1835 (Downpatrick, 1912).

RICHARDS, ELLEN H., *The Cost of Living as Modified by Sanitary Science* (New York, 1901).

ROBINSON, REVD J. M. (Rector of Ovaca), *Facts from Ireland* (Dublin, 1910).

ROLLESTON, T. W., *Ireland and Poland: A Comparison* (1917).

—— *Ireland's Vanishing Opportunity* (Dublin, 1919).

Royal Agricultural Society of Ireland, *Practical Instructions for Small Farmers* (Dublin, 1848).

Royal Ulster Agricultural Society, *Report for 1907* (Belfast, 1908), 1907–8.

ROZ, FIRMIN, *Under the English Crown* (1906).

RUSSELL, GEORGE WILLIAM, *Co-operation and Nationality: A Guide for Rural Reformers from This to the Next Generation* (Dublin, 1912).

—— *Templecrone: A Record of Co-operative Effort* (Dublin, 1915).

—— *The National Being: Some Thoughts on an Irish Polity* (Dublin, 1918).

RYAN, FREDERICK W., *The Preparation of National School Pupils for Technical Training and Industrial Life* (Dublin, 1917).

SAINT-THOMAS, H., *Paddy's Dream and John Bull's Nightmare*, trans. Emile Hatzfeld (*c*.1886).

SALMAN, LUCY MAYNARD, *Domestic Service* (New York, 1897).

—— *Progress in the Household* (Boston, 1906).

'A Scot', *Ireland as it Is and as it Might Be: Being Three Letters on the Land Questions* (Dundee, 1879).

SHAW, WILLIAM, *Cullynbackey: The Story of an Ulster Village* (Dublin, *c*.1913).

SHEARMAN, MRS S. M., *Plain Sewing and Knitting: A Manual for Teachers* (Dublin, n.d.).

SHELDON, J. P., *Dairy Farming: Being the Theory, Practice, and Methods of Dairying* (orig. publ. 1879; 1888).

SHOEMAKER, MICHAEL MYERS, *Wanderings in Ireland* (1908).

SHORT, ISABELLA, *Cutting out by the 'Short' System for Technical Classes and Home Use* (1909).

Short Sketch of the Aims and Purpose of the United Irishwomen (Wexford, n.d.).

Simple Lessons on Health and Habits (Dublin, 1907).

SMITH-GORDON, LIONEL, and O'BRIEN, CRUISE, *Starvation in Dublin* (Dublin, 1917).

—— and STAPLES, LAURENCE C., *Rural Reconstruction in Ireland: A Record of Co-operative Organisation* (1917).

SMITH, AMY K., *Needlework for Teachers: Intended for the Use of Pupil Teachers, Scholarship Candidates and Certificate Students (1st and 2nd Year)* (1899).

SMITH, F. W. (comp.), *The Home and Foreign Linen Trade Directory* (Belfast, 1912).

SMITH, SAMUEL, *The Ireland of To-Day* (*c*.1880).

'Special Commissioner of the *Daily Express*', *Mr Balfour's Tours in Connemara and Donegal* (n.d.).

STITSON, JAMES, *Lights and Leaders of Irish Life* (Dublin, 1889).

STONACH, ALICE, *What Women Are Doing for Ireland: The Work of the WNHA* (1912).

STUART, H. VILLIERS, *Observations and Statistics Concerning the Question of Irish Agricultural Labourers* (1884).

—— *Prices of Farm Products in Ireland from Year to Year for Thirty-Six Years: Illustrated by Diagrams, with Observations on the Prospects of Irish Agriculture* (Dublin, 1886).

Suggestions on the Irish Question by a Resident Agriculturalist (1880).

SYNNOTT, NICHOLAS J., *Proposals for a New Labourers' Bill: An Attempt to Solve the Rural Housing Question in Ireland* (Naas, 1906).

TALLON, DANIEL, *Distress in the West and South of Ireland, 1898: Report on the Work of the Mansion House Committee* (Dublin, 1898).

TEGETMEIER, W. B., *The Handbook of Household Management and Cookery* (1888).

THOMPSON, W. H., *Food Problems: Supplies and Demand in Ireland* (n.p., c.1910).

—— *Food Values: With a Note on the Conservation of Irish Food Supplies* (Dublin, c.1910).

—— *Systematic Food Production: What Could Be Done in Ireland* (Dublin, 1915).

—— *War and the Food of the Dublin Labourer (Issued by the WNHA of Ireland, June 1915* (Dublin, 1915).

Tuberculosis in Ireland (Dublin, 1908).

TUKE, JAMES H., *A Visit to Donegal and Connemara in the Spring of 1880: Irish Distress and its Remedies. The Land Question* (1880).

TYNAN, KATHARINE (Mrs H. A. Hinkson), *Twenty-Five Years: Reminiscences* (1913).

Verbatim Rep. of the 16th All-Ireland Industrial Conference, Held in the Council Chambers, October 4th and 5th, 1910 (Cork, 1910).

WADE, THOMAS, *The Handy Record and Farmer's Account Book. With Notes on Cropping etc.* (Dublin, c.1906).

WALSH, REVD N., *Woman,* (Dublin, 1903).

WALTER, L. EDNA, *The Fascination of Ireland* (1913).

WATTERIDGE, F. W., *Prosperous Agriculture and Home Life: What it Means to the Nation* (1911).

What Mr Balfour Has Done for Distressed Ireland (Dublin, 1893).

Women's Labour League, *The League Leaflet* (Dublin, 1912).

WNHA, *Infantile Mortality and Infant Milk Depots* (Dublin, 1908).

—— *Objects and Constitution of the WNHA of Ireland* (Dublin, c.1910).

—— *Rules of Health which the Mistress of Every Household Should Strive to Bear in Mind* (Dublin, c.1910).

—— *WNHA of Ireland: Organisation of Local Branches* (Dublin, c.1910).

—— *Omagh Branch: Report from December 1908 to July 1911* (Omagh, 1911).

Women's Social and Progressive League, *Open Letter to Women Voters* (n.d.).

WOODHOUSE, THOMAS, *The Finishing of Jute and Linen Fabrics* (1914).

Newspapers and Periodicals

Ark (the Official Farmers' Magazine): Journal Devoted to the Interests of Cattle, Poultry, Pigs, and Farming (1912–16).

Bean na-Éireann.

Belfast Daily Post (1882).

Belfast News-Letter (1902)

Better Business: A Quarterly Journal of Agricultural and Industrial Co-operation.

Cashel Gazette (1885).
Catholic Bulletin (1913–14).
Clare Freeman (Ennis) (1878, 1882–4).
Clonmel Chronicle (1881, 1885, 1887, 1891–1913).
Cork Constitution.
Daily Express (1861).
Derry Standard (1911).
Dialogues of the Day (1900–6).
Dublin Journal of Medical Science.
Dublin University Magazine (1872–4).
Harp (1908–10, 1917).
Health (Belfast) (1893).
Hibernia: A Monthly Popular Review (1882).
Frontier Sentinel (1904).
Kerry Weekly Reporter (1900).
Kings' County Chronicle (1910–13).
Ireland's Own.
Irish Builder.
Irish Citizen.
Irish Homestead.
Irish Educational Review.
Irish Farming World.
Irish Industrial Journal.
Irish Nation (1909).
Irish Peasant.
Irish School Weekly (1900–8)
Irish School Monthly.
Irish and Scottish Linen and Jute Trades Journal (1913–23).
Irish Small Farmer's Monthly Journal (n.d. *c.*1840).
Irish Technical Journal.
Irish Textile Journal (1893–).
Irish Theological Quarterly.
Irish Times.
Irish Weekly Independent (every 5 years from 1893).
Journal of the Dublin Statistical Society (1860).
Journal of the London Statistical Society (1857).
Journal of the Royal Statistical Society.
Journal of the Statistical and Social Inquiry Society of Ireland.
Journal of the WNHA of Ireland (1909–).
Lace and Embroidery Review.
Leader (1908).
Leinster Star (1885).
Nationist (1906).

New Ireland Review.
Nineteenth Century.
Old Grand Limerick Journal (1983–   ).
Royal Society of Antiquarians of Ireland (1905).
Sláinte: The Journal of the WNHA.
Times (London) (1906).
Ulster Folklife (1955–86).
Union (1887).
United Irishman (1902–4).
United Irishwomen: A Journal for Irish Countrywomen.
Warder and Dublin Weekly Mail (1888–1908).
Womanhood: An Illustrated Magazine of Literature, Science, Art, Medicine, Hygiene and the Progress of Women.

SECONDARY SOURCES

Articles and Theses

AALAN, F. H. A., 'The House Types of Gala Island, Co. Donegal', *Folklife*, 8 (1970).

ADAMS, DALE W., 'The Economics of Land Reform', *Food Research Institute Studies in Agricultural Economics, Trade and Development*, 12/2 (1973).

ADLER, HANS J., and HAWRYLYSHYN, OLI, 'Estimates of the Value of Household Work: Canada, 1961 and 1971', *Review of Income and Wealth*, 24 (1978).

ATTWOOD, E. A., 'Agriculture and Economic Growth in Western Ireland', *JSSISI* 20/5 (1961–62).

—— 'Dairying in the Irish Economy: A Review', *Irish Journal of Agricultural Economics and Rural Sociology*, 1/1 (1967).

BAHR, STEPHEN J., 'Effects on Power and the Division of Labour in the Family', in Hoffman, Lois Wladis, and Nye, F. I. (eds.), *Working Mothers* (San Francisco, 1975).

BARRINGTON, THOMAS, 'A Review of Irish Agricultural Prices', *JSSISI* 14 (1926–7).

BECKER, GARY S., 'A Theory of Marriage: I', *JPE* 81/4 (July 1973).

—— 'A Theory of Marriage: II', JPE 82/2 (Mar.–Apr. 1974).

—— 'A Theory of the Allocation of Time', in Gary S. Becker (ed.), *The Economic Approach to Human Behaviour* (Chicago, 1976).

BELL, JONATHAN, 'Harrows Used in Ireland', *Tools and Tillage*, 4 (1983).

—— 'The Improvement of Irish Farming Techniques since 1750: Theory and Practice', in O'Flanagan, Patrick, Ferguson, Paul and Whelan,

Kevin (eds.), *Rural Ireland, 1600–1900: Modernisation and Change* (Cork, 1987).

BENERIA, LOURDES, 'Accounting for Women's Work', in Beneria, Lourdes (ed.), *Women and Development: The Sexual Division of Labour in Rural Societies* (New York, 1982).

BENNHOLDT-THOMSEN, VERONIKA, 'Subsistence Production and Extended Reproduction', in Young, Kate, Walkowitz, Carol, and McCullagh, Roslyn (eds.), *Of Marriage and the Market*, 2nd edn. (1984).

BEN-PORATH, YORAM, 'The F-Connection: Families, Friends, and Firms and the Organization of Exchange', *Population and Development Review*, 6 (Mar. 1980).

BENSON, MARGARET, 'The Political Economy of Women's Liberation', *Monthly Review*, 21 (Sept. 1969).

BERGMANN, BARBARA R., 'Occupational Segregation, Wages, and Profits when Employers Discriminate by Race or Sex', *Eastern Economic Journal*, 1/2 (Apr. 1974).

BLACKWELL, ANNETTE, 'No Role for Women in the Irish Farmers' Association', *Status* (22 Mar. 1981).

BLISS, CHRISTOPHER, and STERN, NICHOLAS, 'Productivity, Wages, and Nutrition, I: The Theory', *Journal of Development Economics*, 5 (1978).

BOSE, CHRISTINE, 'Technology and Changes in the Division of Labour in the American Home', *Women's Studies International Quarterly*, 2 (1979).

BOURKE, JOANNA, 'Husbandry to Housewifery: Rural Women and Development in Ireland, 1890–1914', Ph.D. thesis (Canberra, 1989).

BOYLE, ELIZABETH, 'Embroidery and Lacemaking in Ulster', *Ulster Folklife*, 10 (1964).

BREEN, RICHARD, 'Farm Servanthood in Ireland, 1900–1940', EHR, 2nd ser. 36 (1983).

BREKINRIDGE, SOPHONISBA, 'The Activities of Women outside the Home', *Recent Trends in the United States* (1933).

BROWNLEE, W. ELLIOT, 'Household Values, Women's Work and Economic Growth, 1800–1930', *JEH* 39 (Mar. 1979).

BUCHANAN, R. H., 'Rural Change in an Irish Townland, 1890–1955', *The Advancement of Science*, 14/56 (Mar. 1958).

BUCK, ANNE, 'The Teaching of Lacemaking in the East Midlands', *Folklife*, 4 (1966).

BUTLIN, NOEL, 'A Plea for the Separation of Ireland', *JEH* 28 (1968).

BYRNE, JAMES, 'Some Provincial Variations in Irish Agriculture', *JSSISI* 20/2 (1958–9).

BYRNE, MOLLY, 'The Life of a Servant Girl', *Grand Old Limerick Journal* (Spring 1983).

CAIN, MEAD, KHANAM, SYEDA R., and NAHAN, SHAMSUN, 'Class, Patriarchy, and Women's Work in Bangladesh', *Population and Development Review* (Sept. 1979).

CAMPBELL, F. L., 'Family in Growth and Variation in Family Role Structure', *Journal of Marriage and Family*, 32 (1970).

CLANCY-GORE, CHARLES, 'Nutritional Standards of Some Working-Class Families in Dublin, 1948', *JSSISI* 17 (1943–4).

CLARK, CLIFFORD E., 'Domestic Architecture as an Index to Social History: The Romantic Revival and the Cult of Domesticity in America, 1840–1870', *Journal of Interdisciplinary History*, 7/1 (Summer 1976).

CLARK, COLIN, 'The Economics of House-Work', *Bulletin of the Oxford University Institute of Statistics*, 20 (1958).

COHEN, M. GRIFFIN, 'The Development of the Dairy Industry in Canada', in Innes, Harold H. (ed.), *The Dairy Industry in Canada* (Toronto, 1937).

—— 'The Decline of Women in Canadian Dairying', *Historie sociale: Social History*, 17/34 (Nov. 1984).

COHEN, MARILYN, 'Working Conditions and Experiences of Work in the Linen Industry: Tullylish, Co. Down', *Ulster Folklife*, 30 (1984).

COLEMAN, D. C., 'Proto-Industrialisation: A Concept Too Many', *EHR*, 2nd ser. 36 (1983).

COLEMAN, GOULD, and ELBERT, SARAH, 'Farming Families: The Farm Needs Everyone', *Research in Rural Sociology and Development*, 1 (1984).

CONNELL, K. H., 'Marriage in Ireland after the Famine: The Diffusion of the Match', *JSSISI* 19 (1955–6).

COULSON, MARGARET, MAGAS, BRANKA, and WAINWRIGHT, HILARY, 'The Housewife and her Labour under Capitalism: A Critique', *NLR* 89 (1975).

CRONIN, WILLIE, 'When we Were Boys in Cork: An Exile's Memories', *The Capuchin Annual, 1941* (Dublin, 1940).

CUDDY, MICHAEL, and CURTAIN, CHRIS, 'Commercialisation in West of Ireland Agriculture in the 1890s', *Economic and Social Review*, 14/3 (Apr. 1983).

CULLEN, LOUIS M., and SMOUT, T. C., 'Economic Growth in Scotland and Ireland', in Cullen, Louis M., and Smout, T. C. (eds.), *Comparative Aspects of Scottish and Irish Economic and Social History, 1600–1900* (Edinburgh, 1977).

DALY, MARY E., 'Women in the Irish Workforce from Pre-Industrial to Modern Times', *Saothar* 7 (1981).

DAVIDOFF, LEONORE, 'Mastered for Life: Servant and Wife in Victorian and Edwardian England', *Journal of Social History*, 7/4 (Summer 1974).

—— 'The Rationalization of Housework', in Barker, Diana L., and Allen, Sheila (eds.), *Dependence and Exploitation in Work and Marriage* (1976).

DAVIES, A. C., 'Roofing Belfast and Dublin, 1896–98: American Penetrating of the Irish Market for Welsh Slate', *Irish Economic and Social History*, 4 (1977).

DAVIN, ANNA, '"Mind that you Do as you Are Told": Reading Books for Board School Children, 1870–1902', *Feminist Review*, 3 (1979).

DEANE, PHYLLIS, 'New Estimates of Gross National Product for the United Kingdom, 1830–1914', *Review of Income and Wealth*, 14/2 (1968).

DUNCAN, G. A., 'Rural Industries: An Example from North Carolina', *JSSISI* 14 (1926–7).

DUNCAN, OTIS DUDLEY, 'Does Money Buy Satisfaction?', *Social Indicators Research*, 2/3 (Dec. 1975).

EASTERLIN, RICHARD A., 'Does Economic Growth Improve the Human Lot? Some Emperical Evidence', in David, Paul A., and Reder, Melvin W. (eds.), *Nations and Households in Economic Growth: Essays in Honour of Moses Abramovitz* (New York, 1974).

EHRENREICH, BARBARA, and ENGLISH, DEIRDRE, 'The Manufacture of Housework', *Socialist Revolution*, 5 (Oct.–Dec. 1975).

EHRLICH, CYRIL, 'Sir Horace Plunkett and Agricultural Reform', in Goldstrom, J. M., and Clarkson, L. A. (eds.), *Irish Population, Economy and Society* (Oxford, 1981).

ENGLAND, PAULA, and NORRIS, BAHAR, 'Comparable Worth: A New Doctrine of Sex Discrimination', *Social Sciences Quarterly*, 66/3 (Sept. 1985).

FEE, TERRY, 'Domestic Labour: An Analysis of Housework and its Relation to the Production Process', *Review of Radical Political Economics*, 8/1 (Spring 1976).

FEELEY, PAT, 'Servant Boys and Girls in Co. Limerick', *Old Limerick Journal* (Dec. 1979).

FERBER, MARIANNE A., and BIRNBAUM, BONNIE G., 'Housework: Priceless or Valueless?', *Review of Income and Wealth*, 26 (1980).

FFOLLIOTT, ROSEMARY, 'Cottages and Farmhouses', *Irish Ancestor*, 4/1 (1972).

FITZGERALD, EITHNE, 'The Extent of Poverty in Ireland', in Kennedy, Stanislaus (ed.), *One Million Poor? The Challenge of Irish Inequality* (Dublin, 1981).

FITZPATRICK, DAVID, 'The Disappearance of the Irish Agricultural Labourer, 1841–1912', *Irish Economic and Social History*, 7 (1980).

—— 'Irish Emigration in the Later Nineteenth Century', *Irish Historical Studies*, 22/86 (1980).

—— 'Marriage in Post-Famine Ireland', in Cosgrove, Art (ed.), *Marriage in Ireland* (Dublin, 1985).

—— '"A Share of the Honeycomb": Education, Emigration and Irishwomen', *Continuity and Change*, 1/2 (1986).

—— 'The Modernisation of the Irish Female', in O'Flanagan, Patrick, Ferguson, Paul, and Whelan, Kevin (eds.), *Rural Ireland, 1600–1900: Modernisation and Change* (Cork, 1987).

FOLBRE, NANCY, 'Patriarchy in Colonial New England', *Review of Radical Political Economics*, 12/2 (Summer 1980).

FREEMAN, T. W., 'The Changing Distribution of Population in Co. Mayo', *JSSISI* 17 (1942–3).

—— 'Population Distribution in Co. Sligo', *JSSISI* 17 (1943–4).

—— 'Emigration and Rural Ireland', *JSSISI* 17 (1944–5).

GAILEY, ALAN, 'Changes in Irish Rural Housing, 1600–1900', in O'Flanagan, Patrick, Ferguson, Paul, and Whelan, Kevin (eds.), *Rural Ireland, 1600– 1900: Modernisation and Change* (Cork, 1987).

GAILEY, ANDREW, 'Horace Plunkett's New Irish Policy of 1905', in Keating, Carla (ed.), *Plunkett and Co-operatives: Past, Present and Future* (Bank of Ireland Centre for Co-operative Studies and University College, Cork, Cork, 1983).

GARDINER, JEAN, 'Women's Domestic Labour', *NLR* 89 (1975).

GEARY, R. C., 'Variability in Agricultural Statistics on Small and Medium-Sized Farms in an Irish County', *JSSISI* 19/1 (1956–7).

GERSTEIN, IRA, 'Domestic Work and Capitalism', *Radical America*, 7/4 (July-Oct. 1973).

GIBBON, PETER, and HIGGINS, M. D., 'Patronage, Tradition and Modernisation: The Case of the Irish Gombeenman', *Economic and Social Review*, 6/1 (Oct. 1974).

GLAZIER-MALBIN, NONA, 'Housework', *Signs*, 1 (1976).

GOODE, WILLIAM J., 'Comment: The Economics of Non-Monetary Variables', *JPE* 82/2 (Mar.–Apr. 1974).

GORDON, N. M., and MORTON, T. E., 'The Low Mobility Model of Wage Discrimination: With Special Reference to Sex Differentials', *Journal of Economic Theory*, 7/3 (Mar. 1974).

GREENWOOD, DAPHNE, 'The Institutional Inadequacy of the Market in Determining Comparable Worth: Implications for Value Theory', *JEI* 18 (June 1984).

—— 'The Economic Significance of 'Women's Place' in Society: A New Institutionalist View', *JEI* 18 (Sept. 1984).

GRONAU, REUBEN, 'The Effects of Children on the Housewife's Value of Time', *JPE* 81/2 (Mar.–Apr. 1973).

—— 'Home Production: A Forgotten Industry', *Review of Economics and Statistics*, 62 (1980).

HANNAN, MICHAEL T., 'Families, Markets and Social Structures: An Essay on Becker's *A Treatise on the Family*', *JEL* 20 (Mar. 1982).

HANSEN, BODIL K., 'Rural Women in Late Nineteenth-Century Denmark', *Journal of Peasant Studies*, 9/2 (Jan. 1982).

HARRISON, JOHN, 'The Political Economy of Housework', *Conference of Socialist Economists*, Bull. 1 (1974).

HAWRYLYSHYN, OLI, 'The Value of Household Services: A Survey of Empirical Estimates', *Review of Income and Wealth*, 22 (1976).

HAYDEN, DOLORES, and WRIGHT, GWENDOLYN, 'Architecture and Urban Planning', *Signs*, 1/4 (1976).

HEATH, JULIA A., and CISCEL, DAVID H., 'Patriarchy, Family Structure and the Exploitation of Women's Labour', *JEI* 22 (Sept. 1988).

HEDGES, J. N., and BARNETT, J. K., 'Working Women and the Division of Household Tasks', *Monthly Labour Review*, 95/4 (Apr. 1972).

HERSHLAG, Z. Y., 'The Case of Unpaid Domestic Service', *Economia internazionale*, 8 (Feb. 1960).

HIGGS, EDWARD, 'Domestic Servants and Households in Victorian England', *Social History*, 8/2 (May 1983).

—— 'Domestic Service and Household Production', in John, Angela V. (ed.), *Unequal Opportunities: Women's Employment in England, 1800–1918* (Oxford, 1986).

HOFFMAN, LOIS WLADIS, 'The Decision to Work', in Nye, F. I., and Hoffman, Lois Wladis (eds.), *The Employed Mother in America* (Chicago, 1963).

HOUSTON, RAB, and SNELL, K. D. M., 'Historiographical Review: Proto-Industrialization? Cottage Industry, Social Change, and Industrial Revolution', *Historical Journal*, 27/2 (1984).

HUMPHRIES, JANE, 'Class Struggle and the Resistance of the Working-Class Family', *Cambridge Journal of Economics*, 1 (Sept. 1977).

HUTTMAN, J., 'The Impact of Land Reform on Agricultural Production in Ireland', *Agricultural History*, 46 (1972).

INGLEHART, RONALD, 'Values, Objective Needs and Subjective Satisfaction among Western Publics', *Comparative Political Studies*, 9/4 (Jan. 1977).

JAQUETTE, JANE S., 'Women and Modernization Theory: A Decade of Feminist Criticism', *World Politics*, 34/2 (Jan. 1982).

JAUSSAUD, DANIELLE P., 'Can Job Evaluation Systems Help Determine the Comparable Worth of Male and Female Occupations?', *JEI* 18 (June 1984).

JENSEN, JOAN M., 'Cloth, Butter and Boarders: Women's Household Production for the Market', *Review of Radical Political Economics*, 12/2 (Summer 1980).

JOHNSON, JAMES H., 'Marriage and Fertility in Nineteenth-Century Londonderry', *JSSISI* 20/1 (1957–8).

—— 'Harvest Migration from Nineteenth-Century Ireland', *Transactions and Papers of the Institute of British Geographers* (1967).

JOHNSTON, PROFESSOR JOSEPH, 'An Economic Basis for Irish Agriculture', *JSSISI* 18 (1947–8).

JORBERG, LENNART, 'Proto-Industrialization: An Economic History Figment', *Scandinavian Economic History Review*, 30 (1982).

KATONA, GEORGE, 'The Human Factor in Human Affairs', in Campbell, Angus, and Converse, Philip E. (eds.), *The Human Meaning of Social Change* (New York, 1972).

KENDRICK, JOHN W., 'Expanding Imputed Values in the National Income and Product Accounts', *Review of Income and Wealth*, 25 (1979).

KENNEDY, LIAM, 'Notes and Comments: A Sceptical View on the Reincarnation of the Irish Gombeenman', *Economic and Social Review*, 8/3 (1977).

—— 'Retail Markets in Rural Ireland at the End of the Nineteenth Century', *Irish Economic and Social History*, 5 (1978).

—— 'Regional Specialisation, Railway Development and Irish Agriculture in the Nineteenth Century', in Goldstrom, J. M., and Clarkson, L. A. (eds.), *Irish Population, Economy and Society* (Oxford, 1981).

—— 'Aspects of the Spread of the Creamery System in Ireland', in Keating, Carla (ed.) *Plunkett and Co-operatives: Past, Present and Future* (Bank of Ireland Centre for Co-operative Studies and University College, Cork, Cork, 1983).

—— 'The Rural Economy, 1820–1914', in Kennedy, Liam, and Ollerenshaw, Philip (eds.), *An Economic History of Ulster, 1820–1940* (Manchester, 1985).

KESSLER-HARRIS, ALICE, 'Comments on the Yans-McLaughlin and Davidoff Papers', *Journal of Social History*, 7/4 (Summer 1974).

KHANDKER, SHAHIDUR, 'Women's Time Allocation and Household Nonmarket Production in Rural Bangladesh', *Journal of Development Areas*, 22/1 (Oct. 1987).

KOHN, SEENA B., 'Women's Participation in the North American Family Farm', *Women's Studies Participation Quarterly*, 1 (1977).

KUZNETS, S., 'The Monetary Value of a Housewife: An Economic Analysis for Use in Litigation', *American Journal of Economics and Sociology*, 28/3 (July 1969).

LANCASTER, K. L., 'A New Approach to Consumer Theory', *JPE* 74 (1966).

LANE, ROBERT E., 'Markets and the Satisfaction of Human Wants', *JEI* 12 (Dec. 1978).

LARKIN, EMMET, 'Economic Growth, Capital Investment, and the Roman Catholic Church in Nineteenth-Century Ireland', *American Historical Review*, 72 (Apr. 1967).

LEIBOWITZ, ARLEEN, 'Education and Home Production', *AER* 64/2 (May 1974).

McBRIDE, TERESA, 'The Long Road Home: Women's Work and Industrialisation', in Bridenthal, Renate, and Koonz, Claudia (eds.), *Becoming Visible* (Boston, 1977).

McCLEERY, ALISON M., 'The Persistence of Co-operation as a Theme in Marginal Development', in Sewel, John, and O Cearbhaill, Diarmuid (eds.), *Co-operation and Community Development: A Collection of Essays* (Galway, 1982).

McDOUGALL, MARY LYNN, 'Working-Class Women during the Industrial Revolution, 1780–1914', in Bridenthal, Renate, and Koonz, Claudia (eds.), *Becoming Visible* (Boston, 1977).

MACKINTOSH, MAUREEN M., 'Domestic Labour and the Household', in Burman, Sandra (ed.), *Fit Work for Women* (1979).

MARSHALL, R., 'The Economics of Racial Discrimination: A Survey', *JEL* 12/3 (Sept. 1974).

MINCER, JACOB, 'Labour Force Participation of Married Women: A Study in Labour Supply', *Aspects of Labour Economics* (1962).

—— and POLACHEK, SOLOMON W., 'Family Investment in Human Capital: Earnings of Women', *JPE* 82/2 (Mar–Apr. 1974).

MITRA, MANOSHI, 'Women's Work: Gains Analysis of Women's Labour in Dairy Production', in Singh, Andrea Menefee, and Kelles-Kitanen, Anita (eds.), *Invisible Hands: Women in Home-Based Production* (1987).

MOYNIHAN, DAN, 'Working for Farmers', *Sliab Luacra: Journal of the Cumann Luachra*, 1/4 (June 1987).

MURPHY, DESMOND, 'Derry and North-west Ulster, 1790–1914', Ph.D. thesis (Dublin, 1978).

MURPHY, M. J., 'Four Folktales about Women', *Ulster Folklife*, 13 (1967).

MURPHY, MARTIN, 'The Value of Nonmarket Household Production: Opportunity Cost versus Market Cost Estimates', *Review of Income and Wealth*, 24 (1978).

—— 'Comparative Estimates of the Value of Household Work in the United States for 1976', *Review of Income and Wealth*, 28 (1982).

NORTH, DOUGLASS C., and THOMAS, ROBERT PAUL, 'An Economic Theory of the Growth of the Western World', *EHR*, 2nd ser. 23/1 (1970).

ODDY, D. J., 'Working-Class Diets in Late Nineteenth-Century Britain', *EHR*, 2nd ser. 23 (1970).

Ó GRÁDA, CORMAC, 'The Beginnings of the Irish Creamery System, 1880–1914', *EHR*, 2nd ser. 30/2 (May 1977).

OLDHAM, PROFESSOR C. H., 'The Interpretation of Irish Statistics', *JSSISI* 14 (1923–4).

—— 'Some Perplexities in Regard to the Agricultural Statistics of Ireland', *JSSISI* 14 (1923–4).

—— 'Reform of the Irish Census of Population', *JSSISI* 15/101 (Oct. 1927).

OLLERENSHAW, PHILIP, 'Industry, 1820–1914', in Kennedy, Liam, and Ollerenshaw, Philip (eds.), *An Economic History of Ulster, 1820–1940* (Manchester, 1985).

O MATHUNA, LE SEAN, 'Ellie Bawn, The Sciollaun-Cutter', *Sliab Luacra: Journal of the Cumann Luachra*, 1/4 (June 1987).

O NUALLÁIN, LABHRAS, 'A Comparison of the Economic Position and Trade in Eire and Northern Ireland', *JSSISI* 17 (1945–6).

O RAIFEARTAIGH, T., 'Changes and Trends in our Educational System since 1922', *JSSISI* 20/2 (1958–9).

POLACHEK, S. W., 'Discontinuous Labour Force Participation and its Effects on Women's Market Earnings', in Lloyd, C. B. (ed.), *Sex Discrimination and the Division of Labour* (New York, 1975).

POLLACK, ROBERT A., 'A Transaction Cost Approach to Families and Households', *JEL* 23 (June 1985).

POWER, MARILYN, 'From Home Production to Wage Labour: Women as a Reserve Army of Labour', *Review of Radical Political Economics*, 15 (Spring 1983).

PURVIS, JUNE, 'Domestic Subjects since 1870', in Goodson, Ivor (ed.), *Social Histories of the Secondary Curriculum* (1985).

PYUN, CHONG SOO, 'The Monetary Value of a Housewife: An Economic Analysis for Use in Litigation', *American Journal of Economics and Sociology*, 28/3 (July 1969).

RAVETZ, ALISON, 'The Victorian Coal Kitchen and its Reformers', *Victorian Studies*, 11/4 (June 1968).

RAZIN, A., 'Investment in Human Capital and Economic Growth', *Development and Cultural Change*, 24 (1972).

REIMER, BILL, 'Women as Farm Labour', *Rural Sociology*, 51/2 (1986).

RIDLEY, JEANNE CLARE, 'The Changing Position of American Women: Education, Labour Force Participation and Fertility', in *The Family in Transition: A Round Table Conference, 3–6 1969* (Washington, 1973).

ROBBINS, LIONEL, 'On the Elasticity of Demand for Income in Terms of Effort', *Economica*, 10 (1930).

ROSEN, HARVEY S., 'The Monetary Value of a Housewife: A Replacement Cost Approach', *American Journal of Economics and Sociology*, 33/1 (Jan. 1974).

ROTHSTEIN, FRANCIS, 'Two Different Worlds: Gender and Industrialization in Rural Mexico', in Leons, Madeline, and Rothstein, Francis (eds.), *New Directions in Political Economy: An Approach from Anthropology* (Westport, Conn., 1979).

RUDDICK, J. A., 'The Development of the Dairy Industry in Canada', in Innis, Harold H. (ed.), *The Dairy Industry in Canada* (Toronto, 1937).

SECCOMBE, WALLY, 'The Housewife and her Labour under Capitalism', *NLR* 83 (1974).

—— 'Domestic Labour and the Working Class Household', in Bonnie Fox (ed.), *Hidden in the Household: Women's Domestic Labour under Capitalism* (Toronto, 1980).

SHANKLIN, EUGENIA, 'Donegal's Lowly Sheep and Exalted Cows', *Natural History*, 85/3 (Mar. 1976).

SHEEHAN, KATHLEEN, 'Life in Glangevlin, Co. Cavan, 1900–1920', *Ulster Folklife*, 31 (1985).

SHERIDAN, RITA, 'Women's Contribution to Farming', *Food and Farm Research* (Apr. 1982).

SNOOKS, G. D., 'Household Services and National Income in Australia, 1891–1981: Some Preliminary Results', *First Spring Workshop in Australian Economic History* (1983).

SORENSEN, ELAINE, 'Equal Pay for Comparable Worth: A Policy for Eliminating the Undervaluation of Women's Work', *JEI* 18 (June 1984).

STAEHLE, DR HANS, 'Statistical Notes on the Economic History of Irish Agriculture, 1847–1913', *JSSISI* 18 (1950–1).

STEADMAN, HENRY J., 'Some Questions About National Educational Investments and Economic Development', *Journal of Development Areas*, 6 (Oct. 1971).

STIGLITZ, JOSEPH E., 'The Efficiency Wage Hypothesis, Surplus Labour, and the Distribution of Income in LDCs', *Oxford Economic Papers*, 28 (1976).

STRASSER, SUSAN M., 'The Business of Housekeeping: The Ideology of the Household at the Turn of the Twentieth Century', *Insurgent Sociologist*, 8/2 (Autumn 1978).

—— 'An Enlarged Existence? Technology and Household Work in Nineteenth-Century America', in Berk, Sarah (ed.), *Women and Household Labor* (Beverly Hills, Calif., 1980).

STRAUSS, JOHN, 'Does Better Nutrition Raise Farm Productivity?', *JPE* 94 (1986).

THOMPSON, SIR WILLIAM J., 'The First Census of the Irish Free State and its Importance to the Country', *JSSISI* 15/101 (Oct. 1927).

TOWNE, MARVIN W., and RASMUSSEN, WAYNE D., 'Farm Gross Product and Gross Investment in the Nineteenth Century', *Trends in the American Economy in the Nineteenth Century: Studies in Income and Wealth*, 24 (Princeton, NJ, 1960).

TRIBBOTT, MINWEL, 'Laundering in the Welsh Home', *Folklife*, 19 (1981).

TUCKER, VINCENT, 'Ireland and the Co-operative Movement', in Keating, Carla (ed.), *Plunkett and Co-operatives: Past, Present and Future* (Bank of Ireland Centre for Co-operative Studies and University College, Cork, Cork, 1983).

TURNBULL, ANNMARIE, 'Learning her Womanly Work: The Elementary School Curriculum, 1870–1914', in Hunt, Felicity (ed.), *Lessons for Life: The Schooling of Girls and Women, 1850–1950* (1987).

TURNER, MICHAEL, 'Towards an Agricultural Price Index for Ireland, 1850–1914', *Economic and Social Review*, 18 (1987).

VANEK, JOANN, 'Housewives as Workers', in Voydanoff, Patricia (ed.), *Work and Family: Changing Roles of Men and Women* (Palo Alto, Calif., 1984).

—— 'Time Spent in Housework', in Amsden, Alice H. (ed.), *The Economics of Women and Work* (Harmondsworth, 1980).

VAUGHAN, WILLIAM E., 'Agricultural Output, Rents and Wages in Ireland, 1850–1880', in Cullen, L. M., and Furet, F. (eds.), *Ireland and France, 17th and 20th Centuries, towards a Comparative Study of Rural History* (Paris, 1980).

VINCENT, DAVID, 'Love and Death and The Nineteenth-Century Working Class', *Social History*, 5 (1980).

WALKER, KATHRYN, 'Time Used by Husbands for Household Work', *Family Economic Review* (June 1970).

WALSH, BRENDAN M., 'Marriage Rates and Population Pressure: Ireland, 1871–1911', *EHR*, 2nd ser. 13 (1970).

WARD, MARGARET, 'Marginality and Militancy: Cumann na mBan, 1914–1936', in Morgan, Austen, and Purdie, Bob (eds.), *Ireland: Divided Nation, Divided Class* (1980).

WATSON, MERVYN, 'Common Irish Plough Types and Tillage Techniques', *Tools and Tillage*, 5 (1985).

WEINROBE, MAURICE, 'Household Production and National Production: An Improvement of the Record', *Review of Income and Wealth*, 20 (1974).

WEST, TREVOR, 'The Development of Horace Plunkett's Thought', in Keating, Carla, *Plunkett and Co-operatives: Past, Present and Future* (Bank of Ireland Centre for Co-operative Studies and University College, Cork, Cork, 1983).

WILFORD, W. T., 'Nutrition Levels and Economic Growth: Some Empirical Measures', *JEI* 7 (Sept. 1973).

WILLIAMS, DONALD R., and REGISTER, CHARLES H., 'Regional Variations in Earnings and the Gender Composition of Employment: Is 'Women's Work' Undervalued?', *JEI* 20 (Dec. 1986).

WILLIAMS, FIONNULA, 'Bachelor's Wives and Old Maid's Children: A Look at the Men and Women in Irish Proverbs', *Ulster Folklife*, 30 (1984).

WILLIAMSON, ROBERT, 'Role Themes in Latin America', in Steward, G., and Williamson, R (eds.), *Sex Roles in Changing Society* (New York, 1970).

Other Printed Works

ACTON, JANICE, GOLDSMITH, PENNY, and SHEPARD, BONNIE (eds.), *Women at Work: Ontario, 1850–1930* (Toronto, 1974).

ALBASSAM, DARIM, *Investment in Human Capital and its Contribution to Economic Growth and Income Distribution in Developing Countries* (East Lansing, Mich., 1973).

AMIN, GALAL A., *Food Supply and Economic Development* (Belfast, 1966).

ANDERSON, ADELAIDE MARY, *Women in the Factory: An Administrative Adventure* (1922).

ANDERSON, R. A., *With Plunkett in Ireland: The Co-op Organiser's Story*, (orig. publ. 1935; Dublin, 1983).

ARDZROONE, LEON (ed.), *Essays in our Changing Order* (New York, 1964).

ARENSBURG, CONRAD M., *The Irish Countryman: An Anthropological Study* (1937).

ATTAR, DENA, *Wasting Girls' Time: The History and Politics of Home Economics* (1990).

BANKS, J. A., *Prosperity and Parenthood: A Study of Family Planning among the Victorian Middle Classes* (1954).

BEALE, JENNY, *Women In Ireland: Voices of Change* (Dublin, 1986).

BECKER, GARY S., *The Economics of Discrimination* (Chicago, 1957).

—— *A Treatise on the Family* (Cambridge, Mass., 1981).

BERGER, SUZANNE DORIS, *Peasants against Politics: Rural Organisation in Brittany, 1911–1967* (Cambridge, Mass., 1972).

BERK, RICHARD A., and BERK, SARAH FENSTERMAKER, *Labor and Leisure at Home* (Beverly Hills, Calif., 1979).

BETTIO, FRANCESCA, *The Sexual Division of Labour: The Italian Case* (Oxford, 1988).

Board of Trade, *Working Party Reports: Hosiery* (1946).

—— *Working Party Reports: Lace* (1947).

BOLGER, PATRICK, *The Irish Co-operative Movement: Its History and Development* (Dublin Institute of Public Administration, Dublin, 1977).

BOSANQUET, HELEN, *Rich and Poor* (1986).

BOSERUP, ESTER, *Women's Role in Economic Development* (1970).

BOWEN, WILLIAM G., and FINIGAN, T. ALDRICH, *The Economics of Labor Force Participation* (Princeton, NJ, 1969).

BOYLE, ELIZABETH, *The Irish Flowerers* (Belfast, 1971).

BRAVERMAN, HARRY, *Labor and Monopoly Capital* (New York, 1974).

BUSTEED, JOHN, *Agricultural Bulletin 2: A Statistical Analysis of Irish Egg Production, Prices and Trade* (Cork, 1926).

BUTTERWORTH, ANNIE, *Manual of Household Work and Management* (1922).

BUVINIC, MAYRA, and SCHUMACHER, ILSA (eds.), *Women and Development: Indicators of their Changing Role* (Paris, 1981).

CALDER, JENNI, *The Victorian Home* (1977).

CANTRIL, HADLEY, *The Pattern of Human Concerns* (New Brunswick, NJ, 1965).

CARBERY, MARY, *The Farm by Lough Gur: The Story of Mary Fogarty (Sissy O'Brien)* (1937).

Census of Population, 1926, ii, *Occupations of Males and Females in Each*

Province, County, County Borough, Urban and Rural District (Dublin, 1926).

CLARK, SAMUEL, Social Origins of the Irish Land War (Princeton, HJ, 1979).

COLUM, PADRAIC, The Road round Ireland (New York, 1927).

CONNELLY, PATRICIA, Last Hired, First Fired (Toronto, 1978).

COUSINS, JAMES H., and COUSINS, MARGARET E., We Two Together (Madras, 1950).

COWAN, RUTH SCHWARTZ, More Work for Mother: The Ironies of Household Technology from the Open Hearth to the Microwave (New York, 1983).

Crawford Municipal Technical Institute, Cork, Prospectus: Session 1933–1934 (Cork, 1933), 1933–44.

CRAWFORD, W. H., Domestic Industry in Ireland: The Experience of the Linen Industry (Dublin, 1972).

CROOKSHANK, ANNE, and THE KNIGHT OF GLEN, The Painters of Ireland c.1660–1920 (1978).

CROSS, ERIC, The Tailor and Ansty (1942).

CROTTY, RAYMOND D., Irish Agricultural Production: Its Volume and Structure (Cork, 1966).

CULLEN, LOUIS M., Life in Ireland (1968).

—— Six Generations: Life and Work in Ireland from 1790 (Cork, 1970).

—— An Economic History of Ireland since 1660 (1972).

—— The Emergence of Modern Ireland, 1600–1900 (1981).

—— and FURET, F. (eds.), Ireland and France, 17th and 20th Centuries, towards a Comparative Study of Rural History (Paris, 1980).

DALLA COSTA, MARIAROSA, and JAMES, SELMA, The Power of Women and the Subversion of the Community (Bristol, 1973).

DALY, MARY E., Social and Economic History of Ireland since 1800 (Dublin, 1981).

—— Dublin: The Deposed Capital. A Social and Economic History, 1860–1914 (Cork, 1984).

DARBY, W. D., Linen: The Emblem of Elegance (New York, 1926).

DAVIDSON, CAROLINE, A Woman's Work is Never Done: A History of Housework in the British Isles, 1650–1950 (1982).

DELPHY, CHRISTINE, Close to Home: A Materialist Analysis of Women's Oppression (1984).

DENSON, ALAN (ed.), Letters from AE (1961).

Department of Education (Saorstát Éireann), Report, 1924–1925 (Dublin, 1926).

Department of Industry and Commerce (Saorstát Éireann), Agricultural Statistics, 1847–1926: Report and Tables (Dublin, 1928).

—— Commission of Inquiry on Post-Emergency Agricultural Policy, Second Interim Report: Poultry Productions (Dublin, 1951).

DIGBY, MARGARET, *Horace Plunkett: An Anglo-American Irishman* (Oxford, 1949).

DONOVAN, JOHN, *Economic History of Livestock in Ireland* (Cork, 1940).

DOYLE, LYNN, *The Spirit of Ireland* (1935).

DRUMMOND, J. C., and WILBRAHAM, ANNE, *The Englishman's Food* (1957).

DUDDEN, FAYE E., *Serving Women: Household Service in Nineteenth-Century America* (Middletown, Conn., 1983).

DUFF, FRANK, *Miracles on Tap: The Incredible Transformation of Dublin's Bentley Place* (New York, 1978).

DUNNE, GERR, *Town of Monaghan Co-op: The First Eighty Years* (Monaghan, 1983).

DUNRAVEN, EARL OF, *Cheap Food for the People at Large: An Open Letter from the Earl of Dunraven, KP, CMG, to the People of Ireland* (Dublin, 1925).

DYHOUSE, CAROL, *Girls Growing up in Late Victorian and Edwardian England* (1981).

EBERY, M., and PRESTON, B., *Domestic Service in Late Victorian and Edwardian England, 1871–1914* (Reading, 1976).

EGLINTON, JOHN, *A Memoir of AE* (1937).

Electricity Supply Board, *Report by the ESB Investigation Committee* (Dublin, 1972).

EVANS, ESTYN E., *Irish Heritage: The Landscape, the People and their Work* (Dundalk, 1942).

FIGGIS, DARRELL, *Irishmen of Today: AE (George W. Russell). A Study of a Man and a Nation* (Dublin, 1916).

FITZGERALD, WILLIAM G. (ed.), *The Voice of Ireland: A Survey of the Race and Nation from All Angles, by the Foremost Leaders at Home and Abroad* (Dublin, 1924).

FITZPATRICK, DAVID, *Politics and Irish Life, 1913–1921* (Dublin, 1977).

—— *Irish Emigration, 1801–1921* (Economic and Social History Society of Ireland, Dublin, 1984).

FOWKE, VERNON C., *Canadian Agricultural Policy: The Historical Pattern* (Toronto, 1947).

FOX, BONNIE (ed.), *Hidden in the Household: Women's Domestic Labour under Capitalism* (Toronto, 1980).

FOX, ROBIN, *Tory Islanders: A People of the Celtic Fringe* (Cambridge, 1978).

GAILEY, ALAN, *Rural Houses of the North of Ireland* (Edinburgh, 1984).

GALBRAITH, JOHN KENNETH, *Economics and the Public Purpose* (Boston, 1973).

GALLAGHER, S. F. (ed.), *Women in Irish Legend, Life and Literature* (Gerrards Cross, 1983).

GILLMOR, DESMOND A., *Economic Activities in the Republic of Ireland: A Geographical Perspective* (Dublin, 1985).

GILMORE, FRED W., *A Survey of Agricultural Credit in Ireland* (Dublin, 1959).

GOULET, DENIS, *The Cruel Choice: A New Concept in the Theory of Development* (New York, 1971).

GURIN, GERALD, VEROFF, JOSEPH, and FELD, SHEILA, *Americans View their Health* (New York, 1960).

GWYNN, STEPHEN, *Ireland* (1924).

HARBISAN, F., *Human Resources as the Wealth of Nations* (New York, 1973).

HARDY, EVELYN, *Summer in Another World* (1950).

HARDYMENT, CHRISTINA, *From Mangle to Microwave* (1988).

HARRISON, MOLLY, *The Kitchen in History* (1972).

HARTMANN, HEIDI IRMGARD, *Capitalism and Women's Work in the Home, 1900–1930* (Ann Arbor, Mich., 1975).

HAYDEN, DOLORES, *The Grand Domestic Revolution: The History of Feminist Designs for American Homes, Neighborhoods, and Cities* (Cambridge, Mass., 1981).

HEALY, JAMES N. (ed.), *The Mercier Book of Old Irish Street Ballads* (Cork, 1969).

HOCTOR, DANIEL, *The Department's Story: A History of the Department of Agriculture* (Dublin, 1971).

HOLMSTROM, L. L., *The Two-Career Family* (Cambridge, Mass., 1972).

HORN, PAMELA, *The Rise and Fall of the Victorian Servant* (Dublin, 1975).

Irish Sisters of Charity, *Centenary Brochure* (Dublin, 1958).

IRVINE, ALEXANDER, *The Souls of Poor Folk* (1921).

'Isobel' (ed.), *Things a Woman Wants to Know, with an Illustrated Section on the Folding of Serviettes* (1922).

JOHN, ANGELA V. (ed.), *Unequal Opportunities: Women's Employment in England, 1800–1918* (Oxford, 1986).

JUSTER, F. THOMAS, and STAFFORD, FRANK P. (eds.), *Time, Goods and Well-Being* (Ann Arbor, Mich., 1985).

KATZMAR, DAVID M., *Seven Days a Week: Women and Domestic Service in Industrializing America* (New York, 1978).

KEATING, CARLA (ed.), *Plunkett and Co-operatives: Past, Present and Future* (Bank of Ireland Centre for Co-operative Studies and University College, Cork, Cork, 1983).

KENNEDY, ROBERT E., *The Irish: Emigration, Marriage and Fertility* (Berkeley, Calif., 1973).

KEYNES, JOHN MAYNARD, *The Collected Writings of John Maynard Keynes* (1972).

KNAPP, JOSEPH GRANT, *An Appraisement of Agricultural Co-operation in Ireland (Carried out by the Department of Agriculture)* (Dublin, 1964).

KREPS, J. *Sex in the Marketplace: American Women at Work* (Baltimore, 1971).

KUZNETS, S., *National Income and its Composition* (NBER, 1944).

LANE, JACK, and CLIFFORD, BRENDAN (eds.), *Ned Buckley's Poems* (Aubane, 1987).

LEGHORN, LISA, and PARKER, KATHERINE, *Women's Worth: Sexual Economics and the World of Women* (1981).

LEIBERSTEIN, H., *Economic Backwardness and Economic Growth Development* (New York, 1957).

LEVENSTEIN, HARVEY, *Revolution at the Table: The Transformation of the American Diet* (Oxford, 1988).

LEWIS, JANE, *Women in England, 1870–1950* (Brighton, 1984).

—— (ed.), *Labour and Love: Women's Experience of Home and Family, 1850–1940* (Oxford, 1986).

LEWIS, JOHN P. (ed.), *Strengthening the Poor: What Have we Learned?* (Oxford, 1988).

LEWIS, W. ARTHUR, *The Theory of Economic Growth* (1955).

LINDER, STEFFAN, *The Theory of the Leisure Class* (New York, 1953).

—— *The Harried Leisure Class* (New York, 1970).

LINDERT, PETER H., *Fertility and Scarcity in America* (Princeton, NJ, 1978).

LINDHAL, ERIC, DAHLGREN, EINAR, and KOCK, KARIN, *Wages, Cost of Living and National Income in Sweden, 1860–1930*, iii, I, II (1933).

LIVERNOSH, ROBERT (ed.), *Comparable Worth: Issues and Alternatives* (Washington, DC, 1980).

LUCEY, DENIS I. F., and KALDOR, DONALD R., *Rural Industrialization: The Impact of Industrialization on Two Rural Communities in Western Ireland* (1969).

McBRIDE, THERESA M., *The Domestic Revolution: The Modernisation of Household Service in England and France, 1820–1920* (1976).

McCLEAN, IAN W., and PINCUS, JONATHAN J., *Living Standards in Australia, 1890–1940: Evidence and Conjectures*, (Working Paper 6, Canberra, Aug. 1982).

MACGOWAN, MICHAEL, *The Hard Road to Klondike*, trans. from the Irish by Valentin Iremonger (1962).

McMURRY, SALLY, *Families and Farmhouses in Nineteenth-Century America: Vernacular Design and Social Change* (Oxford, 1988).

MADDEN, J. F., *The Economics of Sex Discrimination* (Lexington, Mass., 1973).

MADDEN-SIMPSON, JANET (ed.), *Woman's Part: An Anthology of Short Fiction by and about Irish Women, 1890–1960* (Dublin, 1984).

MALOS, ELLEN (ed.), *The Politics of Housework* (1980).

MARSHALL, A., *Principles of Economics*, 8th edn. (1930).

MARTIN, M. KAY, and VOORHIES, BARBARA, *Female of the Species* (New York, 1975).

MASON, THOMAS H., *The Islands of Ireland* (1936).

MEHTA, M. M., *Human Resources: Development Planning* (Delhi, 1976).

MICKS, W. L., *An Account of the Constitution, Administration, and Dissolution of the CDB from 1891 to 1923* (Dublin, 1925).

MIES, MARIA, *The Lace Makers of Narsapur: Indian Housewives Produce for the World Market* (1982).

MILLER, KERBY A., *Emigrants and Exiles: Ireland and the Irish Exodus to North America* (Oxford, 1985).

MISHAN, E. J., *The Economic Growth Debate: An Assessment* (1977).

MOFFETT, FRANCES, *I Also Am of Ireland* (1985).

MOGEY, JOHN M., *Rural Life in Northern Ireland: Five Regional Studies Made for the Northern Ireland Council of Social Services Inc.* (1947).

MORGAN, DAVID HOSEASON, *Harvesters and Harvesting, 1840–1900: A Study of the Rural Proletariat* (1982).

MORGAN, J. N., SIRAGELDIN, I. A. H., and BAERWALDT, N., *Productive Americans: A Study of How Individuals Contribute to Economic Progress* (Ann Arbor, Mich., 1966).

MORRISON, GEORGE, *The Emergent Years: Independent Ireland, 1922–62* (Dublin, 1984).

MULLIN, REVD T. H., *Aghadowey: A Parish and its Linen Industry* (Belfast, 1972).

MURPHY, MICHAEL J., *At Slieve Gullion's Foot* (Dundalk, 1940).

MURTAGH, MARTIN, *Proud Heritage: The Story of Imokilly Co-op* (Dublin, 1986).

NAPIER, ELLIOTT, *Walks Abroad: Being the Record of the Experiences of Two Australians in the Wilds of the United Kingdom* (Sydney, 1929).

NASH, JUNE, and FERNANDEZ-KELLY, MARIA, P. (eds.), *Women, Men and the International Division of Labour* (Albany, 1983).

—— and SAFA, HELEN ICKEN (eds.), *Sex and Class in Latin America* (New York, 1976).

NIENBURG, B. M., *The Woman Homemaker in the City* (Washington, DC, 1923).

NORTH, DOUGLASS C., *The Economic Growth of the United States, 1790–1860* (Englewood Cliffs, NJ, 1966).

OAKLEY, ANN, *Sociology of Housework* (New York, 1974).

—— *Woman's Work: A History of the Housewife* (New York, 1974).

O'BRIEN, NORA CONNOLLY, *Portrait of a Rebel Father* (Dublin, 1935).

O'CONNELL, T. J., *History of the Irish National Teachers' Organisation, 1868–1968* (Dublin, 1968).

O'DONOVAN, JOHN, *The Economic History of Live Stock in Ireland* (Cork, 1940).

O'DOWD, ANNE, *Meitheal: A Study of Co-operative Labour in Rural Ireland* (Dublin, 1981).

O'FLAHERTY, LIAM, *Shame the Devil* (Dublin, 1981).

Ó GRÁDA, CORMAC, *Ireland before and after the Famine: Explorations in Economic History, 1800–1925* (Manchester, 1988).

OJALA, E. M., *Agriculture and Economic Progress* (1952).

O'NEILL, DENIS, *On the Land in West Cork: Yesterday, Today and Tomorrow* (Cork, 1983).

O'NEILL, MOIRA, *Songs of the Glens of Antrim* (Edinburgh, 1900).

O'NEILL, TIMOTHY P., *Life and Tradition in Rural Ireland* (1977).

OWENS, ROSEMARY CULLEN, *Smashing Times: A History of the Irish Women's Suffrage Movement, 1889–1922* (Dublin, 1984).

PATERSON, T. G. F. [Revd John Thomas Farquhar Paterson], *Country Cracks: Old Tales from the Co. of Armagh* (Dundalk, 1939).

—— *Harvest Home: The Last Sheaf. A Selection from the Writings of T. G. F. Paterson Relating to Co. Armagh*, ed. E. Estyn Evans (Armagh, 1975).

PEARL, CYRIL, *Dublin, in Bloomtime: The City James Joyce Knew* (1969).

PIGOU, A. C., *The Economics of Welfare* (1920).

PLUNKETT, HORACE CURZON, *Oxford and the Rural Problem* (Oxford, 1921).

Horace Plunkett Foundation, *Agricultural Co-operation in Ireland: A Survey* (1931).

Horace Plunkett Foundation, *Co-operation and the New Agricultural Policy* (1935).

READ, D. (ed.), *Edwardian England* (1982).

REID, MARGARET, *Economics of Household Production* (New York, 1934).

Report of the Council of Education: The Curriculum of the Secondary School (Dublin, 1960).

RIDDELL, C. C., *Agricultural Co-operation in Ireland: The Story of a Struggle* (Dublin, 1950).

RIORDAN, E. J., *Modern Irish Trade and Industry* (1920).

ROBINS, JOSEPH, *The Lost Children: A Study of Charity Children in Ireland, 1700–1900* (Dublin, 1980).

ROBINSON, J. P. and CONVERSE, P., *Sixty-Six Basic Tables of Time Budget Data for the United States* (Ann Arbor, Mich., 1966).

RUSSELL, GEORGE WILLIAM, *Plea for Justice: Being a Demand for a Public Enquiry into the Attacks on Co-operative Societies in Ireland* (Dublin, 1921).

RYNNE, ETIENNE (ed.), *North Munster Studies: Essays in Commemoration of Monsignor Michale Moloney* (Limerick, 1967).

RYNNE, STEPHEN, *Green Fields: A Journal of Irish Country Life* (1938).

SACH, CAROLYN E., *The Invisible Farmer: Women in Agricultural Production* (Totowa, NJ, 1983).

SAFFIOTI, HELEIETH I. B., *Women in Class Society* (New York, 1978).

SAYERS, PEIG, *Peig: The Autobiography of Peig Sayers of the Great Blasket Island* (Dublin, 1974).

School of Domestic Science, Morrison's Island, Cork, *Prospectus, Session 1938–1939* (Cork, 1939), 1939–45.

SCHULTZ, THEODORE W., *Investing in People: The Economics of Population Quality* (Berkeley, Calif., 1981).

SCITOVSKY, TIBOR, *Papers on Welfare and Growth* (1964).

—— *The Joyless Economy: An Inquiry into Human Satisfaction and Consumer Dissatisfaction* (New York, 1976).

SEYERS, WILLIAM CHARLES, *Reminiscences of Old Bangor* (orig. publ. 1932; Belfast, 1983).

SHARKEY, OLIVE, *Old Days, Old Ways* (Dublin, 1985).

SIRAGELDIN, I. A. H., *Non-Market Components of National Income* (Ann Arbor, Mich., 1969).

SMITH, ADAM, *An Inquiry into the Nature and Causes of the Wealth of Nations* (New York, 1937).

SMITH, F. B., *The Retreat of Tuberculosis, 1850–1950* (1988).

SOLOW, BARBARA, *The Land Question and the Irish Economy, 1870–1903* (Cambridge, Mass., 1971).

SOMERVILLE-LARGE, PETER, *Cappaghglass* (1985).

STARKIE, ENID, *A Lady's Child* (1941).

STEARNS, PETER N., *European Society in Upheaval* (New York, 1975).

STEVEN, MAISIE, *The Good Scots Diet: What Happened to it?* (Aberdeen, 1985).

STIGLER, GEORGE J., *Domestic Servants in the United States 1900–1940* (New York, 1946).

STRASSER, SUSAN, *Never Done: A History of American Housework* (New York, 1982).

SUMMERFIELD, HENRY (ed.), *Selections from the Contributions to the 'Irish Homestead' by G. W. Russell—A. E.* (Gerrards Cross, 1978).

SUTHERLAND, DANIEL E., *Americans and their Servants: Domestic Service in the United States from 1800 to 1920* (Baton Rouge, La., 1981).

SWEET, J. A., *Woman in the Labour Force* (New York, 1973).

SYNGE, JOHN M., *The Aran Islands* (Leipzig, 1926).

SZALAI, ALEXANDER, *The Use of Time: Daily Activities of Urban and Suburban Populations in Twelve Countries* (Paris, 1972).

TAYLOR, GEOFFREY, *Irish Poets of the Nineteenth Century* (1951).

TILLY, LOUISE A., and SCOTT, JOAN W., *Women, Work and Family* (1975).

TREIMAN, D. J., and HARTMANN, HEIDI I. (eds.), *Women, Work and Wages: Equal Pay for Jobs of Equal Value* (Washington, DC, 1981).

URDANG, STEPHANIE, *Fighting Two Colonialisms: Women in Guinea Bissau* (New York, 1979).

VAN RAAPHORST, DONNA L., *Union Maids Not Wanted: Organizing Domestic Workers, 1870–1940* (New York, 1988).

VAUGHAN, W. E., *Landlords and Tenants in Ireland, 1848–1904* (Dundalk, 1984).

VEBLEN, THORSTEIN, *The Theory of the Leisure Class: An Economic Study of Institutions* (New York, 1934).

VOYDANOFF, PATRICIA (ed.), *Work and Family: Changing Roles of Men and Women* (Palo Alto, Calif., 1984).

WALKER, KATHRYN E., and GAUGER, WILLIAM H., *The Dollar Value of Household Work* (New York, 1973).

WALKER, KATHRYN E., and WOODS, MARGARET E., *Time Use: A Measure of Household Production of Family Goods and Services* (Washington, DC, 1976).

WEST, TREVOR, *Horace Plunkett: Co-operation and Politics. An Irish Biography* (Gerrards Cross, 1986).

WINSTON, GORDON C., *The Timing of Economic Activities: Firms, Households, and Markets in Time-Specific Activities* (Cambridge, 1982).

YOTOPOULOS, PAN A., *Allocative Efficiency in Economic Development* (Athens, 1967).

YOUNG, KATE, WALKOWITZ, CAROL, and McCULLAGH, ROSLYN (eds.), *Of Marriage and the Market: Women's Subordination Internationally and its Lessons*, 2nd edn. (1984).

Index